To: Therese

Please [accept(?)] my

letters and story.

Best Wishes,

Daniel G. Lloyd Jr.

6/28/04

D1484054

# A BOOT FULL OF MEMORIES

## CAPTAIN LEONARD WILLIAMS
## 2ND SOUTH CAROLINA CAVALRY

**Written by**
**DAVID G. DOUGLAS**

**With**
**Robert L. Brown**

**Cover Art and Annual Sketches by**
**Robert Graham,**
**Charleston, SC-based Civil War Artist**

Published by

Gray Fox
9 Precipice Road
Camden, SC 29020




Printed for

Palmetto Bookworks
P.O. Box 2105
Lexington, SC 29071




ISBN 1-887301-23-2

To Betty Lou, Mom, Tommy, Gordon,
Kevin, Becky and Sophie

*The incarnation of the Old South was he,*
*Clad in the black cape of the old regime,*
*Erect and handsome, picturesque and dominating.*
*Oh! There was a dignity there!*
*Just a touch of hauteur bespoke the aristocrat of plantation days.*
*An easy courtesy completed his charm,*
*He was the breath of the culture…*
*What would have been prejudice in others,*
*In him was the culmination of a delightful provincialism.*
*I drink to him from a crystal goblet,*
*The wine of life.*

…Yates Snowden

# TABLE OF CONTENTS

# MAPS AND ILLUSTRATIONS

# PREFACE

There are exactly one hundred and thirty five of them. Nearly all contain the date and location from where they were written. Some were written in ink, many more in pencil. One was hastily scrawled across a piece of liberated Union stationary. Another filled every inch, margins and all, of one of his blank morning reports. They are far more than the Civil War correspondence from Captain Leonard Williams to his young wife, Anna Olivia Laval Williams. They are windows into history. They are torn, burnt edged, ink-stained, artifacts. According to noted Civil War author Bell Irvin Wiley, "...these faded missives now reposing by the thousands in private possession...constitute a valuably neglected source for the South's social history." For too many years, the personal eyewitness, personal testimony of this brave Confederate cavalry captain was sadly neglected too, until now.

My reason for writing this narrative was much the same as my great grandfather's. He deemed it his solemn obligation to inform dear Anna of his physical, mental, and often spiritual state throughout the war. I considered it my duty to share his words and observations with historians, researchers, and anyone fascinated in those who left the farm for the battlefield. In June of 1861, thirty-seven year old Leonard Williams was one of those who spoke their quiet front porch goodbyes before riding off to danger. Behind him were his wife, infant daughter, and his Negro servants. Ahead of him was the unknown. His youngest brother would lose his foot, blown off in the opening hours at Gettysburg. Another would never return. Though wounded, the Captain survived his bloody ordeal and so did his words.

His letters from the front were meticulously saved by his wife during the war and, upon her death, were handed down from the Captain himself to his youngest daughter, Susie. Susie ultimately passed them on to her son, Thomas Douglas, my father. After his death, my mother placed them in my hands for safekeeping. For twenty years, they rested in the proverbial, musty attic, bound in plastic wrap, alongside scrolls and documents, wedged deep in the bottom of an old black valise. Finally, prodded on by my wife, I ventured up the rickety ladder, brushed aside the cobwebs and dug them out. Thus began my journey back into the past and the life of Captain Leonard Williams, 2nd South Carolina Cavalry, Brooks Troop, Hampton's Legion.

The actual letters are in excellent condition and the handwriting quite legible. My great grandfather was a slave owning, God fearing "sandy hiller" from Greenville, South Carolina. The Palmetto State was the first to secede, and he was never last in offering his opinions about the political, military and social issues pervading the conflict in which 620,000 men lost their lives. Captain Williams was well educated and broad viewed. He wrote intelligently and regularly about troops and turnips, boots and blood, Lee and Lincoln. As a cavalryman, he spent his military service scouting, screening, raiding, and riding the picket lines. Because the reins were in his hands more often than his pencil, tracing and corroborating his exact locations was difficult. Weeks would pass without a message home due to skirmishing, illness, or lack of paper and writing implements. When home on leave there was obviously no reason for him to write and more than a few of his letters were delayed, stolen, or lost altogether. Still, what survived forms a remarkably sturdy chain linking together mighty battles and crucial events that changed the course of a nation forever.

Before undertaking this challenge, I took a literary Hippocratic oath of sorts. I pledged to do no harm to his words. Great care was taken in their handling, deciphering, dictation and transcription. I chose the novel form to display his words, which in no way corrupted the primary source material. With this structure, I endeavored to fill gaps, provide informative bridges between his letters and offer a historical context for the reader. Most importantly, I gave a voice to the Captain forty years after the surrender at Appomattox, which enables him to reflect back on both the war and his words. The most resounding and enduring voice throughout, however, remains the letters themselves.

# ACKNOWLEDGMENTS

I owe a great debt to the many individuals who supported and helped me with this undertaking. My thanks to Robert L. Brown, Senior Lecturer, English, Adjunct Faculty at the University of South Carolina at Sumter, for his persistence, expertise, and guidance in the writing and shaping of the final product. For his encouragement and historical assistance, my thanks to Jim J. Fox, historian, bookseller and reenactor, whose kind and generous assistance throughout was absolutely indispensable. I am most appreciative of the effort and time spent by my second cousin, Anne Kesler Shields, in the unearthing of so many vital materials pertaining to the history and lineage of the Williams and Laval families. For the two memorable battlefield tours, my thanks to historical experts Melody Callahan and Clark B. Hall. For his expertise and guidance rendered most liberally, I thank noted historian and author, Eric J. Wittenberg. Closer to home, I cannot thank enough my mother, Marian Welsh, for entrusting the letters to me, and my wife, Betty Lou, for her transcription, proofreading, and patience.

The following individuals and organizations also have my gratitude for sharing their insights, time and materials:

Patrick McCawley, Reference Archivist, S. C. Department of Archives and History.

Dr. John Coski, Historian, The Museum of the Confederacy.

D. Ray Sigmon, Exec. Director, Historic Columbia Foundation.

Ron Field, Author, Historian, Great Britain.

Anne K. McCuen, Historian, Researcher, Greenville, S. C.

John Bigham, Curator of Education, S. C. Confederate Relic Room & Museum.

Dr. Richard J. Sommers, Asst. Dir. for Archives, U. S. Military History Institute.

Suzanne Case, Librarian, The Greenville County Library.

Fritz Hamer, Chief Curator of History, South Carolina State Museum.

Beth Bilderback, Assistant Manuscripts Librarian, South Caroliniana Library.

Guy Swanson, The Museum of the Confederacy.

Donald E. Lovett, S. C. Comptroller General's Office.

Brenda Hays, Greenville Historical Society, Inc.

Joel Skinner, Greenville Civil War Museum.

John B. McLeod, Historian, Greenville, S. C.

Captain F. Porter Stiles, Reenactor, Fairmont, West Virginia.

Col. Craig Nannos, Military History Expert, Villanova, Pa.

Bertram H. Barnett, Park Ranger, Historian, Gettysburg National
Military Park.

Mike McGaffney, Reenactor.

Calvin Owings and Bruce Quarles, Reenactors.

Detective Salvatore Giafaglione III, Police Artist, Philadelphia Police
Department.

Julia Gabrielle Williams.

Edward D. Sloan, Greenville Historical Society, Inc.

The Staff at Christ Episcopal Church, Greenville, S. C.

Kevin McLoughlin, Joe Orlando, Penny Ashman, Leslie Celia, N.F.L.
Films.

Bob Hoffman, Rene Hangley, Helen Torelli, Eileen Torelli,
proofreaders.

Finally, I owe a debt to the gifted authors whose work I cited and drew
upon. These astute writers have enriched and inspired us all with their words.

Dr. James M. McPherson, Ralph Selph Henry, Bruce Catton, Shelby Foote,
Bell Irvin Wiley, Ulysses R. Brooks, Manly Wade Wellman, Henry B. McClellan,
Robert Paul Jordan, Maurice Matloff, James M. Richardson, T. C. DeLeon,
Frank E. Vandiver, Edward Prioleau Henderson, Craig L. Symonds, Mark
Grimsley, Ron Field, Eric J. Wittenberg, Francis Trevelyan Miller, Burke Davis,
William C. Davis, Carlton McCarthy, Ned Bradford, Noah Andre Trudeau,
John Hennessy, Robert McAllister, Sam R. Watkins, William H. Powell, Joseph
H. Crute Jr., Richard M. Boykin, William A. Frassanito, Stewart Sifakis, Edward
L. Wells, John S. Blay, Joseph P. Cullen, David Donald, Roy C. Basler, John D.
Billings, W. W. Blackford, Samuel S. Cox, Clifford Dowdey, Louis Manarin,
William S. McFeely, Alan T. Nolan, James I. Robertson Jr., Stephen W. Sears,
Gene Smith, Douglas Southall Freeman, Walter H. Taylor, Richard Wheeler,
Steven E. Woodworth, Harry W. Pfanz, Chris E. Fonvielle, Jr., William Woods
Hassler, Edward G. Longacre, and Jim Fox.

# INTRODUCTION

This is the story of Captain Leonard Williams, 2nd South Carolina Cavalry, who served all four years of the War Between the States and saw some of the hardest fighting in the war. His story is told through over one hundred and thirty letters he wrote home during the war. This is a rare historical treasure. Few collections of Confederate soldiers' letters extend through all the years of the war or contain the scope and depth of those of Captain Leonard Williams. Here is an eyewitness to the rise and decline of the Confederate cavalry during the war, as well as the Confederacy as a nation. Captain Williams' letters provide a point of view far different from the broad scope of historians or the biographies of senior officers, giving us a unique insight into the life of a front line, company grade Confederate cavalry officer. The letters also tell us much more than the details of camp life and combat in the field; they tell a story of a young family struggling to survive during war time, and of a young officer struggling to keep his faith in the Confederate cause and himself.

The story of Captain Leonard Williams is also that of the famous Hampton Legion, in which he began his service as a member of the Brooks Troop, and in his letters we meet the many colorful, larger than life figures who filled its ranks and led its regiments. He rode and fought alongside the legendary Wade Hampton and Jeb Stuart. He looked Robert E. Lee in the eye. He bore eyewitness to Sharpsburg, rode around the dead bodies at Second Manassas and led charges at Upperville and Jack's Shop. He galloped full tilt through the woods at the "Buckland Races," and experienced the bloody hand-to-hand fighting at the East Cavalry Field near Gettysburg against George Custer.

In his letters home, Captain Williams tells us not only where he was and what happened, but takes us into the field of combat and provides us with the details of the fighting that made up the life of a dashing beau sabreur. In one of his first engagements in May, 1862, he writes, "An order was given to draw pistols and fire. We did so and advanced on them and then on order to charge, we put them to flight and chased them up a hill...it was a splendid little performance." Later that year he relates a tight scrape for both one of his troopers and himself. "McClanahan's horse fell with him and on him down in the ditch...I leaped off my horse and with my assistance succeeded in rolling the horse off of him, as we mounted and rode off, a number of bullets and shells flew around us." The fighting and close calls would only increase as the war dragged on, and Williams records it all. The letters also provide a candid view of camp and army life, and early in the war he tells his wife Anna about the casualties and poor care of the wounded. "There have been several deaths among the companies from Greenville and I think some have died from neglect. The arrangements for taking care of the sick in the hospitals are deplorably bad..." Williams himself also falls victim to sickness and is wounded, but what seems to trouble him most is lack of supplies, particularly clothing. By the second year of the war he is already running short of basic items. "I'm getting very bad off for shoes...My toes are about out and my hat very bad..." When finally elected Captain of his company, Williams must also worry about the condition of his men, and he takes his new position seriously. "I am determined to have all orders obeyed and to enforce regularity in the discharge of all duties...there are 3 or 4 in my company that endeavor to shirk duty. I am bringing them to a wholesome dread of the consequences."

Williams was an educated man, and his letters reflect this in their clarity, coherence, and imagery. Early in the war his letters have a touch for the dramatic and he writes in the summer of '61 when the Legion is on the move that, "The times are pregnant with stirring events." A year later the letters no longer contain such phrases, but his accounts of movements in the field border on the poetic. "Our crossing the Potomac near Leesburg by moonlight would furnish the painter with a grand subject. We have crossed the mountains and valleys, the most grand and picturesque." The imagery also becomes starker and stronger in a style that has abandoned the Romantic. "I rode through the field on my way here. The dead Yankees literally covered the ground for miles."

Williams was a frequent writer, and each letter touches on more than one subject. In addition to his observations in the field and reports of camp life and battles, Williams provides details on himself and his company, reflects on the war, and attempts to instruct and guide his young wife on how to run the farm, attend to business, and raise their daughter. His letters provide us rare insight into the concerns and details of family life and farm operations. They reveal a writer who has mastered many details and maintains his position as head of the family and interests even while serving in the army. His style is direct, almost dictatorial, yet the letters are filled with the concerns for his wife, daughter, extended family, and servants. "Have you had your turnips sowed? If not, plant in the lower part next to the fence and put all the manure you can get on it...You had better have the clover cut for the calves and not let them into the yard at all...Keep your garden well worked...You can do tolerably well if you can buy more sugar, molasses and rice...Put up all the pickles you can conveniently and buy dried peaches and apples...they are very much needed by the soldiers."

Many of the letters also contain instructions on the care and management of the black servants and field hands, whom Anna must now be responsible for, like so many Southern women during those uncertain times. These particular references are very revealing on several levels. "You must pay careful attention to the cleanliness of the room the Negroes sleep in and that the room is ventilated at night and see that Steve bathes regularly and puts on clean clothes at proper times..." On the surface all of these details may seem unimportant, but together they provide the reader with a rare and rich understanding of the life of the typical small planter and his family. Indeed, it is these concerns and subjects that provide the real insight into Williams' character and life, and underscore the true historical value of this collection.

Leonard Williams was born on his father's Sycamore Grove Plantation, Newberry District, December 15, 1823. He was one of five sons born to Davis Williams and his wife Anne Andrews. He was tutored at home and at a local school until age 17 when he entered South Carolina College, graduating Magna Cum Laude. He returned to Newberry where he became founder and principal of Newberry Academy, later Newberry College. In 1855 he moved to Greenville and settled into the life of a merchant and small planter. His high principles, informed interest in farming, and involvement in the civic and social affairs of the town all served to establish his reputation and position in the community.

As a successful merchant and planter, although on a small scale with but five slaves, he was confident in seeking a bride from one of Charleston's older families and courted Anna Laval, daughter of Major William Laval. The Major carried the badges and scars of 40 years of state and national service, and presented a challenge to the beaux who would take his daughter from genteel and gracious Charleston to the backcountry Piedmont. However, the obvious character and ability of Williams won over the father and in 1858 the match was made. The birth of a daughter, Carrie, only served to further strengthen the families' bonds rooted in mutual respect and admiration.

The Williams family was an old and respected one with deep patriotic roots. It claimed three colonels of the Revolution and a maternal great-grandfather who was a victim of a Tory massacre in 1781. With stories of family heroes and history taught in the home, there was little doubt that Leonard and his brothers would answer the call to colors in 1861 when South Carolina went to war. Leonard was among the first to muster in Greenville's Brook's Troop of cavalry, and in May, 1861, the Troop became one of the four cavalry companies of Wade Hampton's newly authorized Legion. His younger brothers, James and Ephraim, were equally eager to serve and both volunteered for service in infantry regiments. James joined up at Lightwood Knots Springs, rose to the rank of 1st Lieutenant in the 14th S.C. Infantry and served until 1863 when he was captured at Gettysburg. Ephraim mustered in at Clinton and joined the 3rd S.C. Infantry. A year later, he was mortally wounded at Savage Station.

Williams had little time to put his affairs in order and bid farewell to his young wife and baby daughter. Hampton had requested service in Virginia for his new Legion and things moved quickly for the volunteers. They mustered in at Camp Hampton in Columbia in May and were off to Virginia and the training camps in June. Because of his age and experience in the militia, the 37 year old Williams was elected Orderly Sergeant for his cavalry company, a position he would hold through the first year as the army trained, scouted, and skirmished along Broad Run and Occoquan Creek in Northern Virginia. The reorganization of 1862 would see his election as a captain in the troop, which was now part of the 2nd S.C. Cavalry, as the serious campaigns of the army began. During this time mail was sent and received regularly, and Williams was demanding of frequent letters from home, as he reported on his life in the field. His letters with requests for seasonal clothing and purchase of cloth for future use reflect conditions at this early stage of the war. Also present in his correspondence is a form of casualty reporting, giving names, family ties, or other relationships of the men lost—the inevitable price of military service in time of war.

The sending and receipt of mail is an ongoing issue. We find that wherever he rode, Williams seemed to find a way to post a letter, be it in Martinsburg, Pennsylvania, or on the move in Virginia. The frequency and locations of postings and receipts is one of the fascinating features of the letters and, despite Williams' complaints that the mail was sometimes not getting through to him, is an indirect tribute to the Confederate Postal Service.

Captain Williams rode at the head of Company K under Matthew C. Butler as part of Hampton's Brigade during the glory days of 1862-63 and the decline of 1864-65. Yorktown, Sharpsburg, Brandy Station, Upperville, Middleburg, and Gettysburg were familiar places. He participated in 75 battles and skirmishes, and was seriously wounded at Second Brandy Station. He was also personally commended by J.E.B. Stuart for "efficiency and bravery" in leading his squadron in a charge that allowed Stuart to break the Federal line at Jack's Shop and save his men and artillery.

His duties carried him over Northern Virginia, Maryland, and Pennsylvania. A farmer at heart, Williams viewed the land with a critical eye. He noted the worn out soil of northern Virginia, the richness and abundance of Pennsylvania, and the neat and well-tended fields of Maryland that reminded him of French landscapes seen in paintings. When the worn down regiment was sent back to South Carolina for coastal duty, he is distressed at the poor sandy soil of the district where his company's horses cannot find proper forage and he and his men battle malaria. He discovers also that his home state has been drained of men and material, and reports on the boredom of patrolling and camp life when the companies are dispersed in isolated camps along the coast until the unit is called upon to support embattled Wilmington.

By the last year of the war the 2nd S.C. Cavalry, 980 strong in the beginning, was only 150 lean riders and jaded mounts. Williams still clung to the hope that the South could be saved from total defeat. On February 11, 1865, he writes what he thinks should be done to halt Sherman. "Our forces ought to be concentrated and thrown on one and then another of Sherman's columns. It seems to be he ought to be whipped, if he is not, I shall be disappointed. If he should meet with a severe whipping, our cause would revive at once and confidence and hope be reestablished...Bring in every able bodied man and bring absentees back. Let us all work together, forego private interests and send all our energies to one great end, our independence, and we will, I am confident, win success." It was not to be, of course, and Charleston and Columbia would fall shortly after this letter was written.

Captain Williams and his skeleton command would connect with Johnston's army in North Carolina, fighting in the last battles of Averasboro, Smithfield, and Bentonville. They, like the Confederacy itself, had reached the point where valor and endurance were not enough. Despite hard fighting, losses, and dwindling resources, Williams remains ever optimistic and he never lost faith in the Southern Cause. His letters reveal a loyal soldier who would perform his duty and meet his responsibility regardless of odds, or the growing awareness of eventual defeat. The letters cease with the evacuation of Wilmington and Williams finally returns home to put his life back together.

Upon returning to Greenville after the war, Williams devoted his energy to restoring his farm and rebuilding his business. He applied his leadership to assisting in the recovery of the community from years of deterioration through loss of commerce and their best men. He actively promoted improved agricultural practices and fought to reduce the excessive taxation levied by Reconstruction, the brunt of which fell on the farmer and planter. His fight to broaden the tax base led him into politics, and in 1871-72 he was one of the few Democrats in the South Carolina Reconstruction Legislature. Williams was active in Hampton's 1876 election campaign that ended Reconstruction in South Carolina. He remained politically active and served as Auditor of Greenville County and several terms as Alderman, where he played a large role in bringing the Air Line, later the Southern Railroad, to the upper Piedmont. When Anna died, he married her sister Julia. After a long life of service and accomplishment, the old soldier died in May of 1908, leaving five children, a record of 84 years of service, and a growing city as his legacy.

R. L. Brown with J. J. Fox

**Captain Leonard Williams**
**circa 1880**

**Hampton Legion on Parade, Columbia, S.C.**
*Courtesy Confederate Relic Room, Columbia, S.C.*

# 1903

# CHAPTER ONE
# THE DREAM

*...your old men shall dream dreams,*
*your young men shall see visions.*
Joel 2:28

Long after the War many of the veterans had dreams. All too often the dreams were recurring images of lost comrades, or endless marches, or confused and bloody fighting. Often, the images were so real the sleeper would wake with the taste of gunsmoke in his mouth and the screams of the dying men and horses still echoing in his head.

For Leonard Williams, former captain of the 2nd South Carolina Cavalry, the same dream came again and again. It had been repeating itself for nearly forty years now. At the heart of the dream was the horse he had ridden on countless patrols and picket lines, and several times into battle. Her name was Ruby. She was the fire-maned mare he took to war from his Carolina farm to the fighting in northern Virginia. Ruby was a strong and reliable mount during his first year in the field as first sergeant of Company B in the Hampton Legion Cavalry, but by the time he was elected captain a year later, the old girl had been worn down and starved like most of the Confederate cavalry mounts. Eventually there would be a replacement colt that he would be shot off of at Second Brandy Station, then a gelding he would ride home from Durham after Johnston's surrender, but in the dream it was always Ruby...

*Ruby always senses the coming battle first. Flared nostrils pick up the faint tinge of doused campfires and gunpowder wisping in through nearby mountain gaps. Her ears perk up and turn toward muffled gunfire. The bugle sounds. The command to mount up is given. Sabers rattle as the Captain leaps aboard. Soon his spurs would dig into her belly still empty after the night's ride and the cavalry would be off.*

*There were no fits of snorting or sudden upward jerks of the neck. Not one ear even twitched. Both horse and master recognize instantly that this would not be another day of skirmishing with Hooker, scouting the whereabouts of McClellan, or guarding A.P. Hill's ordnance train. This new day dawns almost mystically, not with a cool drink by the*

North Anna, not with a visit to the company farrier, and not with the sound of gunfire from Fleetwood Hill. Instead, both human and equine eyes are entranced by a myriad of colors floating down from a blue spring sky, pastels, bright whites, and shocking pinks. It was a rainbow rain as if sent down from heaven itself. The Captain and his mare had seen each individual color before, but never all together like this.

They had watched swatches of Union blue struggling valiantly then torn apart crossing Burnside Bridge near Antietam. They had seen the brilliant peacock plumes blown straight back atop the hat of Jeb Stuart, at full gallop racing to the front. A few times they even caught a glimpse of the silver-gray beard and the worn black boots of General Lee himself.

But always it seemed, there was red. The ripe red radishes they had eaten on the way to a tiny town named Gettysburg and later the crimson flames that consumed Richmond. There were the red, rough, then nearly raw feet of Stonewall's Brigade, out-marching then out-flanking another shocked regiment of Yankees. Unendingly, it seemed, there was the deepest and dearest red of all...the precious blood of sixteen-year-olds that stained lifeless gray and later butternut brown uniforms.

But this rainbow of color falling down around them now wasn't rain at all. These riders and horses knew rain. For four years it cooled them off during hot summer picketing then chilled them to the bone when it turned to sleet at Fredericksburg. Gray clouds meant for an angry brown Rapidan or a long ride around a flooded, swollen Rappahannock.

As their eyes turned skyward, the riders and horses are showered in the floating colors. Some landed on Ruby's neck and nestled in her mane. A few came to rest on Leonard's old felt hat. Each had a unique, intoxicating scent.

It was unlike the smell of fresh leather, harness and tack. It was nothing like the verdant valley grass that was so lush in '61, then all but eaten out by '63. By the mercy of God, it was nothing like the stench of horse carcasses or mangled privates that lay along the Sunken Road, by the Bloody Lane, on Little Round Top, or below Marye's Heights. This smell was sweet.

The falling colors were fragrant flower petals, a rich mix of china *white magnolias, pink dogwoods, and cherry blossoms. Leonard and his fellow troopers found themselves awash in a watercolor of rose petals, daisies and peach blossoms tossed in the air by wet-eyed South Carolinians who had begun to gather near dawn. Today would be the final reunion ride, the last grand march of the famed Hampton Legion.*

*A band plays "Dixie." General Wade Hampton assembles the men. His many wounds, three from the afternoon cavalry fight above Gettysburg alone, make for a painfully slow move from stirrup to saddle. His closest companion, "Butler," the fine animal that carried him in and out of danger throughout many a campaign, waits patiently.*

*To the General's left sits his gallant younger brother Frank Hampton. To his right is his right hand throughout countless battles, Matthew C. Butler, a Major General by the age of 28. Next in the grand procession are the "Iron Scouts," hand picked by Hampton for risky raids behind enemy lines. And finally, it is Captain Leonard Williams himself who mounts up, ordering Company K to do the same. The flower petals that once danced through the air have now settled on the ground transforming their path into a grand carpet. The Legion is formed and ready. General Hampton raises his right hand to give the command to move out for the last time ever...*

Leonard always woke up before the reunion ride began, and the dream would return on another night to torment him again. Now an old man of 79 years, he had grown used to the images and had almost come to terms with the war and its aftermath. He had lived through the trials and changes of Reconstruction, put his life back together and helped bury many of his fellow comrades in arms. It was now 1903. Wade Hampton had been dead for a year. Many of the other giants had also passed away or were old men now, no longer able to even mount a horse. Even the famous Iron Scouts had rusted away and only a few of these once dashing and daring cavalrymen were still alive.

# CHAPTER TWO
# A BOOT FULL OF MEMORIES

*This is the revelation God gave…*
*that he might show his servant*
*what must happen very soon.*

Revelation 1:1

Wednesday May 13, 1903. Columbia, South Carolina. The remnants of the Confederate Army had come to the capitol of the Palmetto State to participate in one final, grand march. Everyone who could make the journey had come. It was not an event to be missed. It would not come again.

From his window at the Planter's Hotel, Leonard Williams looked down on Lady Street. In a matter of hours, folks would be lined up three-deep to celebrate and honor their veterans of what had now come to be called the Lost Cause. The morning sun warmed Leonard's face. The prospect of riding again with the men of the Legion as little children tossed flowers in the air to form a carpet all the way up to the State House warmed his heart. Whatever the causes of the war—liberty, states rights, cotton, or slavery—in the end all the veterans cared about was to feel that it had not all been for nothing, and there was still honor and respect for the soldiers, dead and alive. Most of the South's boldest officers were long gone. Only their spirits would march today. For the survivors, some would struggle on homemade crutches while others would be pushed in wheel chairs by their arthritic, limping comrades. The amputees would have to be transported in buggies and wagons. Leonard was still able to steady himself in a saddle and he would mount up again and escort them as he had done so many years ago.

Leonard had been awake before dawn. He had tossed and fidgeted for hours. The dream had come and gone again and he awoke disturbed and uneasy. When the first rays of light had appeared over the city, he had slowly sat up and once again felt the twinge in his shoulder, shot clean through at the battle of Second Brandy Station. At least it was proof he was awake and not dreaming. His dented pocket watch read six o'clock. He had made arrangements the night before for the hotel staff to have a pot of coffee brought up to the room at first light. He hoped it would arrive soon. By the winter of 1862 the blockade had squeezed nearly every drop of real coffee out of the Army of Northern Virginia, and he had vowed that when the war was over, win or lose, he'd never again be deprived of a single morning cup.

While he waited for the coffee to arrive, he decided to inspect the uniform he would wear for the grand parade. He reached for his spectacles and noticed that the slight tremble in his hands had gotten worse and remembered the time when he could grip a horse's reins or his cavalry saber for hours at a time without a problem. The uniform had been the best one he had owned and was in fair shape considering the time that had passed and the use it had endured. Anna had carefully repaired it over four decades ago after he had left it behind while on leave. She never thought he'd ever wear it again but had patched it as an act of love, her way of caring for him and doing her part in the war. When he now lifted the dark gray coat out of the corduroy valise, the scent of lilies of the valley filled the room. The smell consumed him. It was as if Anna herself had returned to embrace him one more time.

Illness had taken her from him twenty-four years ago back in 1879, but for an instant she was with him again. He stood holding the heavy coat, then laid it out on the bed. He examined the captain's insignia, the brass buttons, and the slightly faded trim with a critical eye. Suddenly a knock called him to the door where a bellboy stood holding a tray with a silver coffee pot. The boy glanced past the old man and saw the uniform resting on the bed, smiled, and smartly snapped his right hand up to his forehead. Leonard was momentarily startled, then returned the salute and tossed an extra silver dollar to the enterprising young man. Damn cheeky, he thought, then with a half smile, poured a steaming cup of coffee up to the brim of his cup.

After the second cup, Leonard hung up the uniform on the brass hook in the closet and reached into the bottom of the valise for his cavalry boots to give them a brush and a polish. He had worn brogans far more often during the war, but dress cavalry boots were the order of the day for the long awaited march. Then he noticed it, a thick packet tucked deep in his right boot, the very one that was grazed by a bullet during the battle at Jack's Shop. He thought Anna had merely tossed them all away but there they were bound together with her blue linen apron string. Back in 1858 that string wrapped neatly around a young newlywed who weighed but 108 pounds even after the birth of Carrie, their first daughter. Now, it held together his memories. As old Doctor Taylor would deftly undo crusty, blood stained bandages from too many of the Hampton Legion, the Old Captain unknotted his past. In his gnarled and grateful hands he cradled his letters home to Anna from court houses, stations, camps and towns, words hastily scribbled from Virginia, Maryland, and even as far north as Pennsylvania during that most uncivil of civil wars.

He knew all the dates and places by heart. He remembered the ones written on an empty stomach by the light of campfires and the one he wrote on his requisition form when paper was not to be had. Sometimes, he wrote while on horseback, the penmanship a bit shaky, clopping along day after day waiting for McClellan to do something. He wrote a lot of those. He recounted to his worried wife back in Greenville the great victories at Fredericksburg, Chancellorsville and Manassas. His notes from the front took on a far more somber tone after Sharpsburg and Gettysburg. She had even saved a few of the rain-smeared envelopes.

His brittle wire rims rested gently near the tip of his nose but he still squinted a bit as he unfolded the first letter home from cavalry camp. With hours to fill before he'd don his uniform and make his way down to assemble for the grand march, Captain Leonard Williams, Brooks Troop, 2nd South Carolina Cavalry, was going to war again.

**Leaving Home- Orderly Sergeant**

# 1861

Cavalry Camp of Instructions
Ashland Va
July 18th 1861

My Dear Anna

I rec'd your last letter of the 5th yesterday & felt grateful that the blessings of health & comparative comfort was still vouchsafed to you and our little household, and it is due to the continued assurances of your health, the kindness of friends & your own determined spirit to bear up under all adversity in the unusual & trying circumstances in which you are placed, that I am enabled to be content away from you & to discard in a measure my anxieties. There is a probability that we will be moved from here on next monday to manassas Junction to cooperate with the other S.C. forces under Beauregard. There seems to be an impression that a fight is now waging at Manassas & we all look with anxiety for to-morrow's news. No soldier at either Fairfax or manassas is allowed to give any information either in regard to the strength of forces or fortifications, or the probabilities of a fight. You will continue to write to me here until otherwise directed. Letters will be forwarded on from this place to our next point of destination.

**First Letter Written During the War**

8

# CHAPTER THREE
## DUTY

*Another horse came forth, a red one.*
*Its rider was given power to rob the earth of peace*
*by allowing men to slaughter one another.*

Revelation 6:4

The Captain forfeited his pipe this morning, fearful that a stray ash might fall on the fragile papers he now held in his hands. As he settled into his chair to begin reading, he thought back to the fresh spring day when he left Anna, his tiny daughter, and the life he loved behind. He knew then, as sure as he did now, that it was his duty to go to war. There were many reasons not to go but they all crumbled away in the face of duty. Duty, that was reason enough.

A sense of duty, and the notion that its call must always be answered, ran deep in the Williams' family. Great grandfather John Williams emigrated from Shangallon, Wales, in 1700 because he thought it was his duty to do so. Making the arduous trip to Hanover County, Virginia, wasn't easy, but not providing his family with the best opportunity to flourish was a prospect that Leonard's great grandfather simply couldn't accept. In John Williams' eyes, it was his duty to shepherd his clan to a new land of promise. The farther up his family fortunes rose, the farther down south they migrated. Affairs would have been very different, the Old Captain mused, had their move been northward instead. From Virginia, his descendants moved to Granville County, North Carolina, and then, just before the Revolution, deeper south still to the Ninety-Six District of South Carolina.

Leonard's grandfather Daniel Williams had four sturdy sons who played vital roles in the birth of the nation. Three of them— John, James, and Joseph Williams— rose to the rank of colonel in the Revolutionary War. James was shot and killed in a charge. Henry, the eldest son, enlisted in the Continental Army, but his advanced age kept him from continuing in active service. Davis Williams was a son of Henry and the father of Leonard. He too married a woman of patriotic stock, Anne Andrews, whose father Ephraim Andrews was mortally wounded in the Revolutionary War at the "Massacre of Hay's Station" in 1781.

Leonard was born in the Newberry District in the northwest corner of South Carolina on a chilly December 15, 1823. He and his four brothers, Henry, William, Ephraim, and James were privately tutored, and, as the five lads grew, so did "Sycamore Grove." On more than a few summer evenings, their father's old friend and classmate from Dr. Waddel's School for Boys would stop by for a hot dinner and some even hotter conversation. He would become Vice President under John Quincy Adams, and in the years to come, South Carolina's spearhead for secession. His name was John C. Calhoun.

By the age of sixteen, Leonard was off to Columbia's South Carolina College (later the University of South Carolina), and in 1844 graduated "Magna Cum Laude." Leonard Williams was now an astute young man, and while duty hadn't called him yet, destiny did. A college faculty member had suggested that he return home and open a classical school back in the up country. Soon he found himself principal of the Newberry Academy, which afterwards became Newberry College, and both he and the school prospered. He remained there for nine years until the age of thirty before moving to Greenville where he started a fledgling farm and mercantile business.

Overseeing his farm and store filled his days and his pockets, but he had no one to share it with. That all changed one night at the old Greenville Mansion House, site of a grand ball he had reluctantly agreed to attend. There he was introduced to a nineteen-year old Charlestonian named Anna Olivia Laval, who happened to be in town for a visit. She was a petite, blue-eyed graduate of Madame DuPre's school for young ladies, and her intelligence, refinement, and Christian graces mesmerized him from first glance to midnight. Not once did she comment about his awkwardness on the ballroom floor, though she had cause to many times. Afterwards, Leonard, now 34, found himself perched atop North Carolina's picturesque Caesar's Head taking in the breathtaking view. But what awed him was not the vista that lay before him; it was the radiant beauty sitting next to him. It took every ounce of courage he could summon up to propose to her that day in 1858. She had wondered what took him so long.

As the old man unfolded the first letter, Anna's delightful half smile returned again, and he remembered well why he had delayed in asking for her hand. The reason was her father, William Laval, known simply in Charleston circles as "The Major." The Major was no ordinary man. For his valor at the capture of Pensacola in the War of 1812, he had received a commendation for gallantry from President James Madison himself. Later, he became South Carolina's State Treasurer, then Comptroller General, and during the Polk Administration, he served as Assistant Secretary of the Treasury. To Leonard, the Major was a man's man, and more than a little intimidating.

During one of his last visits to Charleston while courting Anna, the nervous suitor listened with deep respect as the seventy year old Major shared with him a brandy and a brief account of his brush with death in the War of 1812. Without the slightest tinge of exaggeration or braggadocio, Major Laval recounted how he and his men stormed the town of Pensacola, then possessed by the Spaniards, and fell wounded while leading a charge against a battery. The enemy surrendered, and afterward he received the commanding officer's sword while lying on the battlefield. For his heroism that day, the young captain gained the rank of major and lost forever the use of his leg. Leonard now knew why the Major walked with a cane and fully understood from whom Anna's quiet courage came. A few hours later, Leonard left the Laval Estate with two things— permission for Anna's tender hand in marriage and an aching head from the six additional brandies required to celebrate the coming wedding with his new father-in-law.

In 1860, after two years of marriage, two events altered the lives of Mr. and Mrs. Leonard Williams forever. First was the birth of their first daughter, Carrie, and second was the secession of South Carolina from the Union. Although his family ties were now stronger than ever, duty called Leonard, as it had for his great grandfather, his grandfather, his three great uncles who became gallant colonels, and his father who helped his four sons thrive.

Now, years later, the letter he held took him back home to Anna in Greenville. He sighed as he noticed that it was written from near Richmond, where his great grandfather had first brought his family over two hundred years ago.

*Cavalry Camp of Instruction*
*Ashland, Virginia*
*July 18, 1861*

*My Dear Anna,*
    *I recd your last letter of the 12th yesterday and felt grateful that the blessings of health and comparative comfort were still vouched safe to you and our little household and is due to the continued assurances of*

*your health, the kindness of friends, and your own determined spirit to bear up under all the adversity in the unusual and trying circumstances in which you are placed that I am enabled to be content from you and to discard in a measure my anxiety. There is a probability that we will be moved from here next Monday to Manassas Junction to cooperate with the other S C forces under Beauregard. There seems to be an impression that a fight is now waging at Manassas and we all look with anxiety for tomorrow's news. No soldiers at either Fairfax or Manassas are allowed to give any information either in regard to the strength of forces or fortifications or the probability of a fight. You will continue to write me here till otherwise directed. Letters will be forwarded on from this place to our next point of destination. Two cavalry companies of this state left here this morning for the scene of war. I expect all will be gone before next week. I have today and yesterday been disabled from riding by a bile on my thigh. It will probably be several days before I can ride.*

That "bile," even though painful as such boils were, at least provided a short respite from endless hours in the saddle. All he had done since he kissed Anna and Carrie goodbye was ride. That first ride took him south from his home in Greenville to the old racetrack outside Columbia that had become Camp Hampton, the mustering point for the Legion. Confederate cavalrymen had to supply their own saddles and mounts, but he knew "Ruby" could stand up to such vigorous duty. Anna had given her the name because of her deep red mane that shined like a beacon as she pulled the plow. Now she'd soon carry Leonard across battlefields. Probably, he conjectured then, they would only be away for a few months anyway. And what a sendoff he and his fellow enlistees had received. Bands played, citizens cheered, and soul-stirring speeches were offered up by young officers promising swift victory. The parting words of Captain Matthew C. Butler, commander of the "Edgefield Hussars," were emblematic of the fervor and resolve that inspired all the South Carolina militiamen as they shook the home town dust from their heels to go to war.

*Ladies and Fellow Countrymen: The feeling and patriotic remarks of Captain Hammond, to which we have just listened, certainly is cheering to us, and in behalf of this company, which I have the honor to command, I thank him and his lovely array of our beautiful women who have honored us today with their presence. In these ranks many of you have sweethearts, brothers and husbands, and we go to the tented fields in defense of our homes and firesides against the invasion of the hireling foe, whose only desire is for beauty and booty. We will go to the front, remembering that we are all Carolinians, and we will return as honored soldiers or fill a soldier's grave. We thank you for your deep sympathies. It is ours to act, and not to speak. You will hear from us. Farewell!*

After such impassioned oratories, cheers rang out throughout South Carolina and all of Dixie, but it was the quiet good byes whispered softly on front porches that echoed the most in the hearts of the departing soldiers. As he held the letter, Leonard's thoughts drifted back to that time when his life changed forever, the summer of 1861. The largest wraparound porch in all of Greenville encompassed his fine and sturdy house at 606 Augusta Street. On June 6, he began the long walk around that house, at a deliberately slow pace, one more time. He paused to examine his garden bursting with turnips, Irish potatoes and butter beans. Part of him hoped he'd be back to hoe it before the weeds attacked. Deep inside, he knew that Anna and the house servants would have to oversee the garden without him. As he rounded the back for an examination of the barn, Anna lost sight of him. It was an absence they'd soon have to face as a way of life. Nearly completing his circuit about the house, he took a long admiring look at the Bailey House next door where he had enjoyed many a prime barbecue on the veranda. Northwest, directly off from the Bailey magnolia trees, hard working churchgoers in Shiloh, Tennessee, were out tending to their crops. Three hundred miles beyond his garden stood the silent heights of Fredericksburg and the weather vane atop the tidy red barn pointed north toward a sedate little Pennsylvania Dutch village that he'd never even heard of.

He reappeared after what seemed a lifetime and his eyes found theirs. He stood for a moment, studying his wife and child, mentally photographing the scene of his two loves as if to permanently burn the image into his brain.

First, he bade farewell to his house servants who would now answer to the lady of the house "Miss Anna." He would miss them all dearly, especially Maum Fannie. She always hummed a joyful hymn as she tended to her chores and never forgot to save him a hefty slice of her blue ribbon sweet potato pie.

Years later, the Old Captain became tickled at the notion that ol' Fannie always fretted over what she deemed an eternal lack of meat on his bones. In truth, both he and Fannie knew it was Anna who was far too frail. She always asked that Fannie serve her a modest portion and rarely did Anna finish even half. Maum Fannie would have to see to her health now.

He then sat down on the front step holding his tiny little angel and looked into Carrie's blue-sky eyes. He twirled then unraveled a dirty blond curl and straightened out her crisp black bonnet that he had dislodged with his goodbye kiss. He whispered something softly in her ear and convinced himself that his tiny, eight-month-old somehow understood. Maum Fannie then carried little Miss Carrie back to the barn to watch servant Ned saddle up the "the big red horsey" so as to give "Massa Wimms and Miss Anna" time to themselves.

But the courtesy was unnecessary, for Leonard and Anna had already expressed their parting thoughts the night before and both had stumbled over a few more angst-filled words over a stack of Fannie's fluffy pancakes. Now the words had become merely nervous fidgets and heavy hearts. Soon the sound of hooves and harness jolted them back to the inevitable as Ned rolled up in the rickety, unsprung wagon. Ruby trotted behind, tied to the sideboard by one of Ned's tight halfhitches.

The house servants then huddled tearfully together as the former farmer and now soldier helped Anna onto the buckboard. Little Carrie was then passed from Fannie to her father and then on to her mother's lap. After a wink and a nod of the hat, Leonard offered a slight tug on the rein as Ned gave Ruby a parting pat on the rump for good luck. Husband, wife, and daughter were off to the Greenville train depot. The last to see them disappear down Augusta Street was Ned, on tiptoes to take in the final glimpse of his master's old felt hat that set like the sun beneath the horizon.

Life with Anna Olivia Laval had been the best three years he could have imagined. Life under Robert Edward Lee would be nothing anyone could have dared to imagine. While the future was uncertain for Leonard, the present was devastating for Anna. With a broken heart, she made the following entry in her diary on the night her dear husband had left her.

*June 6th, 1861*
*Saddest day of my life! And yet there is hope and even joy enough*
*left...for gratitude. Dear Len left me this morning for the seat of war.*

*I bade him farewell at the depot and it seemed my life would go out with the words. My home once so bright and cheerful seems strangely altered now. How I miss his footsteps and his soft kind voice! Many sad hearts are in Greenville today but they are brave and courageous ones. God Bless our loved ones and carry them safely to their destination, crown theirs with victory and honor, and bring them safely back to waiting hearts...But what cause of thankfulness we have that our troops are brave and true and trusting in God alone they go forth to meet the foe. Victory must follow them. The race is not to the swift nor the battle to the strong and if "God be for us who can be against us." None can know the depth of my sadness and the sense of utter loneliness that broods over me. I am blessed with a kind mother and two aunts and friends and above all my own sweet little one who comes like a stray sunbeam over my clouded life. But none can fill his place. I have so leaned upon him, with unshaken trust and security, so looked up to him as my mentor. But something tells me he will come again and come with glory! The glory of victory. I cannot give up my hope or life itself would ebb with it.*

As Leonard made his way toward Columbia, the Legion had already started to organize at Camp Hampton. Three weeks earlier, back on May 20, South Carolinians from every nook and cranny of the Palmetto State had come, man by man, militia by militia. There, he met men from towns like Edgefield, Clinton, Sumter, and the bigger cities of Columbia and Charleston.

It seemed as if there was not one but many legions assembling at Camp Hampton, for each group was clad in disparate garb. There were gray frocks, Bomar coats, eight, nine and ten buttoned coats, brimmed caps, havelocks, blue pants, gray jeans, yellow trimmed trousers, suspenders, and red shirts. Most colorful of all perhaps were the cavalrymen, mounted on their favorite horses, each man an individual cavalier warrior. In time this motley assembly would be sorted out and unified, but for now Hampton's Legion resembled not so much a regulation army as a circus.

When Leonard and his new comrades left for Richmond it was hot and crowds of Columbians, as well as outlying family members, came to see the men off. The coaches were full and the men leaned out the open windows to wave goodbye as the trains pulled out of the station. Young belles beneath parasols waved back and little boys ran alongside as far as they could. The men soon settled down to eating the sandwiches, cakes, and other delicacies that had been pressed on them by the people. Many of the high-spirited recruits passed around flasks of wine and whiskey as the locomotive roared past depots full of handkerchief waving well wishers.

Leonard passed on his turn at the flask and instead chose his pipe. The train smoked along and so did he. He shared his motives for volunteering with fellow planters, merchants, blacksmiths, carpenters, and teachers— future cavalrymen who deemed themselves modern day Minute Men and Paul Reveres, riding out to again preserve their independence. And what a rag tag collection they were. Many whole companies had no sabers at all, and anything that could be shot or saddled had been hurriedly grabbed up by the boys. Shot guns, muskets, duck guns, and pistols of all shapes and sizes would soon be toted by men atop palominos, chestnuts, bays, and black colts. Some would find themselves perched aboard mules. Hunters and riders since boyhood, all bragged they could shoot like hell and ride even better. As Leonard drew on his pipe he knew that soon they'd find out.

In Richmond, as the trains emptied them by the thousands, they were already different men. Perhaps this was because the bond of comradeship had already begun to forge a strange and uncertain human chain. Whether it would break apart or be welded on the battlefield remained to be seen. There were so many on their way to war, and he was older than nearly all of them. He would soon ride alongside tenderfoot Texans, acne-faced Alabamans, teenage Tar Heels, and unripe youths from the Peach State, as well as the many friends from his hometown mustered in back in Greenville in April by Captain John Lanneau. The fact that Leonard was already thirty-seven, a college graduate and respected businessman, meant that he would not share equal rank with the rest of the eager privates in the Hampton Legion. He was elected as First Sergeant, older than most in Company B and, he hoped, wiser as well.

Leonard was one of around 64,000 South Carolinians who would ultimately answer the call. For now, his brother, William Williams, was too young to serve. Brother Henry was too old. Both remained safely behind on their tidy Carolina farms. Unknown to Leonard, however, was the exact whereabouts of his two other brothers. At the age of thirty, Ephraim had joined up back in Clinton while twenty-nine year old James would later sign up at Lightwood Knots Springs. These three Williams men, like their three brave great uncles before them, were battle bound.

On July 5, the Legion received its first review by President Jefferson Davis himself who expressed great satisfaction in the unit's dress and bearing. A brass band and a great parade marked the occasion. Sabers shined bright as did the hopes of each and every man. While Leonard and his newly formed Legion were basking in the glow of adulation, Anna was enduring a bleak, rain-filled evening alone with her diary and her fears.

*July 5th, 1861 Friday*

*Yesterday was the Fourth of July, rumor said the contending armies were to meet in battle. I wait this evening with anxiety. God grant a nobler independence has been won for our dear country and this unholy war may speedily be terminated. It is a dark, rainy day. One would scarcely believe it to be July and yet how time is flying. This is July and today baby is eight months old. Sweet child unconscious of all the troubles around her. God bless her. I have been dreaming a great deal of Len lately- pleasant dreams that I trust soon may be realized. Life seems like a dream to me at times but occasionally I awake to the startling realities to find myself alone, Len on the battlefield. Mother gone. Our village home almost deserted. Sad faces everywhere! Oh sad awakening!*

Before her husband would set foot on that battlefield she had already envisioned him on, he and his fellow Legionnaires had to receive their battle flag and as much training as time would allow. All three cavalry companies of the unit paraded through the streets of Richmond together on their way to the "Cavalry Camp of Instruction" at the old Ashland Racetrack grounds nineteen miles east of Richmond. The infantry and artillery of the Legion were formed into three sides of a square for the presentation of a flag on July 16. President Davis, an old cavalryman himself, watched proudly from the reviewing stand. Two days later, Leonard added a few more lines to his letter to let Anna know that he and the Legion had been honored by their new President.

*July 18, 1861*

*The health of our company is pretty good. There are several cases of slight sickness though none of them in bed but one and he improving.*

> *Willie Thompson is a little ailing but I just see him now hauling hay.*
> *He's riding on the load and McClanahan driving. Jeff Davis presented*
> *a flag to the Legion the other day in Richmond and as we understand*
> *made a deep impression on the soldiers.*

From Richmond, Leonard and Ruby had made the short ride out to the old Ashland Racetrack grounds for cavalry training. The instructors were West Pointers who had resigned their commissions in the U.S. Army and sworn allegiance to their home states and the young Confederacy. There were the two Lees- -W.H.F., General Robert E. Lee's son, and Fitzhugh Lee, the General's nephew. The instructors barked out the commands all day long. Leonard and his fellow South Carolinians were amused by the officers' "West Point drawl," as they called it, and never forgot the command shouted out by one gentleman, "Move out there, you...on the gray horse...move out briskly!"

Move out they did. Under the sweltering summer sun and well into the evening, Leonard and Ruby were put through their paces. Mounting. Dismounting. Jumping fences. Charging. Saddle on at sunrise. Saddle off by nightfall. The new troopers found that their horses learned the drills as fast as the men did. When the bugles sounded "March!" or "Halt!" or "Wheel!" the horses responded even before the pull on their reins. The drummer boys also worked hard perfecting beats known as the double and single drag. In time their crisp snares and deep basses were carrying orders to crack regiments that could parade without shouted orders and on their beats alone. The different camps of instruction vied with each other in contests to determine which was most adept on the parade ground. Much had been accomplished but there was still much more to be learned. The July 18 letter continued.

> *I have no doubt the infantry are well drilled. The cavalry are well*
> *drilled in mere maneuvering but have yet learned nothing of the use of*
> *the sword and will have to depend on our natural dexterity.*

Through it all, rider and horse became a team, an inseparable pair forged together under the harsh heat and drenching downpours. During these demanding daily rigors, Leonard would press his sweaty, cotton-covered legs tightly against Ruby, urging her to leap over ditches, then stop sharply. The result was, finally, some semblance of a real cavalry troop but also that painful boil on his thigh. By July, his boil needed lancing and Hampton's Cavalry needed a fight. Both were ready to burst.

That eruption would take place at a strategic point where the Manassas Gap and the Orange and Alexandria Railroads converged, a prime launching point for a Union attack directly south on Richmond. Jeff Davis and his staff would disagree on many issues before the war was over but not at the start. Troops from North and South Carolina, Georgia, and Alabama, if they were in reach, were ordered to concentrate near Centerville. Through cold summer showers Hampton's infantrymen marched through villages like Gordonsville, moving north, primed for their first encounter, singing and laughing all the way. Everyone but Leonard.

> *Cavalry Camp of Instruction*
> *Ashland, Virginia*
> *July 21, 1861*

*My Dear Anna,*

*I looked for a letter from you last evening and as it did not come shall certainly look for it this evening. I also expected a letter from Henry and Esq. McBee. I think my letters failed to reach them. The bile I spoke to you about gives me a good deal of pain and I shall be unable to ride for about a week yet. Our company moves tomorrow for Manassas. I will have to take a wagon. It will take some six days to make the march. Taylor's company reached there this morning. The whole cavalry force of the legion is now here but Taylor's will remain here a week after the other three leave.*

As the Old Captain read on, he remembered well what had transpired on the very afternoon he had written that hurried letter to Anna over forty years ago. The Federals called it Bull Run, the Confederates, Manassas. Officially it was a battle; in truth it was a chaotic, unorganized riot and a bloody one indeed. Leonard's company and James' brigade were not engaged, but Ephraim was in the thick of it as were many of the Legion. On July 19, the Legion broke camp at Camp Manning for Manassas Junction but Leonard and his fellow cavalrymen were ordered to remain behind at Ashland under Major Griffin for more drilling. After two sweltering days in freight cars without provisions, the infantry battalion of the Legion, numbering 627 officers and men, finally reached Manassas

Junction about 4 a.m., Sunday, July 21. Ephraim was one of those who would be on the battle line for the first time, just six hours after they had arrived, already worn out and hungry. The old veteran's heart became heavy again as he recalled how he had prayed on the eve of battle for God to shelter his brother and the men of Bonham's Brigade.

# CHAPTER FOUR
# FIRST BLOOD

*Today you are going into battle against your enemies.*
*Be not weakhearted or afraid;*
*be neither alarmed nor frightened by them.*

Deuteronomy 20:2

Manassas would be the Legion's first battle, and its debut drew quite a crowd. On that hot summer Sunday, wealthy Washingtonians had arrived by carriage near Centerville, Virginia, with picnic lunches, champagne, and field glasses. These ladies and gents had traveled the eighteen miles not to watch a battle really, but to take in a spectacle of sorts, pitting Brigadier General Irvin McDowell's raw Northern Army against West Point classmate Brigadier General Pierre Gustave Toutant Beauregard's band of upstart Southerners. There had been some smaller battles before Manassas, including a pair of minor Federal victories in western Virginia. Beauregard had already become a hero by capturing Fort Sumter back in April and John Magruder had repulsed a Union attack at Big Bethel Church on June 10. But now two large armies were about to meet head-on for the first time in the war.

Actually they weren't quite armies yet. Both sides were filled with amateur militia units, unseasoned recruits who had never experienced battle. On July 16, McDowell had begun marching his roughly 30,000 men toward the rebels. The Northern commander was a large man who it is said had the appetite of ten men. So did his troops, who stopped frequently to pick berries, washing them down with leisurely drinks from streams as they strolled casually toward the battlefield. The supreme commander of the Confederate Army at the time was General Joseph E. Johnston who had directed 11,000 troops in the Shenandoah Valley. By the morning of the 21st, three brigades of Johnston's men had arrived to join Beauregard and a fourth would soon be there. Although Johnston outranked Beauregard, he allowed the flamboyant Creole to retain command of the field. At 8:30 on Sunday morning, the two sat astride their horses on a high hill opposite Mitchell's Ford as the clash began. By midday, they thought, victory would be theirs and McDowell's men would be hightailing it back to the capital.

Nothing that day went as either side had planned. Orders were vague, late in being received, or never received at all. Units cut across one another. Soldiers moved haphazardly. Strategy became reactionary. Cohesion became chaos. Commanders rode to the sound of the guns only to have their horses blown from beneath them. Men screamed as minie balls tore holes in the ranks. Cannon blasts boomed across Henry Hill. For the stunned onlookers, the grand picnic suddenly unraveled into an out-of-control slaughter field of charging, retreating, regrouping then fleeing troops. Close by the main battlefield, Leonard's brother, 30-year old Corporal Ephraim Williams, Company I, 3rd South Carolina Infantry, and his fellow South Carolinians tensely lay by a fence line waiting for the command to go forward. Their lives were about to be changed forever.

The Old Captain grew misty-eyed for a moment and pondered once more the different fates that awaited him and Ephraim that Sunday long ago. While his young brother was preparing for battle, Leonard was attending a church service back in Ashland. A baby boy was baptized that morning and the young lad squirmed then screamed as the water streamed over his head. Leonard knew that Ephraim and the Hampton Legion were soon to face a far different baptism that very afternoon. Screams would be heard there too as bullets, not holy water, rained over them.

Because of his boil and orders to the company to remain behind for more drilling, Leonard and his unit were not at Manassas. The drilling was over for the Legion's infantry, however, as they lay flat on the ground, faces down, hidden from the enemy on a grassy knoll. Orders were given not to stir or even twitch. Unable to stand the suspense, one of Hampton's men rose up to peek at what was happening. Immediately a shower of shells fell among the discovered infantrymen. Forced out from cover, they were assaulted by a withering fire of round shot, shell, musket, and rifle balls that fell like hail among them. It was as if a great hurricane was sweeping the valley. Bushes and trees were cut to pieces. Here the Legion suffered its first casualties as three Manning Guards were cut down by canister. They were terribly mangled but did not suffer as they were immediately killed.

The Legion then took up a new position along a rail fence near the Warrenton Turnpike. Moments later, a line of Federal skirmishers advanced and fired. It was by this volley that Lieutenant Colonel Benjamin Johnson, a forty-five year old native of Beaufort, S.C. who commanded the left wing of the Legion, fell dead from his horse. A minie ball had ripped through his temple and out the back of his head. Hampton held his position for two hours as the battle raged on in favor of the bluecoats.

As the battle continued, Brigadier General Barnard Bee and his shocked South Carolinians were on the verge of being overrun. Bee ordered a retreat that soon turned into utter panic. The Yankees began to celebrate, but an unearthly sight and sound never before seen or heard quickly drowned out their premature cheers. The sight was that of Brigadier General Thomas J. Jackson, a quirky, former V.M.I. professor, leading a charge straight into the Federal lines. Jackson was a Bible- thumping, lemon-chewing, born fighter, and his men would follow him into hell itself. The sound was the famed Rebel Yell, a high pitched, banshee-like scream, that would terrify many a Federal on this day, in the battles to come, and in the nightmares of Union veterans long after the war. It was as much a part of a rebel's fighting gear as his musket. Many described it as a blood-curdling cross between a scream and a holler, and more than a few believed it was unleashed by the devil himself.

Amidst this godawful yelling, Jackson first earned the nickname "Stonewall," a name that, like him, would stand firm forever. Inspired by Jackson's boldness, Bee's men halted their retreat, turned, and rallied behind Stonewall. Bee was killed in the advance but the charge allowed Beauregard and Johnston to stem the tide and form a new line. McDowell, meanwhile, did his damnedest to lead a counterattack. A shell killed his horse so he mounted another, his fourth of the day, as he pressed on in what would become thirty-two straight hours on horseback. More of Johnston's fresh troops from the Shenandoah Valley began to reinforce the nearly spent army that had fought the Federals and the heat since early morning. Meanwhile, the Legion infantrymen were near exhaustion, but still Hampton and the South Carolinians fought on. The Colonel would later relate in his official report that,

*We advanced to the Spring Hill farm house...under heavy fire of cannon and musketry. In the face of this my men advanced as rapidly as their worn out condition would allow, and after delivering a well-directed fire, I ordered them to charge upon the battery under the hill. In leading this charge I received a wound which, though slight, deprived me of the honor of participating in the capture of the guns which had done us so much injury during the day.*

The Federals then launched an attempt to recapture those guns. The Legion withdrew, then reformed alongside the 18th Virginians, and charged yet again, driving the enemy beyond the hill. This action roughly coincided with Beauregard's final effort, and victory was at hand. The Confederate line pushed forward, captured the Federal guns near the Henry House and turned them on their retreating owners. McDowell's men panicked and ran.

The road back to Centerville was clogged with correspondents, officials from Washington, ladies, and other picnickers who had driven out with their luncheon baskets to see a glorious victory. Like their army, they too ran now. A Confederate shell struck the bridge over a creek, overturning a wagon and blocking escape. A group of congressmen trying to halt the stampede, drew their revolvers, jeered the men as cowards, and threatened to shoot them. But it was all in vain as panic possessed the soldiers. The heat was awful even now at six in the evening. The defeated Federals streamed back to Washington with frenzied eyes, gaping mouths, and cracked lips blackened with cartridge powder. While McDowell's six-day campaign was a disaster, the Legion was proud of its showing and rightly so. Over 600 strong had stood tall in their first taste of action and fought to the finish. General Beauregard and President Davis came to Hampton's tent to congratulate the Legion on its opening encounter. The first blood of the Civil War's first great battle had been spilled and the Legion had proven itself worthy.

"On to Richmond!" had been the northern cry. Now the only cries headed to the new capital were the screams of the wounded and proclamations of a great Southern victory. Back in Ashland, early reports of Beauregard's heroics were beginning to drift in and Leonard passed on to Anna what he heard in his July 21 letter. Now, as the Old Captain read the words he had written so long ago, the events were still fresh in his mind.

*The infantry companies of the Legion went on to Mannasas day before yesterday and I suppose probably participated in the fight of yesterday which we hear by rumor was going on at Bull Run or near there. I hope Beauregard was as successful as in the first engagements. It's believed here that the enemy must have lost nearly 1,500. I have not been able to get any of the details. The regiment Ephraim belongs to was engaged in the fight and cannot hear whether he was hurt or not. It is said our regiments suffered most. Last night heavy cannonading was heard at Aquia Creek about 55 miles distant. The firing lasted over ten hours. The big fight I expect will be over before we can reach the field but that will be only an opportunity lost. There will be plenty of work still to be done even if our army was victorious. I find the people of this place very kind, the ladies in particular. They offered to do any work I might need. They made me an apron to wear when carrying my horse. A gentleman made a present today of a horse to Austin, one of our troopers who lost his and another gentleman a fine shotgun to another one of our men. There is nothing of importance transpired in the company since I wrote you. There are three or four cases of measles. All of our neighbors are well. Mr. Cline recd a letter yesterday and told me you were all well. I asked you some time ago to send me an oil cloth for an overcoat. I have found one at Richmond, India Rubber, which will keep me dry. Write to me at Manassas Junction. Next time I write I can be more certain as to the point to direct me at. My bile pains me so much it gives me the headaches. This evening I think it will be ready to lance tomorrow and then it will get well directly. Write often and tell Henry to write.*

*Yours,*

*L. Williams*

*My love to Aunt Susan and to all and tell me about baby and hope she will soon be able to talk to you and receive the good instructions you will be sure to give her.*

Four decades later, as the old veteran glanced out his hotel window, he shook his head at the inaccuracy of his casualty estimates. He had always taken great pride in the detail and fairness of his business dealings. Why, he wondered, were his figures rarely even close to the actual tally?

Later historians would estimate that 500 Union troops were killed at Manassas with another 1,400 wounded. The total losses, including those captured, were about 3,000. The Confederate losses in killed, wounded, and missing were about 2,000. But Leonard was right about the high price paid by the Hampton Legion. It had suffered greatly. Nineteen were killed. One hundred were wounded. Two were missing. In the cavalry, four were killed and eight more wounded. Ephraim Williams survived Manassas as the 3rd

S.C.V. Infantry was not engaged. Leonard's prayers had been answered. Anna's prayers were answered too and thankfully expressed in her diary.

*July 25th, 1861 Thursday*

*On last Thursday 18th a battle was fought at Fairfax and on Friday one at Bull Run. In both the Confederates were victorious, the loss of life on the Federal side was over nine hundred. The Confederates lost but a hundred and a few over. On Sunday 21st a great battle was fought at Manassas. The victory was ours but the loss of lives great. Many brave men fell among them Col. Johnson of Hampton's Legion. God has given us the victory! Oh may they be spared through coming conflicts. Len has not been engaged yet. Something tells me he will not be hurt. God grant it. I pray for strength whatever may come. "Deal courageously & God shall be with the good" II Chronicles.*

It would be her last entry for the duration of the war, because she knew well that regular letters to her husband were far more important than reminiscences to herself.

While Leonard and Ephraim had been spared, an opportunity had been lost for the victors. Only a half-hearted attempt was launched to cut off the panicked Union retreat as the spent rebels, dead on their feet, let McDowell and his shattered army limp back to Washington. Two days after the battle, First Sergeant Leonard Williams, Ruby, and the rest of Company B were ordered north toward the Manassas battlefield.

*July 24, 1861*
*Junction, VA*
*Hanover County*
*8 miles above Ashland*

*My Dear Anna,*

*The cavalry of the Legion moved yesterday morning from Ashland. Myself, Maj. Norwood and Absalom Blythe and Westmoreland on act of indisposition were permitted to go by rail. We came here last night to go to Manassas this morning but the cars were so full we could not get on and besides the conductor told us that another train would come in soon and take us. We have been deceived. We have therefore to stay here till morning. We will be at Manassas tomorrow evening at 5 o'clock if nothing unforeseen prevents. The times are pregnant with stirring events.*

Stirring events indeed. President Lincoln, his cabinet, and the citizens of the industrial north were devastated, but the defeat also galvanized them. They grasped fully that it would not be a short war after all and would fight on resolutely. Poet Walt Whitman was one of those who saw it happen.

*The defeated troops commenced pouring into Washington, over the long bridge, at daylight on the 22nd, a day drizzling all through with rain. The Saturday and Sunday of the battle had been parched and hot to an extreme...but the hour, the day, the night passed; and whatever returns, an hour, a day, a night like that can never return again. The President, recovering himself, begins that every night, sternly, rapidly sets about the task of reorganizing his forces, and placing himself in position for future and surer work...he endured that hour, that day, bitterer than gall – indeed a crucifixion day – but did not conquer him – he unflinchingly stemmed it and resolved to lift him and the Union out of it.*

Jefferson Davis and his military advisors now turned their attention to the casualties being transported from Manassas to Richmond. The dead were sent south in narrow boxes of rough plank, carried on the shoulders of grim-faced soldiers. The wounded were carried on stretchers, gripped by tired hands straining to balance the broken bodies of those so full of hope just a few days ago. Their clenched teeth and matted hair distorted blood covered faces. Their eyes strained for comrades they hoped would transport them back home. Leonard did not look into the deep eyes and deeper wounds of his friends. Assigned prisoner transport duty, he was looking directly at those who were responsible. His boil now clean and healing, he sat stoicly aboard Ruby as they passed by. He kept the prisoners in line and ordered them to briskly move along. At a resting point, he offered them a few pinches of his tobacco in the hopes of sparking a discussion, which might reveal their motives for fighting.

*A whole train of prisoners has just passed by to be taken to Richmond. I talked to a great many of them and gave them all the tobacco I had and an apple and everything I had in the way of refreshment. They looked most dispirited and generally an inferior sort of men. Some of them were good looking. I asked them why they were making war upon us. I told them we simply wished to govern ourselves and wished them to do as they pleased. Some said it was very fair, another said a country or city might secede if the doctrine was sound. None of them seemed to understand any other doctrine than that the majority must rule.*

Now, in 1903, Leonard was nearly 80, yet he still wrestled with that doctrine. Why must the majority rule? Independence is what his ancestors had fought and died for. Weren't he and his fellow Southerners doing the same? Four of the first 5 and 7 of the first 10 Presidents were sons of the South. Each and every one of them would have clung resolutely to the sanctity of states' rights. Over 80 years ago, the colonies had urged that taxation was unfair without representation. The South paid far more than its fair share, yet its voice fell on deaf ears in the Senate. As for the slavery issue, President Lincoln himself knew that it was protected in the Constitution and his own wife came from a family of slave owners. In 1860 there were some three and a half million slaves living in the South, but all were purchased from northern traders over the preceeding hundred years who had profited handsomely. To be sure slavery was a scourge, but it was a practice born in the North. Who was right? Who was wrong?

After the war, Leonard did everything in his power to help resurrect a state that had been decimated and severely punished by the Federals, all the time wondering what the lives of so many thousands had achieved. The 1900's had arrived and there was still distrust. The country in many ways was still as divided as ever. In the end, he recalled, it came down to duty. Lincoln was doing his and so was Jefferson Davis. Leonard and his two brothers from the upcountry had no choice but to do theirs. But back then there was no time to delve into the reasons for war because the winds of war were upon them and ever changing. So were the events and casualty counts following Manassas. He included those estimates and his own impressions as he finished up the letter written just three days after the battle.

*President Davis also passed down this evening from the battlefield. I suppose you have heard by this time that the Legion suffered terribly.*

*Lt. Col. Johnson was killed and his body was carried down this evening. I have not yet heard the particulars. I do not yet know who are killed but the loss is not quite as great as I supposed. I hear this evening that 500 of our men were killed and 1,000 wounded and that 4,000 or 5,000 of the enemy were killed and a great many taken prisoners probably 1,000 or more. It was a magnificent and glorious victory. I regret our cavalry was not present. I think we could have done service.*

*This place reminds me very much of the country inns you read about in Spanish romances. There are now 25 soldiers belonging to several different regiments all waiting like ourselves to get away to join their companies. The farmers around here all come in to hear the news. I have just got up to hear the news from Richmond by the cars just from there and I read an extra giving the northern act. Their statement makes the matter worse with them than we had expected. There is a great gloom over in Washington and I believe for the first time the Washington papers give a correct account of the fight. Our company had a bad day yesterday for the march. They started in the rain and it rained all day and the tents being sent by cars, they had not shelter at night. It is a bad wind that blows nobody any good. My bile that has given me so much pain brought me an exemption from yesterday's march in the cold rain. I am now much better, the bile has broken and been running today and feels much better. It will be well now in two or three days. We will get to the junction one or two days before our company. I was anxious to get there today to learn who of my friends were wounded and killed to give them any assistance I could. I do not apprehend another fight for some time. You must have the baby's likeness taken. I can hardly call to mind how she looks. Keep one and send me one. Take yours and hers together. Write to me at Manassas Junction. Give my love to all.*

*Yours as ever*
*L. Williams*

On his way to the still smoking but now quiet battlefield where the Confederates had prevailed, Leonard had been filled with a newfound sense of pride. Before, he viewed himself more or less as part of a South Carolina militia, but Manassas was a victory achieved by common blood and those amorphous legions so recently detrained at Richmond had fused into the semblance of an army and had won a national victory. There was an atmosphere of triumph in the camps, and troops like himself who had missed out on the action were eager to fight. He had always possessed a quiet confidence in the ability of the South to beat back any advance. After Stonewall's charge and the Union retreat, he was certain of it. That conviction was strengthened all the more when the spoils of the enemy were counted up following Manassas. The Confederates captured 26 pieces of artillery, 34 caissons and sets of harness, 10 battery wagons and forges, 24 artillery horses, several thousand stand of small arms, and numbers of wagons and ambulances, as well as army supplies of all kinds. Less than a week after that first action, Leonard wrote home from the battlefield to tell Anna all that he had heard and seen.

*Manassas, Virginia*
*July 27, 1861*

*My Dear Anna,*

*The cavalry companies of the Legion arrived here day before yesterday. One, two, or three others reached here the day before and were guests of the Davis Guards. We were too late for a place in the great fight of Sunday. The first word of all that I met was a wish that the cavalry and artillery had been with them in the fight and all the probabilities are had we been here we could have taken a thousand more prisoners. And the rout and flight was so complete that the pursuit with cavalry would have been safe as the enemy threw down everything that encumbered their speed. It's amazing to look at the spoils of the enemy. It was perhaps the best provided army ever marshaled. It was the very flower of their army. All the soldiers had three days' provisions and their wagons were full of supplies. They took over 100 wagons, several wagonloads of knapsacks, clothing, blankets, shoes, about 100 cannon, 15,000 or 20,000 muskets and munitions of all sorts, horses in great numbers, and in fact, I think everything they had. You will, however, see the details in the papers as well as the part the several regiments acted. The Legion has won great distinction and also the 4 Regt. S.Cv.*

*It is amazing that more of our men were not killed and that victory crowned our army is attributable to nothing else but the benign*

*30*

*interposition of the Almighty. They had the advantages in situation, in artillery, and numbers and 10,000 of their troops were regulars. They had made arrangements to have a grand revel at our camps and a great many ladies and congressmen were to join them. They had many wagons loaded with timber for building bridges and they had no other idea but that their march to Richmond would be uninterrupted. A great many letters were found with words of caution as to the health when they got to a southern climate especially at N.O.*

*It's not thought they will offer us another battle for several days. We do not know anything of Davis' plan of operations. It may be that Washington will be attacked. I have seen a great deal of suffering among the wounded. They are sent off to the towns nearest by to be attended to and also several of the enemy are sent off. They took four or five of their surgeons who have been put to work to wait on their wounded.*

*We have now reached the naborhoods of the enemy and hard times are looked for. There is nothing to buy and it is out of the question to have washing done. We will have to do it ourselves. It will be rather awkward for most of us. Your foresight in providing me with sewing material has been of great service to me. I keep patched up pretty well. Our clothes are getting pretty seedy. We will get new uniforms in a week or two.*

That uniform now hung on his closet door. It was 42-years old. It had been slept in, cut up, shot through and bled on. It had lost two buttons, much of its original gray, and by the summer of 1862 it had almost worn out entirely. But Anna had patched it up and preserved it in first-rate fashion years ago, and the bullet hole in the shoulder was mended so invisibly that only the trained eye of a seamstress could notice. He had fared rather well with the sewing kit she had sent along, he remembered, but her skill with the needle far surpassed his. He poured himself another cup and once again returned to his letters. Like his coffee, things had cooled down a bit since the battle, so he had time to write a second letter on July 27 and he added it on to the first.

*My Dear Anna,*

*If ever I get home I think I shall appreciate the comforts of home and the pleasures of your society and kindness more than I ever did tenfold. Every house I pass seems to me to be the home of comfort and happiness. I know now that I never knew the extent of the blessings and the means of happiness with which I was surrounded to such a degree and so far beyond what I deserved. I hope I will get a chance at the enemy soon and that our army may win another brilliant victory and that peace may soon be restored and that we may all in a few brief months be permitted to return to the endearments and delights of our respective homes.*

*This leaves us all well except a few left at Ashland with measles. I have not heard from them since leaving but I judge they are doing very well. It is now reported that we will go in a few days to Leesburg (a pleasant place it is said). I recd yours of the 16ᵗʰ and two from you tonight. The whole face of the country for miles around is covered with tents. I judge there must be near 100,000 soldiers in our army within 25 miles. Write to me at this place. I will write to you when we make a move. I am nearly well I think I can ride in a few days. I hope the next time we move I may be able to go with the company. Leesburg is about 25 miles from here and near the Potomac. I do not know its locality, perhaps 15 miles from Alexandria. Kiss baby for me and give my compliments to all.*

*Your own*
*L. Williams*

On August 16, the Legion was ordered from Camp Johnson near Brentsville to Bacon Race Church where they established Camp Griffin. There, they formed part of the Confederate right wing behind the Occoquan River. James Conner an infantry Major in the Legion described the church as "a regular old Methodist looking building, like a thousand other churches or meeting houses. For the past three months it has been a temple of war, not peace. We have half of it ruled off for a store house and the other half for the guard room."

The surroundings seemed custom-made for the Legion. Three hills rose up as if intended to provide lodging for the three departments of infantry, cavalry, and artillery. In the rear of each of those gentle mounds was a thicket of trees that served as a sort of natural barn for the stabling of their horses. The woods were also quickly transformed into a large, shady kitchen where the men could rest and eat. In front of the camp ran a broad stream, which served as both bathing tub for the men and watering trough for the horses. After a fine fish dinner, the men also used the clear stream water to dilute their rather stiff whiskey. As Ruby relaxed in her natural barn of a pine thicket, Leonard sat by the rapids, rapidly writing a letter home to inform Anna of his present situation and what he sensed was soon to come.

*Bacon Race Church*
*August 29, 1861*

*My Dear Wife*

*We recd orders last night to hold ourselves in readiness to march at a minutes notice and to carry provisions for three days. We subsequently fell to cooking and feeding horses and we got ready our provisions and packed our blanket in our oil cloth and had everything in readiness to march and today we are under the same orders to be ready. It is now 4 ock in the evening and still no further orders. It may be I will be called up before finishing this but my impression is that we will not be moved for the present at least. There is a probability of a fight near Fairfax but there are 50,000 troops I understand between us and the enemy and unless there is apprehended a pitched battle we will not be needed. We, however, can know nothing of the designs of the generals in command. It may be that an attack upon Arlington is intended. Maj. Perry will probably leave tomorrow and I write to send by him. I am still in good health and so are the majority of our company. But a few cases now on hand they're going on about and improving. I saw Dr. Gaunt yesterday. Miller Thompson is still near Brentsville and nearly well. We look for him in camp daily.*

Over five weeks had passed since the clash at Manassas and brother James was getting the itch to fight after drilling day after day back in Aiken, S.C. Ephraim was also frustrated as his regiment just missed the Manassas fight. Drill and more drills was now the routine. The energy and euphoria that once cascaded through the regiment had long since dissipated. Boredom was setting in and many turned their attention to those that were being neglected back home. Leonard was no exception.

*Bacon Race Church*
*August 30*

*Today the weather has cleared after two or three days of steady rain. We have recd no further orders and there seems at this time no probability of an engagement here very soon. It may be that we will remain here another fortnight. We are encamped on a pleasant ground and fare very well, no other regiment being very near us. We have therefore a monopoly of the country luxuries. I recd your letter by Maj. Perry and expect another by Mr. Burgess. We look for him tomorrow. I am anxious to hear from you and hope the baby will pass through the trial of teething without any unusual sickness. I am anxious to hear. You must pay attention to the cleanliness of the room the negroes sleep in and that the room is ventilated at night and see that Steve bathes regularly and puts on clean clothes at proper times. I know to carry this out will be troublesome but from what you tell me about Steve I think it is necessary to take particular care of him and also see that he is warmly clothed and shod and kept out of bad weather. You had better begin now and secure enough woolen cloth to make all of them clothing for the winter. Also, get shoes for them, heavy ones and lay them by til cold weather. It will, I have no doubt, be difficult to get them a little later.*

*I am now wearing a pair of Brogans and I find them excellent for mud and rain. We are near Dumfries on the Potomac, the next oldest town after Jamestown in Va. It has gone to decay now but was formerly an important place, an importing town. I am well and so are all the company. Maj. Perry is now telling goodbye and I must close. My love to all. Write often, my dear Anna.*

*Your husband*
*L. Williams*

Shoes, coffee, clothing, all necessities for that matter, were becoming harder to come by with each passing day. The Federal blockade, part of Winfield Scott's "Anaconda Plan," was beginning to take hold in earnest, tightening like a noose along the Southern coastline. Faster and smaller Confederate ships could still slip unnoticed between Northern patrols, but the Federal navy was being strengthened and in time the blockade would become just that.

Anna now had to oversee the farm and her seven slaves with only occasional assistance from Mr. Whitmire, her husband's business partner down at the mercantile store. While he still could, Whitmire would put aside a few items for her, baby Carrie, and the house servants. Ned, Clough, Steve, Lucy, Bill, Nan, and Maum Fannie were family property as much as the house, garden and store. Now, Anna had to keep an eye on everything and everyone while her husband was riding picket duty and keeping an eye on the Federal army.

While Anna set about the job of organizing her household, a general was in the midst of building up and reshaping the largest, best-trained army in the world. His name was George B. McClellan. They called him "Little Mac" and "The Little Napoleon". An impatient Lincoln urged him to have his army ready to attack Richmond as soon as practicable. Between McClellan and the Southern capitol were an army of ornery Rebels and Leonard, Ephraim, and James Williams.

# CHAPTER FIVE
## ALONG THE OCCOQUAN AND POTOMAC

*Send men to reconnoiter the land...*
*Go up into the highlands and see what kind of land it is.*
*Are the people living there strong or weak, few or many?*
*...Are the towns in which they dwell upon open or fortified?*
Numbers 13:1

Autumn leaves would soon start changing but nothing else seemed to be except for the health of Colonel Hampton who was now nearly fully recovered from his wound suffered at Manassas. Doing nothing and hearing little from home had Leonard in a foul mood.

> *Bacon Race Church*
> *Camp Griffin, Virginia*
> *September 9, 1861*
> *Monday Morning*
>
> *My Dear Wife,*
> *It has been something over two weeks since the date of your last letter from Mr. Burgess. I have heard nothing except by Willie Thompson. I attend to his letters closely as I always hear from him about you. He has recd 3 or 4 letters in the last week, however, in the last no mention was made about you. I am more anxious than usual, as the last letters from you inform me that baby was unwell and also that Steve was sick. We've been stationed here about three weeks and a few days over and the monotony of duties is becoming tiresome. I believe it is best to change frequently being the orderly sergeant and therefore, having all the details for picket to make and guard duty as well as all other details, it is difficult for me to get out of camp. Genl. Johnson says that we occupy the most important post on the river but so far we have been inactive.*

But not all were without their fair share of excitement. Twenty-five men from each company had been handpicked by Major Matthew Butler to mount a reconnaissance expedition in pouring rain towards Mount Vernon on September 5. Learning that George Washington's backyard was not occupied by the enemy, they changed direction and proceeded along the muddy Accotink Road towards Alexandria. Surprising Federal pickets in Gibb's Lane on the outskirts of the town, they took three prisoners, captured three ambulances and a number of arms and knapsacks, and returned unscathed to camp the next day.

Matthew C. Butler, to Leonard then and even more so now, was the consummate leader of men. Leonard never saw Butler order a soldier to go where he would not go himself. He loved his brave men and they loved him. No one was any cooler under fire and like Leonard, he was a "sandy hiller." His uncle was the famous Commodore Perry and his wife was the fourth daughter of Colonel Pickens, afterwards Governor of South Carolina. Butler would rise from captain in the First Battle of Manassas to major general.

Butler was only twenty-five, twelve years younger than Leonard and a hard riding, hell-for-leather cavalryman. Ruby was fortunate she was under Leonard's care and not Butler's, because the cavalry leader couldn't seem to keep a horse a long time. Leonard was sure that he had more horses shot from under him than any general in the army but on this raid, captain and mount returned together, safely leading the scouting party back into camp. Four days later, Leonard added to his September 9 letter, describing the raid.

> *A few days ago a scouting party from our squadron went to within three miles of Alexandria and encountered and drove in the enemy's pickets and took four prisoners, two wagons, four horses and 8 or 10 muskets. We do not know where or when the next fight will take place. We rarely get a late newspaper. We can form opinions from newspaper accounts better than from the rumors we hear.*

But one little tidbit making its way around Camp Griffin, even faster than the measles, was not a rumor at all. President Lincoln had indeed authorized the enlistment of 500,000 volunteers. The enemy would soon be a much larger and well-armed force than what lollygagged out to Manassas only to retreat in fear two months ago. What Leonard and his fellow troopers weren't aware of was the state of affairs over in western Virginia. There, a 54- year old general found himself on a muddy road heading toward Cheat Mountain. A former

West Pointer who had graduated in 1825 second in his class without a single demerit, he was a handsome man of commanding presence, with a brave face, covered by a graying beard. Men looked up to him, loved him, fought for him. He was the father of seven and ultimately he would be revered as the true father of the Army of Northern Virginia. His name was Robert E. Lee.

Lee's orders were to turn affairs around in the west. It hadn't been easy for other commanders in that area and it wouldn't be for Lee. The country was hostile and his supplying railhead was seventy miles away. To make things worse, torrents of rain were an everyday occurrence and measles and mumps were epidemic. The army's chain of command was also weak as Lee would issue orders only to have them misinterpreted by his subordinates. Such was the case at Cheat Mountain where Lee failed to defeat General John Reynolds when a flanking force did not fire the agreed upon-signal because their ammunition was soaked by a mountain storm in the night. Winter finally ended the botched campaign, and Lee came back to Richmond. The newspapers berated him and editorials dubbed him "Evacuating Lee."

While there was plenty of activity in the western states and on the Virginia seacoast, Ruby spent her days eating grass while Leonard watched it grow. In the mornings he posted guards, assigned picket duty, and kept a watchful eye on the mail delivery. He continued his letter in the hope that Anna's trials had not been as difficult as those of Ephraim.

> *September 9, 1861*
>
> *A few members of our company paid a visit to the Butler Guards and returned last night. They bring news that all on hand are well, a great many being absent on furlough. I also recd a letter from Ephraim. He is quite well now but after the great battle and fatiguing marches and exposure has taken sick and went to near Culpepper. He says he was waited on as a brother. They refused remuneration and begged him if again sick to come back. He boasts of a good many other invitations of the same sort. James is near Columbia. I do not know whose regiment he will be attached to. If Williams' health admits of his joining the army and he does so as I know he will as soon as he can, I will be satisfied. In the defense and maintenance of our sacred rights, if any of my blood were to hold back without good cause I would feel exceedingly mortified.*

In the end, his youngest brother William was unable to answer his call to combat duty, but he did transport goods and shuttle letters back and forth from soldiers to families. Now, many years later, the Old Captain realized that his brother had served the best way he could, and it was good enough. He returned to the letter.

*Say to Mr. Thompson that Miller is well and will be on duty in a day or too. He is allowed a few days to recover fully. There is no sickness on any account in camp at present. We have had a great deal of rain and the wet and cloudy weather has been most disagreeable. It is now bright and clear. I am much obliged for the socks. They are everything I wanted. The preserves and pickles were excellent. Our fare is getting scant and very often we make meals without meat. We, however, by marketing make do, manage to do very well. There is a prospect of being paid soon and then we can have what we like to eat. This is a very poor country and the people poor and the crops have been much neglected this year. Put up all the pickles you can conveniently and buy dried peaches and apples, say three bu apples and two bu peaches. They are very much needed by the soldiers. I expect they are cheap. They will be fine to have in scarce times. Flour and corn I understand are cheap in Greenville. I expect you can provide well at present in everything except coffee, tea, sugar, and I suppose these are very scarce. Get Mr. Whitmire to save you twenty-five pounds or fifty pounds to keep for hard times. Unless the blockade is broken it will be impossible much longer to get coffee. Give my love to Uncle Adam and say to him his boys are well. I will answer his letter soon. Tell Mr. Whitmire to lay aside ten pounds coffee and keep it til he hears from you. I still enjoy good health. You must write oftener. I get uneasy and disappointed when I fail to get letters at least every week. But I would like to hear twice a week. Tell the girls I would like to see them and must stay til I get back. Give my love to all.*

*Your husband,*
*L. Williams*

Here the Old Captain paused. He now had plenty of coffee and found the need to use the hotel's water closet. He shook his head when he pictured some of the fields, swamps, and creeks he had pressed into service but never really become accustomed to back in those four hellish years. He chuckled as he recalled the old words of a fed up corporal in his company who defiantly proclaimed that he'd rather face General Sherman's entire army himself, armed with nothing but a pea shooter, than to have to relieve his pee shooter in one of those fetid camp latrines one more time. Leonard returned to the letters with a wry smile. It was only seven-thirty and the great final march was still many hours away. He lost himself once more in his words and the War.

*September 10th, 1861*

*Dear Anna,*

*I intend to send today by Mr. Garrison this letter but he had deferred his departure and I will send this either by Mr. Moore, who is now at Manassas trying to get a furlough. If he fails, will send it by the mail. I am again disappointed in not getting a letter from you. It has been nearly 2 weeks since I have recd a letter from you. I would like for you to write me twice a week and tell me about your affairs, whether you are supplied with the table necessaries, poultry, mutton, beef & c and about your garden and cow and all about yourself and baby and everyone about the house, white and black. How's the baby getting? Has she teethed yet? You had better get a bu of salt and put it away in your closet. It may be out of your power to get it after the present stock is exhausted. I don't know whether we will be able to buy hogs next winter on account of the great number of soldiers to be fed. It is for this reason I advise you to take care to provide seeds and put up dried fruits (preserved) and also to keep a close eye upon the meat in your house. It is well to provide for the worst, let me know what you are doing in these respects. Has your aunt bought Mr. Fleck's house? When will she occupy it? I wish to see you very much. I have forgotten how the baby looks. I feel the better satisfied in being away from you that you are good Aunt Susan is with you and your sisters. I hope your father will give you a visit this fall. It would relax his mind and improve and rest him very much. He needs rest. Everybody gets some vacation and I think you ought to have a month or so. William can attend to his business for him.*

Sergeant Williams and his fellow men were good scouts. They picketed, guarded prisoners, and took fine care of their horses. All of this they did with little complaint and with little news from home. The mail was sometimes lost and always late. Newspapers were like diamonds, rare and cherished. Even more so was a visitor who would arrive with developments from Richmond or a box from home. There was a long undated letter that told of Leonard's excitement at receiving a rush of letters and items, but also how quickly camp routine again took over.

> *Bacon Race Church*
> *Camp Griffin, Virginia*
>
> *The various packages you sent by Mr. Burgess came into camp safely and I believe had something for nearly every member of the troop. His arrival produced a great sensation. In addition to the blankets and other things, I recd four letters all of which were exceedingly gratifying. The pantaloons came in good time. I was reduced to a pair of cotton ones, my uniform pants being entirely worn out. The blankets I cannot carry with me. The blue blanket you sent with the trunk as I told you came to hand. I had, therefore, enough with the last. They are needed, however, by others, and I will let Willis Benson have them. The pickle sauce is exceedingly nice today. We had beef soup and with the blessing of the sauce it was as good as I have ever tasted and was so generally pronounced. I am now as comfortably off as I wish to be excepting that I am out of boots. I took a pair of government shoes (Brogans) which are the thing for the wet and muddy in camp but I cannot get them in my stirrups nor put my spurs on them. They are, therefore, useless in the march. I look for a pair in a box of guns on the way for our company. Alex McBee took my order for a pair and he wrote me they were on the way. When I get there I will be well furnished. We are getting a new uniform. I have recd mine and fits tolerably well. Most of the uniforms are failures and some of them will be useless. The pants you sent me fit beautifully.*
>
> *The excitement in camp which prevailed when I last wrote you has entirely passed away and we have elapsed into the usual monotony. It*

*is probable we will be kept here some time. We are right of the Army of the Potomac and it may be that an invasion may be attempted from Occoquan Bay about ten miles from our camp. The bay is entirely navigable and the landing from the Potomac might be easily affected through this little bay. We keep our pickets out in that direction all the time. Last night signal rockets were seen by our pickets on the river.*

*I recd a letter from Uncle Adam and he says business is pretty good. Burgess says everything is cheap, chickens worth 10 cts., 12 ½ cts. You will I hope provide abundantly with such things. There have been several deaths among the companies from Greenville and I think some have died from neglect. The arrangements for taking care of the sick in the hospitals are deplorably bad and it is impossible to get such things as they need. Poor McDaniel, a son of Madson McDaniel, my particular friend, is dead. He was in the Davis Guards. He was left behind at Brentsville at ten miles off and I could not get to see him. He was a handsome, stout young man and very promising and of excellent character. I feel for his parents. If I should get sick, I intend if money can procure it, to get accommodations in some family and I intend to do the same for others as far as my power.*

*We have now a larger turnout now than we have had for several weeks. Our sick are all nearly well. We left two at Ashland and I do not know how they are doing. The rest are all fit for duty. Will Thompson has not got into camp yet but I think he is about well. My friend, Silas Johnson, is still with us and I enjoy his society very much and I hope his stay may last a week or two yet. I got the newspapers you sent but have recd none very lately. Henry wrote me that the baby has teeth, but I expect he was mistaken as you did not mention it. How is Steve's health? You said you thought he was in bad health. I think attention to his cleanliness and sleeping and some care from exposure will likely restore him. I advised you in my last to commence early to get clothing for the winter. Mr. Whitmire can buy it for you. Do you get milk enough? Mutton, beef? We are now getting very good peaches at 10 cts. per dozen. I haven't enjoyed the luxuries of a watermelon yet. They begin to come into camp but they are too high. I may indulge when they get cheaper. The fruit and vegetables, milk and c we are now getting [        ] I have no doubt to our health. I am in prime health but no fatter or but little more than when I left home. I was amused at the idea of your making my pantaloons larger. There is no need. But I like my clothes loose. My love to all and remember me when you write to Charleston.*

*Your husband*
*L. Williams*

The Old Captain remembered that his state of good health did not last. His next letter home revealed a change.

*September 16, 1861*
*4 Miles from Bacon Race Church*

*My Dear Anna ,*

*I wrote you by Moore and also Lieut. Gaillard who had all the papers signed necessary to make up his furlough excepting the signature of Gen. Johnson. He had, however, moved his headquarters and he failed to get off on Friday as he expected. In the letter now in his hands, I enclosed you 2 twenty notes issued by the Confederate government, a part of the proceeds of my service, which I hope will reach you safe. If Mr. Gaillard fails to get off I will forward you by mail.*

*I have been threatened with jaundice and have a slight attack of it. I got permission to leave the camp and now I'm in very comfortable quarters and improving and will be able to return to my duties in 2 days I think. My case has been very light and possibly but for the precaution of getting a quiet nice place might have been sick. The house I am in was built in 1781 by Col. Ewell, a revolutionary soldier and friend of Washington. Gen. Washington has frequently slept in the house, maybe in this room I occupy. The house is of brick, built in a most romantic spot and in its day I have no doubt the admiration of the country. Having changed hands often it has become somewhat dilapidated. The people I am with are very kind and this table is as well supplied as I have seen anywhere. The cooking is excellent. The lady and her daughters nearly grown, does the cooking, the gentleman the milking. They have no negroes. Everything about them looks neat and comfortable (their name is Howard ). It has been a long time since*

*I have received a letter from you not since Mr. Burgess returned. I have been anxiously expecting one every mail for the last 10 days. I know you have written me but I suppose the letters must be lost. I wish you would write to me twice a week. Tell me how you are getting along and how is baby and all. Give me market prices for poultry, butter, eggs, beef. How is your garden?*

*We do not hear at present of any immediate movement on the part of the Legion. We may be at the camp sometime yet. I am tired of the inactivity. There will be a scout of 200 men sent out tomorrow for what kind of work on hand no one knows. I would like very much to go but it would be improper now to take a long ride and lay out in the open air during the night. We are within 20 miles of Alexandria and about 6 from the Potomac. Give my love to all and remember me to your father and mother when you write them.*

> *Your husband*
> *L. Williams*

To this day, the Old Captain never took for granted the sacrifices made by the Old Dominion. A week after the firing at Fort Sumter, the spark that lit the fuse back in April, Virginia quickly joined the Confederacy and Arkansas, Tennessee and North Carolina followed her example. Virginia also brought heroes named Stonewall, Jeb, and Bobby Lee. She understood when she left the Union that much of the war would be waged on her soil as indeed it would be. The Virginia folk had been kind to Ephraim, and now they had opened their doors and offered everything they had to Leonard. Across her valleys, mountains, and streams, the Army of the Potomac and the Army of Northern Virginia would soon flank, attack, and slash at each other in small skirmishes and great battles. Caught in a swirling whirlpool, they would circle back upon one another, in a bloody vortex chewing each other up and nearly all of Virginia in the process.

Upstate Virginia would be the cockpit of the eastern theater for many reasons. First and foremost was its shape and location. The strategic triangle of northern Virginia shielded invasion routes. Its point aimed right at the Federal capital. The Potomac River, along which Leonard was camped, and the lower Chesapeake Bay formed its right leg. To the west rose the Blue Ridge and the Shenandoah Valley. The base of the triangle followed the basin of the James and Appomattox Rivers while Richmond stood halfway between the bay and the valley. For most of the war, Federal commanders would be beaten on the edges and in the middle of this triangle as they attempted to capture Richmond and defeat the Army of Northern Virginia. In three neighboring counties within this triangle more than half a million men would fight in deadly battles. Remarkably, more would perish in those counties than in the Revolutionary War, the War of 1812, the War with Mexico, and all the Indian Wars combined. But in the summer of '61, Virginia was still a pristine paradise, not the burned, stark wasteland it would become, the perfect place for Leonard to rest and gain strength.

> *Bel Ayre, Va.*
> *Near Bacon Race Church*
> *September 17, 1861*

*My Dear Anna,*

*Being still at this pleasant retreat where quiet and plenty abound, comfortably seated in a well furnished parlor with abundance and leisure, I begin to write another letter to you today. Although this is the 4ᵗʰ since I have recd one from you. There are 4 of us here on the sick list but all up and improving, none of us have been in bed but still too unwell to be out in the sun or to undergo much labor. I think we will all be back into camp very soon. I find this to be so pleasant a place and Mr. Howard's such an agreeable family. I propose staying till I am quite well. I am surrounded by books with which I can be amused and also beautiful walks and rides around about. I walk in the morning and ride in the evening. Mr. Howard is a capital farmer and he has revived in me a strong desire to get on a good farm. His horses and cows are fat with only the feed they get in pastures. His barn is full of hay and oats. I am pleased with his entire management but I can improve I think in some of the details. I would like very much to find a place that suited me within 25 miles of Greenville. This, however, is all speculation. The war must first be fought out and peace won and how many may be left to enjoy its blessings is hidden in the womb of the future.*

*I have been out riding and feel much invigorated; this evening in the distance we have heard heavy cannonading but do not know where or who are engaged. It may be our own scouts who were to have gone out this morning. There have been a good many Yankees in our naborhood, but on the breaking out of war, most of them left their property and fled back. There are few of them left who seem to be true to their adopted state and will take the oath of allegiance.*

*I do not know yet where we will be quartered this winter but I think will be impossible to live out in tents and to keep our horses out in the open air without shelter. It seems to me if the exigencies of war require our presence and services in this part of the country, we will be compelled to go into the enemy's territory and take some of their cities to quarter in. If we can get into Baltimore, I think it would afford us admirable accommodations. It may be, however, we will be ordered back to S.C. This I would like very much as it would enable me to see you perhaps often if not actively engaged and I can get off and will try to get off in December for a short furlough. I want to see you and baby very much. How is the baby getting? Has she got through teething? How is Steve? Are you making any progress towards getting their winter clothing and shoes? Have you had your turnips sowed? If not, plant in the lower part next to the fence and put all the manure you can get on it. Mr. Whitmire will assist. What are potatoes (sweet) worth? Did the Irish potato patch yield any? If there are any left in the ground make Steve dig them and put them away. You remember year before last we saved a good many. Mr. Howard is waiting to go to our camp and I must close. My love to all. I would like in an addition to the hat I wrote for if you could mail me two shirts, colored of some woolen material. These I have are good but I am tired of the sameness. I want them equally as heavy as these but lighter color. I cannot describe what I want but leave the thing to you. Write soon.*

*Your husband*
*L. Williams*

On the same day he had written the above letter, there was one hell of a thunderstorm at camp. The regimental history later recorded this incident.

*On 17 September 1861, Lieutenant-Colonel Griffin was struck by lightning, and by the end of October was still on furlough, the results proving more severe than was supposed. His arm is almost paralised by that lightening stroke. He was standing by a pole at the entrance of his tent, supporting it until the gust blew over, while his servant was standing at the opposite end doing the same thing. The bolt struck the head of the pole in the hands of Col. Griffin, passed down, across his breast, leaving a bright red streak, and entering the body of the Negro, killing him instantly. Another servant in the tent was also stunned, but has since recovered.*

Nine days later, some of the Legion unleashed a little thunder of their own. The first fight of the artillery branch took place on December 26 when a group from Hart's Battery, a part of the Washington Artillery under Captain Stephen D. Lee, were sent to Freestone Point on the Potomac. Their orders were to attract fire from Federal gunboats. In their possession were two rifled 6-pounders and a rifled 30-pounder nicknamed "Long Tom," a captured trophy from Manassas. After three hours of shooting, Lee moved his guns up to a high bluff. Soon, a gunboat approached until it got close enough so that Lee's artillerists could see the buttons on the Union officer's coat. Finally, Lee gave the order to fire and shelling forced the side-wheel tug *U.S.S. Jacob Bell* to withdraw. An hour later it returned with no less than five additional armed boats but after about four more hours of spirited fighting, the union flotilla began to limp off, taking one of their gunboats, a disabled screw steamer named the *U.S.S. Valley City* in tow.

While the boys of Hart's Artillery Battery were out firing away at Federal gunboats, Leonard had returned to camp and could hear the echoes of their handiwork in the distance.

*Camp Griffin, Va.*
*September 26, 1861*

*Dear Anna*
 *I am still in command of our company at the old camp and have nothing at all to do except seeing to posting the guards in the morning which does not occupy more than ten minutes. The rest of our company as I mentioned in my last are encamped 8 miles off near the Potomac. The batteries that have been put up lately in the neighborhood of their camp offered fire on the vessels yesterday and it was returned. They*

*had a pretty sharp brush and one of their vessels was disabled and had to be carried off by a tugboat. The firing was renewed this morning. The Legion and also many other regiments are stationed nearby from 2 to 5 miles distant in order to pounce upon the enemy if they land, but I have no idea they will attempt to do so. Our men, though within 2 miles of the firing cannot see nor know anymore of what is going on there. We who are 10 miles off, we can hear the guns and if they should make a landing or camp here will be deserted.*

*Everyone is now impatient for the fray and we will be immediately sent for if an engagement is likely to take place. Our generals are, I think, exceedingly cautious and I do not know what they are waiting for. It may be they propose acting entirely on the defensive and if so, it may be months before they attack us. I do not, however, know that they intend to pursue strictly a defensive policy, if offensive, this onward movement may be commenced at any moment. We know nothing here of what is on foot. If it be the purpose of those in authority to carry the war into Africa, I think they have no time to lose. The weather is now pleasant and we should make hay while the sun shines. I see some of the Richmond papers and also I believe The Charleston are censoring the apparent inactivity of our forces but I think they are incapable in these kinds of affairs and are worthless. I regret to see this fault finding.*

As the Old Captain reread these words, he remembered that when he wrote this letter, it had been over five months since he had so zealously enlisted, and he still had yet to fire a single shot. The only time he had seen the enemy was when he guarded the prisoner transport from Manassas to Richmond. Worse, while Anna was alone, frail and prone to lapses of illness, he had suffered but a tiny boil and a touch of jaundice. Jaundice…was he yellow? Would he have the courage when needed? Would his fellow troopers? For now, he was getting soft, and perhaps the papers were right in criticizing their lack of effort and not taking the initiative. Camp life was almost too easy. The old man noted how much of his September 26 letter revealed this.

*The mail brought me yesterday your letter of the 17th and soon afterwards Oscar Mauldin brought me another dated the 13th and also the sugar and tea and crackers and oysters in Willie Thompson's trunk.*

*The oysters were a grand treat. I stewed them with butter and pepper and crackers and they were fine. I assisted in the preparation of them by several interested cooks and not withstanding the old saying "too many cooks spoil the broth" ours was excellent. The sugar came in the nick of time. We had just finished a pkage sent by Dr. Long. We get no rations of sugar. The tomatto catsup as usual was lost but enough was left in one of the bottles for dinner for the whole mess. I am afraid the tea was spoiled by the accident. I have however most of the tea on hand that you sent me before. I am obliged for the palmetto tea but it too was stained by the catsup. I have just washed and put it out to bleach. The letters were of more concern and interest to me than the delicacies. It had been a good while since I had heard from you. And I was glad to be assured of the health of you and all and pleased with this account you gave of baby of its teething, its trying to talk and of its vivacity and I may say of its smartness for I am very sure it is a very smart child and that I am sorry I cannot have the pleasure of witnessing and assisting the developments of its mind and affections. I would be glad to have yours and her picture together. I have yours but I do not have a good one. I want yours and baby's taken together.*

...

Little Carrie...were her eyes still sky blue like her mother's or had they since changed to the slate gray shade of his? Was she taking those tentative first steps yet? Would she even remember who her father was? These were the constant anxieties of Leonard and all the others, North and South alike, who had left brides and babies behind. It is in those first critical years that a child's notions, curiosities, and outlook are shaped, and he knew he wouldn't be there to help guide her.

Today, the Old Captain still marveled at how Anna somehow managed to raise their daughter in those formative years, alone and on a foundation shook by chaos and suffering. The unsung heroes of this war, he thought as he continued to scan his words, were the Annas who maintained their homes and sustained their faith in the face of four years of despair. Back then, however, there was no time to dwell on his wife's circumstances because the Legion was preparing to head north for a raiding expedition across the Occoquan.

On October 4, 1861, the entire Legion advanced on Pohick Church in Fairfax

County, where a Federal force was posted to protect what was believed to be a large stock of oats and fodder. Both the Legion's artillery and cavalry started off at two o'clock in the morning, marched about ten miles that night and bivouacked in the woods at about eight o'clock. An attack at first light was set, but by then the Federal troops and supplies were long gone. Hampton's raiders had been discovered.

Leonard and the Legion returned to camp empty-handed. There would be no fresh fodder for Ruby. Frustrating him even more was learning from Anna that events back home were not going as he'd hoped, because she was not receiving the sorely needed assistance from all her slaves. Leonard had always cared for his Negroes who were a vital part of his family, separate and unequal, but family just the same. He had made certain at all times that they were properly clothed, fed, and housed. He saw to their needs and expected them to reciprocate. Now that responsibility, in addition to Carrie's proper growth, fell solely to Anna. He wrote to her less than a week after the failed raid with those thoughts in mind. His letters were sent from what was Camp Griffin, renamed Camp Conner because Major Conner was now second in command, temporarily replacing Lieutenant Colonel Griffin, who was still indisposed from his lightning strike.

> *Camp Conner, Va.*
> *October 10, 1861*
>
> *I recd one letter by Lieut. Moore and another by mail from you last night and also one from Henry and another from uncle Adam. I was proud to get them but I would have liked them better if they had been distributed over a week. The mail, I think, never has yet failed to bring letters safely through and had they not waited for Moore, I would have recd them as I expected a week ago. Henry writes to me that Steve is a bad and worthless boy and I expect he has given you a great deal of trouble. When you go to Charleston, it will not do to let him stay at home. I believe I will have him sent to Wm. Mills or Robert to keep a year just to learn him how to plow and make him work. They will put a curb on him. I will write to William Mills and see if he will take him. I do not know what to do with Nan. Probably it would be as well to send her also with Steve to learn how to work. Fanny and Bill and Clough can stay at home and try to take care of the place and the cows.*

*You by all means should visit them and will bar no objections if things go on well at home for you to stay 2 or 3 months. But I should feel badly if I shall be permitted to go home on a furlough to find that you were in Charleston. In the meantime I will make arrangements to get Steve and Nan off. It will not due to leave either one of them at home. I would also like to get rid of the Brindle cow. It will be too expensive to feed her during the winter and if Fanny should get sick there would be no one to attend to them.*

*Alexander McBee writes to me that there is no bacon in Greenville and that it is very high. I think you had better get Mr. Whitmire to sell it saving only enough to do them at home till 1st of Jan. and keep the money to buy hogs with while you are gone. The only embarassment connected with your trip to Charleston would be in the case of sickness but I have no doubt Henry and Joseph Whitmire will cheerfully give you the place and the negroes some attention but if the state is invaded this winter I would much prefer you to be at home and your folks with you. We cannot tell what is ahead of us but if possible I will be at home the 1st Dec. Apart from the motive of seeing you, my business requires my attention and if a furlough can be had I will be at home in the early part of Dec. I would like you to postpone your visit til that time and if successful in getting home will after staying a week or 10 days at home, go with you to Charleston. But if I do not get home I will notify you in time to make your visit to Charleston at any rate, by the 10th Dec. I hope this suggestion may be agreeable. This is a rainy gloomy day and bids fair to continued rainy.*

*October 12th. I recd another from you last night and was glad to hear of the good health of you all and of the exploits of the baby. I know it will be a pleasure to your father and mother to nurse and watch her amusements and pleasures and I want from the Drovers. I want him to buy about 3 hogs for you. The bacon, I understand is worth 25 or 30 cts. per lb. and it would be a good exchange at this price for pork this winter at 8 or 10 cts. per lb. See Mr. Whitmire and ask him to store it for you. Besides in these scarce times while you are gone, I do not think it would be safe at home. I will write to Mr. Mills and Robert this week about Steve and Nan and also to Henry. I wish to remove all the obstacles I possibly can so that you may be freed from anxiety as much as possible while you are from home.*

*The shirts and gloves and necktie all came safely to hand and please me exactly for which I am much obliged. I am now comfortably supplied with bedding and everything else and occupy with Lieut. Prince a tent by ourselves. The money also came to hand. I would have preferred small bills but I can use it. It is hard to get change and that is the reason I do not always prepay my letters. Write soon and let me know if it will disarrange your plans to postpone your visit til Dec, I never tire of hearing about the baby so you must tell me all about her. My love to all. Remember me to Jno. & Mrs. McKay.*

> *Your husband*
> *L. Williams*

A month later, the mood of the Legion and all South Carolinians turned as gray as the skies overhead. Down on the coast of their home state, Port Royal Harbor fell into the hands of the Yankees on November 7. Now the North had a base on Hilton Head from which they could strengthen the blockade and launch an assault on Charleston, Columbia, or perhaps even as far west as the upcountry. Three days after Port Royal fell, Robert E. Lee arrived in Savannah to personally oversee the defense of the South Atlantic coastline. When news of the defeat and Lee's arrival on the coast reached the Legion, the men wished to return to South Carolina as a unit and defend their home state. In particular, the officers of the Beaufort District Troop, who came from the occupied area, asked Colonel Hampton and General Beauregard to order their company back down to South Carolina. Their pleas were denied.

Two and a half weeks later, the Legion still fumed about the prospect of having to remain in Virginia while the coast of South Carolina was now crawling with bluecoats. When Leonard wrote home, he accentuated the positive and shrugged off the defeat at Port Royal. As he would in future letters, he put the most optimistic spin he could muster in the next envelope home.

> *Camp Butler, Va.*
> *November 24, 1861*

*My Dear Anna,*

*I recd yours of the 16ᵗʰ day before yesterday. I am inclined to believe you and the people of Charleston overestimate the enemy's success at Pt. Royal. I regret that the inhabitants of the islands and country in vicinity of Pt. Royal did not dispose of their cotton and Negroes out of their reach. I see by extracts of northern journals that they are rejoicing most extravagantly over their success and the Secy. of the Navy has ordered a national salute at all the Navy yards. This shows their desperation and they are endeavoring to buoy up the public mind by holding up this achievement as a brilliant victory when in reality the odds against the little garrison was so overwhelming there. The wonder is they held out so long. The only real damage to our cause consists in the destruction of property in the neighborhood. If proper measures are taken it matters not what force may land. They can never reach Charleston. Indeed I do not believe they would attempt a march toward Charleston with 50,000 troops. I am not acquainted with all the modes of attack the enemy can make on the city nor the means of its defense but if the harbor and its surroundings are properly fortified and garrisoned I have no fears of any serious injury they can inflict upon us. If the people of Charleston are compelled to leave the city or if it is in any way endangered, of course, I would be glad if Billy's family would take refuge and as many of your relations as you can accommodate and if your father would reconcile it with his feelings I would be very glad if he and his mother would go up and stay with you.*

*Col. Hampton applied to Davis for a transfer of our Legion to S.C. but under present circumstances he could not grant it. It may be if the present threatenings here pass off we may be sent back but it is quite uncertain. I think it is likely we will have to defend these passes during the winter. We are yet making no preparations for the winter. I am quite well and no great ordeal of sickness at camp. It is now quite cool. I am standing it so far very well. Write soon. Tell me about baby and all the news. My love to all.*

*Your husband*

*L. Williams*

*P.S. I sent by Arnold in Lieut. Moore's trunk a bundle of summer clothing, 2 coats, 2 pair pants and 3 shirts.*

As 1861 drew to a close, Leonard wondered how long the South's apparent inactivity would drag on. Worse, he read of the steady stream of new Federal recruits who were pouring into Washington where vast supplies awaited them. Still, he felt confident that if his troopers weren't allowed to rust too long, they would once again reclaim the spirit they were first flushed with four months ago. Fort Sumter and Manassas were over and far bloodier battles were to come. While George McClellan was drilling and re-drilling an army that now numbered well over 100,000, the Old Captain recalled that back then he was celebrating his 38th birthday and his first Christmas away from Anna and Carrie. For the cavalry and the entire Hampton Legion, it was time to settle into their first winter quarters and find out if they really were good scouts in the face of snow and ice. Now Leonard and Ruby would have to endure some tough campaigning at Camp Wigfall, Virginia.

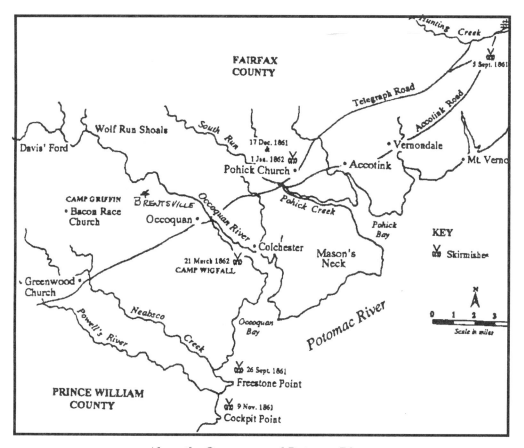

Along the Occoquan and Potomac Rivers

**General M. C. Butler**
**Commanded 2nd S.C. Cavalry in 1862-63**

**Captain of Brooks Troop**

# 1862

**Letter Advising of the Death of Leonard's Brother, Ephraim**

# CHAPTER SIX
# THE COLD WAR

*I know your deeds, your labors, and your patient endurance.*
*You are patient and endure hardship for my cause.*
Revelation 2:2

On January 1, 1862, James Williams and the men of McGowan's 14th Regiment were in deep trouble along the shallow waters of the South Carolina Coast. Near Pocotaligo, shells from Federal gunboats were ringing in the New Year and ringing in the ears of the 14th S. C. Volunteer Infantry. One shell exploded right in the heart of their ranks killing nine and wounding another fifteen. James was not one of them. Leonard knew nothing of his brother's predicament or of the exact whereabouts of his youngest brother Ephraim. He thought about them often on picket duty, and when riding near Pohick Church, he'd stop and offer a short prayer for both of his brothers before heading back to his new winter encampment.

Camp Wigfall, located near the village of Occoquan, was in essence the first and last true winter quarters for the 2nd S. C. Cavalry. Subsequent winters would be spent on the move or only in brief periods of encampment. From Camp Wigfall, Leonard and Ruby would still pass by Pohick Church where General George Washington once worshipped, as Mount Vernon was located just twelve miles away. Sudden snowstorms were waited out in the home of kindly Mrs. Violet, which also served as their reserve picket post. Almost every frigid morning was spent splashing across rocky Selectman's or Davis' Ford on scouting parties with Colonel Hampton. Leonard sucked on icicles he would break off his cabin overhang until he could fill his canteen at those fords. Coffee was scarce. Grousing was plentiful. That first winter in the field was hard.

The Old Captain shivered as he recalled it, and his frostbitten little finger still never felt right in cold weather. But it was the lack of proper quarters and supplies more than the cold that created hardships, especially on the horses. Leonard confided in his letter to Anna his concerns and the cost in animals.

*Camp Wigfall, Va.*
*Jan 13, 1862*

*Dear Anna*

*I recd yours of Jan. 4th last night and one from Henry tonight written the 6th. Both were highly gratifying to me giving me continued assurance that you were all doing well considering the times. I was amused at your dreaming fancies as to my eu-bon-point (I have no French references). I will have to undeceive you. I do not weigh a lb. more than I did last winter but I have better health. I expect this sort of life has changed my appearance somewhat. I have not shaved since I left home. The winter so far has been mild and there is less rain than usual. We hear no talk of winter quarters yet, nor of moving soon. It is difficult getting supplies being over 20 miles from Manassas. Our horses are going down every day and unless they are better supplied, many of them will die. The health of our troop is pretty good at present. Mr. Gaillard left again today on a furlough. He's been quite unwell since his arrival and the next day left camp for a farmhouse. I have seen very little of him. His fatiguing trip with the boxes he had in charge, I expect made him sick. If he does not improve within a month so as to have a reasonable hope of standing the service, he will apply for a discharge. I am sorry that he cannot be with us and I hope he may yet recover and return to us.*

*A few days ago I heard that the women and children had been ordered to remove from Charleston under an apprehension of an attack. The same night I wrote a letter to your father urging him to make Greenville his home, but learning next day that the report was false, I did not send the letter. If he and your mother should ever be forced to leave the city, I hope they will take up their abode with you. Our house is large enough and if you should feel any reluctance I would be glad to give him the premises and for you to turn guest. This idea of course is upon the presumption of a long sojourn (a year or so) if any misfortune befall them, or if they are forced to leave the city, I wish them to make our house their home.*

*I will write you about the fences. I have not talked to Mr. Cline but I judge he will be willing to join me in a fence and I believe you said your aunt was. The fence must be built on both sides. I am glad to hear you talk of your stock of provisions. This is worth bragging about. It was very kind of your father to send you such a valuable and nice*

*present. I'm glad you are bidding defiance to the blockade in the mat-
ter of coffee. Really Rye makes a very good substitute. The first opportunity you have, please send my old overcoat to me. If no earlier
opportunity offers, put it in with the uniform Mr. Ira Williams is cutting. I directed him to send mine to you and also, I believe, recommend
you to get Mr. Taft to make the coat. I'm using a blanket with a hole in
the middle instead of an overcoat, but it is not quite so convenient. My
old one will do me the balance of the winter.*

With a hole in his blanket and a hole in his heart, all Leonard could really
do was take care of Ruby. He gave her apple cores and what mess remains he
could find, but the lack in quantity and variety of fodder along with the chilling
morning rides of picket duty were making her weak and bound up. He, like the
other cavalrymen, knew he could do little for his horse and, worse, for his
loved ones back home. Yet, even from 400 miles away, Leonard was determined
to help assist his wife in the development of young Carrie. He may have worn
the gray but he always saw things in black and white. Children, no matter what,
must be taught right from the start to be respectful and obedient. Anna now
held the rod and, in the same letter, he instructed her not to share it or spare it.

*Henry seems to take as much pleasure in writing about the baby as
you do. He thinks it an extraordinary child. I would like to be at home
to enjoy its prattle and to see its timid steps and assist you in giving
guidance to its young thoughts and disposition. Early impressions
exercise a life long influence and I hope above all things that you will
teach her implicit obedience that your commands must in no instance
be disregarded. You must teach it self-denial of other things as the
inculcation for the love of truth, justice, unselfishness, charity and there
is no need to make even a suggestion but to teach it that your wishes
must always be obeyed and unquestioned. It will require firmness and
decision and I hope you will make all tenderness and reluctance to
punish if punishment ever be necessary yield to that higher love that
looks through its happiness throughout life. I have no fears save one
on this point, as I know so will your reluctance to inflict pain. There is
another matter to which I think parents do not generally attach enough
importance. I refer to the habit of nurses and others of controlling*

*children by exciting their fears of unseen things. You know, dear Anna, that you have yourself suffered and so has almost everyone from fears conjured up by the imagination, and I have no doubt for the most part, they have their origin in early false impression caused by imprudence or ignorance of nurses. Another common error is the practice of deterring children or influencing their motives by falsehoods. Though apparently innocent, nurses ought not to be allowed to speak a falsehood to a child. I only wish to put you on guard believing you will agree with me in these views.*

*I sent you in my last an order on Mr. Cox for $50, which was sent by express to his care. Have you recd it yet? Write soon. Give my regards to all.*

*Your husband*

*L. Williams*

*I send my letters unpaid because we cannot get silver.*

The Old Captain angrily cast aside the letter. Instinctively, he found his pipe and his homemade concoction of cherry and hickory tobacco. In such vexing moments, a smoke seemed to either help him forget or focus more precisely on what troubled him so. In this case, it was that letter he had just finished. In it, and all the others he'd yet to read, he never addressed his first and only daughter by name. Carrie was "baby", or "she", or "her", and many times even an "it". A mule is an "it". A rat is an "it". Hell, he called his horse by name. Is an infant not a complete being and thus not worthy of a name? Was "it" just a lump of clay to be molded or truly God's gift to be cherished? Of course he loved Carrie and Anna more than life itself, but that affection was held at bay many times by that stubbornness of his, that iron ideal that a Williams must at all times act like a Williams, even at age one. He knew that Anna did famously in coaxing out Carrie's first words, supporting her in her first steps, and nurturing her curiosity without him...and that's what hurt. But that stern sense of moral rightness was deeply imbedded in him, and as he took a final puff, he realized it was in all of Dixie as well. Southern pride— it was the source of her strength... and ultimately her downfall.

He emptied his pipe, tamped out the ashes and reread the letter that had caused him such consternation. This time, however, he smiled at himself and something else he found hidden in the words. *"Timid steps"*... *"your commands*

*can be in no way disregarded"*... *"it will require firmness and decision"*...
*"reluctance to punish"*... *"fear of unseen things"*... *"fears conjured up by the
imagination"*... *"false impression caused by imprudence or ignorance"*...
*"influencing their motives by falsehoods"*... *"reluctance to inflict pain."*
Ironically, these phrases were not only watchwords for Anna, they were the
many plagues of a Northern general, a commander with over 100,000 troops
under his direct authority, a general who should have won the war in months
with a huge army that the South couldn't match. His name was George
McClellan, and as 1862 began, he would be called upon to help shape the
year's outcome. At only 35, McClellan was the second highest General in the
U. S. Army. Glory, he told his wife, would be his. "You have no idea how the
men brighten up now when I go among them. I can see every eye glisten…you
never heard such yelling... I believe they love me...God has placed a great work
in my hands… I was called to it; my previous life seems to be unwittingly
directed to this great end." Behind all this cock crowing was really a mother
hen. His base became a nest and the men became his eggs. He sat on them day
after day. He obtained more and more fine eggs, and they were eager to hatch
and fly. Instead, he sat on them refusing to budge off his nest. On January 27,
President Lincoln issued an order authorizing a mighty onslaught against the
Confederacy. It was to be unified, uncompromising, and sweeping. Richmond
was the target. McClellan would take it. The war would soon end. Instead,
McClellan ignored the order.

Once more the Old Captain recalled those words he had written that oddly
applied to both young Carrie and the Federal General. *"Your commands can
never be disregarded".* Instead of taking the necessary risks required to win,
McClellan always took *"timid steps".* As for leading men into danger every
officer without question knew *"it would require firmness and decision."* But
despite his genius in drilling and tactics, "Little Mac" was consistently *"reluctant
to punish"* and never attacked with his entire force, if he ever attacked at all.
*"Fear of unseen things"* ran rampant within him. The enemy, though less than
half his size, he imagined to be twice his, with twice the artillery and twice the
cavalry. In his '62 campaign, he had eternal *"fears conjured by the imagination"*
and a crippling hesitancy fostered by *"false impressions brought on by
imprudence or ignorance".* But there was some cause for McClellan's fears
and indecision. Like those nurses back home who might fill little Carrie with
fears of unseen things, the General's intelligence gatherers created a false picture

of the Confederates' force. They reported to him that the enemy had built up more than 200,000 troops in order to defend the capital, and had amassed an array of mortar and cannon that would blast the entire U.S. Army right back to Washington. In reality, the Confederates possessed less than 100,000 and their prodigious artillery was in many cases, merely tree trunks, arrayed to look like cannon. This fake firepower was given the name "Quaker Guns" and they struck fear in the heart of McClellan. With "Chicken Littles" for spies, and no killer instinct, the hen sat and Lincoln stewed. *"Fear of unseen things"* indeed.

For Leonard and the rest of the Hampton Legion cavalry, 1862 would be a most trying year, but in January and February the toughest enemies were the bitter gales and snow. With his windblown tent flap pounding out an eerie night rhythm, Leonard shivered as he wrote. That night, as his bunkmate Alex Payne snored and his candle flickered, Leonard gave Anna a crash course in buying goods and running a farm.

*January 22, 1862*
*Camp Wigfall, Va.*

*My Dear Wife,*

*Yours of the 14th came to hand last night. I also recd in proper time yours of the 10th last. I asked you in one of my last to inquire of Henry and Mr. Whitmire what insurance offices it would be best to insure in. I think it probable that there has been organized and chartered in Charleston a company very lately and I expect if so would be as safe as any. I would like to insure for about half at least on both houses, say $1,500 each. Let me hear from you on the subject. I fear Mr. Whitmire's health is getting precarious and also that the business has dwindled to a small matter. If so, and the war lasts, it will be hard getting along and it behooves us to economize as much as possible. This I know you are doing but the times require us to study how to expend most advantageously. You are now manager and being inexperienced, it is necessary that you study and keep posted on the prices of all kinds of provisions. To assist you, I will make a few suggestions.*

*1st a good milking cow is important. To have one, you must feed without stint. Buy if you've not already 300 bundles of fodder. Feed night and morning, that is for each day. Stable the cow at night and keep the stable well cleaned and dry. Next buy 6 bu wheat bran. Give* her plenty and whatever vegetables can be had and every day or two a feed of boiled peas or meal. It is cheaper to feed well. You will be enabled to make butter and have plenty of buttermilk. In the next place, corn is cheap now, worth I understand 65 cts. per bu. Get Mr. Whitmire to buy you 12 bu. Put in one of the front basemant rooms and see to it that it keeps dry. This will do you for bread, hominy and to feed the cow on for several months in the spring. I have no doubt it will be worth 300 per bu. It will at the same time save Mr. Whitmire trouble of measuring out ½ bu and charging. Also, get 5 gall. molasses for the same reason of lessening trouble both to you and Mr. Whitmire. The little negroes are fonder of molasses than anything else. You will thus be the better enabled to see what the current expenses are. Also, buy 2 bu Irish potatoes at a time or sweet potatoes, however, sweet potatoes are apt to spoil. You have already a pretty good start in the way of meat, sugar, rice and I hope by examining my suggestions you will be enabled to do very well for the next six months.

The garden is an important matter in living. Save all the manure and have it spread over the land. Get up in time all the seeds and when the time comes, hire a good hand to prepare the ground and plant for you. Aunt Edna can give you good ideas on the subject. Keep the cow and calf out of the yard. Let the milking be done in the lower lot. I saw Mr. Cline on the subject of a joint fence. He will pay half the cost between us and I believe you said your aunt would also. So send for Mr. Gibbs at once and get him to put up a plank fence as soon as possible. Your aunt will need one on both sides. It had better be done at once. Get Mr. Gibbs at it right away. I almost despair at getting oaks to live. I think you had better put out some fruit trees. They will soon grow and be useful and ornamental. Did the little cuttings I set out next to Mr. Cline's fence live? If you could see Mr. William Hawkins and Mr. Whitmire will send him to you, he will bring you peaches and set them out for you or you can buy them about and get Henry to set them out.

You said to me sometime ago that your teeth needed working on. I forgot to say anything about it. Of course, you had better attend to it at once. Dr. Anderson is in debt to me about $30 or $40 so you will not have to pay him the cash.

*We are all getting on finely in camp. Our sick list is less now than it has been for the 4 months. It has been either raining, snowing or cloudy for two weeks and mud is very disagreeable. We cannot walk ten steps without getting shoe deep in mud but our tents are very snug. I and Alex Payne occupy a large sybley tent and have a good chimney and a good bed of straw. We sleep perfectly comfortable and sit up til 10 ock by the fire and while away the time reading, conversing or playing chess. This is a very popular game in our company and there are some fine players. My horse has been sick and is very poor but is now beginning to eat but on account of bad roads and the long distance to Manassas our horse feed is very insufficient. Our own supplies are very good. We have the very best beef, coffee, but no sugar. We however buy a little from the country stores. It is out of my power to send you any jars. A great many valuable articles in this time are lost for the want of means to send them home. There is nothing new in camp and from the bad conditions of the roads I expect all military movements of all sorts will be stopped for a while and possibly for the next two months. Has Mr. Ira Williams sent my coat and pants to you yet? Send my old cloth overcoat with them. It will do me very well and I expect a great deal of cold weather in February and March.*

*What progress is baby making at walking? I gave you in my last some of my ideas in regards to its training. I will make another suggestion that I regard it a common fault of making a child believe that everything it does is a prodigy of smartness. A good deal of injury is done to older children by this kind of training and I judge the same bad effect may be produced on the infant mind. Write often. Give my remembrances to all at home and to your father and mother, Aunt Linny and all. Tell Uncle Adam to write to me and also Mr. Whitmire. Say to Henry I recd his letter and will write him soon. Give my respects to Mr. and Mrs. McKay.*

*Your husband*
*L. Williams*

*I panic because I cannot get a stamp or a piece of silver and I expect it is about as difficult for you to get it. I will try, however, to get $5 worth of stamps and will send you some. Can they be had at Greenville?*

*I hear they cannot.*

In the morning, Leonard posted his lengthy letter as January wore on. Two minor scouting parties were sent out that month, both led by Colonel Hampton. On the first reconnaissance, a Texas scout named Burke warned the colonel just in the nick of time that he was riding right into a swarm of Yankees. One trooper along on the venture was left with an indelible recollection of the confrontation.

> *How well I remember to this day that sight. The whole valley was blue with Yankee cavalry...When they found out that we were not going to charge them, and enter their trap, they were mad indeed. They taunted us in every way, shaking their sabers at us, and 'cursing us to boot.' Then they commenced firing on us, and we with our pistols, for the men at that time had no rifles, only the sword and pistol. They of course had the best of this long range firing. We had only one man seriously wounded, Corp. Lip. Griffin, Edgefield Hussars, shot in the face; one or two others slightly wounded, and several horses struck. Col. Hampton, knowing he could not contend with the force on his front, retreated across the Occoquan, sorely regretting he did not have the entire Legion with us. If it had not been for Burke's timely warning, how different it might have been for many of us, who are alive today.*

A few weeks later, Hampton again led four cavalry companies out toward the enemy. His advanced guard spotted them first, a swarm of mounted bluecoats headed directly for them. While Hampton was off leading a detachment on another road with the aim of meeting up in Alexandria, command of the remaining force fell to Matthew C. Butler, senior captain of the four companies. True to form, Butler led an immediate charge. Saber raised, he dashed up the steep, slippery clay hill. Leonard put the spur to Ruby as enemy fire whizzed around him. Bullets poured down from atop the hill but Butler pressed on and routed the Yankees who quickly galloped off to the safety of their picket lines. In mere minutes it was all over. In the brazen attack, many Federals were killed and even more were captured. Leonard helped to round them up. Not a single Confederate trooper or horse had been lost, although it was a tight scrape to be sure for the man who had ordered and led that decisive charge in the first place. Just before reaching the top of the hill, Butler's horse slipped up and fell, falling on the Captain's leg. Butler writhed in pain on the verge of going into shock. Quickly, several of his men unsaddled to help their pale-faced captain to his feet. Dizzy but undaunted, the Edgefield Hussar remounted and maintained command. Butler's close calls were common. Sometimes the horse returned without Butler. Sometimes Butler returned without his horse. This time both came back, but in no way near the condition in which they departed. The Old Captain smiled. There was never a doubt as to Butler's courage, and because of it, never a dull moment for his men.

Leonard admired and respected his immediate commander and his mood always seemed better when he was involved in some sort of action like that recent raid. The excitement and danger energized him and helped him forget the minor annoyances of camp life. The Old Captain noticed almost immediately that his next letter, written not long after the raid in which his fellow Greenvillian was nearly crushed by his own mount, was almost light in tone and did not even make reference to his having been under fire. As with so many of his letters home, he wrote of home and concerns of family.

> *Camp Wigfall, Va.*
> *Jan. 25, 1862*

> *My Dear Anna,*
> *Mr. Gower leaves in a few minutes for home and although I wrote you a few days ago, I will send a line by him. I am still in first rate health and so are the company generally. The roads are so bad I do not expect we will get away from these camps for several weeks. We have permission to move nearer Manassas in order to be more accessible to horse feed, but at present we are detained by bad roads and deficient teams. Maj. Butler is sick and will leave for home as soon as he is sufficiently well. I do not look for any movements of a military character for several weeks at least in this section. We are just as comfortable here as I could wish although it sleeted and blew last night. We sleep perfectly warm. I have a good fireplace. How is Willie Thompson and Mrs. Thompson and Miss Sallie? Give them my respects. I have no news to write. I wrote you in my last to have the*

*fences built and to get fruit trees and have them planted in the yard.
You can also, if you can. Have the walk reset with trees and also then
along the bank near Mr. Flick. Have any of the trees lived? Now's the
time if you cannot do better, fruit trees will do well along the wagonway
between us and the Flicks. Remember me to Uncle Whitmire and Aunt
Edna and all.*

Winter in cavalry camp. The Old Captain recalled quite vividly it could be dreadful one moment then great fun the next. Ingenuity went a long way in coping with hardship at Camp Wigfall. Canteens, tack, utensils, and virtually everything lying around could be made into something of use with a little imagination. Saddles became headrests, logs and plank were placed across two barrels for a table for eating or writing home. Boxes "borrowed" from the quartermaster served as seats, and some privates were adept in the art of whittling, creating pawns from pine and bishops from birch. There were better chess players than Sergeant Williams, but some he could finish off before Ruby was ready to saddle up for morning picket duty. In the evenings, he could spin a yarn with the best of them and not get tangled in it after more than his fair share of spirits. He was allowed a few more sips because the code in this camp and all camps was such that the provider be allowed an extra turn at the bottle. He revealed where those spirits came from and shared a bit of camp news in the remainder of his January 25 letter.

*I forget to tell you that I recd as a present from Miss Sue Wright a
beautiful large scarf, all woolen and 3 and a half feet long and also a
bottle of wine from Dr. Thompson of Newberry and also 2 bottles of old
peach from William. Everything is high here. Butter is selling at 75
cts. per lb. and molasses at $2 for a gall. Our fare is pretty good. We
have excellent beef and good bread and coffee. I have not yet touched
the coffee you sent me. I'm keeping it for hard times. We still get
coffee but no sugar. Transportation is so difficult. Have you heard
anything from our uniforms yet? Kiss baby for me. My respects to all.
Write soon.*

> *Your husband*
> *L. Williams*

Spirits from home raised the spirits of Williams and his comrades, but only temporarily. Inactivity and confinement soon led to boredom. They ran out of jokes. Conversation grew dull, then all but disappeared. Discipline, once accepted as a matter of course, now began to get on their nerves. The days were long and tempers were short. Officers who were eagerly obeyed on the battlefield were now criticized for their lack of movement and blamed for the lack of fruits and vegetables. Gossip ran rampant. Quarrelling and resentment were the order of the day. In the Legion, however, ill feeling never lasted long and the uprisings that did occur more often involved the hurling of snowballs rather than harsh words. At 38, Leonard still had a strong arm and a fair aim in a snowball fight, but at the start of February, a pencil was at the end of that arm and his aim was to inform Anna that he had left Camp Wigfall.

As he opened it, the Old Captain noticed that the letter was written on his morning report form and the address was Bacon Race again. An odd name for the place, he puzzled, for there was no bacon and the pace there was anything but a race.

*Feb. 2, 1862*
*Bacon Race*

*Dear Anna,*

*So you will see by this caption we have left the Occoquan and we have been here 3 days and will leave, I expect, tomorrow on the RR near Bristow. We had to leave our comfortable quarters at Camp Wigfall on act. of the impossibility of hauling supplies for our horses. We will still have to keep up the same piquets beyond the Occoquan and therefore, will be under the necessity of keeping 15 men from each company. Now all the time the men will relieve each other every week so that for the balance of the winter I hope the service will not be so hard. It will take some time to get fixed as comfortably as we were at Camp Wigfall. We have had snow on the ground for 2 weeks and as yet partially covered but it has now cleared off.*

As the Old Captain read along he was struck by the notion that he had enlisted to fight, not care for horses, build cabins, and transport supplies. So much of the early war, he realized, was spent on many things other than fighting. He recalled that he had kept his pistol clean and well oiled yet rarely fired it. Rarely also did his saber leave the scabbard. He kept Ruby fed and groomed as he best he could only to wear her down by mindlessly riding in circles around camp. War, he had thought, would be a grand, heroic thing. Instead it had proved to be a tedious series of insignificant little things. He noticed that this letter, like many of them to date, was filled with the minutiae of camp life and the mundane concerns of expenses. He had even resorted to listing the men on his morning report.

*We have had a most disagreeable time since we moved but hope in the course of a week to report good quarters and a country where we can get good butter and c. There is nothing new in camp. The health of our men pretty good. I am by a smoking fire and cannot write with any satisfaction so I will make this letter a short one. I recd your last and also the papers. You need not send me the papers except one Mercury each week, the copy that contains the market report and also the Enterprise. Try to send as soon as you can after reading them. If you can get a gardener to lay out the front yard and can manage to pay him out of your little assets, I would be glad you would do it and also spend a little, if you like, for shrubs or evergreens. I will probably in the course of a few weeks, be able to reimburse you. I do not want to call on Mr. Whitmire for anything more than we are obliged to do as his business, I have no doubt, is much diminished. I judge you can now, with plenty of cow feed, be able to get milk and butter enough. Don't feed roughness to your cows sparingly. When summer comes, you can have your milk and butter cheap.*

*We have now but little over 4 months to go on when I hope to be with you. I was much disappointed at first in not getting a furlough. I did not apply for one, however, but from number refused, I supposed it would be impossible to get one. When did you get your instrument? You speak of music but tell me nothing about the price or who you purchased from. I understand that paper and envelopes are high and very scarce in Greenville. I sent to Manassas for $5 worth stamps but they were stolen before reaching me, else I would send you some. Paper is scarce here. I write on one of my blanks. Had I thought of it sooner, would have sent you my report for this morning. I will however, give it to you marked in the columns which will give you an idea of our condition. We have in camp for duty, 39 privates and 7 non comd. officers off in detached service, 10 privates, 1 non comd. officer due. On act of difficulty of getting paper, I must put up with one letter a week. I will write now when we get to our next camp.*

The Old Captain paused to finish off his now lukewarm cup of coffee. He found the bitter grinds in the final sip as disagreeable as that first winter. Down went the cup as did his squinting eyes to the bottom, last paragraph of the rather long letter. He did not fail to notice that the tone had become negative, and that he had chided Anna again for not writing often enough.

*In consequence of a snowstorm setting in this morning, we do not send to the office today. It commenced snowing this morning about dawn and now 2 ock in the evening. The ground is covered about 4 in. deep and still snowing but not so rapidly. I am now at Mr. Arrington's. I came here this morning to spend the day and have just finished a good dinner and am now sitting in a chair by a good fire as comfortable as possible. We are present in a bad plight at camps. Our tents were left behind and now the ground is so wet we cannot stretch them. We are using some old tents but having no place to keep fires except out of doors. It is very disagreeable, with chimneys such as we had in our last camps, we were almost as snug as in houses. We cannot say now when we will resume our march but I hope in a few days. I am anxious to commence building again. Our next camp will probably be our quarters til spring. We may expect nothing but hardships til we get settled again. I recd. yours without date last night and was glad to hear you were in good health and spirits. Can baby walk cross the house with assistance? I think you had better get large paper instead of note. I said I would put up with one letter a week from you but it must be a long one. My respects to Mrs. Thompson and all the neighbors and also to Mr. Carlisle. Tell him to write me also and tell Dr. Dean I would be glad to receive a letter from him.*

*LW*

While Leonard, Ephraim, and James Williams were bearing up as well as they could through February ice and snow in Virginia, a storm of a different kind was brewing out in the western theater. It was a bad wind indeed for the Confederacy. On the east bank of the Tennessee River lay Fort Henry and 12 miles away on the west bank sat the much larger Fort Donelson, two Southern strongholds. Both fell into the uncompromising grip of Ulysses S. Grant. At Fort Donelson, when asked what his terms for surrender were, he sent his famous message: "No terms except unconditional and immediate surrender can be accepted. I propose to move immediately upon your works." With those words, a lion was born, who would growl and later roar as the war lingered on. The loss of the two forts was a serious one for the South. It meant the opening of a large part of Kentucky and most of Tennessee to the Union, the loss of nearly a third of Johnston's army, and an operations base for the North in Nashville, the first Confederate state capital to be taken in late February.

In March, Southern forces were preparing to evacuate their camps around Manassas in the freezing cold, and winter was taking its toll on everyone in the Hampton Legion. Williamsburg was their ultimate destination and a showdown with McClellan's army was all but assured. Leonard informed his wife, who was visiting her family in Charleston, about the movement in a long letter that covered the latest war news and rumors, advice on health and economics, and comments on the virtue of homespun dresses.

> *Camp Evans, Va.*
> *Catlett's Station*
> *Orange and Alexandria RR*
> *March 3, 1862*

*My Dear Anna,*

*I have recd 3 letters from you since I have been at this camp but all through Manassas. I do not know how it happened but I must think you have not recd any of my letters from this place. I hope, however, to get one this evening. It snowed and sleeted all day yesterday and the ground is still covered. We are under marching orders and so I believe is the whole army. What is on foot we have no way of finding out. We are ordered to send all our superfluous baggage to Culpepper, all our sick and disabled horses and the rest to hold themselves in readiness to march. We have an idea our movement will be toward Fredericksburg on Aquia Creek, but this is conjecture. It is possible on account of bad weather, we may not move from here in a week. You may continue to write me at this place until I advise you otherwise. I have sent off everything but one change of clothes. I have heard nothing from Greenville for about 2 weeks. Mr. Whitmire scarcely ever writes and Henry but seldom. I think I must insist on you writing oftener than twice a week. I am more anxious now than when you were at home in the midst of the dangers that threatened Charleston, but so long as your father decrees your stay safe, I will be satisfied, and in the event that you're having to run, I will expect all of the family to go with you. How is your brother getting? If you see Nath or Whitfield, tell them both to write me. I know nothing about the organization of their regiment or where they are stationed or what kind of duty they are doing.*

*We are well except some 3 or 4 are complaining a little. There is* *nothing of importance in camps. We have had a very pleasant time here. The people are obliging and supply us with poultry, eggs, butter and c at reasonable prices. I will not close this until I see whether I get a letter from you. I have not been disappointed. Your letter of the 26th came this evening. The box has not yet come. I understand no freight for soldiers is allowed to be brought and I expect it is at Richmond. What was in the box? I am sorry I did not tell you I had leggins. Esq.McBee sent me a present of a pair of elegant ones some 3 months ago. Not only the box but the expenses ($2.25) I expect are lost. Henry sent me a bundle of papers. Mr. Gower put them in his carpetbag. It was opened and they were stolen. I expect the rascal was mad enough to find nothing but a pkge of old newspapers.*

*Nothing definite yet has transpired as to our movements or what is on foot. Genl. Johnston is getting up a thousand horses and from this the army around Centreville may be preparing for a forward movement. I am pained to hear of the extent of the sickness in the army around Charleston. From all I can learn, the up country soldiers must have and are still suffering most severely. I fear they were but poorly supplied with blankets. I am surprised to hear of the high price of corn in Charleston. Farmers all over the south should this year use all industry and devote themselves almost entirely to the production of provisions. You speak of returning home very soon. Unless you are forced to fly, I do not see the necessity of your returning before the 1st of April. It will then be time enough to garden. But I know the life you lead in Charleston is injurious to your health. You stay in the house too much and keep the rooms too close. Fresh air, sunshine, and exercise are what you need. The more you can accustom yourself to endure, the better it will be for you. You have a motive now I might say, a necessity to take outdoor exercise in seeing about your garden. Fanny is a first rate weaver. I wish you had a loom and cards. She and Nan could make cloth enough to clothe them all. I hope the ladies will wear homespun dresses. You can get baby and you nice ones woven when you go home. To me, they always appeared handsome and becoming. I was amused at your exhibit of expenses. I think you have been economical but you must study by the science and profit by the experience and practice of others. I have no doubt it is a pleasure to you. But for this, I would be pained at the thought of your denying yourself. You remember I used to laugh at you about your economical expenditures for the baby. If I remember right, it is really amusing. If*

*I were with you I could laugh an hour about it.*

*Tonight it has been raining furiously and is still raining moderately. I will write you as soon as I find out our destination. I would like for you to write twice a week. I hope baby is well again. I am glad she's so fond of her grandpa and that she amuses him. My love to all.*

*Your Husband,*
*L. Williams*

Leonard had surmised correctly concerning the army's movement and his words *"the more you can accustom yourself to endure, the better it will be"*, would indeed be proven true. That axiom was echoed by a fellow cavalry soldier on the move with First Sergeant Williams.

*...We remained several weeks at Catlett's...to see what move our army at Manassas, under command of that gallant soldier, Gen. Joseph E. Johnston, were going to make. Nothing of consequence happened while we were camped here, except an awful wind and rainstorm, which blew down every tent and horse shed in the entire command. The men sought shelter from the storm in the houses surrounding the station, with a few exceptions...In a few days we got orders to report to Manassas. We knew our army was falling back, for we were encamped in a few hundred yards of the railroad. We proceeded to Manassas, I suppose to act as rear guard, also to get some of the spoils that could not be carried off. What a sight when we left there— every man's horse loaded down with things most needed. I remember for one thing, I had a fine ham, slung on each side...Many a day, in the future days, have I thought of the good things burnt up at the evacuation of Manassas.*

As always, resourcefulness was indispensable in making the best out of difficult situations. But far more than creating a deck of playing cards out of pieces of requisition forms or turning munitions crates into chairs, ingenuity was taken to new heights by the South in two instances in early spring. The first was in the naval war.

When Virginia seceded, the Federals had hurriedly but only partially destroyed the new steam frigate *U.S.S. Merrimac* to keep it out of Southern hands. Confederate engineers went to work on it adding iron plating to her hull. Re-christened the *Virginia,* she promptly made a name for herself by sinking two of the Union's finest steamers. Word had leaked northward about the South's clever recycling and the U.S. Navy had soon developed an antidote for the *Virginia*, the *U.S.S. Monitor*. Unlike the *Merrimac*, the *Monitor* was made entirely of iron and together the two creations changed the landscape of the sea war.

The *Virginia* ventured out again on March 9, the same day that Leonard and the Legion were in the midst of evacuating Manassas, but this time it was met by the *Monitor* at Hampton Roads. The two circled one another, got in close, and then fired away furiously. The *Virginia* tried to ram once, but the blow was futile as her iron beak had been twisted off the day before in the process of sinking a Federal frigate. At day's end, each craft hauled off, battered but fully operational.

A few days later, Leonard read an account of the ironclads in the *Charleston Mercury* aloud to his fellow troopers over breakfast. One private mischievously clanged two tin cups together to serve as background sound effects as Leonard dramatically orated the portion of the attempted rammings at Hampton Roads. The duel of the two ships spanned only four hours or so, but the draw meant that the Union fleet was no longer in peril as was McClellan's plan to ferry a force a few weeks later by sea for an attack on Richmond.

A second instance of Southern ingenuity was nothing short of magic. The great prestidigitator was Confederate commander John B. Magruder who masterminded one of the greatest April Fools jokes ever when he mystically transformed 13,000 men into 50,000. Magruder was in charge of the defenses at Yorktown, site of the surrender that ended the Revolutionary War. His opponent was McClellan who had finally launched his Peninsula Campaign. Magruder's problem was age-old. The enemy had four times as many troops, but Magruder had a plan. "Prince John," as he was called, loved attending the theater so he decided to stage a masterful performance of his own for his counterpart. He marched his infantry in continuous circles and moved his artillery noisily from location to location in order to deceive McClellan into thinking that the Southern defenses were far more stout than they truly were. The pageant was a smashing success, and McClellan reacted as Magruder had hoped. Instead of attacking with his superior force, McClellan hesitantly laid seige to Yorktown.

Magruder's grand illusion bought Johnston's army time, as his demonstrations along with those dreaded "quaker guns" convinced the Federal "mother hen" to hold fast to his chicks. McClellan's procrastination allowed Johnston to transfer his entire army down to the peninsula with the Hampton Legion cavalry riding the flanks. "Old Joe's" forces were brought south slowly by way of Trennis Crossroads to Grove Church about twelve miles north west of Fredericksburg. The Legion cavalry went into camp there and picketted toward Manassas and the northern fords of the Rappahannock. After about two weeks, Leonard and his company then followed Johnston's infantry to Fredericksburg where they subsequently acted as rearguard. He, like the others, believed they were headed to protect the Southern capital, but upon reaching Richmond, the Legion passed on towards the Peninsula. Soon they heard that they were going to Yorktown to reinforce Magruder, whose small army was still miraculously holding McClellan at bay. Finally, a hungry and exhausted Ruby and rider trotted into Caracoa Mills, a few miles above Yorktown.

The Old Captain recalled his first hard ride of the war as if he had embarked on it yesterday. It took over five days to go but fifty miles. He had to often stop in driving rain to dismount and tend to Ruby after a brier or a sharp piece of shale wedged itself in her shoe. He would reach into his trusty pommel holster and fish through it in the dark for his hoof pick. A moment later, the offending object would be pried out and they'd gallop up to get back in place with the rest of the outriders. It was a tough ride, but a tougher march for the infantry, one of whom recalled the muddy ordeal.

> *The distance was about fifty miles, over the worst roads that were ever traveled. Our company lost tents, cooking utensils, and everything except blankets, which, fortunately for us, we preserved. For two weeks, we were without tents and on cold ground. A great many have been made sick by the exposure...*

When a soggy General Johnston finally arrived to inspect what Magruder really had hidden behind his curtain, he knew at once the position was far too weak to defend. Luckily, McClellan remained timid. Day after day, Little Mac stared through his field glasses still beset with *"fears conjured up by the imagination,"* but Johnston knew that eventually even McClellan would soon follow up his siege and attack. As the pensive Northern general was busy counting the same enemy troops and cannons over and over again, Jefferson Davis and his military staff were in the midst of a reevaluation of their own. The Southern army needed a reorganization; it was too fragmented, top heavy with smaller brigades and in need of larger, more powerful units. In the spring of 1862, sweeping changes were made in Johnston's army as regiments were fashioned into brigades and brigades into mighty divisions.

With the reorganization of troops came elections of lower officers and appointments of higher echelon commanders. It was time to weed out the green and the aged and replace them with seasoned and capable leaders. As in such affairs, however, some were deservedly elected while others went about buying votes with dubious enticements that ranged from a new cap box to promises of more rations, furloughs, less picketing, or lighter duty. As one cynical soldier observed:

> *Our election has not yet come off, and to one who like myself is not a candidate it is a time replete with feelings of disgust and contempt. The candidates of course are interested and busy. I could start out here now and eat myself dead on "election cake," be hugged into a perfect "sqush" by most particular, eternal, disinterested, affectionate friends. A man is perfectly bewildered by the intensity of the affection that is lavished upon him. I never dreamed before that I was half as popular, fine looking, and talented as I found out I am during the past few days.*

On March 29, one of the more even-handed of such elections was held in the Hampton Legion cavalry, and Leonard had a surprise to tell Anna.

> *Camp Bartow*
> *Near Fredericksburg, Va.*
> *March 30, 1862*

*My Dear Anna,*

> *Some 3 or 4 days ago, I recd both your letters. One on the 10ᵗʰ and the 14ᵗʰ and also one from Henry and another from Esq. McBee. It was the 1ˢᵗ information I had recd of your return home since coming to this camp. I have written you three letters to Charleston. I'm glad you have gotten home safely and Aunty with you. I could have written you earlier but an election was ordered yesterday a week ago to take place on yesterday for 2ⁿᵈ Lieutenant to fill the place of Lieut. Prince. I was a candidate. I have waited to give you the result. There were four candidates at first, two of them during the week withdrew and the race has been run by Blythe and myself and a close race it was. Many times during the canvass, I would have been glad to be out of it. The canvass was warmly but fairly conducted. The vote cast was 62. Several refused to vote not wishing to vote against either. I recd 35 votes and Blythe 27 giving me a majority of 8 votes, just as many as I wanted. Blythe is a capital young man, a student at Furman University and very popular. It will be several days before I am commissioned, you need not therefore address me "Lt." but "Mr."...*

Not all were as satisfied with the results as the newly elected 2nd Lieutenant, especially one member from the Beaufort District.

*I did not approve of throwing good and tried officers out, and putting others in their places, who lacked experience. Time proved it hurt our cause, more than anyone supposed at that period. Many a good and efficient officer lost his "stars and bars" from this reorganization. And though time and service proved that their places were filled by worthy men, "The Cause" felt their loss for some time, for in the near future incredible wonders had to be performed by this army, commanded by Gen. Joe Johnston. Here Capt. M.C. Butler was appointed Major of the Legion Cavalry. The brave and efficient Capt. Lanneau, Brooks Troop, lost his position, and several others of the cavalry companies...I regretted at the time, hearing of the 'throwing out' of two of our Legion artillery officers-Capt. Stephen D. Lee, of Charleston, S.C., and Lieut. Paul Hamilton, who were fitted to command in any cause, both by efficiency and bravery.*

Despite the faults of the election system, "incredible wonders would be performed by this army," for McClellan was finally on the verge of action. Leonard swapped his three stripes and a diamond for a new bar on his collar and prepared to move off with his company into battle. He concluded his March 30 letter with details of the unit's actions and his personal situation.

*Yesterday, it sleeted a good deal and today it is rainy and sleet on the ground. It is very disagreeable and cold and what makes it worse, we have no fireplaces to our tents. I am quite well. Several of the troopers are sick with diarrhea and the sick are being moved to Richmond. All the troops in the vicinity are under marching orders but we do not know for what destination. It may be several days before we are moved. You may write to me to this place. Address me as formerly so that if we are moved, the letter will be sent to Mr. It will be known in Richmond where the Legion is and the letter forwarded direct from there. I miss very much the regular letters I used to get and I think strange that you have not recd or answered any of my letters from this camp. I suppose they have never reached you. If not, I expect you think it strange I do not write: the last 3 letters I wrote to you were to your father's care, Charleston.*

*I have been to Fredericksburg several times. It is an old town, the head of navigation and has been a large place of business. I judge its population to be six or 7,000. I believe it is only sixty miles to Richmond. McClellan is said to have a larger force in the field on its way to Richmond. May the Lord grant we may be able to turn them back in confusion and defeat. I will write you again in 2 or 3 days if we are not moved. Do write oftener and tell me all about baby. I never tire of reading what you say about her: you and home are constantly in my thoughts and tell Franny and all the children I often think about them and hope they are doing well. Tell Mary Susan I am much obliged to her for the box. Give her and Mr. Whitmire my respects. My overcoat came safe and I am glad it came today. I made a kettle of preserves with the fruit and sugar. It was capital. Give my love to all. Tell Billy W. I want him to wait and join the same company I do. Write soon.*

> *Your husband*
> *L. Williams*

The Old Captain put down his letters for a spell, rubbed his eyes and then wiped away a smudge on his wire rims with his handkerchief. For both him and Anna, 1862 had been a hard year.

## CHAPTER SEVEN
## A CAPITAL SAVED AND A BROTHER LOST

*For thus says the Lord…*
*Behold, I will bring them back*
*from the land of the north;*
*I will gather them from the ends of the world*
*with the blind and the lame in their midst…*
*They departed in tears,*
*but I will console them and guide them;*
*I will lead them to brooks of water,*
*on a level road, so that none shall stumble.*
*For I am a father to Israel,*
*Ephraim is my first born.*
Jeremiah 32:7

Late spring, 1862. George Brinton McClellan finally moves against Johnston. Little Mac transports his force of over 100,000 men via 400 ships down the Potomac to the southern end of the peninsula. With him are over 300 pieces of artillery and 25,000 animals. He lands safely on the coast under protection of his gunboats and now he prepares to take Yorktown then march the seventy miles or so to capture Richmond. Facing him is Gen. Joseph E. Johnston's army of less than 60,000 and the Hampton Legion.

June 6 would mark the one-year anniversary of Leonard's enlistment. In just over two months, his duty requirement would be fulfilled and he'd be free to return to his farm and mercantile business back in the Carolina up country. All he had to do was survive the confrontation with the Federal Little Napoleon, which was sure to come to pass before that date. Other developments bothered him also. Many of the wounded and sick had already returned home and with them went disease, theft and trouble. Their presence added to concerns he already had about his home and the high prices and privations brought about by the Federal blockade, which was tightening its grip slowly but surely like an anaconda.

In early April, Leonard shared his concerns in a long letter home, and also his need for news from home.

*Camp Bartow*
*Near Fredericksburg, Va.*
*April 2nd, 1862*

*Dear Anna,*

*I recd yours of the 21ˢᵗ before yesterday. I was sorrowful that you were all complaining. I hope it's nothing more than colds. There are so many sick soldiers returning I feel they will scatter disease all over the country. A good many citizens here who were kind enough to take in the sick soldiers have lost members of their families with the camp fever. I would advise you to keep them all in the yard as much as possible and not let them go to the depot where the cars come, especially the baby and the Negroes. I hear through Mr. Burgess that Mr. Whitmire had corn and things stolen. Was it from the store or from his house? I fear it is dangerous to have no one sleep in the store at night. I expect corn is high, perhaps as it will be til mid summer. Leave it to Mr. Whitmire. It is too late now to buy hogs to kill. If your bacon runs low, you must buy but you may have meant you wanted another hog to feed. If you think you can feed another, get one while you can. I hope you will soon get an abundance of milk when spring sets in. It is well proper enough to sell anything you can spare.*

*It seems to me you write very seldom. I have only recd one letter sent to this place and we have been here 3 weeks. Did you call in the doctor to see baby? Say to Dr. Dean I wrote him a month ago and would be glad to hear from him. Tell Henry I will write him soon and tell him to put Steve out somewhere with someone who will mother him, work and make him know his place, at least until the middle of June at any price, or if he will take him and attend to him for nothing, I would be glad. I fear he is a trifling boy. Now is the time to train him, else he will probably be ruined. We've had two or three fine days but now is cloudy and threatens a cold rain. Yesterday I was inaugurated into my new office. We hear no news. The enemy are about 25 miles from us in strong force. We are under marching orders but cannot tell when or where we will move. I sent to Mr. Whitmire $60 a few weeks ago to pay as far as it would go my taxes. I will send you what I can next pay day. All I can share I will send you knowing if you do not want it immediately you will take care of it til you do.*

*We cannot tell what is ahead of us. I know you are as economical as you ought to be and perhaps more so. You must do the best you can. I hope you have learned to do very well on rye coffee and sassafras tea. We are not getting coffee now and I hope the government will not pay the exorbitant price any longer for it. We can do very well without*

*it.  Give my respects to Mr. Thompson and Miss Sallie, to Mr. and Mrs.
McKay and remember me to Uncle Nath and Aunt Edna and Sallie and
Billy and Fanny and all.  We will no doubt have hard fighting before
the 6th of June and may the Lord give us victory and spare my life to see
you and baby and all I hold dear once more.  I hope you are all again
well.  Do write twice a week to me.  Send my love to all in Charleston
and remember me to Aunt Susan.  I am in good health and so are the
troop and generally Mr. Cline's as well.*

*Your husband*
*L. Williams*

The Old Captain noticed that he had added on to that letter the very next
day, sensing that it would be a while before he'd have a spare moment to take
pencil in hand. He had been right.  It would be over a month of dodging minie
balls, galloping away from cannon blasts and nightlong rides before he'd have
a moment to write Anna once more. The letter was badly worn, with some
words now unreadable.

*April 3rd, 1862*

*Dear Anna,*
*I will add a few more lines this morning before the mail leaves
while our breakfast is cooking and a good one it will be.  Mr. Burgess
went yesterday to town and brought for our mess several large shad at
50 cts. each. I wish you could get them so low.  Fish are the only cheap
thing we can get.  Eggs sell here at 75 cts. per doz. and butter same
price.  They are luxuries I do without.  Molasses is 2.50 per gall.  Don't
buy anything for me.  It is uncertain whether I would ever get it if you
send.  I did think, probably, if we ever become stationary again, I would
get you to send me some butter but I beg you to send me nothing else at
least until I write you to do so.  The sugar you sent me was very fine.  It
makes sassafras tea drinks as well as [       ] or Rye, as well as Rio.
I told you I made an excellent kettle of preserves with the peaches and
pears.*
*Wm. Perry succeeds in my office of 1st Sergt.  Edward Stokes rises
to a sergeancy.  I am indebted to these two gentlemen very greatly for
my election. I am proud that I recd every vote in my mess and all the*

*old members of the troop. I shall continue to mess with my old mess although it is usual for the officers to mess together. My horse is now improving and looks very well. I think will last me this campaign and probably another if I can get into a cavalry company that I like or if ours can be reorganized satisfactorily. If you see Mr. Westfield, give him my regards. I would be glad to see him back with us but I would prefer he stay at home. We need such men at home. If Mr. Whitmire cannot spare you Nathan to work your garden, you must get him to hire you another hand and you are right to plant your Aunt's garden. You can get a hand for 75 cts. a day. I'm not homesick, but I think constantly of you. I had no idea when I left home that I would be away so long. I sent a few old clothes and some other articles in a trunk by express to Joseph Whitmire. Mr. Burgess has a great many more things in it than I have and Mr. [ ] also about as much. Tell Mr. Whitmire to pay expenses and store the trunk until we get home. Send him the enclosed receipt. There is nothing very valuable in the trunk. My own goods are not worth more than 8 or 10 dollars, but I did not want to throw them away. Write soon and oblige your husband.*

*L. Williams*

Three days after these words were written, a bloody battle was fought out on the rainy western front at Shiloh, a name that means "place of peace," situated near the banks of the Tennessee River. The first twelve hours of this carnage were carried by the Confederates who had launched a surprise attack, and in the process had driven Grant's army nearly into the frigid river. While spearheading that afternoon charge, Confederate General Albert Sydney Johnston received a minieball in his leg. Thinking it merely a flesh wound that could easily be tended to later, the General refused to leave the field. He should have. Shortly after, he fell from his horse, faint from the loss of blood, and died. The highest ranking Confederate field general had an artery severed and bled to death, but the hero of Manassas, Pierre Beauregard, assumed command and sustained the momentum. In a location known as the Hornet's Nest, the Federals put up a stubborn and lethal defense. There, 2,300 bluecoats were slaughtered and another 2,200 surrendered as the sun began to set on the field.

Grant was doomed if the attack continued into the darkness but that attack never came. That night he was reinforced but his situation was still uncertain.

His subordinate commanders, including one William Tecumseh Sherman, who was earlier in the day shot twice and had three horses blown out from beneath him, wondered if a retreat was in order for the coming morning. Grant answered him sharply, "Retreat? No. I propose to attack at daylight and whip them." And whip them he did, ripping through dank swamps and reclaiming a battlefield heaped with dead the likes the war had never seen. Broken gun carriages, gutted horses and men contorted in a freeze frame of death covered the bloody ground. Twenty years after the war, Grant attested in his memoirs to the horror he had sown. "I saw an open field, in our possession on the second day, over which the Confederates had made repeated charges the day before, so covered with dead that it would have been possible to walk across the clearing, in any direction, stepping on bodies, without a foot touching the ground."

In the largest, most brutal battle ever fought in the United States up to that time, the Union sustained 13,000 casualties while the Confederates suffered more than 10,000. After Shiloh, critics in the north called for Grant's ouster, decrying his lust-for-blood tactics and senseless sacrificing of men. The President replied, "I can't spare this man; he fights."

Shiloh proved resoundingly that it would indeed be a long, hard war. The Old Captain had thought about going out and walking those killing fields for himself some day. He was eternally grateful that he wasn't there back on those rain-soaked, blood-filled two days. He now knew that it was on tide-turning, savage afternoons like those near the "place of peace" that the Civil War was ultimately decided.

None came any grittier than Ulysses S. Grant, an irascible West Pointer from Ohio. He was a natural horseman and fighter who could stoically order thousands into the jaws of death. He was a short man with a shorter temper, who loved black stallions, strong whiskey and bad cigars. Grant believed that the way to win was not by capturing supplies or destroying railroads, but by killing his opponent's men. "War was hell," and killing soldiers was his and his army's sole purpose.

Back in the eastern theater, capturing Richmond was the prime objective for President Lincoln and the Union Army. Preventing McClellan from achieving this was the stern task facing Confederate President Jefferson Davis, military advisor Robert E. Lee, General Joseph E. Johnston, and the three Williams brothers. But it was the striking if somewhat strange figure known as "Old Blue Light" who would soon alter the course of events in Virginia.

Thomas Jonathan Jackson was a quirky loner who kept to himself and believed that God Almighty controlled the fate of his Virginia army and the destiny of the war. He disdained fighting on the Sabbath, although nearly all of his battles seemed to take place on Sundays. He was a gawky, shabbily dressed, hypochondriac and undoubtedly one of the oddest generals to ever command the field. He still wore the old army coat and broken-visored kepi he had sported back in the Mexican War. He sucked on lemons because he believed they alleviated his indigestion. He never used pepper because it made his left leg ache. He was a devout Presbyterian and considered a religious fanatic by his staff. Certainly, he was fanatical when it came to discipline and secrecy. His orders were final. He had little patience for the weak and kept his colleagues in the dark about his tactics until the very last minute. He sought to mystify, mislead and surprise, and during the next month, "Old Tom Fool" proved crazy like a fox. Robert E. Lee would trust no commander more.

It was Lee who advised Davis to use Jackson to tie up the Federals in his brilliant Shenandoah Valley Campaign of the spring of '62. The movement was designed to strike the fear of God into Washington, draw northern attention away from Richmond, and keep McDowell's 50,000 men in front of Lincoln instead of alongside McClellan. With him, Jackson brought Jedediah Hotchkiss, a cartographer and guide unmatched in the war, and a cavalry force led by the fiery Turner Ashby. To this day, military experts deem Jackson's Valley Campaign as one of the most brilliant in any war. Between March 23 and June 9, with as little as 4,200 and at most 17,000 near bare-footed men, Jackson marched 676 miles, skirmished nearly every day, and fought five pitched battles. He out-thought and out-fought three different Union commanders who pursued but never caught him. The opponent he flummoxed most was Nathaniel Banks, who lost enough wagons, arms and supplies to keep Jackson's men sustained for months. "Commissary Banks" was the name pinned on him by Jackson's "foot cavalry," who were so named for their limitless endurance on long marches. Throughout those remarkable weeks, Jackson came to be revered by his men, although he drove them mercilessly. He was indeed a "stone wall" and after the Valley Campaign, his rock-hard men were just as tough.

The result of Jackson's action in the mountain passes was precisely what Lee had hoped for. It relieved the pressure around Richmond and meant that Leonard and his fellow troopers would not have to contend with McDowell's forces left to defend Washington. While Jackson was befuddling the Union in the valley, John Magruder's quaker guns and magic act no longer held McClellan spellbound. Johnston anticipated that the Federals were about to move against him and ordered a withdrawal of his 15,000 men from Yorktown on the night of May 3.

On this night, the real fighting, shooting, and dying war began for Lieutenant Leonard Williams. His terrified wife now scoured the local papers for the names of the dead and wounded, praying she wouldn't become a widow. In early May, she almost did. The Old Captain opened the letter he had written following what had been the most ferocious and deadly combat he had experienced since riding off to war. Gone were the instructions on running the home front; this was all war.

*May 8th, 1862*
*New Kent Co. Ct. House*

*My Dear Wife*

*On account of the impossibility of mailing a letter to you, I have not written for almost two weeks and as the whole country has been looking with painful anxiety for the result of operations about Yorktown, I have no doubt your anxiety has been great especially as you have heard nothing from me lately. My last was written to you from camp near Williamsburg, Friday last the 2nd our squadron was ordered to report at Yorktown. Our generals had come to the conclusion that our redoubts and batteries along the York River could not stand against the attacks of the enemy'gunboats and that it was best to yield to them without a fight. We were called to assist in the retreat of our army. The retreat commenced on Saturday and on Sunday morning the last forces were put in motion towards Williamsburg. In consequence of an accidental explosion of ammunition just as the troops were leaving, the evacuation of Yorktown was known to the enemy at once and they, therefore, took immediate possession and started several regiments in pursuit of our army and also sent up the river (York) one or two regiments of cavalry and artillery who were landed within 3 miles of our road. They came very near intercepting the cavalry of our rear of which we were a part and we numbered only some three or four hundred.*

It was at this time that Major Matthew C. Butler, Leonard's immediate superior for the next three years and with whom he was riding, almost met his maker. As Butler rode through the cobblestone streets of old Williamsburg, a young drummer boy perhaps from A. P. Hill's division, yelled out to him to look out for a mine that had been planted in front of him. Sure enough there it was, right in his path just inches away. Butler gingerly rode around the deadly device and directed his column to do the same. That blasted mine couldn't have missed old Ruby by more than a few yards, the Old Captain mused. Shaking his head, now deep in his words and recalling the peril of that night, he returned to the streets of Yorktown and his May 8 letter.

*From this time until we reached Williamsburg, a distance of 3 miles, we were much annoyed by their artillery. Of course, their shots were wild, not being in sight, but their balls whizzed over our heads. Just as we got into Williamsburg, they planted several pieces of artillery at the extreme end of the open ground and commenced throwing shells at us. Our artillery had been sent for immediately and there commenced a most exciting artillery duel. We, in the meantime, had retired under cover of some hills nearby and 2 or 3 regiments of infantry came to support our batteries. Shortly, an order came to the cavalry to charge their battery.*

That order came from none other than twenty-nine year old General James Ewell Brown Stuart, the boldest and most daring cavalry commander in all the war. He was a true cavalier and dressed the part. He crisply barked out orders while clad in shiny knee-high cavalry boots, elbow length gauntlets, a red lined cape with a yellow sash, and a felt hat with pinned-up brim and ostrich feather plume. Yet beneath this glitter was a fine horseman and born cavalry leader. To his Confederate brothers he was known simply as "Jeb," to the Union he was known as a deadly enemy and called every invective known at the time for his uncanny ability to damage them then vanish into thin air. He would now prove again just how deadly he was. When one of his Virginia regiments was cut off from entering the town, Stuart ordered Butler and Leonard's company to lead a charge, every cavalryman's dream. "See them across that valley," yelled Jeb. "Charge and scatter them, so that my men may be able to join us." The letter described how the men were deployed in preparation for battle.

*Major Butler, hearing the order first took the lead. We had only 72 men in all, the balance of the squad now being away upon various services. Col. Davis had 250 or 300 Va. Cavalry, Butler's command being independent of Davis. Our squadron led a long ways in front. We made a circuit away to the left in order to attack the battery on its flank and came right upon a regiment of the enemy's cavalry who perhaps was intending to attack our battery. We came within fifty or sixty yards of them before seeing them. They were in sort of a ravine. There we were face to face about seventy-five on our side, fronting some 300 of the enemy and about 500 or 600 a quarter mile distant on the top of the hill.*

The Old Captain stood up and began to pace as he read. He was reliving his first defining moment as a cavalryman. In a flash of memory he once again held the reins in his left hand and his 44 colt in the right. He took a mental inventory while pouring over the words, preparing to lead that charge again right across his hotel room. His six shots were packed and rammed, 30 grains to a ball. The spare pistol was primed and ready, jammed in his boot and, as always, two extra, preloaded cylinders waited in his pommel holster. His saber was sharp with its clean blood groove ripe for the staining for the very first time. This was the precise instant in time he and Ruby had prepared for back at the Ashland Cavalry Camp of Instruction. The Old Captain's heart was pounding anew, just as it did over 40 years ago. For the then young Lieutenant...destiny was at hand. The words on the paper transported the old man back.

*An order was given to draw pistols and fire. We did so and advanced on them and then on order to charge, we put them to flight and chased them up a hill under cover of their reserve but we had to retreat. It was a splendid little performance. The killed, wounded and prisoners were between 25 and 30. We captured and brought from the field 8 horses and several other horses were afterward taken by the infantry. Our boys got several army pistols and saddles & c. We got their colors and trumpet and killed 5 horses on the spot. How many men were wounded we do not know, as I have no doubt when we retired, they moved as many as they could. We got the enemy at a disadvantage and it was used well. We were even cheered most vociferously by all the regiments as we passed and have been highly complimented by all the officers who witnessed the charge. We have to mourn the loss of one of our best men, Mr. Boggs, who was killed in the fight. Mr. Boynton of the Beaufort District Troop was also killed. Thornwell of the Congarees was wounded and 2 or 3 others none however, too seriously.*

...

His first charge remained an indelible image years later. First Butler ordered his command to form platoons. They did so swiftly despite the day's marathon march and no supper. The Major then ordered King, their old English bugler, to sound the charge. Off they raced down the hill and across the swamp beneath it, hitting the Sixth Pennsylvania Cavalry nearly dead center. After desperate hand-to-hand fighting, the South Carolinians drove the Pennsylvanians to the top of the next hill but Leonard and the men of the 2nd South Carolina were counterattacked by another regiment and pushed back to the muddy crossing where they had first started. Dead and wounded men and horses clogged the ford. One of the fallen was S. D. Boynton who lay in the mud with a mortal wound beneath his arm. The men attempted to carry him away but he died before they got him to the top of the hill. Steve Boynton was buried that night in Williamsburg. He had been a good friend. The Old Captain sighed once more.

Covering the retreat of General Johnston's forces from the onslaught of a far larger army was fraught with danger. It was in that ordeal that Second Lieutenant Williams first heard the pledge that he and his mates would honor forever, "Go ahead Major Butler, we will follow you to hell!" Hell was just a day and a few miles away down the road in Williamsburg where General James Longstreet fought furiously to delay McClellan. There, Leonard and Ruby battled driving rain and overwhelming odds before falling back grudgingly to New Kent Court House. A letter hastily added the next day, described what took place there.

*May 9th*

*Early in the morning in the camp, the enemy have been hanging on our rear all the time. The day before yesterday a considerable fight took place with the enemy that were landed at West Point on the York River. After some four hours fight, they were driven back under cover of their gunboats. They were worsted and suffered severely. Also on Monday a severe fight took place at Williamsburg in which they were driven back. Now they are said to be within 3 miles of us. I do not apprehend, however, any more fighting soon. I think the balance of the retreat will be affected without much annoyance. We are now in 28 miles of Richmond. I did not expect to have an opportunity of sending you this for several days but just now have learned a mail carrier is going to Richmond, so I will have to make this short. I expected to write you 2 sheets and say a great deal about the reorganization but I have time to merely to state the results.*

Those results were based largely on what a man did and didn't do during the Yorktown retreat and subsequent battle at Williamsburg. If he ran, hid, dawdled, feigned injury, or disobeyed orders, he was deemed a liability, shirker and a coward. If he fought from start to finish, stood his ground to the last, and saw to the well being of his fallen comrades; then, and only then, was he considered a brave and honorable soldier. Those that didn't do their duty were ridden harder than their horses. Those that did were commended, respected, and stood the best chance of promotion during the latest reorganization. The May 9 letter continued.

*I am now Captain Elect of the Brooks Troop. W.H. Perry, 1ˢᵗ Lieutenant, Ed. Jr. Stokes, 2ⁿᵈ, no election for 3ʳᵈ, the vote was a tie for third. I wish I had time now to explain my motives for continuing in service. Sufficient to say at present that I thought I was right I should do so, although my heart yearns to see you and baby. I hope the war will close this summer and that if lasts long, I can get a furlough, or if I think proper, can resign next winter or fall. I saw Ephraim and Billy W. lately. Ephraim this morning all well. I will write you more fully as soon as we get to camps, I expect near Richmond.*

*I intended to say more of the skirmish. It was surprising more of us were not killed, as the bullets whistled in showers around us. Write soon to Richmond, my dear wife. I hope the Lord will continue to bless you and give you a strong heart to bear up under these threatening times and the day may not be too far distant when I will be permitted to return home and enjoy your society with the proud consciousness of having done my duty to my country and family. And my dear Anna, I must now close. Write soon. My love to all.*

*Your husband*

*All our company are doing pretty well, no sickness scarcely. Jno Austin of our company died last week near Richmond. I will write you soon.*

The Old Captain studied the words he had written that lifetime ago, and paused to wonder now at the immensity of it all. Had he really lived through such a time? It all seemed almost a dream now. How young he was then, and how idealistic. "*...with the proud consciousness of having done my duty to my country and family*"... My God, had he really written that? Yet it was all there. It had happened and he had been a part of it. He picked up the next letter and read on, the words carrying him back into a time and place that now seemed almost unreal.

*May 10th, 1862*
*Bivouac*
*24 Miles from Richmond*

*My Dear Anna,*

*We will probably remain here to rest til towards noon and as I conclude the letter I sent you yesterday hastily, I will occupy a portion of this leisure time writing, which I may add to for 2 or 3 days, as I have opportunity or until I can mail it. I recd yours of the 1st May last night and was truly gratified to hear from you that you were all well and that baby was growing and learning. I will give you a detail of my labors for the last week of occurrences. The army commenced its retreat from Yorktown on Friday a week yesterday. Today we (that is the squad now of cavalry) was ordered from near Williamsburg to Yorktown on Friday the 3rd. We reached there in the evening at night. I was sent with fifteen men to picquett the roads leading toward the James River. I was up all night and returned to camp about 9 ock next morning. Sunday we were called up at 2 ock and fell in the rear of the army, but while the infantry were getting off, our cavalry went back to Yorktown and was the last troops to leave. While there the enemy's shells were thrown into the town, but the place was tenantless. All the inhabitants*

92

*gone, it was sad to leave this beautiful and historic old place to the enemy. Its whole precincts seemed to me almost sacred.*

*As I said in my letter yesterday, the enemy pursued our army and when we were 3 or 4 miles of Wmsburg. commenced firing on our rear at about 4 ock sundown. When they came in sight of Wmsburg., our batteries met them and a lively contest kept up til near night. It was at this junction we charged the enemy cavalry. Probably four times as large as our squadron and supported by the balance of their regiment in position on the summit of the hill, we fired into their dense ranks and then pursued them with sabers. After running them near the top of the hill, an order was given to fall back. The enemy then sent after us a perfect volley of balls, fortunately, few were hurt. This was our first fight and resulted most fortunately. The only sad occurrence being the loss of our fellow trooper Mr. Boggs, one of our best soldiers. After the fight we rode some 4 miles to get with our wagons. We reached them 4 ock, having been on horseback 20 hours. The next day we came in front of the army when aroused at 2 ock and marched 30 miles in the rain and mud and reached New Kent Courthouse about night. We, however, got bread and bacon about 10 ock. For several days we could get nothing but cold bread, not enough of that but we have not suffered. Once a day we have been able to get a pretty good meal.*

*May 11th, here an order was given to saddle. We marched back some 4 miles and waited for the enemy to advance. Some 6 or 8 regiments remained in battle all day til night. The enemy came up within a mile or two but fell back. We returned here last night and occupied the same bivouac we did night before. On last night a considerable fight took place at Williamsburg between our rear forces and the enemy's advance. Our army drove them back much worsted. On Wednesday, the enemy's gunboats landed a pretty considerable force at West Point. 5 of our regiments were sent to meet them. They were badly whipped and driven in under cover of their gunboats. Since then (now Sunday) our rear has been comparatively unmolested except on Friday Genl. Stewart's cavalry were attacked and lost several men.*

It was here that the Old Captain suddenly thought of Ruby and how she held steady in the pitch black of night amid the almost surreal blasts of cannons, and how she didn't flinch from the sparks of pistols and the moonlit flashes of sabers. In the crisis he knew they both had drawn on the lessons learned on the drilling field. He remembered to aim low because his 44 recoiled about 8 inches up and not to lead his target when riding parallel, for both he and the enemy were progressing at the same rate. Ruby must have known that the gun fired by her master, sometimes right behind her ears, while certainly a jolt, wouldn't harm her. Leonard knew too now that somewhere on that muddy ride to catch up with the wagons, man and horse were not so different. In some strange way both needed to fight the war in order to see if they could fight the war. He continued on, intrigued by his longest letter yet.

> *I recd your last of the 5th and 6th just yesterday while in battle line and was made happy to know you had heard of my election and was pleased with it and had acquiesced and made it your mind to give me to the country still longer. Indeed the great business of our country is war, war for our independence and the right of self-government and I deemed it my duty to stand by the country as long as my life might be spared. I do not apprehend any further molestation from the enemy in our rear. I do not know how near Richmond our lines will be established. We are now a little over 20 miles from Richmond.*
>
> *We have a splendid army and it looks to me that it is invincible. I have seen nearly all the brigades. The soldiers are in prime health and in high spirits. I recd a letter from Mr. Gaillard last night. He speaks highly of baby and says he will visit you as often as he can and requests me to command his services. I hope you will visit his family as often as convenient. I esteem his family most highly. For several days on account of the wagons and supplies being ahead, all the army had been living on very short rations and frequently on parched corn. They joke over it and I vaguely believe are proud of an opportunity of showing their devotion to the cause by submitting most cheerfully. Now, however, we are getting supplies by wagon by the RR but few miles distant.*
>
> *I sympathize with the people of Charleston in the hour of their apprehension and I still hope the city will prove impregnable. I am glad your family or part of them will be with you again this summer. I am pained at your father's embarrassing situation but believe his philosophy will bear him up under all adversity. I know it will be*

*painful for him to leave Charleston, but I trust he will not allow himself
to be harassed but will yield to circumstances that he cannot control
without murmur or grief.*

*Mr. Greenfield joined us today and had letters for a great many.
We have heard that Beauregard was driving the enemy back and also
that France was in the act of recognizing our independence. I think
matters are favorable with us at present. This may, however, reduce us
to a much greater extremity yet, but we will come out triumphant, I
have no doubt. Remember me to your father and mother and all, to
Henry, Cousin Frances, Uncle Whitmire and Aunt Edna, Mary Susan
and Mr. Whitmire. Tell Mr. Whitmire to write to me again soon. This
leaves me in prime health. Hard work agrees with me. My respects to
all our neighbors.*

*Your Husband*
*L. Williams*

After settling into camp, the first order of business was to take Ruby to the
company vet. He had noticed that while driving her up that slippery precipice
he had cut her with his right spur. As he had with Carrie eleven months earlier,
he whispered into ears that he hoped would understand. It never ceased to
amaze him how these animals endured the hardships and injuries inflicted upon
them by their human masters. A few stitches later, Ruby put her nose deep into
a field full of sweet timothy while Leonard put a point on his stubby pencil to
write to sweet Anna.

*Cavalry Camp HQ*
*2 Miles from Richmond*
*May 20, 1862*

*My Dear Anna*

*I recd your letter of the 14ᵗʰ last night and was made glad to learn
that you were all well. I hope you enjoy your growing occupations,
gardening, housekeeping. This is the first day of leisure I have had
since the 4ᵗʰ last but have had no very severe labors for several days. I
have heard today nothing of the enemy's movements. On Saturday, the
enemy's gunboats came up to within 10 or 15 miles of Richmond. They
were even attacked by our land batteries and driven back. I have heard*

*of no other movement since the enemy, I understand, have landed about 20 or 25 miles from this place on the Pamunkey since, but I do not know whether they have commenced an advance or not. It is thought now that the defenses and obstructions of the James River can keep in check the gunboats, and if Richmond is to be attacked, it must be by land. The fight at Williamsburg on Monday (in the retreat) was a complete success. The enemy lost some 4,000 and our loss less then 1,000. It was the day previous Sunday evening we had our fight. Some of the prisoners said the impetuosity and recklessness of our charge struck terror into their men on account of the difficulty of passing the marshy and narrow pathway but little could be done with sabers.*

In truth, much was done with sabers that night but Anna need not ever know. The gory specifics are cited in the Hampton Legion Regimental History.

*The enemy in their haste to escape over a very rough boggy place were piled three deep— men and horses indiscriminately together— those in the rear endeavoring to rush over those that went down...There was no time to pause, such of our members as could pass the obstacles, dashed upon the foe, many a horse and live man were overtaken by the swift bullet and some were made to taste our cold steel.*

As if it happened just moments before, the Old Captain recalled with grim detail that it was here in the mire that he saw his first man die. The man wielding the saber was the one who first mustered Leonard in back in Greenville, the man whom he was elected over as captain of the company. Indeed, it was John Lanneau who "at the first blow, severed the head of a Hessian." Such an image remained Leonard's and Leonard's alone. That shocking scene stayed with him forever as would the question of whether or not he, like Lanneau, had sent a young man to a swampy grave that night. The lengthy letter continued.

*Most of the work was done with pistols. I had 5 as fair shots as I could wish. The most distant shot not more than 40 yards. My horse performed most admirably and in passing and crossing back leaped the marsh when many bogged up and was as tractable as a lamb. I send this by Sergt. Alex Payne who leaves tomorrow for home having got a substitute.*

At the word "substitute," the Old Captain halted abruptly, as Ruby would when she sensed danger. The idea that a man, if wealthy enough and influential enough, could pay another to serve in his place and perhaps die for him was wrong. To him, home was heaven and the battlefield was hell, and it is written that no man shall buy his way into heaven. Over the years, his contempt for those who bought their way out of duty remained unchanged, as did his anger over the law and lawyers who created it. He sniffed about it again then finished reading the letter.

> *I have no doubt you are in want of money. The government owes us for nearly 5 mo. service. We will be paid soon. I will send you more. Did you tell me the trunk I sent from Fredericksburg reached home? Let me know as Mr Burgess is uneasy about it. Did you not buy me a hat last fall? If you did, please send it to me first opportunity, probably some recruit can bring it to me. It won't do for a captain to wear such a shocking bad hat as mine. I intend to get a Confederate uniform as soon as I can get into Richmond. It will cost me nearly $100. I will be very glad to get Miller Thompson and Mr. Gibbs into our company. Say so to them. The Confederate state and city authorities have determined to defend Richmond to the last. I believe every soldier endorses them. McClellan is afraid of this army and if his gunboats fail him, I don't believe he will fight here. We are looking with great anxiety to hear from Beauregard if we wiped out the Yankees near Corinth and their army there. I doubt not it will be done if they leave the water far enough. I think peace will be made very soon.*

Like Leonard, many aimed their eyes west to Corinth in Mississippi. Southern generals considered Corinth the key to holding the entire Missisippi Valley and they knew that losing it would mean disaster. In early May, Beauregard had 70,000 men there, many still recovering from their wounds at Shiloh or dying from typhus. Fearful of being starved out by siege, Beauregard evacuated Corinth leaving the vital railroad to Memphis in Union hands. Leonard shook his head when the morning courier informed him of the dark news drifting up from Ole Miss.

If Richmond were to fall like Corinth, the Confederacy was doomed. Presidents Lincoln and Davis both knew it. Generals McClellan and Johnston knew it too. So did Robert E. Lee along with 9 million citizens of dear old Dixie including three named Williams. To do his share in preventing such a lethal outcome, Leonard kept a careful eye on the enemy out on picket duty. But he also kept a hopeful eye on the well being of his company and Anna. The letter reflected this.

> *Everything quiet this morning and no intelligence from the enemy. Troopers are in good health. I enjoy prime health, but thin as usual. I have a good appetite and can make as good a meal on bread and bacon and Irish potatoes and enjoy it with as much zest I could formerly the best of breakfasts. I appreciate your advice to me in regard to my men and make it my endeavor to carry it out in all respects. Write me soon. I saw Ephraim and Billy Whitmire lately. Billy was anxious to join my company and has been making efforts to get a transfer and also many others. I could have raised my company to over a hundred if transfers from regiments out of the service had been allowed. Some 7 or 8 from the Butler Guards and boys of the most influential families in the dist. have applied to me and desire very much to get in my company. As provisions are high, and you have not a way to buy conveniently, I think you do very right not to take boarders. I wish you could send me a statement of your accounts for provisions, say for two weeks. It will give me a better idea of how you are getting on in the way of living than in any other way. Sergt. Payne is about to leave, so I must close. Write soon and often. My love to all.*
>
> *Your husband*
> *L. Williams*

The Old Captain could still recite Anna's advice on "being a proper officer" as she called it. "Be prudent." "Share your packages from home with them." "Lead by example." "Ask the men to join you in camp prayer meetings." He heeded it all to the letter and since so many wished to transfer under him, he reasoned, he was fairly regarded. He considered himself a square man yet with the monotony and the aftermath of his new election, a tinge of resentment sometimes filtered through the smoke of nightly campfires. Some rancor was almost to be expected so he warned Anna that if she should ever hear rumor of any bitterness from his camp, she should simply ignore it.

*Cavalry Camp HQ*
*May 21, 1862*

*My Dear Anna,*

*I sent you a letter this morning by Sergt. Payne. Mr. Cline will leave for home this evening. He arranged with Campbell Williams to take his place, being liable for only 2 or 3 months longer. I have nothing new to write you but dislike to let such a fine opportunity pass without saying something to you. We are again quiet today with nothing to do. I believe I prefer activity. It is astonishing how much labor, loss of sleep and food a man can endure without suffering when there's excitement and responsibility. The retreat from Yorktown was a masterful performance and would be surprised if it took McClellan a full month or two to get his affairs in train for another battle, if he fights at all near this place. If he approaches by land, his progress will be very slow.*

*If anyone should come on soon, I wish you would send me the saddle cloth Ira Westfield gave me and also the hat I spoke of. I am not sure that you have a hat for me but think I remember you mentioning having one. I hear Mrs. McCullough has sold her house for $6,000. If you wish to sell yours and can get $4,500 or $5,000 for it, you may do so and buy a plantation with it but I expect you had better wait til after the war. Lieut. Jas. P. Moore is at home now. He cannot be reelected, the committee appointed to nominate officers were named by himself, the said committee ignored his claims. He did not receive a nomination. Probably up to this time, he said he would not serve under Lanneau, but now on failing to get the nomination, he turned against us and privately avowed himself in favor of Lanneau. He was previously nettled by my being run and elected Lieut. over him. I have no doubt he is now bitter against the company and will do so privately all the harm he can by representing extreme divisions in the company. If you hear any insinuations to this effect, pay no attention to it and let it give you no uneasiness. I have no fears of my ability to conciliate all opposition since all of Lanneau's friends have already voluntarily expressed their satisfaction at the result. Lanneau had many warm, personal friends, and their disappointment and regret for his defeat was quite natural and I expected it.*

*How is your yard doing and the trees and the hedge? I wish I had planted fruit trees instead of oaks at first. They would now have been pretty large. I fear you will injure them by letting in your calves. You had better have the clover cut for the calves and not let them into the yard at all. The clover will go further by cutting it than by grazing it and then there will be no danger to your shrubs and flowers. You must visit your neighbors and take plenty of outdoor exercise. Keep your garden well worked. Hire Nathan one day a week or so and hope you will have a good garden with plenty of vegetables, dried fruit, milk, rye coffee, butter, hominy, rice and bacon. You can do tolerably well if you can buy more sugar, molasses, and rice. You had better do so. I have a pretty good idea of the bacon you have on hand. Let me know how much sugar, rice, molasses, coffee and c you have on hand. Hereafter, I will be able to draw my pay monthly and then I intend to send you all I do not need and make you my banker. Major Butler and nearly every officer in the squadron was in favor of my election. I have no news to write you. I rather regret there are so many people going to Greenville. It will make it so difficult to get poultry, eggs, beef &c. You must do the best you can. My love to all. Kiss baby for me.*

> *Your husband*
> *L Williams*

Three days after finishing this letter, Leonard quickly penned another to take advantage of a personal courier going home. Little did he know it would be his last for three weeks. In four days, the battle of Seven Pines, would be raging just five miles south of Richmond.

> *Cavalry Camp*
> *Near Richmond*
> *May 24, 1862*

*My Dear Anna*

*Although I have written you twice since your last letter, as Dr. Long, discharged, leaves this morning, I will send you a few lines by him merely to say that I am well and everything quiet. I am getting on smoothly as yet in the administration of my office and apprehend nothing else for the future. The health of the company is very good at present, with some exceptions of slight cases of sickness. The enemy are making no developments yet that we know of. It is still believed that the Jas. River up to the city can be defended and that the enemy if he chooses to attack Richmond, must do so by land. All the citizens about Richmond and vicinity seem to be calm and apprehend no danger. Capt. Scriven was the only captain who retained his place in the squadron. The others there drew for places and it was my luck to draw 4th, but the War Department has decided that all must be placed on equality, consequently, we will draw all over again. I may be luckier next time and get the 1st instead of the 4th place. We have a beautiful camp and well fixed at present. Dr. Long will leave directly so I will close hoping you are all well. Has your father moved yet? Give him and all my remembrances. Write soon. My love to all. Kiss baby for me. Tell the servants I think of them often. They must be good children, and tell Fannie that she must be watchful and careful.*

*Your affectionate husband*
*L. Williams*

With the Union army within sight of the spires and sound of the church bells of the Confederate capital, General Joseph Johnston would strike a week later on May 31. The plan for his bold counter stroke was to assault the southern most regiments of McClellan's forces, which were divided by the muddy and swollen Chickahominy River. Unfortunately for the veteran general, the details were neither written down nor effectively communicated to those who would carry them out. The results were missed chances and delays. Assaulting columns were indecisive and disjointed, and attacks came in drips and drabs. The Federals ultimately held their ground and bloodily repulsed the Confederates. Most of the 42,000 men engaged on each side fought in isolated pockets lost in thick woods and flooded clearings. Some of the wounded had to be propped up against fences or tree stumps to save them them from drowning in the mud. If either side gained an edge it was the Union which suffered 1000 less casualties. For Leonard, and a fellow trooper who wrote of the battle, Seven Pines was a soggy nightmare.

*What a scene— the roads for miles, blocked with artillery and ambulances, mired down over the hubs of the wheels in mud and water.*

*And that night, how it rained. The thunder rolling, and the lightening flashing, until after midnight. I remember we were all halted beside the road, those of us not on vidette duty to rest for the night, the water nearly knee-deep, and worse than all, no feed for man nor horse.*

Luck was not on Dixie's side, especially the side of its commander. A later historian would write:

*Probably no one in service carried more lead in his body than Joseph E. Johnston. He collected bullets in Indian Wars, in the Utah campaign, in Mexico, on almost every hostile field he knew. On the peninsula below Richmond during the afternoon of May 31ˢᵗ, 1862, Johnston's luck ran typically...Old Joe was hit and unhorsed. Badly wounded, unable to keep the field, he was sent to the rear under the saddened eye of Jefferson Davis.*

It was under Johnston's supervision that the oddly assembled, untrained, raw enlistees had become an army. The Old Captain remembered the worries they all had. Who would replace him? Who could drive off a mass of bluecoats twice their size poised only a few miles from Richmond? Whoever replaced Johnston had to first take stock of the army, because after Seven Pines, every tattered Confederate regiment was full of overworked, ill, and homesick men. Worse, these men knew well that had it not been for the damned conscription act they'd all be home plowing. Leonard's one year was up too, and his letter was much like all the others sent back from the lines a week after Seven Pines.

*Camp Near Richmond*
*June 6ᵗʰ, 1862*

*My Dear Wife*
*This day 12 months ago I left Greenville for the war and though sad enough, could the veil that then shrouded the future have been removed and the present condition of the country and the vast proportions which the war has assumed, been revealed to me, still sadder would have been my heart on leaving my cherished home. I had no idea the last short night I spent with you, that so long a time would have elapsed without having an opportunity of spending a month*

*with you, but now dear Anna, everything is obscure and I can see no time when I can calculate on getting home. I should be very unhappy but for the encouragement I get from you-never have I read a letter from you that did not cheer and encourage me to persevere in duty.*

For the next six days, Captain Williams and his company did persevere, dodging raindrops and shells, but morale was sinking as deep as the horses in the swamps and bogs. The army knew it had to make a stand around Richmond soon. In the meantime, the men had to contend with the elements and deteriorating equipment.

*Camp Near Richmond*
*June 12<sup>th</sup>, 1862*

*Dear Anna,*

*I fear you have been disappointed in not hearing from me sooner. I have been busy for several days and out on picket and twice had the misfortune to stay out 24 hours in wet clothes. I have been unwell with cold and diarrhea but am now improving. I have been up all the time however. I had hoped to go home on recruiting service but learning from a note from Maj. Perry that it was very important at once to have recruits mustered in at once I telegraphed him yesterday to have it done. This will render a recruiting officer unnecessary. I have hopes of getting my company to its full standard. If transfers were allowed I would get 125 men. I am glad Willie Thompson and Wm. Gibbs are coming. I have already here four recruits and have no doubt can get 20 more of good material.*

*I have never seen so much rain. The enemy are no nearer than they were two weeks ago and the lines are at present quiet. I ran the gauntlet of their shells the other day in going the rounds of my picket posts. I had to pass between a body of our soldiers at whom they were firing and their batteries. They did not however explode nearer than 50–100 yards of me-one shell fell without exploding in a short distance of me. I lost the needle and pincushion you gave me in the retreat from Yorktown and some clothing. If you have the time to make me a plain one and put in a few pins and needles and a skein of thread I would like it. My love to all. Has your father moved to Columbia yet? My remembrances to him and your mother. I saw Billy W. yesterday in Richmond. He was well. Ephraim is well. Wm. East is doing well. You know he was wounded in the fight of the 31ˢᵗ. Kiss baby for me. Write soon.*

*Your Husband*
*L. Williams*

Why hadn't that shell exploded, the Old Captain wondered. Why were he and Ruby spared while others just as brave were not? Was there some greater destiny that awaited them? Shots that missed by a whisker, sabers that grazed instead of pierced, a chance tree that deflected a once dead-on minie ball, a saving ravine that provided shelter ...all were fortunes cast and controlled by God alone perhaps. The Old Captain had also seen men hit right between the eyes when behind apparently safe defenses, and he had seen even more die of invisible, terrible diseases. In the end, he concluded, it was fate and fate alone that determined who would live and who would die.

He had hoped that God's benevolent hand would rest on James whose brigade was now a part of A.P. Hill's famed Light Division, the largest in the Confederate Army. Ephraim was now under the command of John Magruder busy building up the defenses around the capital. Finally, all three brothers had converged on Richmond to help defeat McClellan, and it wouldn't be long before they'd be firing at more Federals than they'd ever laid eyes on. For the present, Leonard and Ruby hoped to simply remain upright and semi-dry as they slogged around the capital. Leonard was on the verge of being sick in the rotten weather, but the mail from home lifted his spirits and thoughts of Anna sustained him.

*Near Richmond*
*Sunday, June 15ᵗʰ, 1862*

*My Dear Anna*

*I recd with gladness your letter of the 8ᵗʰ and 9ᵗʰ this morning. I have been unwell for several days. I was out on picket a week ago yesterday, started at 2 ock in the heaviest rain and got thoroughly wet and remained wet all night and most of next day. It gave me the dysentery. On Thursday, I left the camp and have been staying here at a pleasant farmhouse in a ¼ of a mile of our camp. I enjoy very much its quiet and good fare. I think the Virginians are the best cooks in the* world, especially of bread. I am now nearly well and may return to the camp in a day or two. I am staying with a family named Randolph, a relation of the celebrated Jno. Randolphs, a very pleasant family. I was out on picket on the 8$^{th}$ with rifles and cannons roaring in my ears all day now and then a shell bursting near me and being wet and cold.

The pleasant memories of the anniversary of our wedding day did not come into mind although for weeks before I had often thought of it. It was a fitting way to call to mind and retain the solemn pledges we mutually made. But, dear Anna, those solemn vows have not lost their force yet they are superceded by sentiments of admiration and love I bear to you, more enforcing than all the vows and I humbly pray to God in his mercy will see fit to unite us again and that we may spend our lives happily in each others society and our dear baby's, cultivating the graces and the sentiments calculated to make us all and we associate with happier. My heart yearns to see you and baby. Of all the earthly wishes, next after the independence of our country, is my wish to be with you. It seems to me now I would be satisfied to live the balance of our days in Pickens or Buncombe or any other out-of-the-way place happy with you and baby and servants around us.

There is a good deal of sickness in our company at present. The Yankees, I understand, have fallen back a mile or two. They have been occupying a miserable, swampy ground and I hear they have a great deal of sickness. I do not think they will make any effort to get to Richmond soon. We are sending off some 9,000 or 10,000 troops from here to Gen. Jackson and possibly more will be sent yet. I have pleasant company here. Captain Gary of Edgefield and Capt. Henry Smith, you remember, he used to accompany me in my visits to you, and Mr. Hamilton, a nephew of Mr. Westfield's, who was wounded in the last fight. His wound was slight and is now about well. It has been very warm for several days but a shower is just commencing which cools the atmosphere delightfully. I wrote you in my last to send my hat and saddle cloth and socks, if you had them furnished, and also, if Mr. Jennings has any number of shoes to send me a pair. There will be several leaving soon. You had better divide them probably between Mr. Gibbs, Willie Thompson and Robt. Adams. You need not send anything else. It will be troublesome and maybe lost.

*I'm glad your garden is prospering. You must keep planting, and especially Irish potatoes. I hope your dried fruit is answering a good purpose. From your monthly expenses, I think you are managing most admirably. The cows and garden are a great help to you. You have been very careful of your meat. I am glad your aunts are with you. They will be such good company for you. Give my love to them all and to your father and mother, whom I now love almost as a father and mother. Write soon, dear Anna and tell me everything. I like your long letters the best. As ever.*

*Your husband*
*L. Williams*


The Old Captain had missed Anna terribly. He missed her then. He missed her now. He missed her always. She had offered up her heart and proclaimed her deepest love and devotion in her letter to him on the very anniversary of their union. But back then he had to focus on many different unions. Foremost was the cherished union of his young country, perhaps unsalvageable. There was the union of the men he led, whose lives he was responsible for. And finally, there was that Union Army now staring them in the face, a sea of relentless, royally equipped, infinitely funded, constantly reinforced men. His union with Anna could withstand everything save a bullet or saber slash. They both knew it. Still, their anniversary had come and gone without the new captain even giving it an inkling of a remembrance. Years later, with Anna no longer at his side, the Old Captain paused once again to ask her forgiveness.

It could have been worse, he pondered, at least he never rode up to a young artillerist whose face was blackened with powder and asked "Who are you young man?" only to discover to his chagrin, that the boy was his own son. That man was Robert E. Lee...or so the story goes. As for that Union army perched at Richmond's doorstep, it now faced a new guardian of the gate. It was Robert E. Lee again, and he knew well the men he faced. He knew what they'd do before they did. He knew how to save Richmond and whip them. How did he know? As superintendent at West Point, he watched future Union generals like a tentative young cadet named McClellan. He met a braggart named Pope, full of bombast but short on tactics. He knew that "Fighting Joe" Hooker played a mean game of poker but lacked the same nerve in battle. He knew of the intelligence "Old Brains" Halleck possessed in mathematics and

Latin but his weakness in grasping the big picture in conflict. As a captain in the Mexican War, Lee once commended a young lieutenant named Grant for his aggressive fighting instincts and knew they'd serve him well in the years to come.

Lee also understood his own subordinates, once marveling at Cadet Tom Jackson's work ethic, rising from close to dead last to nearly number one in his class. He knew James "Old Pete" Longstreet was steady as rock and he marveled in the swashbuckling air and unmatched horsemanship of Jeb Stuart. But above all, Lee knew the heart of the Southern private and he knew himself. Had Lee accepted the offer of U.S. Army General-in-Chief Winfield Scott and accepted command of the North's massive army, few doubt the war would have lasted much more than a year. Instead, Lee had remained true to Virginia, and now the Federals would have to face the ultimate general, a perfect man in the eyes of loyal southerners, the messiah in the eyes of more than a few. But it wasn't this way at first.

When Davis first named Lee as Johnston's replacement, his countrymen shook their heads and the enemy rejoiced. Southern newspapers grilled him and dubbed him "Granny Lee" and "Evacuating Lee" for his lackluster performance in western Virginia. George McClellan cackled at the appointment, berating Lee as "cautious and weak under grave responsibility...likely to be timid and irresolute in action." Perhaps McClellan's self-describing, completely off-the-mark remark can be blamed on delirium from typhus, from which he was in the midst of recovering. Regardless, Little Mac's words smacked of the pot calling the kettle black and very soon Lee would have the hen boiling in it.

The South had a bold new general and he gave his forces a brand new name, "The Army of Northern Virginia." He put the army to work with picks and shovels to strengthen the defenses around Richmond. As his trenches and earthworks were being fortified, Lee then set out to ascertain the exact size and location of the enemy.

To that end, he dispatched General J.E.B. Stuart, with twelve hundred cavalry and a section of artillery, to see what was behind McClellan's front. On June 11, Stuart headed north for Ashland then quickly turned east and rode behind McClellan's right and far to his rear. Near the Federal commander's base at the White House, Stuart's men created quite a ruckus, blocked the railroad at Tunstall's Station, and gathered information about the enemy's fortifications and supply lines. Stuart knew he could ride circles around the disorganized

Federals and the venturesome maverick did just that. With visions of heroic headlines in his head, Stuart rode out, won skirmishes, and captured 170 enemy soldiers. He snatched up almost twice as many horses and mules and destroyed wagonloads of critical supplies. He burnt bridges behind him, performed harrowing escapes, and tormented Union cavalry officers for four days. Stuart and his horsemen finally completed their audacious 100 mile round trip and returned to Richmond on June 16.

The cool commander got his headlines. Lee got his headcount. Leonard and Ruby missed the whole thing. The Old Captain remembered how disgruntled many of the Legion cavalrymen had been that they had missed their chance for glory, but their time would come. In the meantime, life went on and Leonard enjoyed an interesting diversion.

> *Cavalry Camp*
> *Near Richmond*
> *June 19th, 1862*

*My Dear Anna,*

*I wrote you some 3 or 4 days ago and I expected a letter from you this evening but have been disappointed. Robt. McKay stayed with me Tuesday night and entertained me a great deal with matters that had and were taking place in Greenville and a recitation of his poetry describing the scenes of camp life and the troubles of a soldier's life. His pictures are quite true to nature and animated. I hope he will have it published. He left me promising to call again. Tomorrow (Friday) he expects a leave for home on next Monday and I commence now to write to be sure of having a letter to send by him.*

*Yours of the 6th is the last letter I have recd from you and just now have read it again with increased gratification. You tell me I have never confessed to you in such terms. If not dear Anna, it is because I intended it to be inferential (I allude to your reflections on the anniversary days of our marriage) and I now confess the pride and happiness with which I was filled in your confessions as you term them and can truly say that I cordially reciprocate every sentiment. June 20, 1862. I was interrupted from yesterday and today have been into the city. I now find Mr. McKay in the act of starting for home and have therefore to make this a short letter. I left Mr. Randolph's yesterday*

*morning, am now quite well again. I send by Mr. McKay to you $100.
I must close. Write soon.*

*Your affectionate husband*
*L. Williams*

Affairs were becoming white hot around the capital. The bloody and pivotal Seven Days' Battles were only five days away and the new captain found himself in charge of a squadron.

*Cavalry Camp HQ*
*Near Richmond, Va.*
*June 21st, 1862*

*My Dear Anna*

*Lieut. Perry will start home this evening for volunteers and conscripts to fill up our company. I was very anxious to go two weeks ago but Col. Hampton was not willing for me to go being the commanding officer of the company. I sent Perry 1st Lieut., whose father has been interesting himself very much in behalf of the company and through him I hope he will do more than I could. I sent you a short letter yesterday by Robt. McKay and also gave him $100 to hand to you. I am getting strong again and ready for duty. There is a good deal of sickness in camp at present but none of a serious character. Maj. Butler is sick and I am now, since some other captains have left to get conscripts, in command of the squadron about the responsibility of which I feel somewhat timid and diffident. I hope the Major will return soon. The affairs along the line are about the same condition. The recruiting officers have only 20 days leave of absence, only 10 or 12 days at home, and that time must necessarily be mostly occupied. I hope that I may in the course of the summer get a quiet furlough for 30 days or more. Perry will bring the recruits by land on horseback. I hope you will send me by Mr. Greenfield or Robt. Adams the articles I wrote for [     ] the hat, shoes, and saddle cloth. There are no shoes or hats in Richmond or but few and very high. Everything is high here. You will please pay Mr. Scruggs for the shoes. Our squadron will soon have an ascension of two companies, Capt. Lipscomb's and a company from Camden. It has been a week today since I heard from you. I hope*

*I will get a letter this evening.*

*I engaged a Confederate uniform yesterday to be made. I alas bought the cotton undershirts and a pair of cassimere pants. I am nearly out of boots but hope they will last til those you send me come to hand. I would like to send home my two winter undershirts. They will do me another winter if I live. I will do so if nothing prevents by Mr. Burgess. We are all quiet in camp. The weather is warm. The days will soon begin to shorten and then time passes rapidly. Last winter I hardly knew how time passed and it flew so rapidly. I think the War Department will owe me a furlough under all the circumstances and I have no doubt will get one this summer or early in the fall. Kiss baby for me. I wish I could find some plaything to send her to give her something to talk about. My love to all your aunts and hope they will enjoy their visit in Greenville and I expect your aunts will probably, after getting acquainted, will likely stay. My remembrances to your father and mother and also to Uncle Whitmire and Aunt Edna. Tell them I think of them. Write often.*

*Your affectionate husband*
*L. Williams*

Meanwhile, Lee was finishing the final touches on a battle plan that everyone would be talking about. He would move swiftly, with great strength and at great risk. Boldly, he divided his smaller force in the face of superior numbers. His target was the 25,000 man Fifth Army Corps under General Fitz-John Porter, which rested north of the swollen Chickahominy. Lee would strike this force with more than 55,000 men, but to do so he would have to take a chance. McClellan had 80,000 well-armed men just south of the river facing Richmond and Lee proposed to leave only 20,000 in the trenches to face him. He prayed that McClellan would not attack while Porter was being thrashed. If Lee's gamble paid off, the rest of the Confederate army could go north of the river, Stonewall Jackson could lead his army down from the valley, and Porter's exposed corps would be wiped off the map. McClellan, of course, was in his usual disposition. He believed that 200,000 graycoats awaited him instead of about 90,000, which included Jackson's men marching south. The battle was looming and Leonard could smell it.

*Cavalry Camp*
*9 Miles from Richmond*
*June 26th, 1862*

*Dear Anna*

*This day 12 months ago I was spending my way from Columbia to Greenville. I believe I am right in the date and tomorrow will be a year since I left my happy home. It seems to me to have been a long time, yet a portion of the time has passed very rapidly. I am somewhat uneasy for fear you may be sick and yet I hope you have been waiting to write by someone coming on. A good many are complaining that they do not get letters and it may be the fault of the mail. We left our camp near Richmond on the 24th. We are now near the James River or near it 9 miles below the city. Yesterday I took out the squadron to picquet on the river near the boat landings and along the roads that lead toward the enemy's left wing, their extreme left. Genl. Casey's division is about 2 or 3 miles from our piquet post and their picquets and ours about 1 mile apart; now and then each party sends out scouts. This morning a small scout came in sight of our videttes. I am now in charge of the entire squadron, the Maj. and senior captains being absent.*

*A great battle is looked for every day and before this reaches you it may take place. Genl. Jackson is in Hanover County and will probably force Genl. McClellan to change his front. I think he will be attacked very soon by Genls. Lee and Jackson simultaneously and I do trust we may whip him most severely. I regret to see our newspapers taking such pains to make the public dissatisfied with our generals continually finding fault with their slowness and urging an immediate attack. It does no good. The authorities will have their own way and it tends to produce distrust in the minds of both soldiers and public. I was rejoiced to hear of the victory of our forces in Charleston. I think Charleston is safe, at least til the winter.*

*I hope your garden is turning out according to your expectations. I can appreciate now more than ever the advantages of a garden. I have had 2 or 3 messes of green peas and 1 of cabbages and while I have been here I have had buttermilk and sweet milk and also butter, the first I have had for months. It seemed to me that buttermilk was good enough for anybody and that I never would want anything better.*

*I hope your cows are doing well and giving you plenty of milk and butter. How much do you get at a milking and what vegetables are you using now? Have you any tomatoes growing? I was glad to hear that marketing was getting a little easier. I was surprised to hear you had so much bacon on hand. Is it all in sound condition? If so it will last you til winter or nearly so. Your expenses are incurred with a due regard to economy and it is less than I expected. If coffee is selling at 80 cts. per lb. you ought to indulge in the luxury of a cup. While I was able to get it at $1.00 a lb., I had my morning cup and thought it tolerably cheap. It now sells for $2.50 to $3.00 per lb., sugar for 75 cts. I have, therefore, dispensed with them both. I hope to see several friends from Greenville.*

The day that letter was written, Richmond reporters who had been bemoaning indecision had a hot new scoop to write about. On June 26, "Evacuating Lee" became "Attacking Lee," unleashing his forces at Mechanicsville, initiating the Seven Days' Battles. No one scribbled more furiously than Leonard. There wasn't even enough time for his usual "My Dear Anna," just an instant to fire off some random, choppy sentences after the Mechanicsville fight.

*June 27th*

*A fight took place yesterday between Genl. Jackson and some of McClellan's forces. It was a very heavy fight. We could hear the cannonading, about 50 rounds to the minute. We have heard nothing from it. I am in good health. Since we have changed camps there is less sickness. My love to all. Write soon. I am very anxious to hear from you. The mail is waiting and I must close. Kiss baby for me.*

*Your affectionate husband*
*L. Williams*

For a week the fight raged on through forests, fields and swamp. Richmond held its breath and Washington awaited any news. Once serene spots like Mechanicsville, Gaines Mill, Savage Station, White Oak Swamp, and Malvern Hill were transformed into hellish places echoing with canister, minie balls and clashing sabers. It would come to be known simply as the Seven Days' Battles.

During those battles to save Richmond, the Regimental History would later state:

> *The Hampton Legion Cavalry battalion was commanded by Captain Thomas E. Screven...and formed part of the cavalry brigade of Brigadier General J.E.B. Stuart. Attached to the 5th Virginia Cavalry under Colonel T.L. Rosser, they operated south of the Chickahominy River thereby preventing the Federals from advancing from White Oak Swamp to the James River.*

In the end, Lee's Army of Northern Virginia drove the invaders out, saving Richmond against overwhelming odds. McClellan had retreated 18 miles to the south, but to his credit he had done so brilliantly saving most of his army and nearly all his weapons and supplies. The South rejoiced, but Lee and the men of the Legion knew they had squandered a golden opportunity to squash the hen, who now nested comfortably under the cover of his gunboats at Harrison's Landing south of Richmond.

Throughout nearly every day of these critical Richmond fights, one commander known for his poise, skill, and gallantry in the field was inexplicably slow, late and ineffective. "Old Blue Light" looked more like "Old Red Light," stopping, sputtering, and getting to the battle line late three times. Perhaps the six weeks of strain in the Valley, the lowland heat, and the long marches had finally taken their toll on Stonewall and his weary warriors. Stonewall himself may have been suffering from what is termed battle fatigue today; regardless, he was not his usual daring and effective self during the battles around Richmond.

The third of his failures occurred on the fourth of the Seven Days' Battles on June 29 at Savage's Station. This time Jackson never showed up. Instead, he spent his Sunday rebuilding the Grapevine Bridge, despite having available to him a nearby ford where he could have crossed rather easily. Jackson's dawdling was one of several key, random events that led to calamity and defeat for the Confederates that day.

While Jackson was building his bridge, John Magruder was heading east from Richmond. Under Magruder was Brigadier General J. B. Kershaw, who in turn ordered Colonel James D. Nance to march the Third South Carolina Infantry out to the battle line where the tail of McClellan's army might be bitten off. If Magruder's eastbound forces could have struck simultaneously with Stonewall's southbound forces, McClellan's rear guard could have been squeezed in a deadly vise. But with Stonewall nowhere to be found, the plan resulted in disaster, especially for the companies of Colonel Nance's Third South Carolina Volunteer Infantry.

It was near dusk on that hot Sunday evening, when young Ephraim Williams and the men of the 3rd S.C.V.I. were hurled into action. Nance later reported the details, when his men dashed uphill into a foreboding, dark woods.

*We received the command forward and immediately thereafter the command to charge. The commands were obeyed with alacrity and great enthusiasm. My regiment dashed up the ascent in front through the woods, yelling as they went, and into the thick undergrowth, in which it was impossible to discover either friend or foe over twenty yards. We were not aware of the exact position of the enemy until we received his galling fire at a distance of 25 or 30 yards...The fire checked us for a moment, but we pressed on slowly, returning the enemy's fire and making him yield gradually, when I ordered a charge, and pushed him out of the wood and some distance across the open field beyond. We had scarcely emerged from the woods before I heard, to my surprise, the command, 'cease firing.' I immediately went to the right of the regiment, where I heard an officer giving this command, of whom I inquired by what authority he spake. He replied that it came from the right, and that he understood we were firing at our friends...I could not with certainty determine, on account of the approaching darkness and smoke of battle-might be our people moving on the enemy's flank, I ordered the regiment to cease firing. We had scarcely ceased fire before the enemy...rallied on a hill opposite us and renewed the attack with great vigor. Suspecting the command to cease firing was either a ruse or an error, I withdrew a short distance in the underbrush, and reformed my line the best I could under an extremely severe fire...As they advanced they poured a deadly and incessant fire into my line. I met them again, pushing my line almost to the edge of the undergrowth, when, besides the fire in my front, I was subjected to a threatening fire on my right flank. In this emergency...I deemed it prudent to retire, which I did. I...collected the scattered, reformed the line, and took position, by order of General Kershaw, on the edge of the wood in front of our first position, where, after throwing out pickets, we slept on our arms without fires until morning.*

That night, 2,500 sick and wounded Union Soldiers and nearly the same number of Confederates lay out in the open field unattended except by horseflies and bloodthirsty mosquitoes. Swirling around the carcasses were questions as well. Where was Stonewall? Who yelled out the command to "cease fire"? Why did Magruder only send in half his force that day?

The next morning, only a mile or two away, as Leonard and Ruby kept tabs on McClellan's move south toward Malvern Hill, somewhere on the outskirts of the underbrush or deep in the wood near Savage Station, lay the motionless body of a 31-year-old orderly sergeant from the doomed 3rd S.C.V.I. His musket was still loaded. His eyes were still wide open. But his heart, once full of hope, was now as empty as his canteen.

The Old Captain wiped away a river of tears he knew time could never damn up. He took a deep breath then walked slowly to his hotel window. Like his tears, folks were beginning to trickle down Lady Street. In five hours or so, the few old soldiers left standing years later, would march proudly in front of them one final time. Brother Ephraim, the Old Captain knew, would not be one of them.

# CHAPTER EIGHT
## FOLLOW THE LEADER—1862

*He shall wipe away every tear from their eyes,*
*and there shall be no more death or mourning, crying out or pain,*
*for the former world has passed away.*
Revelation 21:4

*Bivouac*
*30 Miles from Richmond*
*3 Miles from the James River*
*July 7, 1862*

*My Dear Wife,*

*I have no opportunity of writing but a short letter. We have been out on the flanks of the enemy now for over a week, constantly on the move with no opportunity to write. I have sad intelligence to give you. My dear brother Ephraim was killed in the battle of Sunday, the 29th June. He fell at his post doing his duty, as he ever did through life. I mourn his loss but trust his spirit is at rest with God. I very much desire his body to be carried home, but I could not attend to it. I have written to William about it and hope he will come to convey his remains home. He was a beloved brother. My bro. James is somewhere near here but I have not seen him nor do I know but he may have been killed or wounded. I am most anxious to hear from him.*

James was safe as was Richmond. The Seven Days' Battles were over and President Jefferson Davis had issued an official proclamation of thanksgiving. Yet Southern gratitude for Lee's achievements was tempered by an outpouring of grief. Ephraim was one of the 20,614 men Lee lost, nearly one fourth of his army. The losses among his officers were staggering also as 10 brigade commanders and 66 regimental commanders were killed or wounded. The Federal toll of 15, 849 was considerably less, but it was still a Union defeat. McClellan called his tactical movement a "change of base," but he had indeed retreated and Lincoln had finally had enough. On July 11, he plucked overall Federal command from the hen and turned it over to Major General Henry Halleck, who turned his army in the west over to Grant. McClellan would keep his army, but now Lincoln and Halleck would tell him where to take it.

For the time being, Lt. Williams was doing his part to make sure it wasn't going anywhere. A fat white sun baked a thin gray rider as he held tight to the reins and Ephraim's memory. He grieved for his brother and yearned to see his wife and daughter. Leonard received some small comfort, however, in the form of a new saddle he had recently come across. Not only did that saddle come courtesy of McClellan's retreating army, it was invented by none other than Little Mac himself. The "McClellan" was lighter and more upright with a hole in the middle to lessen saddle sores and aching backs. Ruby seemed more content now, but it was her master's back that was sore, the McClellan being much stiffer than his roomy, old plantation saddle. It would take some getting used to, especially that odd hole at the top. As he rode along, he looked down through it and he could see straight through to Ruby's blanket and almost into her happy heart. After a few picket circuits, the new saddle felt fine, but unfortunately, another painful boil had appeared. Leonard added to his July 7 letter the next day.

*I thought on commencing this letter I would have had the leisure to finish it but the bugle sounded and we spent the balance of the day in sight of the enemy. At night we came back and are now 1½ miles from the Yankees. Our horses have been saddled for over a week and we have slept most of the time with boots and spurs on. The enemy have been driven 20 or 30 miles from Richmond. We do not know what they intend to do. They are now under cover of their gunboats. In the past week I have been twice under the most terrific fire shells but by the mercy of God have escaped harm. We have been in no charge. There has been no opportunity for one. One of our squadron only has been killed during these fights. I do not think this state of things will last more than 2 or 3 days longer.*

*I am now in prime health. When ordered out, I was almost too unwell to start but have been improving all the time and am now as well as I ever was. I have had a bad bile on my thigh but I have not withstanding, kept to the saddle and it is now about well. I recd your letter of the 18th June by Moore, the only letter I have recd from you since the 8th and it only came to me on the 5th inst. It has been 3 weeks four days since I have recd a letter from you by mail. Do write me at*

*Richmond every few days. Did you receive the money I sent you by Mr. McKay? I am always low spirited when I fail to get your letters, do write twice a week. I may at least get one.*

> *Your affectionate husband*
> *L. Williams*

While Lee and his new Army of Northern Virginia were being praised in the press, McClellan sulked in his tent. Lincoln had replaced him as overall Union commander with Halleck and, worse, imported Major General John Pope from the west to infuse new life into the Union army. Pope immediately insulted friends and foes alike in an address to his newly named "Army of Virginia."

> *I have come to you from the West, where we have always seen the backs of our enemies; from an army whose business it has been to seek the adversary, and to beat him when he is found; whose policy has been attack and not defense...I desire you to dismiss from your minds certain phrases, which I am sorry to find so much in vogue amongst you. I hear constantly of 'taking strong positions and holding them,' of 'lines of retreat' and of 'bases of supplies.' Let us discard such ideas...Let us study the probable lines of retreat of our opponents, and leave our own to take care of themselves...*

Pope's bombast angered Lee and created a tug of war between the old Federal commander and the new. Although Pope had come east to assume command of the Federals' Army of Virginia, McClellan wanted the general to reinforce him down on the Peninsula, while Pope wanted McClellan's forces shipped back to Washington to strengthen him. Lee was in the middle, keeping his eye on both. It was Leonard's lot to picket south of Richmond for a few more days to make sure Little Mac made little trouble. The sooner the hen flew, the better. Except for the gunboat shelling, Leonard and his men had not been in direct contact with the enemy, but the constant patrolling in steady rains was taking its toll on clothing and equipment.

> *Camp Near Richmond*
> *July 10th, 1862*

*My Dear Anna,*

*Our squadron just returned last night from its reconnaissances on the Jas. River on the enemy's right some 30 or 35 miles from Richmond. We had a most laborious time. We were out 10 days with nothing but a blanket and no food but bacon and crackers, but this kind of diet is very good. We rest today til 2 ock and then we move. We're going into Hanover County. I do not know exactly how far from Richmond, but probably 20 or 30 miles. I write you this short letter merely to inform you of my safety so far and good health. I'm getting very bad off for shoes and a hat. I hope you have already found means of sending them. If you lose all opportunities, you will please box them up and send them by the express to Richmond. My toes are about out and my hat very bad so use all dispatch. I cannot get a hat in Richmond except straw.*

*I regretted to see the announcement of Mr. East's death. It is sad to think so few of our poor wounded soldiers ever get well. I have not seen Billy Whitmire but understand he is safe and well. Your letter of the 20th last month came yesterday evening about 20 days on the road. I know you must write me oftener. I have recd only one letter by mail from you and in 4 weeks Saturday next. I know you must write oftener, do write often. I wrote you by Robt. McKay and also by Lieut. Perry and twice by mail since. Did Mr. McKay hand you the remittance I sent by him and did you get the small draft on Mr. Cox cashed?*

*I think the recent victories about Richmond and the repulse of the enemy for 35 miles into and under the cover of his gunboats will create a good impression abroad and will procure our recognition soon & Lincoln's call for 300,000 additional troops will certainly call for intervention. I would like very well for you to pay your parents a visit in Columbia. I know it would gratify them and I expect baby would interest your father very much. I write in haste amidst noise and confusion. Give my love to all and write soon and often.*

> *Your affectionate husband*
> *L. Williams*

As the summer of '62 wore on, Anna's situation at home was also deteriorating. The house servants were doing their best to help as was Mr. Whitmire down at their store, but provisions were growing scarce and disease more prevalent. The sick weren't getting better at the battlefront or the home front. Still, the young captain had no choice but to ask more of his wife in the way of clothes and letters while sending less and less good news and money home. Pay was meager and never regular. The mail was sometimes stolen or undelivered. A few weeks leave, let alone a furlough, seemed impossible. But at least brothers James and William were still among the living as he discovered during a chance visit on his way up to Hanover County.

> *Camp in Hanover County*
> *9 Miles from Richmond*
> *July 14th, 1862*

*My Dear Anna*

*This is a bright beautiful Monday morning. The sun is just up and will employ the half hour before breakfast in complaining. I have only recd from you since the 8th of last month, one on the 18th and the other the 20th. I am really much put out and must think it is carelessness in the mail agents, for I know if you are well, you would and do write much oftener. Do write me every day for 3 days and it may be I will get one of them. On my way from James River (Chas. City C.H.) to this place I went to several S. C. regiments. William has been here over a week. He was with James. I saw them both, took dinner with them and spent several hours with them. I met Billy Whitmire along the way. He had been worn down but was then well and ready to rejoin his regiment. Ephraim's body has been removed by kind friends from the battlefield and buried near Richmond. I shall never forget their kindness. He had many warm and attached friends and I was told no man had more. He was orderly Sergeant of his company. William will take his remains home with him if the RR authorities will allow it, if not we will have to wait til next winter. I visited his grave.*

*We do not know what movement will be next on hand. The enemy are under cover of their gunboats on the James River. What will be their next step, I can hardly form an idea. I think it will be sometime before McClellan can get ready for further operations. The wounded in the late battles have died and are still dieing fearfully. I have stood the fatigues of the last few weeks firmly. I have never had better health. The health of the company is much improved lately. My uniform is* *finished but still in the shop. I am waiting for my hat and shoes- my toes are out and my jacket indecent. I would have bought a pair in Richmond the other day but they asked me $12 for a common pegged shoe so I thought I would wait. If no one is coming on by RR at once, you will please put my chattels in a box or small trunk and send them express to Richmond. We will likely be here a week or two. Prepay the expenses and send me the receipt. I have been in command of the squadron for 3 weeks. Maj. Butler is now here. We are attached temporarily to the Jeff Davis Legion, Col. Martin. Everything now very quiet. I am anxious to see the recruits. I have now an opportunity of sending this off and must close. My love to all.*

*Your affectionate husband*
*L. Williams*

The Old Captain knew the tone of that letter was due to displaced aggression, or more accurately, it was the result of the pressure of his rank. General Stuart demanded more of him now as company captain, and in turn, Leonard had become more impatient with his men. Regrettably, when he'd write home that chain of stress wrapped, in the end, around poor Anna. The real targets of his anger were the imperfect mail system, the inefficient quartermaster, and the whole damn war. He knew it now but he didn't recognize it then, irritated by no letters coming and not knowing where the army was going. In his letter three days later, the "Dear Anna" was omitted. He knew this was not because of hurriedness but distress over a lack of news of any kind from 606 Augusta Street and the stress of his responsibility as an officer. Be that as it may, the Old Captain now regretted the almost curt tone his words had taken.

*July 19th*

*I am again disappointed, no letters yet. Send your letters to Columbia and have them mailed there. There possibly, I may get them. The 20th last month is the date of the last of your letters I have recd. Possibly the government is interfering in the transmission of the mails. Someone is no doubt, but whether authority or otherwise, I cannot say.*

*I wrote you in my last that I had spent a day with William. I hear he has erysipelas and is with James some 5 miles beyond Richmond from this place. I must try to see him. I wish him to spend a few days with me here before he returns home. We have just heard of the brilliant performance of the Arkansas. It equals the achievement of the ill-fated Merrimac. I hope her career is not destined to such a short existence and that she may have many another equally as splendid encounters with the Yankee fleet.*

*We are in a quiet out-of-the-way place where we see no one but troopers. There are 6 or eight regiments of cavalry near us today. We had a brigade drill under General Stewart. We are drilling twice a day, on foot and in the saber exercises. The officers too are attempting to institute a rigid discipline among the soldiers. Being under orders myself, I am compelled to exercise some rigor. I am determined to have all orders obeyed and to enforce regularity in the discharge of all duties. Good soldiers, as a matter of choice, discharge every duty with compulsion and they are glad to have all the others do the same. There are some 3 or 4 in my company that endeavor to shirk duty. I am bringing them to a wholesome dread of consequences. I have to maintain discipline and you may hear complaints from some parties but it will not last long. You need not give yourself any trouble about anything you may hear. I am tightening the cords and there will be as a matter of course dissatisfaction for a time, but for the better and more numerous class of soldiers, it is approved.*

*All is quiet yet. I hear of no movements on foot yet. I wrote you to send the shoes and hat by express. If you have not already done so I wish you would do so at once. Kiss baby for me. My love to all. Tell the servants howdy. I am in capital health and so are most of my company, but Stokes is unwell. I think of you almost constantly and I am anxious to get a letter.*

> *Your affectionate husband*
> *LW*

The Old Captain had become familiar with many sites during the war, but perhaps the most lasting image was that of the roaring Rappahannock. He picketed its fords. He camped by its banks. He filled his canteen from it. Ruby consumed gallons of its crisp cold water. What the Mississippi was in the western theatre, the Rappahannock River was in the east. Bisecting Richmond and Washington, it flowed northwest to southeast, and slicing across it and nestled next to it were important railroads and supply points. It was this key logistical artery, that both North and South would control, give up, cross, re-cross, picket, defend, attack, or fall back along its banks, throughout the war. Historians would later point out that Lee, Meade and Grant would all headquarter there and lay plans near its rapids. The greatest cavalry battle in North America would be fought near its banks in '63 and from it, the Wilderness Campaign would be launched in '64. For now though, in the summer of '62, the Rappahannock was Leonard's home, and toward the end of July, two armies were descending upon it once more. Fremont's and Bank's forces had been ordered east to link up with Pope's, and soon, despite his protests, McClellan's forces would be sent back north too. Lee not only knew of this mass movement, he had anticipated it. Again he boldly divided his forces and sent Stonewall with 12,000 men back up to the valley with another 13,000 under A.P. Hill close behind. Lee himself would ride beside steady James Longstreet with thousands more. In all, well over 100,000 men from both armies were Rappahannock bound, huge gray and blue snakes, winding their way beside the Blue Ridge, across the valley and along the Rappahannock, feinting, slipping through passes and hissing all the way because of the damned heat.

Captain Williams was now in the saddle continuously. On long rides, he'd nod off but Ruby knew the bugle commands by heart. Day after day, they screened their army, watching its rear on one day and scouting what lay ahead the next. They served as outriders, guarding flanks, supply wagons, and ordnance trains. At night, they picketed, eyes peeled while the exhausted infantry stole some richly deserved sleep.

Jeb Stuart launched raids behind enemy lines in the hope of striking terror in the enemy and cleaning them out of food and supplies. It was dangerous work, but Ruby was a good horse, and she never balked on the long rides that began with reveille and ended long after dusk. The Captain remembered how she could lap up about twenty gallons of water a day, about a gallon to the mile, and he made sure she got her full ration. He worried over her just as he did over every tiny detail that frail, little Anna could possibly be overseeing back at the house. The rich fields they traversed provided fodder for Ruby and food for thought for her master.

*Camp Near Hanover C.H., Va.*
*July 24th, 1862*

*My Dear Wife*

I recd yours of the 15*th* yesterday and was pained to hear that you was not well. I was in hopes you would pass this summer without your usual debility and nervousness. I still hope it is not as bad as it has been for the past 2 or 3 summers and that before many weeks the weather will be bracing and restore you to health. The weather here is very warm and plenty of rain. I fear a drought in the south, the wheat crop has failed and if the corn crop too should fail, it would place our people and our armies in a desperate condition. If there is an abundant corn crop, however, the people can live; how is your bacon doing? Has any of it spoiled and how much have you on hand? Beef, I understand is worth 25 cts. per lb. I am sorry your cows have begun to fail. I supposed the grazing in the woods was very good. Do you turn them out? It is too expensive to keep them up and feed them entirely. If you can manage to give them a tolerable feed night and morning and then turn them out soon before it gets too hot, I think they will still give you plenty of milk. You must, by all means, try to get milk and butter enough. With an abundance of milk and butter and with the products of your garden, you can do tolerably well.

Don't forget to have turnips sowed at the right time and in all the ground you can spare. If any of the crops are done, for instance, the English pea or beans, use the same ground, manure it as well as you can. Turnips are excellent diet and fine food for cows. How is your Irish potato crop and okra? I'm doing pretty well as to my eating. I am furnished at government prices. We can get molasses at 20 cts. a gall., sugar at 5 cts. a lb., only however, a limited quantity and sometimes the commissary can't supply any at all. No coffee. Ham's at 35 cts. per lb., flour at 4 or 5 cts. per lb., fresh beef occasionally at 12 ½ cts. I have denied myself the luxury of a fried chicken. They sell at a dollar apiece, butter at $1 to $2, eggs at $1 per dozen. I did buy some butter the other day at $1, but chicken and eggs I have nothing to do with. I had to buy a pair of boots and had to pay $35 for them. I could find no hat. I am still waiting for my shoes and hat. I need shoes and boots both. I wrote you in several of my letters to send them by express and if you have not already done so, and no one is about to leave, say, within a week, box them up and send them by express to Richmond. I *am very much in need of a hat.*

Though ragged and far from home, trying to maintain some sort of order amidst the chaos of war was most important to him. In looking back, the Old Captain realized the sheer folly and futility of it all. For in war there is no order, just disorder. Yes the columns were neatly aligned and the orders were clear. But the only thing living, breathing men had in common with those perfect pointed arrows on a battle map, were sharp tempers. It was survival and nothing more. The Old Captain had been near the command tents overhearing the Stuarts and the Hamptons discussing where they thought best to hit the enemy. But all the time, he and they knew well that men were not mere arrows. Men laughed. Men cried. Men sweated. Men bled. And they had opinions about the sharp arrows, sins, and spins of war. The July 24 letter continued.

> *You asked my opinion about the war. We cannot, I think, as yet see the beginning of the end to it. I do not see much probability of its closing before the Lincoln administration goes out or their present army and the 300,000 new lives are destroyed. There seems to be a madness in the north that drives them to the employment of every means lawful and unlawful to accomplish their purposes as to intervention. I begin to look at it as a baseless hope. I did think on the termination of the late fights around Richmond, we would be recognized by European powers. But now looking to the disappointments of past hopes, I begin to doubt immediate recognition. I think our wisest policy is to work for our independence, fight and act as if there were no other powers but the ones we are engaged with. To have no hopes of intercession and if recognition comes at all, let it come spontaneously without seeking it because I think no diplomacy we can set afoot can move Europe to act before she is ready.*
> *Our chief object should be to give them merely a true and correct account of the progress of the war and the events as they transpire. This is about all we can do, to keep them informed as to current events, a portion of the press of the country are in favor of carrying the war into "Africa" and are denouncing the administration and military authorities for their supineness. Only on two conditions can I give my*

*consent to such a policy. The first is if our crops fail and provisions cannot be procured for the army without consuming the entire substance of the people. In that event, it will no doubt be good policy to invade and subsist on the enemy. But I trust no necessity may come upon us. The other condition is impracticable at present. It is that we get a many to go side by side with our army along the Ohio River or Potomac and other rivers to transport reinforcements when needed, and also supplies a dernier resort to fall back on in case of being pressed by overwhelming numbers.*

*If McClellan's gunboats had not been on the Jas. River, the last man of his army would have been captured. I don't care what army he may bring. If he carries it into the interior fifty miles from his boats, we can destroy it before he can get back with it and so I fear if we're to invade with no control of the rivers or bays and push our armies to the interiors of the enemy's country, they could and would concentrate forces enough by aid of their boats and RR either to overcome them or cut them off from supplies. I think at present, with the present lights before me, our policy is to act on the defensive, to meet the enemy wherever he invades. There is some hope that when the north is compelled to have recourse to drafting to raise these new levies lately called for and (I think it very probable) that public opinion will begin to change and also new taxes and heavy ones must be imposed to meet the increased army. This too may probably have a good effect in checking their military enthusiasm by these influences. Public sentiment may be revolutionized before Lincoln's administration closes. Kiss baby for me. My love to all and my sincerest sympathy and regards to Sallie East. I hope you will visit your mother and father and as you return, stop with Mary a few days.*

> *Your affectionate husband*
> *L. Williams*

McClellan was not the problem. Pope was. The braggart "must be suppressed," as Lee once said, and he was about to be. Just as clover strengthened Ruby and letters from home invigorated Leonard, the Valley was rejuvenating Stonewall. On August 9 at Cedar Mountain, he rode out in front of his troops and rallied them to defeat his old adversary Nathanial Banks once more. A.P. Hill's division led the slashing counterattack that cost Banks 30 percent of his force. Over the next two days, Jackson pulled back to Gordonsville to avoid a collision with Pope. Along the omnipresent Rappahannock, then along the railroad toward Manassas, Stonewall marched his men, all 24,000 of them, an incredible 50 miles in two sweltering hot days.

James Williams of the 14th S.C.V.I. was one of the barefooted troops who plodded stoically through the rain subsisting on little more than roasting ears, and like the rest he was bone-weary and near starving when he finally arrived at Manassas. But great rewards were discovered at the end of that march as he and the worn out "foot cavalry" feasted on Pope's supplies then torched the few leftovers. While brother James was full, the James River was now almost completely empty of invaders. Only a few deserters from McClellan's beaten army were left behind. With the hen's chicks headed back to Washington, Captain Williams and his faithful mare were glad to be rid of them and the ever-present flies and nasty gnats of the swamps below Richmond. The Old Captain carefully unfolded the next letter. He noticed that it was postmarked from a new location below Richmond and deep into August.

*White Oak Swamp*
*15 Miles below Richmond*
*August 19th, 1862*

*My Dear Anna,*

*I recd yours of the 13th yesterday. I fear you made your visit to Columbia at a disagreeable time. Col. is a very warm place, more than Charleston, and since you have been there we have had the most oppressively warm weather. Now, however, the nights are cool here and I expect the weather has changed considerably in S. C. I hope baby will get through the whooping cough before winter sets in. I would not physic her much but let the cough take its course. Nor would I change her habits any. Let her take the air and sunshine as usual. The only thing I would guard against is measles or the contagious complaint until she got well enough. How long do you expect to stay in Columbia?*

*I came here from Hanover C.H. on Saturday. On yesterday, we went out on reconnaissance on the James River to see whether the enemy were gone or not. From deserters we learned that all of*

*McClellan's forces were gone and leaving and from prisoners taken yesterday and from citizens living in the vicinity we found out that this part of Va. has been evacuated by the enemy. They have all crossed the Chickahominy and on their way towards Williamsburg, and thence probably to Pope's army in the valley. The great bulk of the forces in and near Richmond have been sent up to Jackson and everyday I expect to hear of a fight. The battle on the 9th was a larger matter than we thought. The Yankees admit a loss of 3,000, our loss was less than 1,000.*

*I am much gratified with being with Captain Westfield's company and a Spartanburg company. I have a great many acquaintances among them. In fact, I know nearly all of Westfield's company. I have known Lieut. Thompson of the Spartanburg company for a long time. He is an eternal friend. I never knew he was here til this morning. He called on me. These old friends I am much strongly attached to than to new ones. My resources for social enjoyment are greatly enhanced. Lieuts. Latham and Kent of Westfield's company and Thompson I have been doing business with for several years on the most pleasant terms. Every man in Westfield's company knows me but I have forgotten several of them, being boys. We are now under marching orders. I expect we will go back towards Hanover C. H. and possibly in the course of a few weeks, to the valley. We will leave here tonight or in the morning.*

*I wish you would get, if you can, enough fine dark gray homemade jeans to make a couple of winter shirts for me and also enough plain country wove white woolen goods to make two pairs drawers. My heavy undershirts will do me next winter. The whisky you sent me I found out accidentally when in Richmond last Thursday, it was prime. Ira Westfield and 2 or 3 others with myself, enjoyed it very much. The pincushion came safely packed in the shoes for all, which I am very much obliged. If you can find any other cloth for heavy warm shirts you prefer to the jeans, get it. The weather now will soon begin to change and I expect a severe winter, the last few winters having been so mild.*

...

One week and 70 miles later, Leonard and Ruby found themselves north of

Richmond back up in the lush valley fed by the Rappahannock. Just north of them, the armies of both sides were parrying for last minute positions, but Pope was in a fix. Jackson's 24,000 men had vanished into thin air and McClellan's two powerful corps, now within marching distance of the battlefield, were being held back to defend the Capital rather than provide him with an overwhelming edge in manpower. Halleck, like Lincoln, couldn't get the hen to budge. McClellan was jealous of Pope's promotion and he told his wife that he would leave his replacement "to get out of this scrape himself...[If] Pope is beaten...they may want me to save Washington again. Nothing but their fears will induce them to give me any command of importance." While the two Union generals were backstabbing one another, Longstreet, Jackson, and Lee were planning their final thrust. The safety of the Confederate rear and its railroad supply line were in the solid hands of Jeb Stuart, to which Leonard Williams and the 2nd South Carolina Cavalry were now attached. "Second Manassas," as it would be called, was just three days and a short ride away. For Leonard, this was the final opportunity before the critical battle to get off a rapid note home. He wrote to Anna from the banks of the North Anna.

> *Camp on North Anna*
> *35 Miles above Richmond on Central RR*
> *August 26, 1862*

*My Dear Anna*

*I recd your letter of the 18th 3 days ago. I fear you selected a very bad time for your visit to Columbia. It has been so oppressively warm. I think it is best for you to get back to Greenville as soon as you can and make another visit in the winter. I hope the change now taking place in the weather may restore you to your usual strength and health. I feel at times very uneasy about you. Regular exercise and employment for a certain time every day in the open air will do you more good than physic. Plenty of air and sunshine will do the baby more benefit than anything else. You spoke of returning home early in Sept. Write me and let me know the day you expect to be at home.*

*We are stationed between Richmond and Gordonsville and within 25 or 30 miles of Fredericksburg. Of what is transpiring on the Rappahannock, you're no doubt informed through the papers. Jackson, it is said, is pressing Pope and his forces and is crossing the river in pursuit of him, that the Yankees are throwing away everything that retards their flight, that the roads are strewn with knapsacks, clothing, commissary stores and broken wagons and that McClellan and Burnside have baulked in effecting a junction with Pope. What movements we may make depend upon results on the Rappahannock. We may move any hour towards the scene of conflict. My company is small now. Some dozen have been and will be discharged being under 18 and over 35 years of age which will leave me less than 60 men. When Perry went home recruiting, he got some 35 or 40 recruits, but they have been enrolled among the conscripts. Col. Preston would not suffer him to bring them on and I suppose some 50 applications have been made for transfer to my company but the authorities have refused. I'm trying to get Billy Whitmire into my company. I saw him yesterday. He had chills and looked rather worsted. I think if he can get into the cavalry he could get well.*

*We have just now recd orders to be ready to leave this evening for the up country but do not know to what point, probably towards Fredericksburg. You may still write to me at Richmond until further notice. The nights are becoming cool but the sun is still very hot towards noon. Lieuts. Perry and Stokes are both sick, have not heard from them for several days. Have you sowed turnip seed yet? They ought to have been sown the middle of this month. I have nothing of news to tell more than you see in the papers. I think it is highly probable Jackson will continue his pursuit and cross the line. My love to all. Write soon. We are constantly on the move, I scarcely have time to write.*

*Your affectionate husband*
*L. Williams*

It would be twelve days until he could write again. Second Manassas was at hand and it was time for Pope to put up or shut up. But perhaps even the supreme braggart himself sensed that he was overmatched against the likes of Stonewall... Old Pete ...A.P...Jeb... and of course Old Bobby. The ultimate showdown would take place back on the battlefield of Manassas, but this time the Federals held the position similar to Beauregard's, while Lee controlled the ground formerly held by McDowell. Thirteen months earlier, overexcited, dry-mouthed militiamen trembled on the trigger, now battle-hardened veterans were locked, cocked, and ready to do business.

On August 29, the battle was on and the Hampton Legion, attached to Hood's Division, was involved heavily. Leonard's respected friend, Lieutenant Colonel Martin Gary, with whom he had shared many a campfire chat, revealed the true mettle of his fellow South Carolinians when his regimental flag fell momentarily into the hands of the Yankees. The Colonel of the 22nd New York foolishly demanded the surrender of the Legion. "Surrender hell!" thundered Col. Gary. "If you don't deliver your sword up I'll blow your brains out, sir! These are South Carolinians!" The Yankee officer, surprised and suddenly prudent, gave up his sword and was taken prisoner.

The boastful Pope came nowhere near matching the decisiveness and true elan of Gary that day. Not only was he unaware of the exact position of the Confederates, he had only the vaguest notion of the disposition of his own troops. Reinforcements he was counting on weren't coming. Foes that he assumed were retreating were regrouping for the next day. Still, the delusional general believed he had the rebels on the run. In grand Pope-esque fashion, he sent a victory telegram that night to Washington informing Lincoln and his advisors that by this time tomorrow, the Army of Northern Virginia would be no more.

The next morning, Pope launched his chase to round up Stonewall's "retreating" army only to find them still at-the-ready in their railroad trenches. Instantly, the leading Federal regiments were lost in a cloud of dust and a hail of bullets, yet somehow, kept pressing forward and nearly gained the upper hand. The exhausted Southern line bent and nearly collapsed. Some units resorted to hurling rocks when their ammunition was used up and Jackson held doggedly on until Longstreet brought up his artillery and five divisions. Longstreet's shells and men tore Pope's surprised army to pieces, sending it in full retreat back toward the Henry House where the hardest fighting had taken place at Manassas the year before. By nightfall, over 1,700 dead Federals and nearly 1,500 dead Confederates littered the field. Nearly 16,000 wounded wailed in hastily erected hospital tents tended by overworked and undertrained surgeons. In the 14th Regiment, 8 were killed and 57 more were wounded. First Sergeant James Williams was not among them.

That night, Pope decided to retreat, like his First Bull Run predecessors had, back to Washington. There, a bit less boastful to be sure, he blamed his defeat on his subordinates and a lack of killer instinct in his men. The general who had counted his chickens well before they were hatched, was instantly replaced...by the hen. As many as 30,000 battered Federals were strung out along the pike leading back to Washington and there to meet them was the man who had kept his army in reserve and left them out to dry. Ironically, his was still the only face that could restore their dashed hopes. McClellan rode forward to meet his retreating army. His soldiers still revered him. Despite his tactical faults, he still possessed many fine leadership qualities. He was a superb organizer, trainer and provider, and he always put the welfare of his men first. For that, they still loved and trusted him.

For the Southerners, respect for their commander was absolute and unwavering after Second Manassas. In the months to come that affection and loyalty would grow to such a degree that perhaps no army assembled before or since ever revered their commander more than the Confederates did Robert Edward Lee. Lee made them feel almost invincible, and his army would follow him wherever he cared to lead them. When a Prussian observer once asked Lee about his apparent genius in managing armies in the field, Lee offered this humble response: "I plan and work with all my might to bring the troops to the right place at the right time; with that I have done my duty. As soon as I order the troops forward into battle, I lay the fate of my army in the hands of God." In two short months, Lee had completely reversed the fortunes of war. Back in July, McClellan was ten miles from Richmond, now in September, Lee's army was a mere 20 miles from Washington. The pendulum had swung, but at a severe price for both sides. A worn out Captain and a near starving Ruby witnessed that cost first hand as they methodically sidestepped the dead strewn all over the hallowed ground at Second Manassas.

*Camp Near Urbana, Md.*
*September 7, 1862*

*My Dear Wife*

*We crossed the Potomac Friday night and am now near Frederick, a town of some 2,000 inhabitants, 25 miles this side of the river and about 21 miles above Washington. We have been resting this Sabbath day, the first rest we have had in 2 weeks. The last 2 weeks have been the most laborious and severe we have had. No rations have been issued for some 10 days until yesterday. The wagons of our cavalry could not keep up, the men had to support themselves the best they could, living mostly on green corn, apples, getting sometimes a piece of bread. Our men have been nearly worn and punished out but now resting and eating Johnny Cake. Genl. Jackson occupies Frederick. I do not know what next is on hand or in what direction the army will move. My powers of endurance have been pretty severely tried with short rations and none at all sometimes and hard marching with a bile on my knee. I have had a rough time but today's rest has put me all right again. I am in good health. I only write to tell you where I am. Our brigade was not engaged in the last battles about Manassas.*

*I rode through the field on my way here. The dead Yankees literally covered the ground for miles. Our victory was complete, our losses light, that of the enemy most terribly heavy, but you can know all about them by the papers.*

*I send this by Carson who undertakes at some risk to carry the mail to Richmond. I do not know when next I shall have an opportunity to write, perhaps not again for 2 or 3 weeks. I will write you at length as soon as I get an opportunity of sending a letter. I think from all I have seen that the people of this state do not like to see our army. Yet an intelligent Union man told me yesterday that if Maryland was left to decide for herself, he had no doubt she would cling to the south by a large majority. Monday Morning 8th. This is two nights we have rested here and I feel entirely rested and ready for the saddle. I will write you again soon. Still write to Richmond and expect the RR will be repaired soon and communication will soon be established. Write soon. My love to all.*

*Your affectionate husband,*
*L. Williams*

The Old Captain sat back, removed his spectacles, and closed his eyes for a moment. The scene of those grotesquely mauled bodies after Second Manassas came back to him. It was a spectre he'd never shaken. He could still hear the echoes of distant groans as well as the incessant buzzing of flies crawling over blood-caked arms and legs that had been ripped from their owners. The smell of death too still lingered, a fetid mix of gunpowder, sweat, urine, feces, and blood. But above all, he was still haunted by their faces...faces of men he was sworn to kill. Some were contorted in agony, while strangely others wore a veil of sweet serenity. They had been resourceful carpenters, tough factory workers, scratch farmers, aspiring poets and silly dreamers, not mere numbers, casualty counts, or replaceable arrows. Yet, for both Leonard and those that lay there, it had become almost too easy to charge pell-mell into a sea of blue or gray because there were no faces, only a blur of enemy cannon, sabers, and rifles. But back then, in September of '62, on the outskirts of Henry Hill, he had looked deep into the lifeless eyes of the enemy. If it is true, the old veteran mused, that the eyes are indeed the window to the soul, then their empty eyes revealed the true darkness of that brutal, soul-less war. Moreover, he realized those eyes were just like his, full of dread and hope at the same time. For them, the work was over; for Leonard, the sternest tests were only just beginning. Now, it was time for the 2nd South Carolina to follow their leader once more and that leader was taking them into Maryland.

# CHAPTER NINE
# FROM SHARPSBURG TO FREDERICKSBURG

*You have wandered round these highlands long enough:*
*turn and go north.*
*Give this order to the people:*
*You are now about to pass through*
*the territory of your kinsmen... .*

Deuteronomy 2:3

On September 4, Lee took the war and his 60,000 men north because, as Leonard had predicted, they needed *"to invade and subsist upon the enemy."* President Davis and General Lee hoped to not only win battles but to convince Maryland to consider joining the Confederacy, and a mighty victory on the enemy's turf just might be enough for France and England to recognize their cause as well. The final reason, and perhaps the most critical for Lee's invasion, was to break the will of the northern citizenry to fight on and send off more men to die. Quite simply, Lee thought, another smashing Southern victory over the Federal army they'd just torn up in their own back yard might just hasten the end of the war.

The sight of Lee mounted on "Traveler," leading his great gray column north across the moonlit Potomac, made a powerful impact on his men. The image certainly made for poignant, unforgettable letters home from all who crossed with him. Leonard was one of them and a portion of a letter dated September 25 recalled that memorable crossing vividly.

*Our crossing the Potomac near Leesburg by moonlight would furnish the painter with a grand subject. We have crossed mountains and valleys, the most grand and picturesque. I wish I had time and paper to give you a sketch of what I remember. We commenced the passage about dark, the entire brigade in column. The banks of the river were shaded by dense forest and before getting to the river we were shrouded in darkness. So thick was the foliage on reaching the bank the whole scene was lit up by the brightness of the moon and the winding column could be scene for several hundred yards. At various depths from knee-deep to swimming, after first entering the river, the column went down near the bank some 100 yds., then straight across for some 50 yds., then right down again some 75 yds., and then again directly across. Some of the horses swam and a good many lost their saddlebags, the water floating them off.*

With the crossing at Leesburg, Lee was in the midst of the most audacious exploit of his career. He had only 55,000 men while McClellan commanded more than 80,000 with another 70,000 at his disposal back in Washington. In the face of overwhelming odds, Lee again daringly split his smaller force. Jackson was sent off with 12,000 men to capture the garrisons at Martinsburg and Harper's Ferry, while the remainder waited with Lee in Boonsboro. If Jackson could defeat the garrisons quickly, then link up with Lee before McClellan could attack, the fox, though still outnumbered, would take his chances with the hen.

At this time, Leonard was taking orders from his esteemed friend Colonel M.C. Butler, who was receiving his orders from the aggressive Wade Hampton, who received his from risk taker Jeb Stuart. All four were dispatched to ensure the safe and timely return of Jackson from Harper's Ferry. Jeb knew the roads, passes and towns around Harper's Ferry like the back of his hand. Leonard, however, was galloping through hamlets that he was only vaguely familiar with, and soon he'd be skirmishing in towns he never even knew existed. He recorded his observations and experiences in his letters home to Anna.

> *Camp Near Martinsburg, Va.*
> *September 28, 1862*

*My Dear Anna,*

*This is a quiet still Sabbath day. The first quiet day we have had for many, and we know not now but that before night we might be moved. I promised you in my last hasty letter I wrote you to give a full account of the campaign in Md. We left the North Anna near Hanover C.H. about the 25th of August, passed through Culpepper, Manassas, Centreville, Warrenton, Dranesville, Leesburg, and on the 5th just crossed the Potomac a few miles below Leesburg. We then marched 5 miles to Poolesville; the crossing occupied some 2 or 3 hours. Poolesville is a considerable village. Here the merchants sold our men hats, shoes & c at old prices and were generally kindly disposed to us taking Confederate money in pay for their goods. We left Poolesville next morning and marched some 20 miles to Urbana, a small village. We stayed in this neighborhood several days and near there had several skirmishes with the enemy. We next went to Frederick, the 2nd largest city in Maryland. The enemy were pressing us all the time. Here we camped all night. The people, it seemed to me, sympathized but little with us. Next day we moved off towards Middletown, our regiment had charge of the rear and just as the front squadrons were moving out of town, the Yankee cavalry came in. 2 of our rear squadrons charged them in the sts., routed them, took their Col. and several privates prisoners, killed and wounded several others. We kept back this army that day and the next. The country around Frederick City is beautiful. It is in a valley nearly surrounded by mountains...*

The skirmish in Frederick was most spirited, especially to the rear of Hampton's Brigade as they withdrew through the streets. Union infantrymen were pressing the Legion severely, supported by a gun they had placed on the outskirts of town. The Federal cannon was booming, ripping up the thoroughfare, which Hampton's men had to use. Colonel M.C. Butler was ordered to attack the gun, which was defended by two companies of cavalry. Lieutenant Meighan's squadron made the charge and swiftly rode over the gun, dispersed its support, and captured the officer in command, Colonel Moore of the 30th Ohio. Meighan would have absconded with the powerful piece had five of the horses that transported it not been killed in the fight. Regardless, the gun was silenced, seven prisoners were captured, and Hampton's escape route was clear.

The Old Captain recalled all too well that instant danger came with assignments like covering Hampton's rear, scouting with M.C. Butler, or just being in the same county as the 29-year old, glory seeking Jeb Stuart. All three were hair-trigger fighters who never gave orders from the rear or missed out on a charge. Whoever rode with them fed off their energy and became a hell-for-leather, thrill seeker too...whether he wanted to or not.

The Frederick fight was unremarkable in the grand scheme of things, but remarkable indeed was the extraordinary discovery made in a field near that little town. In an incredible coincidence, a Union private in the 27th Indiana Volunteers found wrapped around three cigars a copy of Lee's "Special Order Number 191," the overall troop movements of his Maryland Campaign. These lost orders were quickly sent up the chain of command until they rested in the hands of an overjoyed McClellen. "Here," he boasted to one of his generals, "is the paper which if I cannot whip Bobby Lee, I will be willing to go home. Tomorrow we will pitch into his centre and if you people will only do two good, hard days' marching, I will put Lee in a position he will find hard to get out of." McClellan now had the advantage; soon he'd have to prove if he had the nerve to exploit it. Had Lee known of this crucial turn of events, he would have massed his forces. As it was, Jackson continued on his mission to reduce Harper's Ferry. Leonard was right behind his division and recorded what happened in detail in his letter of September 28.

> *...On leaving Frederick about 5 miles distant, we came to the summit of the mountains and here I had the finest view I ever beheld. It was less grand than the view from Caesar's Head but more interesting as far as the eye could reach up and down. The whole valley was studded with beautiful, and in many instances, elegant and costly dwellings. It looked like a scattered city. The land is very rich and productive. Here the grim visage of war had never intended itself before and every farm presented the appearance of undisturbed tranquility and peace in striking contrast to the desolate farms of Va. In this valley land is selling at $100 an acre.*
>
> *We next came to Middletown after dark about 5 miles from Frederick. This town is larger than Greenville. Here we recd no sympathy, all the houses being closed. Next day our brigade had another skirmish near Middletown. The Cobb Legion this time engaged. The enemy were again routed though we probably suffered most. At night the brigade encamped around a little village, the name of which I have forgotten.*
>
> *I was sent ahead with a squadron to guard certain roads leading to Harper's Ferry. I was requested by Genl. Hampton to be particularly vigilant. I had no alarm during the night. Next morning their advance guards came in sight and I judged from the dust there was a regiment. I sent Genl. Hampton an account of what was going on and he sent*

*another squadron to support me. We then drove them back a mile or so and kept them in check until noon when the whole brigade came on. We then went to Knoxville, a little town on the Potomac-4 or 5 miles below Harper's Ferry. We camped near this place and next day heard of the surrender of Harper's Ferry. It was the intention of our cavalry to hold the enemy at bay until the reduction of Harper's Ferry. This done, the next day we marched into this place. Here were all kinds of stores in great abundance. There were about 13,000 prisoners taken. Here next day we recrossed into Md. and was on the flank while the terrible fight was going on at Sharpsburg...*

The South called it Sharpsburg; the North, Antietam. Those who fought in it or even witnessed it, called it Hell Incarnate. It was the single bloodiest day of the entire Civil War. Had McClellan acted swiftly upon discovering Lee's lost orders, Sharpsburg would have remained a quiet, unmolested village of churchgoers. Instead, McClellan hesitated, giving Lee just enough time to gather up his fanned out armies, which would ultimately transform Sharpsburg into a slaughterhouse. For the first time in the war, both sides were satisfied with the ground and both thought they would win there.

The Dunkard Church. Burnside Bridge. The West Woods. Bloody Lane. They all still sit there quietly today. But at dawn on September 17, all were scenes of the most desperate fighting the war had ever seen. By nightfall, they would become graveyards. On the flank of Jackson's corps, on the left, Leonard sat atop Ruby bearing witness to the grim reaper himself.

McClellan outnumbered Lee two to one and his tactics were sound. He'd attack the left, then the right, then send in his reserves and slam Lee's army right in the gut. The weakness of the plan was that McClellen was reluctant to bring his entire force to bear in one massive, decisive blow. As a result, Lee was able to deftly move his men from left to right then back again. Like the Little Dutch Boy, the resourceful general desperately but brilliantly moved his units, plugging the holes and staving off defeat.

Leonard was horror struck and transfixed at the same time as he watched the scene unfold. Joe Hooker tore down the Hagerstown Turnpike then slashed like a mighty scythe shredding division after division and turning the west wood and the cornfield into killing grounds upon which 12,000 lay dead and wounded. Dunkard Church became the crucifixion point at midday, as gray and blue mingled together then turned to red. From his vantage point, Leonard could not see the ghastly spectacle of D.H. Hill's dead and mangled bodies that filled the "Bloody Lane." Nor could he glimpse the deadly Confederate sniper fire that ripped through and mowed down General Ambrose Burnside's regiment as they tried again and again to cross a stone bridge that spanned a crimson Antietam Creek. But he witnessed enough to last him a lifetime.

Jackson, Longstreet, and later A.P. Hill, fought until it was pitch black and night fell over the gruesome field. Nearly 6,000 men lay dead or dying, and another 17,000 wounded offered up silent prayers or groans of agony. The casualties at Sharpsburg numbered four times the total that would be suffered by Americans on "D-Day" in World War II. More than twice as many Americans lost their lives in one day at Sharpsburg than in the War of 1812, the Mexican War, and the Spanish-American War combined. The Army of Northern Virginia was spent and now hung by the barest of threads, but Lee stubbornly held his ground. All he could do was wait for the inevitable, crushing blow that even McClellan would certainly order the next morning. But despite two fresh Federal corps in reserve who were eager to fight, McClellan's morning attack never came.

That night, the battered Confederates followed their leader again, but this time, Lee was glumly taking them back to Old Virginny. His invasion was over and Davis' hopes of European recognition were just as dead as those that lay along Antietam Creek. McClellan, in Pope-like style, wired Washington about his resounding victory, but Lincoln knew better. Lee's army was there for the taking, and had McClellan used all the forces at his disposal, his counterpart would have been signing a document of surrender instead of issuing new orders to an army that still had plenty of fight left. Lincoln, meanwhile, had been busy doing a little scribbling of his own, and six days after Antietam with Lee no longer an immediate threat, he finally deemed it appropriate to unveil what he had written months earlier. On September 23, President Abraham Lincoln issued his Preliminary Emancipation Proclamation, and for that alone, Antietam is considered a Northern victory and a pivotal point in the war.

Years later, the Captain would make his way out to his wraparound porch in the evenings and sit quite still on his favorite wicker rocker to enjoy a slice of Maum Fannie's sweet potato pie. With each bite, he'd relive what he had witnessed first hand and what soldiers on both sides had endured on that grim day at Sharpsburg. When his neighbor, Mr. Bailey, or the Whitmires would stop by the conversation would often lead back to that afternoon back on September 17. Sometimes he'd deflect such inquiries with explanations like "Jeb had sent me off with Colonel Butler," or "I was too busy picketing and tending to my horse." Sometimes he'd say nothing at all pretending that his squeaky rocker made it difficult to hear. After a while, his neighbors, friends, and even Anna herself realized that Sharpsburg was a subject the Captain simply did not and would not talk about.

Years later still, back in the Planter's Hotel, a subdued Old Captain returned to his letters of that fateful September.

*Camp Near Martinsburg, Va.*
*September 28th, 1862*

*You have no doubt recd all the particulars of the recent fights. Our army, though severely cut up, gained the day. This fight cost us a great many lives but the enemy were much worsted. The Yankees admit a loss in the Md. campaign of 25,000, but I think they must have lost 35,000. We are in the celebrated valley of Va., the most famed, I expect in America. This is a most interesting country. Everybody seems comfortably situated but none exceedingly rich. I find by observation in Md., that the enemy have not suffered much by the war. Their supplies, I believe, they buy cheaper than ever, except perhaps luxuries.*

Two days later he added:

*Yesterday we went out on a scout towards Wmsport. but could find no enemy. I think they are still beyond the Potomac. This morning at 10 ock. we go out again and picket. We are just finding out what war is. Our first year was so quiet and everything so abundant. We knew nothing of its hardships but I stand it well. In fact, I'd rather be in motion than laying up in camp. The weather for the last month has been beautiful. I do not know when this will reach you. There is no mail communication with Richmond. I suppose you cannot account for not hearing from me. I had to leave Douglas Holloway of my co. at Frederick. He was sick, unable to ride. I hired a spring wagon to carry him but he was too sick to ride and had to go to the hospital at Frederick. I suppose he is in the hands of the enemy. We have seen no papers since the 1st this month and know nothing that is going on either in or out of Congress. Write soon. I dreamed last night I was at home and had baby in my arms kissing her and that she knew me almost at once and was full of talk. My love to all.*

Your husband
L. Williams

Captain Williams was riding on a dream. Actually, he was riding on many. First there were his little dreams of a simple cup of coffee, two fine eggs, or a new felt hat. Then there were his big dreams. He dreamed that he'd have a house to come home to and that dear Ephraim was finally at rest in his eternal home. With his dreams he prayed. He prayed that Anna's faith would sustain her through the privations of war. He prayed that tiny Carrie would not fall victim to disease, and he hoped that she'd recognize the haggard figure of her father that someday might again ride up Augusta Street. Although tougher to maintain with each passing day, he somehow held fast to his impossible dreams. He dreamed that slavery, once an institution in the South but now the undeniably single most divisive issue in all of America, could somehow be accepted and sustained without more bloodshed. He dreamed that a fellow Democrat or Peace Party candidate could defeat Lincoln's Republicans and bring the war to an end. With all his might, he prayed that though outnumbered, out supplied, and out funded, his shrinking army could somehow emerge victorious.

Finally, there was his hidden, deepest dream and prayer. He never uttered a word about it. He chased it quickly from his mind whenever it tried to creep in. It was everywhere and nowhere. So precious was it that he only offered it up to God. He asked for his life. He beseeched that his almighty hand would deflect the bullet and shield him from the saber and cannon. Yet, if he was to be sacrificed in the end, he prayed only that God do it swiftly and judge him worthy to someday sit by his side. Leonard shared this dream with no one, but he was not alone. His dreams and prayers were those of 200,000 other men who wore the Confederate gray.

As the soon to be 39-year old cavalry captain rode through the wildflowers of the Virginia valley, it seemed to him that heaven itself couldn't be a more breathtaking place. The dogwoods, sycamores and maples were just beginning to drape themselves in their myriad fall colors, creating a blazing tapestry that would stay with him forever. It was almost possible to dream again with the terror at Sharpsburg now almost a month behind him. Leonard and Ruby had successfully done their duty in protecting Lee's divisions back across the Potomac without further harm. They had done so not by following their leader, but by drawing attention away from him in a diversion behind enemy lines.

Stuart personally led the brigade as they splashed across the Potomac and marched northeast fifteen miles. At night they crossed at Williamsport and returned once again to Maryland. Union cavalry scouts were dispersed and prisoners were taken. Captured Federals would later state that McClellan's entire Twelfth Corps was turning to deal with Stuart's commotion. Leonard and the 2nd had ridden hard and fought even harder to slow down and divert the closing Federals. Finally, they recrossed the Potomac in a windy rainstorm, comforted by the knowledge that their diversion had allowed the main army to reach Virginia safely. Now they could enjoy some well-deserved rest amid the pleasantness of Virginia's pastures and people.

*Camp Near Martinsburg*
*October 9th, 1862*

*My Dear Anna*

*I recd yours of 11-12th several days ago but have not had time to write until now. I returned yesterday from a two days piquet at Hedgesville near the Potomac, a little village of four hundred inhabitants in the gap of the mountains, a most picturesque village commanding a view of all the adjacent valley. This village is about 8 miles from Martinsburg. I found the people very polite and intelligent and generally are almost universally secessionists. The ladies are particularly so. I had invitations on all sides to dinner and tea, which of course, I never declined. The people have been universally kind to me everywhere, scarcely ever charging me for meals even when called for. This valley is certainly the most productive region in Va. not withstanding the immense armies it has fed for months. Provisions are still abundant and wherever you go you will get a good meal. At present, the country appears to be at a disadvantage. There has been an unprecedented drought here but crops are still good. Almost every farmer in this country lives in a rock or brick house and have barns of the same material but 2 or 3 times as large as their dwellings. There are but few negroes in this section of the country. Everybody works.*

*Young ladies are brought to do all kinds of domestic work. All the better class of people here are secessionists, but there are a large class for the Union. At Martinsburg, 3/4ths are for us. The place has been built up by the Ohio and Baltimore RR and a great many Yankees live here and employees of the RR Co. This accounts for the Union sentiments.*

*Today a large scouting party went out with 5 days rations for distant service. 175 men from each regiment of the brigade and for all I know from other brigades. On what service, no one knows. It may be a dash into Pennsylvania. I was desirous of going with them but only two captains were detailed to go from our regiment. I would have volunteered but my horse had just lost one of its shoes. It may be they are only going on a raid into Maryland...*

The Old Captain remembered the day that Stuart, Hampton and M.C.Butler, three of the bravest men he's ever known, had assembled those 1,500 men for their daring mission into Chambersburg, Pennsylvania. As a captain, he was ordered to stay behind and oversee the duties of Company K, but that didn't stop him from saddling up Ruby after hammering in a new shoe and galloping out to the rendezvous point. There he overheard Jeb's stern, pre-raid address.

*Soldiers! You are about to engage in an enterprise which, to insure success, imperatively demands at your hands coolness, decision and bravery; implicit obedience to orders without question or cavil; and the strictest order and sobriety on the march and in bivouac. The destination and extent of this expedition had better be kept to myself than known to you. Suffice have not a doubt of its success- a success which will reflect credit in the highest degree upon your arms. The orders which are here published are absolutely necessary, and must be rigidly enforced.*

With that, they were off. Leonard contemplated falling in quietly at the rear of the column. With Colonel Butler near the front, he wouldn't be noticed until nightfall, and with a ban on campfires it might not be until they moved out the next day when he would be discovered. But orders were just that, and as the column slipped away, Leonard reluctantly turned Ruby around to head back to camp. On the way back he noticed that she seemed listless and her gait was uneven. Despite the lighter McClellan saddle and even though he was ten pounds lighter now, Leonard knew her back couldn't take much more punishment. He dismounted and walked her slowly back to camp vowing to look for another horse to spell her in the coming winter picketing. There would be no rest, however, for those in the raiding party.

Stuart's 1,500 men had left on October 9 and were headed deep into enemy territory. Their destination was Chambersburg, Pennsylvania, where they hoped to find supplies, especially sorely needed artillery horses to replace those shot up at Sharpsburg. When travelling out to the great enemy unknown, he that leads the way is in the most danger. On the way back, with the enemy nipping at the tail, the risk is transferred to those in the far rear. True to form, M.C. Butler led the way out and commanded the rear guard on the way back. In between, he himself lit the fuse to a Union storehouse in Chambersburg, blowing up ammunition that would never be used against them.

Three days later, on October 12, with well over 1000 captured horses in tow, Stuart's raiders rode 65 grueling miles in 24 hours and were almost home free…everyone but Butler's rear guard, who were being pressed severely by Union cavalry. An edgy Stuart sent back a stream of couriers to ascertain what was holding up Butler, fearing he had been overtaken and captured. Captain William Blackford, a member of Stuart's staff, had been stationed to expedite a fording when Jeb encountered him and warned, "Blackford, we are going to lose our rear guard." "How is that General?" asked Blackford. "Why I have sent four couriers to Butler, and he is not here yet; and see there the enemy closing in behind us!" "Let me try it," said Blackford. Stuart paused a moment and then, extending his hand, said, "All right, and if we don't meet again, good-bye, old fellow," and Blackford rode away on his mission. Blackford finally found his way back to Butler who was endeavoring to move off a heavy gun he had captured. Unfortunately, its tremendous weight was too much for his horses to budge, and Blackford urged the young Colonel to leave the gun and save his rear guard. Butler calmly responded, "Well, we'll see what we can do." To the surprise of everyone, the mired and worn out Union horses answered the call of the whip and spur and the gun went speeding down the road. Butler's men galloped off behind it but as they roared around a bend in the road they were hit by a smattering of fire from the distance. Federal infantry were closing in, but with minutes to spare, Butler's spent men found themselves safely on the Virginia side in a cloud of dust with their captured prize. After a quick watering of the horses and a few nervous laughs over Butler's close shave, the men returned through Leesburg to their camp west of the mountains suffering only one man wounded on their daring, four day Chambersburg raid.

Jeb's second ride around McClellan's army was of little military significance; however, it did create a tremendous aftershock. The foray had tied up McClellan's cavalry thereby delaying his advance until October 26. By then the Confederates had distributed their 1,200 new mounts between units, and Lee had adroitly distributed his army between McClellan and Richmond. Stuart's high jinks and McClellan's hesitation were the last straw for Lincoln who soon fired McClellan for the second and last time. On November 7, after a few emotional parting words to his precious, blindly loyal, "outnumbered" chicks, the humiliated hen left the army for good.

With Ruby tender and tired, it was probably just as well that the Captain was ordered to remain with his company. He had indeed missed out on a fine expedition, but while they were away, he had a bit of spying business of his own to attend to. The October 9 letter recorded the details.

*...While out yesterday, the brigade brought in a man who presented himself to be a Canadian with the Secret Service of our government. He had dodged the Yankee piquets and crossed the river in the night. I sent him on to Genl. Hampton under a guard. He said he had important intelligence to give at Richmond. He showed me several extracts from British papers of a late date, all of which were urgent for recognition and spoke in the highest terms of the skill of our generals and the bravery of our troops.*

*I have forgotten where Steve is. I think he is now large enough to make a good plowboy and I would like to have him hired out when he could be learned to work. He ought to be worth something next year. I engaged last summer from Mrs. Rufus Smyers enough jeans to make me a suit of clothes. He lives near Williamston. I wish you would go to it as soon as possible and get enough material to make me 2 shirts. Make shirts for me and send the first opportunity and keep the rest until I tell you more about it. You told me your aunt came to Columbia to have her funds examined but did not tell me whether any of it was counterfeit nor whether she returned or not.*

Later, Captain Williams added on further detail and comment, both personal and professional.

*My Dear Anna*

*I cannot tell when I shall have the satisfaction of seeing you. It is now near 16 months since I left home and the prospect of peace as distant as ever. When I left baby had just begun to open her eyes in wonder and delight at the beautiful green trees and birds and now she talks and runs about the yard. I am very anxious to see her. I am grateful at your accounts of her smartness and sociability and hope you will be able to restrain her temper within proper limits and mould her disposition as you would like it. I have a good deal of business on hand today, so I must close. I am going to draw pay for my company. I will be able to send you some funds the 1ˢᵗ opportunity. I have to buy another horse as soon as I can find one and it will cost me $300 or $400. Horses are very high here. If seldom now can I find time or materials to write so you need not look for letters often. I have recd very few letters from you lately.*

> *Your husband*
> *L. Williams*

By the time he had left home, Carrie had mastered the art of crawling and was dabbling in the notion of walking. In order for her to make her way from Maum Fannie's back kitchen, through the dining room and across the parlor to the front porch, she'd employ virtually every form of conveyance and assistance. In endeavoring to make this epic journey, Carrie transformed the three rooms into her personal three-ring circus. At the start of the trip stood steady Maum Fannie, like a spotter next to the balance beam, always ready to break her fall, but only if absolutely necessary. At the finish line was her father pretending to read the paper but focused on every single calamitous moment in her attempted advance. Crash! Carrie invariably knocked over her glass of milk while lowering herself from the breakfast table. Maum Fannie's scream resulting from said crash served as the unofficial starter's gun. The first leg of the mission around the milk puddle to the dining room doorway was accomplished with ease, but then affairs got a bit dicey. Next, she'd pull herself up by the door molding and just sway back and forth. There she studied the dining room, the next trial, wobbling on legs not quite up to the task. After sizing up the terrain, she'd suddenly drop down on all fours and using the rug as a lilypad she'd catapult herself, like a bullfrog from the shore, over to the nearest seat at the dining room table. Halfway through the gauntlet now, she'd monkey swing her way, letting go of one chair as she grasped the next until she had come around full circle to the parlor threshold. It was at this point that the Captain would hide behind his *Greenville Enterprise* so she couldn't see him vainly trying to restrain his laughter. Leaving the dining room she picked up the pace, crawling madly but crookedly, as if she had accidentally gotten into Maum Fannie's old jug of back medicine. From the parlor to the porch she wiggled and squiggled, leaving behind wrinkled up throw rugs strewn haphazardly in her wake. At last, she had made it to the front porch screen door. There, the Captain would feign great surprise as if startled by his little daredevil and then swoop her up into his arms. Mission accomplished. Memories made. Milk wiped up.

A year and a half later, Carrie was now running in the back yard while he was 500 miles away fighting the Yankees through snowy mountain passes. He had not only missed out entirely on her successful transition from knees to feet but also in her forming her first words. Maum Fannie was more influential in her rearing than he was, and it saddened him deeply. The captain had many a melancholy mess conversation with corporals and sergeants who had lain in trenches awaiting both the enemy and the birth of their first son or daughter. He was comforted to a small degree in that he was at least able to hug Carrie before he rode off while others had to settle for a blurred daguerreotype of a child they'd never once held in their arms. Still, he lamented he had never heard Carrie speak a single word...let alone "Dada" or "Papa."

After the war, soldiers on both sides were commended for leading bold charges or valiantly saving their comrades, but the Old Captain held in the highest esteem those silent soldiers who simply fought on without ever having seen their own offspring. Occasionally and far more frequently as the war wore on, some would flee for their home and loved ones, knowing well there would be harsh consequences if they were caught. Some faked illness or injury. A prevalent trick was to leave one's own regiment during the chaos of skirmishing and then avoid duty by pretending to vainly search for the unit purposely abandoned. Irate commanders would curse these weaklinks, threaten them with their swords, or even have them beaten and imprisoned. Generals would place file-closers in the rear with strict orders to arrest or shoot down those who attempted to flee. Courts martial sentenced many of the spineless to hard time.

To the Old Captain, file-closers killing their own was the darkest aspect of the entire dark war. He had never witnessed the ultimate consequence of their task, but once he had seen a guard fire in the air and order a terrified private to double quick it back up to the line. The practice was absurd for he believed his army needed every able bodied man they could muster, even if he did possess a yellow streak. To murder one's own to maintain discipline seemed utter insanity. As a cavalryman he never was subjected to such a practice nor did he ever have to order such a deadly rear line guard. Still, there was no place for cowardice or desertion and while attending many a courts martial, the Captain dealt with shirkers sternly despite fully understanding their motives. One precious furlough per man, he often thought, would have put an end to all file-closers and many a military trial.

Like the others, it had been a year and a half since he had enlisted, and he yearned for a few weeks of leave. But for now, Lee's army needed protecting and there was plenty of work to be done, which thankfully focused his thoughts on blue coats instead of the tender blue eyes of his wife and daughter. After three straight days in the saddle, he found a pencil and a flat board. Once situated, he poured out his observations on the present and revealed his dreams for the future in a rambling, long letter home.

*Camp Near Martinsburg, Va.*
*October 21, 1862*

*My Dear Anna*

*I recd your letter of the 4th on last Friday morning just as the bugles sounded the assembly to go out to meet the enemy we had just heard had crossed the river at Sheperdstown, so I recd your letter on the way again, while in position to charge the enemy. They had crossed in considerable force but for some reason or other did not advance more than 5 or 6 miles before they turned back and recrossed the river, our cavalry pursuing til night. He took advantage of the darkness to recross. We lost but few men and our regiment only one. The enemy must have lost a hundred or more. I was then left with 60 men to piquet along the river-from all my posts I could see across the river hundreds of Yankees. They were very anxious to get into a talk with my men but I forbid any communication.*

Here the Old Captain paused. He knew quite well that a few exchanges between soldiers did indeed take place. He remembered one shouting match word for word because again the Legion was the clear winner.

"How are ye, boys?' called a Yankee late in October. "Don't you want some coffee over on your side?"

"Not any, thank ye," yelled back a Carolinian. "Got plenty from Pennsylvania."

"Don't you want some clothing over there?" persisted the Federal, touching a spot generally sensitive with the ragged rebels.

"Not a stitch," the Carolinian was able to answer for once. "We got a good supply at Harper's Ferry and over in Pennsylvania."

"Why do you fellers wear our blue clothes?" came the next jibe. "You've got a brand new government, why don't it furnish you in its own glorious gray?"

"Economy, egad," rejoiced the Carolinian, becoming a little stuffy. "We get yours so much cheaper."

Verbal honors rested with the South, and the two waded out to meet in midstream and drank from the same whiskey flask. Wearing a good natured grin, the Old Captain then returned to the letter.

*I remained out 3 days and got into camp last night. Everything is now quiet along the lines. What is next we know not. Our army is now in fine condition and in good spirits and perhaps fuller than it has ever been. At Sharpsburg, the regiments were very meager, many not numbering more than 125 men and many of those unwell from hard marching, scanty fare, and exposure. Notwithstanding this, the day was as much ours as the enemy's though they claim a victory. The spirit of our army now is as confident as it has ever been and perhaps before another week, we may be in Md. again. Today our army is destroying the Ohio and Baltimore RR depot, workshops, bridges, etc.*

*The expedition I mentioned in my last letter was into Pa. It was a brilliant performance. They went right through the enemy's lines a distance of 125 miles or more and back again to someplace in close proximity to large bodies of their forces, recrossed the river in open day without the loss of a single man. They made the longest of marches on record in one day. They traveled 94 miles. They brought back* *about 1,500 or 2,000 horses taken in Pa. and also pistols, clothing, etc. and destroyed perhaps $300,000 or $400,000 worth stores.*

*I am more pleased with the valley everyday. It is a grain and provision country and I am making observations everywhere I go taking lessons from every farm I have the opportunity to visit. The people are very thrifty and live most luxuriously everywhere. I do not mean foreign luxuries, but merely the products of their own teeming lands. They live better here than in S. C. and it seems to me with far less trouble. Here everyone makes what they term apple butter, peach, plum, and pear butter which is better to my taste than any imported preserves and this too without the onlay of a cent, except for a copper kettle. They diet more generally on fruit here than with us. They scarcely ever have warm bread for any meal. They have the best raised bread. Indeed I never saw as good bread in S. C. as they have here everywhere. I fare elegantly when out on duty. I get meals at 25 cts. each such as would cost at Richmond $2 or $3.*

As reasonably comfortable as things were, Leonard's thoughts still would return to his family and the home in Greenville.

*You must ask Henry to put Steve out somewhere where he will be made to work and obey. He will be ruined at home with hardly anything to do. Where is Nan? I forgot who she is staying with. I am delighted with your accounts of baby. I have no doubt she is a very smart child and I hope she may be a good tempered one, obedient and tractable. I trust your health will get better as the winter comes on. I have been uneasy about you but have been hoping that the bracing weather could restore you.*

*I would like above all things to be with you a month or two in the winter but I will not suffer myself to be influenced too much by such hope-as it is very uncertain. They grant no furloughs except to the sick and I trust I may never have to ask for a sick furlough. My health has been excellent ever since I left here with slight exceptions although the arduous Md. campaign, I lived in a great measure on apples and green corn and I stood it all most wonderfully, better perhaps than 5/6ths of the regiment, the last night we were in Md. Having had no breakfast*

151

*but a small piece of bread and apples, no dinner and at night getting 2 or 3 roasting ears and a piece of mutton, I ate a very full supper which made me sick the next day. I marched, although feeling quite badly, and then went to a farmhouse and stayed 3 or 4 days, took a good rest and no medicine and returned to the company for duty again.*

*The old gentleman with whom I stayed and also his wife and daughters, treated me with the greatest kindness. The young ladies made me a haversack and when I left filled it with loaf bread, cheese and c. They invited me to call, if possible, and spend some time with them and to write to me. If I could have reconciled it with my conscience to have shirked duty a little, I would have liked to stay a week longer. They had everything that was nice to eat and yet nothing they did not produce themselves except sugar and coffee. Here I find that the farmer, which I have pictured to myself for years, he is not a creation of fancy, but actually does exist and industry and intelligent enterprise might convert thousands of now common farms into just such as I find here. It is my chief recreation to thinking upon and developing in my mind agricultural schemes. But while doing so, I know the uncertainty of the future. This miserable war hangs over us as a thick cloud concealing everything from view and stands between us and our fondest hopes. My love to your aunts and all my relations and friends. Write soon. I believe I recd all your letters. I would write oftener if I could get materials. Willie Thompson is well. My respects to Mrs. Thompson and Miss Sallie.*

> *Your husband*
> *L. Williams*

The Old Captain was grateful for the positive outlook the Lord had given him and also for the kindness of others. Both had sustained him through the horrors and hardship of war so far. He knew then and now that those who resolutely clung to some sort of vision of what could be, as they struggled to survive what was, stood the best chance of survival. Yet layers of hope were stripped away with every battle. Only the rare visionaries who could see through the smoke of cannons, beyond the approaching columns and back to their beloved homes, might return as nearly whole beings.

A few sharp and bloody skirmishes would break out soon in early November, but the captain and Ruby had obtained yet more support to help see them through. Leonard had just hired a slave boy and purchased a packhorse.

*October 24ʰ*

*I have an opportunity this morning to send this to Winchester. I will add a few lines to say that I recd your letters of the 9ʰ and 13ʰ this morning and was much gratified. I'm glad you secured the cloth for my overcoat. Get Mr. Pickle to cut it out and perhaps you had better get him to make it also. Get the two jeans shirts I spoke to you about. Mrs. Rufus Smyers is leaving. I engaged a suit but keep it until you hear from me and send the first opportunity. I lost my woolen undershirts in Md., but I have good cotton ones and with heavy overshirts I can do well. The weather now has become quite cool here. I have a boy and I'm glad the one Henry engaged for me did not come. I also have a packhorse and can now carry my tent and baggage. My love to all. Write soon.*

*Your husband*
*L. Williams*

During his final week of command, McClellan had tried desperately to unleash a knockout blow on Richmond once more. Like two mighty heavyweights, Lee and his counterpart jabbed and counter punched, but in the end, Lee cut off the ring every time sending McClellan back to his corner in frustration. With the Rappahannock Valley the scene once more, Leonard and the 2nd South Carolina Cavalry were directly involved in three sharp fights with McClellan's cavalry. There were feisty clashes at Berryville, Flint Hill, and Barbee's Cross Roads. Another skirmish at Little Washington was waged in a snowstorm. A rather strange incident took place at Barbee's Cross Roads as the Legion was falling back before a heavy force in the morning. Hampton retreated grudgingly, leading charge after charge against the oncoming Federals. Hart's Battery gave them grape and canister as well as shells until suddenly there was a cease fire by both sides. The two faced each other for over an hour when all at once a rabbit hopped along between the quiet lines. Privates in gray and blue began yelling at the poor disoriented hare as if to see which side could yell the loudest in order to get the floppy-eared fella's attention. After about ten minutes, the rabbit disappeared and the fighting continued until Hampton's men had driven the Yankees back.

A rabbit's foot would have come in handy for many a man during those skirmishes and certainly those in Leonard's active company.

> *Rappahannock Co.*
> *Near Little Washington, Va.*
> *November 12, 1862*

*My Dear Anna*

> *We left Martinsburg on the 3rd and since then have had constant labor and a good deal of hardships. The 3rd we were saddled by daylight and ready for the march. We were in the saddle til 9 ock without any rations. Most of us however, on the way, managed to get a piece of bread. The next day we entered the Manassas Gap and towards evening encountered the enemy. He was in position, our course was changed and we traveled a mountain road westward. That night we camped almost in sight of the enemy and next day had a fight in which we were rather worsted by their sharp shooters. We had to fall back. We lost some twenty killed and wounded most of them of the N.C. Cavalry. The next day we had another skirmish and again the next day, in both of which the Yankees were driven back.*

At the skirmish at Barbee's Cross Roads, a Confederate private named Eldred Simkins had his horse shot dead from beneath him. With Simkins stuck beneath his dead mount and with the enemy fast approaching, Sergeant Mickler raced back to the rescue, extricated the shocked private, threw him on the back of his gray colt, and carried him off to safety. Mickler wasn't the only hero in those chilly autumn fights of '62 as the remainder of Williams' October 12 letter revealed.

> *...In the 1st days' fight we were falling back out of reach of their sharp shooters and we had to cross a wide and deep ditch. Several horses fell in the crossing. Jas. McClanahan's horse fell with him and on him down in the ditch and was so cramped the horse could not move and McClanahan under him, the Yankees in 200 yds. advancing. I was in the rear of the squadron and found 2 of my men endeavoring to extricate him but perfectly unable to do so. I leaped off my horse and*

*with my assistance succeeded in rolling the horse off him. As we mounted and rode off, a number of bullets and shells flew around us. 2 minutes more and McClanahan would have fallen into Yankee hands.*

*We are still in the mountains. There was a snowstorm. Since we have been in there, the weather was extremely cold. The Yankees ceased following us after the third days' fight. On Monday our regiment went back to look them up. We came upon their picket post and captured 9 of them and then advanced til we came up with them. We had 3 or 4 hours artillery and sharp shooting fight with them and then returned to camp. Yesterday, we had a few days rest and also today. I have no knowledge of the whereabouts of our army. It is scattered from Winchester to Culpepper and the enemy are also scattered. Jackson's said now to be crossing the mountains from Winchester, Longstreet to be near Culpepper, the Hills in or near the mountain, our brigade is in the mountains, General Lee's, toward Culpepper. The next fight will be one of generalship.*

...or the lack thereof. For the Union, that next great fight would be orchestrated and led by a new general named Ambrose Everett Burnside, he of the long muttonchops from which, by inversion of his name, the term "sideburns" is derived. McClellan told the men, as they yelled their affection for the leader who had created them as an army, "Stand by General Burnside as you have stood by me and all will be well." One of those who most regretted McClellan's ouster was Burnside himself. Although he had some successes in North Carolina earlier in the war, he lacked confidence in himself to lead an entire army. His concern would soon prove justified. He had twice turned down Lincoln's offer to command the Army of the Potomac, but now he had grudgingly accepted. He was popular and respected, and unlike his predecessor, modest. However, much to the North's chagrin these qualities would be nowhere near enough against a fox like Lee. The reluctant 38-year old Burnside lacked both the tactical skill and instinct possessed in abundance by his Confederate opponent.

While the new Union commander was pondering his options about how to capture Richmond or defeat Lee, Grant had begun his Vicksburg Campaign. It would be an arduous one full of unexpected twist and turns, but regardless of the ordeals, Grant was unrelentling in his desire to take the key Mississippi River fortress. Vicksburg's fate, however, would not be decided until the following summer. Burnside was no Grant, but on November 15 he had his forces south of the Rappahannock on a resolute march toward Fredericksburg, the same day that Leonard had a brief lull in which to add to his previous letter to write Anna.

*November 15th*

*Since writing the above, our camp had been moved. The enemy has fallen back some seven or 8 miles and we have moved up towards him. The citizens tell us that the enemy's loss in our late skirmishes was very severe. The first shell on the last day's fight we understand killed at least 25 of them and also a col. or genl. Lieut. Perry came to camp last night and brought me your letter and I was delighted with it, being the only one I have recd for 3 weeks. Of course, I am proud to hear of baby's acquirements. I am more and more each day anxious to see you and her. I would not make any effort to increase her powers of memory at present, but give her information about things tangible and visible and learn her to reason as well as remember. Lieut. Perry left the trunk with my shirts and socks at Richmond with Mr. Barnwell. I am about out of shirts. Perry has a handsome uniform of the cloth I engaged Mrs. Smyers. Please get enough of it to make me coat and pants. I will send you my measure to have my coat and pants cut and you can get the coat made by Mr. Taft. I wrote you to get Mr. Pickle to cut my overcoat and have it made. Keep them all until I can find a good opportunity to send them. I have a Yankee overcoat which will do me a while.*

*I know I have several letters on the way for me. Your letters came very regularly until we left Martinsburg. I do not know what my chances for a furlough will be but I shall apply and appeal to their sense of justice. It will soon be 18 months since I left you. I am more desirous than ever to see you. If I can select my time for going home, it should be the later part of Dec. but if granted I do not expect it earlier than Jan. I am in good health and so is the majority of the company. Will Thompson is complaining a little. Write often. Remember me to all.*

*Your husband*
*L. Williams*

Over three weeks would pass before he'd next have a spare moment to take pencil in hand. Reins and saber would be constantly in his grip as late autumn raiding missions were the order of the day. This time the leader of the brash expeditions wasn't Jeb Stuart; it was his second in command, Wade Hampton, who had risen to the rank of Brigadier General.

Wade Hampton III was South Carolina's first and finest soldier. He stood six feet tall, and despite having forty-three hard years under his pistol belt, he was perhaps the best pure horseman in all the cavalry. Few were as brave and none possessed more strength and agility. In his biography, <u>Giant in Gray</u>, Hampton's brute strength and athletism are described as follows.

*He was more than commonly large and strong by nature, and constant exercise gave him thick, hard muscles. He could lift prodigious weights, and was a mighty jumper. Occasionally he stood with his hand set edgewise upon his head to measure a palm's breadth above his own height. A bar set at that level, even with a sagging center, was a good six feet above the ground. Then, moving back, the young athlete would run and leap high, clearing the bar. It was a feat that none in all the surrounding county could match.*

Years later, he would often go bear hunting on the grounds of his sprawling winter estate and commonly perform deeds that no one in the county would even dare to attempt. Anyone with a fair aim could shoot a bear, but Wade preferred to slay them up close and personal. One that accompanied him on such hunts recalled that:

*He would pursue bears with a pack of hounds. The leaping, bugling pack was well-trained in scenting and chasing this particularly perilous quarry. The hunter followed it at a gallop to where, its back against a trunk or thicket, the bear reared on its hind legs and lashed out with its front paws, boxer fashion, at the clamoring ring of the hounds just out of reach. Then Wade Hampton swung out of his saddle. With one hand he drew from its sheath a long, keen and heavy knife, almost a sword in size and design. Commanding the dogs to get out of the way, he charged in. It was always over in a moment- a darting swing of the huge talon-armed paw, a quick dodge by Hampton to avoid it, a deadly counterstroke with the steel...Not only once did he kill a bear at close quarters, but fully eighty times...Sometimes he failed to dodge quite clear of the raking claws, and bore the scars on his body throughout his life...and on one occasion at least he displayed the derrick-like strength of his arms, legs and back, by stooping, lifting unaided a big furry carcass that weighed 400 pounds, and with a sudden surging effort throwing it across the saddle of a horse.*

You did not want to be the bear prowling about the Hampton sty or hen house, nor was it wise to be the upstart bluecoat in his path on the battlefield.

Throughout his entire life, the Old Captain held no one in higher regard than the man who first assembled the Legion. Hampton was one of the wealthiest men in all the South, and his generosity and courage were as boundless as his sprawling cotton and sugar cane plantations. He armed every man at his own expense, then led them off to war. At first Leonard was naturally impressed by Hampton's intimidating physique and fearlessness, but later it was his inner strength and no nonsense demeanor that he came to admire above all. The Old Captain respected the way he fought but respected far more why he fought. Leonard wasn't the first to realize that Hampton was the direct antithesis of his commander Jeb Stuart. John Esten Cooke, Stuart's ordnance chief, contrasted the two cavalry legends.

*Stuart seemed a god of battles to his comrades, and perhaps to himself. He laughed and sang in action as at a picnic. Hungering for glory, he sought it in the very smoke of Yankee guns. He was ready to die for military fame. Hampton, on the other hand, fought soberly from a mature sense of patriotic obligation. He was foremost in every fight and everywhere did more than his duty; but evidently martial ambition did not move him. Fame followed him. He did not follow it.*

Riding with Wade Hampton was fame enough for Leonard Williams.

Fame followed the "Iron Scouts" too, so nicknamed by the Federals who found them hard to kill; a title the scouts both cherished and richly deserved. Hampton often sent them off behind enemy lines under the leadership of Sergeants Bill Mickler and Jack Shoolbred. On their perilous missions, the cool scouts befriended Southern sympathizers in Union territory, slept and ate at their farmhouses, and, it is said, wooed their innocent daughters. Sergeant George B. Shadburne, a tough Longhorn, rose to become Hampton's chief of scouts and was equally admired for his raucous behavior as his raiding. Shadburne's men were deadly with both pistol and shotgun and routinely dressed in captured Federal uniforms. When occasionally captured, no stockade could hold them as they bribed guards, surprised sentries, or snuck away in shackles that would be later hammered off.

They were an odd collection of coon hunters, turkey shooters, trackers, rogues and cads, and nothing pleased Leonard more than listening around the campfire to the tales of daring escapades and hair-raising rescues of the Iron Scouts. It was Brigadier General Hampton who first unleashed them, and no one was more appreciative of their liberated supplies, creative diversions, and deadly accurate reconnaissance. For the same reasons, the Yankees despised them.

For the Old Captain, the life of that eclectic detachment still retained its romantic, swashbuckling air years later, but he wouldn't have traded, then or now, the adventures he shared with Wade Hampton and the gallant M. C. Butler for a single foray with the Iron Scouts. Back then he'd always trade some pipe tobacco for a page or two of writing paper, however, and after yet another mission with those two salty South Carolinians, he put that newly acquired paper to use.

> *Camp on the Rappahannock, Va.*
> *15 Miles above Fredericksburg*
> *December 6th, 1862*

*My Dear Anna,*

*It has been several days since I have had an opportunity to write. I recd your last with Uncle Adam's statement and also a letter from Mr. Whitmire last Saturday. I wrote them the same night but still have them on hand to send with this. I find by the schedule Mr. Whitmire has paid out a good deal on my debts and collected but little comparatively on accounts due me. I left my share of the stock on hand, $3,200 and now I am in debt to the establishment over $4,000. I still hope the business may go on and make enough to pay home expenses. There are now but few outstanding debts against me, now at least, that Mr. Whitmire will be called on for. I hope he may collect enough and make* *enough to keep me in about the present status. He has made some money if he collects well. I will be able to pay Capt. Westfield the last note he holds on me for the house.*

*I just returned a day or two ago from a 3 day scout. I had command of the first squadron. There were in all about 1,000 troops. Went in the rear of the grand Yankee army around Fredericksburg, ascertained their whereabouts, took the 8 or 10 piquets and intended to attack a Yankee camp at night but the firing on the piquets, Genl. Hampton supposed, put them on the alert and therefore did not make the attack. We were in the saddle all day and night til 2 ock and the night before slept in the woods without fire for fear of drawing attention, being near the enemy.*

*Our labors have been most trying for the last few months and I think now we will have some rest. I made the acquaintance of Col. Black, 1st S. C. Cav. on the last scout. He is an intimate friend of your brother and I brought a letter from him for me, which was sent to Hd. Qrs. and has been lost. I am very sorry I did not get it. Col. Black is a very agreeable gentleman. I will write your brother to acknowledge his attention though the letter is lost.*

*Winter has now set in in earnest. It has been snowing all day. Looks like continuing for some time. I fear my shirts are lost. Lieut. Perry put them in his carpetbag with his uniform and put it in Mr. Barnwell's care in Richmond and cannot now be found. I hope it will turn up soon. I bought a couple of pretty good shirts yesterday, being out I could not wait much longer. Pickle is out here and as he is the only tailor that has my measure, you had better keep the jeans til you hear from me on the subject. I'm wearing out my uniform and would like to have another pair of pants but things sent are so liable to be lost I prefer that you do not send til safer conveyance is obtained. The health of the army is good. I am quite well. I am looking for a letter from you. I hear there's a good deal of sickness in Greenville. Write soon and often. My respects to all.*

> *Your husband*
> *L. Williams*

That grand army he had recently passed behind numbered 110,000. Burnside was on the march to Fredericksburg where he hoped to find transportable pontoon bridges waiting for him there to enable his army to cross the Rappahannock. But the bridges were delayed a week because Burnside had not clearly defined when and where he needed them deployed. That week was critical indeed for it gave Lee's 78,000 men plenty of time to settle in on the steep, unconquerable hills south of the river.

One of those digging in was First Lieutenant James Williams, who had traveled 180 miles to get there in time. Brother James and the rest of Maxcy Gregg's 14th S.C.V.I. had marched 15 miles a day for 12 straight days through the bitter cold, and now he and his exhausted comrades anchored the Confederate right flank south of Marye's Heights waiting for Burnside's inevitable attack. Finally, on December 11, Burnside's bridges were in place, and the Federals launched their attack with a deafening artillery barrage. It had little effect on Lee's men, but it ravaged the city of Fredericksburg as blasts ripped the old city to shreds. The cannon blasts shook James down to the quick, and more than once caused Leonard to jerk his pencil across the letter he was hurriedly writing during that very barrage.

*Camp on the Rapidan, Va.*
*December 11, 1862*

*My Dear Anna*

*William is now with me. He has been with me 2 nights and will stay 2 or 3 days longer perhaps. He brought my shirts, drawers, socks and scarf, which I was needing pretty badly. I am now very well off. I like the shirts and drawers very much. They're just the thing I needed. I prize them very highly and will last me if I do not lose them, the 2 years. Lieut. Perry is wearing a suit of clothes made by Mrs. Smyers, gray or mixed, it is rough, but looks very well. I suppose the cloth he left with you is the same kind. How many yards did he leave? When Mr. Pickle gets home, he will cut them by the 1st Feb. it will be time enough. I have now plenty of clothes for a while.*

*A few days ago, an order was published requiring all applications for leaves of absence to pass through the hands and receive the approval of the Col., Brigadier, and the Major General and also General Lee's. The routine puts it almost impossible to get off. I still hope that sometime during the winter some plan of granting furloughs will be adopted, if*

161

*so, I will undoubtedly be favored. I shall not, however, allow my hopes to get too deep a hold on me.*

*If Mr. Whitmire fails to get a home in Greenville, I ought, by all means, to be at home to make arrangements for renting the storehouse. I could also hire out Steve and Nan for something when they would be taught how to work, and I could also put my notes and accounts in better shape and perhaps collect some. I left with you my notes private, apart from the business transactions at the store, and also a paper containing a list of my notes and acts. connected with my mercantile transactions. I wish you would draw off and send me a copy of that list so that if I fail to get home, I may put in train proceedings by which some of the debts may be secured. I have forgotten who owes me. If I could be at home, I could straighten up and shape my business matters in 2 or 3 weeks, satisfactorily. I have had several days' rest here but do not know how long it will last.*

*This morning from daylight until 10 ock, the cannon has been booming most terrifically near Fredericksburg. It has now ceased...*

The Old Captain slowly placed the letter on his nightstand. His eyes were moist and he was ashamed. The letter seemed harmless enough, but when read in the context of the grim events and contretemps of the day, it vexed him deeply. Ephraim was cold in his grave. James was shivering and praying not to join him too soon. One hundred and ten thousand courageous Yankees were preparing to march steadfastly to a certain death. Brave Anna was suffering silently and wearing down more by the day as the naval blockade inexorably tightened its grip on her and all his countrymen. Yet there he was clad in brand new, hand-stitched apparel, safely away from the impending slaughter, selfishly inquiring about his business dealings. His letter seemed a bit self-absorbed, tinged with greed, and blithely and callously dismissed the imminent danger besetting his brother, his wife and his army. In time, he and all those who deluded themselves with the notion that they could balance their accounts while dodging bullets, experienced a sort of epiphany. They came to accept that there was only one bottom line, and that line couldn't be found in a ledger. The business at hand now was somehow finding food, shelter, a durable pair of shoes and, of course, a way to go on. The Captain rationalized that while the idea that he could manage his finances from afar may have been ludicrous, by attempting to do so, a brother that lay in the ground and another whose finger twitched on a frozen trigger could, to some degree, be put out of his mind. It was a senseless exercise, but in many ways, so was the war.

On the morning of December 13, 1862, the sheer futility of war was revealed as never before. Fog veiled the plain in the early morning hours as many divisions of Federal troops got into position below the heights. Steeples and chimney tops were all that could be seen by the confident Confederates waiting on the hills. Slowly, the sun baked the fog away revealing a grand vista of blue columns, one hundred thousand fighting men in all. Soon the troops began their advance. Their banners uncoiled in the sunlight. Gun barrels gleamed. Lee watched from high above and was momentarily transfixed. "It is well," he said, "that we know how terrible war really is, else we would grow too fond of it." Those perfectly arranged blue columns were exactly where Lee wanted them and he wanted Burnside to attack for Lee knew there was no chance that the heights he defended could be conquered. Indeed, the Confederates were ready. Longstreet asked one of his artillerists about an idle cannon. The man informed him that the other Confederate guns already covered the ground and added that, "A chicken could not live on that field when we open fire on it."

But Burnside did attack... not once but six times. Swarming out of the Fredericksburg streets, Burnside's men crashed into the stone wall and were decimated. Perfectly aligned division after division kept pouring up toward the wall only to be slaughtered and driven back in hails of unbroken fire. For hours they kept coming, like lemmings to the edge, until the plain was covered with dead and wounded Yankees. Not a single man ever even reached the foot of the hill. Morning mist had once sheltered the forming columns. Now smoke embraced the dead.

One of Kershaw's young soldiers gazed down on the twisted and bloodied men that lay in front of the stone wall and was overcome. His name was Sgt. Richard Kirkland of the 2nd South Carolina, and he could no longer ignore their groaning. Having gained permission from his commander, the brave young sergeant crawled resolutely out onto the deadly plain expecting to be shot by a Union sniper. Not a shot was fired as he gave water to the wounded Federals. Again and again he returned with more water. For over an hour and a half he never ceased until all on his section of the front had their fill.

The Yankees kept pouring across and one mighty blue wave crashed on the Confederate right where James and the 14th S.C.V.I. were deployed in the second line. There was an interval between the 14th and the front line and not expecting an imminent attack, some had their arms stacked. Commander Maxcy Gregg misinterpreted the approaching force as his own front line falling back and ordered the 14th not to fire. Realizing the mistake at the last moment, James and his comrades scurried to their guns, held their ground, then wheeled to the right to front the enemy. The 14th helped drive the invaders back, suffering 28 wounded in the repulse. Failure to recognize the enemy at once cost Gregg his life as he fell mortally wounded. James Williams, however, lived to fight on.

The Battle of Fredericksburg ended as Lee knew it would, with an easy Southern victory and the worst defeat in the history of the U.S. Army. It could have been even worse when on the next day Burnside considered leading yet another suicidal assault, but his subordinates wisely convinced him to abandon the ill-fated notion. Afterward, the stubborn general blamed himself for the doomed attack and held himself personally accountable for the thousands of sleet-covered corpses that were frozen in time beneath the heights. The plain and town were littered with corpses. One overwhelmed mother was found in her cottage surrounded by the bodies of six men as she stood in shock where her front door used to be. Fredericksburg became a vast burial ground where bodies were hurriedly thrown into shallow holes in any piece of frozen ground. One empty icehouse was filled to the rafters with corpses, which remained there until the war ended.

In the end, Burnside sacrificed over 12, 500 men while Lee's losses totaled fewer than 5,500. Because of the terrain and limited size of the area, Lee could not follow up his rout. Instead he had to be satisfied with watching the defeated horde limp back across the icy Rappahannock. "We had really accomplished nothing," Lee later lamented. "We had not gained a foot of ground, and I knew the enemy could easily replace the men he had lost."

Safely west of the river and excused from duty, Leonard added a brief note to his December 11 letter on the same day the Battle of Fredericksburg was in full bloom. The Old Captain noticed that the letter was signed near the lower right corner and still smelled a bit like charcoal.

> *William has left me for home. I have just returned from carrying him to Mitchell's Station. He stayed with me 4 nights notwithstanding the scouting and piqueting has been very heavy. Col. Butler very obligingly excused me from duty while Wm. was here. It was the 1st*

*time I ever asked to be excused and it was most cheerfully allowed. The fighting is still going on at Fredericksburg. The scout will be back tonight. I expect we will move nearer the scene of conflict tonight or tomorrow morning. I forgot to tell you in my last that I suffered but little from the fire. My oil cloth was burned nearly up and 2 of my blankets burned a little at the edges. The letter describing the conflagration never reached you as well as several others. I wrote you several long letters, which I think you never received.*

*I have heard nothing yet from the package Lieut. Perry left with Mr. Barnwell. What was it you gave him? I recd the socks he put in his trunk. Wm. gave me a sole leather valise which holds all my clothes and enables me to carry them more safely. I left one of the same kind at home, if you can find it. It may be at the store. Send it to William. He deprived himself by giving me his. Wm. will take back with him Ephraim's remains and also Willie Thompson's, son of Dr. Thompson, with whom William is boarding. I recd your brother William's letter of the 2nd Oct. just a day or two ago. I was gratified at his kind expressions and must take the earliest leisure to write to him. Harvey Gaillard has been discharged and will leave for home in a few days. If I can get to see him, I will send you some funds. I know you must need some. My love to all. Write soon. Kiss baby for me.*

*Your husband*
*L. Williams*

As he prepared to unfold his final letter from 1862, the Old Captain re-lit his pipe. As the smoke floated over his head his mind drifted back over his first full year of war. It had been over a year and a half since he had bid farewell to his precious wife and infant daughter. Over that time he had seen young men beheaded, blown apart, sabered across the face, and left to die gruesome deaths in filthy hospitals. He had somberly crossed the battlefield at Second Manassas, staring down at the dead and mangled then raising his eyes skyward to God in wonder and anguish. He had witnessed first hand the single bloodiest day of the war from the flanks at Sharpsburg. He had seen his ill equipped but steadfast army defeat McDowell, McClellan, Pope, and Burnside. He had risen to the rank of captain and, more importantly, he had become a respected leader who was looked up to by all those in his battle-tested but shrinking company. Yet, like Lee himself, he realized that the Confederacy hadn't progressed an inch, hadn't gained European recognition, and hadn't put a dent in the Federal blockade. Ruby was wearing down as were many other hungry mounts in the cavalry, and the men themselves, despite their morale heightening victories on the field, now had to face another grueling winter with little to wear and even less to eat.

And of course, there was Ephraim, killed at the tender age of 30 in a frenzy of bullets in the Seven Days Battles at Savage's Station. Savage indeed, the old Captain lamented, and so young to be taken. As he puffed and pondered, Leonard's thoughts wandered back to Greenville when Carrie, so young to be deprived of her father, was somehow learning and growing up without him in 1862. And lastly, there was dear, diminutive Anna, managing to bear up thanks in large part to the loving care of Maum Fannie and her own abiding faith in God. As he began that final letter from 1862, it occurred to him that he turned 39 just three days after he had written it, and that five days later he'd spend yet another bleak Christmas separated once more from the loves of his life.

*Camp Near Raccoon Ford, Va.*
*December 20, 1862*

*My Dear Anna,*

*I recd yours of the 12ᵗʰ two days ago. I was glad to hear you were all well and hope Clough may not be much sick. Try to make him as comfortable as possible. I am writing a short note to Mr. Whitmire and enclose you a few lines. I wish I could be with you at Christmas. We have never spent a Christmas together. I do not wish you to build up any expectations of my getting home. I do not expect to ask for a furlough until the enemy develop their plan of operations and then if matters become quiet and we are allowed to go into quarters, I shall apply for a leave of absence. I do not expect that affairs will assume any permanent situation for 2 or 3 weeks at least.*

*Burnside has had a terrible chastisement and I regret he did not renew the attack. Where Burnside will next turn up, we have no idea. I have made the acquaintance of Col. Black, your brother's intimate friend, and found him a very agreeable and sociable gentleman. I was with him on picquet when the news came to us that Burnside's army had been thrashed and driven across the river. He said if the Major knew of it that we were setting by the fire talking and laughing, he would have been delighted. I have no news of any importance. The health of the company is very good. My own health is still good. The weather is today excessively cold but I am sitting by a good fire. Sergt. Beattie has returned. Mr. Gaines was here yesterday. He spent a day with me a short time ago. Tell Lizzie he is very well. My love to all. Write soon.*

*Your husband*
*L. Williams*

Leonard, the Hampton Legion and the members of the 2nd S.C. Cavalry had followed their leader honorably. They had picketed day and night along the Potomac, the Rapidan, and the Rappahannock. They had successfully evacuated Yorktown and ridden entirely around McClellan's bewildered army, not once but twice. They had helped to defend Richmond against superior numbers, screened Lee's army on its way to a resounding victory over Pope at Second Manassas, and led daring raids behind enemy lines. They had led divisions to retire safely from Sharpsburg. He and Ruby had done everything asked of them with little complaint. In 1863 they would be asked to do even more in what would prove to be the most pivotal and crucial year in the entire Civil War.

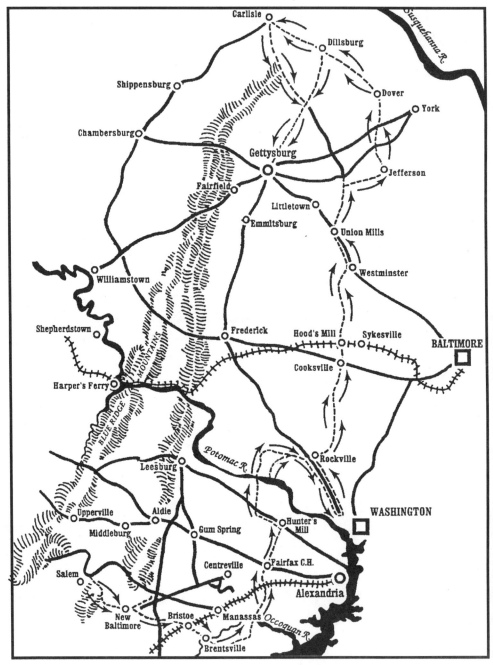

**The Route to Gettysburg**

**Mid-War- Commanding Veteran Riders**

# 1863

Camp near Culpeper Va
Aug 2nd 1863

My Dear Wife:

"Yesterday we had another of the most desperate fights of the war for the number engaged! The yankees Crossed the Rappahannock in large force one or two divisions of Cavalry & one of infantry. Our Brigade met them. The entire brigade did not number more than ___ men we were opposed I judge to five times our number. The fight lasted from 12 ock till near night; we lost a good many men. Iw ____ received a flesh wound in the ___ part of the neck & shoulder from a pistol shot; the wound is slight, & I hope to be well in 10 days or two weeks. I re___

**Letter of Leonard's Wounding**

170

# CHAPTER TEN
## EGGNOG, WHISKEY AND BRANDY STATION
### EARLY 1863

*Their cavalry troops whose count I heard,*
*were two hundred million in number...*
*Now, in my vision, this is how I saw the horses and their riders.*
*The breastplates they wore were fiery red, deep blue...*
*The horses' heads were like heads of lions,*
*and out of their mouths came fire...and smoke.*
Revelation 9:16

In January, 1863, the icy Rappahannock again divided Billy Yank from Johnny Reb. The two armies were encamped on opposite banks and pickets warily watched each other. Then one evening, a strange joining of spirits took place. It started out faintly at first but soon it echoed throughout the valley...the crisp high notes of fifes and the rattle of snare drums piercing the cold winter wind. An enthusiastic band of Union musicians had appeared at riverside. They were playing Northern tunes but to the Confederates it was certainly better than listening to the lonely crackle of the campfire, the endless drone of coughs brought on by the fever, or the pleading whinnies of their hungry horses. One of the Southerners nearest the players shouted out a request for one of his own songs. Immediately the shivering band struck up the stirring bars of "Dixie," "Maryland, My Maryland," and a rousing rendition of "The Bonnie Blue Flag." A hearty cheer rang out from the Confederate side. Then, after a moment of thoughtful silence, the band finished up their impromptu winter concert with the melancholy strains of "Home, Sweet Home." A river of tears welled up in eyes on both sides and even the Rappahannock seemed to sigh. Much separated the men of the two armies, but in their shared misery and the yearning to return home, blue and gray shared common ground.

The last winter had been uncommonly cold but food, clothes and shelter had been in abundance. Not now. Veterans on both sides had long ago cast off anything that they deemed superfluous on the march. Blankets, tents, spare clothes, and full haversacks had weighed them down during the hot campaigns of summer. Now, as they huddled by smoldering ashes with nothing in their cooking pans and tattered threads covering their backs, how they longed for the belongings they shed months ago. For months, skinny Northern privates ate little more than salt pork and hardtack, poor defense for the scurvy that had made its home in both camps. The Confederates fared even worse. General Lee himself complained about the meager amounts of rice and flour being so sparingly distributed, but even his pleas fell on deaf ears back in the capital his army had saved just months ago. On occasion, crooked purveyors gave the men spoiled meat, which killed them as surely as any enemy bullet ever would.

But undeniably man does not live on bread alone, and Captain Williams was keenly aware of that old adage. That winter, his spirit sustained what the commissary and quartermaster couldn't. Old newspapers and Anna's letters kept his mind off his growling stomach. Conversation and the sharing of childhood tales helped speed the time as well. His imagination became his greatest friend and ally. He dreamt of Anna and Carrie, and he held to the dream that he, his family, and his extended family of house servants would someday enjoy the rewards of a grand plantation like the fine Virginia farms he had seen. Still there were those around him who could not read, did not open up to their comrades, or would not dare to dream. For them he felt deep sympathy, then and now.

The Old Captain's trusty pocket watch now read 9:30. By the time he'd completed the next year's worth of letters, he figured he'd still have time to put a quick shine on his dress boots before Lady Street would be lined with onlookers eager to bid a final salute to the old men who had fought so hard four decades ago. As he carefully opened his first letter of '63, he noted that it was written on New Year's Day. What a year of fireworks it would prove to be.

*Camp Near Raccoon Ford, Va.*
*January 1, 1863*

*My Dear Anna*

*It has been nearly or quite 2 weeks since I have written, for the last 10 days I have been on picquet duty on the Rappahannock. My Christmas was spent on the picquet lines without even a dinner. I, however, had an eggnog on the next morning. Two of my adventurous men desired permission to go over within the enemy's lines after something for Christmas. They succeeded in getting 2 canteens of brandy, but before the 3rd was filled, the Yankees were after them. Being, however, well acquainted with the country, having operated in that section last winter, they easily gave them the dodge & came back flushed with success & the prospect of an eggnog. We are picqueting in conjunction with the 1ˢᵗ S.C. Regt. I have made many pleasant acquaintances with the officers and men while on duty, while out.*

*Genls. Hampton and Stuart have taken about 10 men from every company and are now beyond Dumfrees. They took 5 days rations and have now been out about 8 days. They have sent back several gangs of prisoners. I have not heard from them for several days. I am looking for their return with great anxiety.*

The weather was the first cause of his anxiety. The winter wind bit into the faces of the raiders and the snow-covered roads had become difficult to follow. But the prime concern plaguing the Captain on the days the men were out was the notion that once again the big three, Stuart, Hampton, and Butler were leading the way. With these three hard riding fighters, danger didn't just wait around the next bend, it rode alongside them. Although these trips were merely to gather information and supplies, they always seemed to result in shots being fired. The men picked to go knew damned well it wasn't due to their horsemanship and sharp eyes; they were chosen because they had a steady aim and a steadier heart. Leonard Williams possessed both, but again as a ranking officer in charge of a company, he was ordered to remain behind and see to the posting of guards and pickets, and the hundred other duties that were the responsibilities of a company grade officer.

The raid towards Dumfries was the second such foray and despite the danger, only one mishap was encountered on the entire mission. Not surprisingly, it was Colonel Butler and his 2nd South Carolina Cavalry who found themselves in peril. Butler was leading a detachment of 150 men toward Bacon Race Church where a body of the enemy was lying in wait. The Colonel first encountered the Federal cavalry pickets about a mile from the church and quickly drove them back upon their support, which proved to be a considerable mounted force and two large guns. Despite harsh artillery fire, Butler staunchly held his ground anticipating that the rest of his command would join him from a parallel road as planned. For critical, harrowing minutes, Butler's men waited and prayed for support, which never came. Finally, realizing the jeopardy his detachment was in, Butler attempted to fall back to Brentsville. After moving but a short distance, however, the Confederate cavalrymen quickly reined up in the face of a large Federal cavalry force on the road. It suddenly seemed that Butler was trapped, but he quickly sidestepped past the enemy and safely rejoined his brigade at Selectman's Ford. Later, both Stuart and Hampton congratulated the resourceful commander for his expert maneuvering. Butler's poise under pressure saved his men in a raid that ultimately netted 20 sutler wagons, 200 Federals killed, and over 100 more taken prisoner. The Confederates lost but one man and suffered just thirteen wounded.

The raiders returned to camp about the time Leonard was finishing up his New Year's Day greeting to Anna.

*Yesterday the Yankees in heavy force, attacked our picquets on two of the fords we are guarding and crossed over, but returned at night. We lost one or two men and the Yankees also had a few killed. Everything quiet along the lines. Lieut. Williams brought me your letter of the 15th. He told me everybody expected me at home. I'm sorry I disappointed them. After the fight at Fredericksburg, if our affairs permitted my leaving, I intended to press my claims, but our operations are still active. I shall bide my time. One of the officers in the regt. made application with a pretty good showing but Genl. Stewart disapproved and said 500 applications have already been refused. I still think the time will soon come when I may apply with propriety and not be refused.*

*Has Mr. Whitmire obtained a house yet? I sent by Harvey Gaillard a hundred dollar note, has he handed it to you? I see Mr. Gaillard has offered his house for sale and I am sorry he intends to leave Greenville. Give my respects to him and all his family. I hear corn has somewhat declined and also pork. You had better get Mr. Whitmire to buy you two hogs and after they give out, buy bacon. I wish you had a good cow. You had better sell the calf and get a cow. One well fed will yield more than both. How does the hog thrive? Do you intend to bacon it this winter? You ought to do so and buy another hog. How much dried fruit have you? It helps out very much these scarce times. Make Steve spread out all the manure and litter about the yard. Over the garden, broadcast and spade up thoroughly about the yard. It is time he begun preparations. I hope you may have better luck next year. The first essential in a garden is richness, manure the best you can. How are*

*your shrubs doing and the hedges? My respects to all. Write often.*
*Your husband*
*L. Williams*


In his mind, his property along Augusta Street remained in the immaculate state in which he left it, and the livestock too were blue ribbon, county fair contenders. In his gut, however, he knew the grounds, house and out buildings were in disrepair, and the animals were in dire need of nourishment and attention. In his heart, he merely hoped that he'd get back there to save something of his former life.

While he and Anna were unable to be together, the winter of 1862-63 was the only time in which all the branches of the Army of Northern Virginia weren't separated. Stonewall Jackson's headquarters were below Fredericksburg, at Moss Neck. Stuart was situated by the Telegraph Road, near the town and his commander Robert E. Lee. One day Leonard might see one of General Lee's children arriving by carriage, the next, perhaps Jackson's wife and daughter. Jeb's bride and little daughter were fixtures at camp. Being Virginians, these fortunate spouses and youngsters had only a short distance to travel in order to be with their husbands and fathers. A weak wife and fragile one-year old, four hundred miles away tucked deep into the far northwest corner of South Carolina, stood no chance of such a much dreamed about reunion.

As the Old Captain reflected back on that tedious, testing winter, he recalled that some of the men paid for their pleasure, as certain women roamed from tent to tent at night then quietly disappeared from camp at the sound of the morning trumpet. After such trysts, many soldiers were racked with guilt, which created another plague. Religious zealots full of fire and brimstone, swarmed into camps like locusts, passed out tracts and threatened young privates with eternal damnation if they didn't repent and convert. Cavalrymen didn't find religion. Religion found them. So did crooked merchants filled with goods and greed called sutlers, who sought to lighten the wallets of the young riders. Exorbitant fees for ginger cakes, half-moon pies, dried fruit and tobacco angered the officers, who sometimes ran the crooked venders out of camp, while keeping their provisions of course. To the Old Captain, those card sharks, shysters, and prostitutes who preyed on the all too human weaknesses of his men revealed that while the war brought out the best in some, it brought out the worst in others.

If the winter was bleak for Captain Williams, it was even more so for President Lincoln. After the severe Union whipping at Fredericksburg, Lincoln had lost faith in Ambrose Burnside. Burnside had lost faith in himself. Northern citizenry distrusted their Republican led government and blamed them for conscription, rampant corruption, and indecisiveness on the part of their hand picked generals on the battlefield. Peace Party candidates were growing louder and more voters were listening to these so-called "Copperheads" now. The war was expensive. Inflation was sky rocketing. From Maine down to Pennsylvania and out west in Ohio, there were murmurs of discontent and pleas for a compromise that might end the war. Worse, over 100,000 Yankee soldiers in Virginia wondered if they'd ever find a general who could match "Bobby Lee" in the coming spring campaign.

There were smoldering tensions down in Dixie as well. Richmond had been transformed into a colossal field hospital, and the wounded from Fredericksburg were sapping the citizenry of food and supplies. Violent hunger riots were commonplace. Southerners offered no protest over the meager yet critical amounts of rice, pork, and salt sent up to sustain Lee's army, but they grumbled over prices that had risen tenfold. The shrinking Confederate dollar was buying far less grain and cloth with each passing day. Overseas, Europe was beginning to turn its back on the young Confederacy, and along the coast, the naval blockade was becoming almost impenetrable. Most troublesome of all was the realization that slaves were now legally free. Strong, obedient men who once picked cotton had picked up rifles and were now aiming those guns in the faces of those they once served. Still, the Southern boys seemed in a far lighter mood than their shivering enemy as the winter took hold for real.

In the field and camps, it was the little things that raised the spirit and gave comfort. The Dumfries raiders had returned unscathed and with them arrived some prized Union stationary. A few coveted sheets of that writing paper fell into Leonard's thankful hands. Each pilfered page featured the Stars and Stripes, a snare drum, a mighty black cannon, and a bald eagle etched across the top. In his sharp talons, the eagle clutched a banner proclaiming that "The Star Spangled Banner Must Be Upheld." Deep in his haversack, he finally found his stubby old pencil and beneath the eagle atop one of those sheets of liberated Union stationary, wrote to his beloved Anna.

*January 3, 1863*

*I neglected to mail yesterday and will add a few lines this morning. The scout has returned without any mishap of any importance. Took one or two hundred prisoners. I fear you will hardly be able to decipher this when you get it. I have no ink and am obliged to use pencil. The health and spirits of the company are capital. We last night recd intelligence of the result of the first day's fight near Murfreesboro, which tends to heighten the already joyous hopes of an early peace. I think I see the tone of Lincoln's message in the spirit of the Yankee press service, their disaster at Fredericksburg, and lastly Bragg's victory, the foreshadowing of peace. Everything is now bright. I have hopes too that Charleston is impregnable and also Savannah and Mobile. The news too from Vicksburg is favorable. All the Yankee prisoners we take seem delighted with the idea that their warfare is over and all of them are for peace. None of them have their hearts in the war but are miserably tired of it. I recd yours of the 25th and 26th yesterday. Was sorry to learn you were not well, hope it is slight. My remembrances to your father and mother and all.*

*Your husband*
*L. Williams*

Murfreesboro was a brutal affair pitting 42,000 men under Union Commander William S. Rosecrans, a devout Catholic who sipped whisky far more often than communion wine, against the irascible Braxton Bragg and his smaller Army of Tennessee. Bragg evened the numbers a bit by virtue of a larger cavalry force and on early New Year's Eve morning, he surprised the bluecoats who were in the midst of breakfast. Thirteen thousand of Bragg's screaming men descended upon the Yankees in a mighty gray wave and after several hours of fierce fighting, pushed the Federal flank back three miles. Rosecrans aborted his attack on the Confederate right and rushed up reinforcements to shore up his own smashed right. "Old Rosy" was at his tenacious best, however, yelling orders down his lines while splashed with blood from a fellow officer who had been riding by his side and beheaded by a cannonball. Bragg assumed that the battered enemy would retreat the next day but Rosecrans stubbornly held fast. Equally as determined, Bragg advanced again near Stones River on the 2nd only to have Union cannons tear up fifteen hundred of his men in a single hour. The following day, Federal reinforcements poured in and it was Bragg who had to retire before superior manpower. This was the second time in only three short months that the Army of Tennessee had retreated after its commander claimed to have victory in hand.

Coincidentally, a relentless Ulysses S. Grant was in the process of launching four separate assaults on Vicksburg down in muddy Mississippi. The fate of Vicksburg weighed heavily on the hearts and minds of Davis and Lincoln alike. For now, this critical Southern stronghold stood firm, but so did Grant, unyielding in his resolve to see it fall.

Leonard and his troopers constantly kept themselves apprised of military developments in the west as they rode outpost duty along a 50 mile front in the east. He and Ruby patrolled both the Rapidan and the Rappahannock, guarding fords and shadowing every unit of Burnside's massive army. The weather was unusually mild, roads were now clear, and a winter movement by the Union was not entirely out of the question. Back at camp, Jeb, with his lovely wife and daughter, were posing for a portrait. Leonard meandered over to see the local artist's work up close. For an instant, Leonard imagined that it was he, Anna, and Carrie who were posing for the old painter. He smiled then sighed as he wandered over to a small pine table. Leonard sat and wrote of many things, though the prime reason was to inquire about the state of his distant, 23-year old wife's fragile health.

*Camp Near Kelly's Ford*
*January, 8th, 1863*

*My Dear Anna*

*I recd your last of the 27th a few days ago and was sorry you were still unwell. You must put on warm clothing and take regular exercise in the open air when it is not raining as much as you can without fatigue. You will be less apt to take cold and let baby have as much outdoor amusements as possible. Another preventative of cold is always to have your room more or less ventilated night and day. Plenty of clothing and air and daily exercise and more attention to diet, I think, are worth more than all physics. As to diet, I need not, however, make any mention as I have no doubt yours is such that the most abstemious Dr. would not forbid. I think all dispoeptics will certainly be improved if not perfectly cured. I have often felt a little inconvenience from it at* home but since I have been in the army I have never felt the least symptom of it and the same is the case with all I know.

The weather has been delightful for 3 or 4 weeks. I never knew so long a spell of fine weather this time of year, this winter has been far more favorable than the last. We have had only two snows yet and the 1st soon melted away. It's now clear and the air bracing. The road's in good condition. But I look for hard weather enough yet and bad roads while in camps. I am very comfortably fixed. I sleep with Sergt. Beattie, Lieuts. Perry and Stokes also occupy the tent with us. We have plenty of blanketts between us and straw to sleep upon. In dry weather, I sleep as comfortable as I could wish.

Our fare is at present very plain, beef and bread. We are at present in a country where everything has been brought up and its impossible to get butter, lard, or pork. But I am perfectly satisfied with it, I relish it well and never eat too much. I now and then get out and take in a good dinner or supper. While on the fatiguing labors of the last 4 months, we were so poorly supplied with rations that I got so I could eat enough at one meal and I could get by to last a day, and many a time I had breakfasted on a piece of dry bread and made supper of the same and enjoyed it and my hunger just as much satisfied as if I had a variety.

Often too, we have been in the saddle almost night and day without rest or sleep in the cold, sometimes in the rain. Yet in a day or two we forget all our hardships. I used to when a boy almost shed tears in reading about Marion's dining on potatoes and my heart swells with pride in contemplating his patriotism and devotion to liberty. I believe our army, or a portion of it at least, have been exposed to as many hardships as Marion's men in the Revolution, but our hardships so far have been of short duration and to a person sparing, they are not so trying as what appears to one who merely heard of them. As soon as we get a good meal, we forget our hunger or a night's sleep, forget cold and fatigue.

Bragg's fight in Tenn. has turned out as have all the western battles, a grand victory the 1st day and then a retreat. I think, however, from all the information I have recd that the Yankees were most terrifically slaughtered and that our army got much the best of the fight and that

*Bragg retired on the account of the reinforcements brought against him. I've heard of no movement of Burnside's army lately. I think it is still near Fredericksburg. I cannot apprehend they will attempt another onward movement this winter.*

*I have not much hopes of peace very soon but there is every indication that there is a peace party forming at the North, which will gain strength every day. The 300,000, nine months soldiers' time will be out in a few months and I think it will be very difficult for them to raise another army. An effort to do so will give strength to the peace party. Our skies are evidently brighter, I have strong hopes that Genl. Johnston will turn the tide against the Yankees in the west.*

*My pantaloons are about worn out. On account of having no transportation, I reduced myself to one pair. If Mr. Pickle is at home, have him to cut my coat and pants. Have them made a trifle larger than he has been in the habit of cutting them and if the opportunity offers, send them, if not box them up and send them by Mr. Barnwell's agency. I can get them from Richmond. Have the box marked distinctly to me and not on card- it is apt to be torn off and I do not want a vest. I have a good one.*

*I have not seen a list of the killed and wounded in the S. C. Reg.'s at Fredericksburg. On the 3rd I see Jno Feltz among the listed. I expect it is my cousin as I know of no other family of that name. I did not know he was in that regiment and he may have joined it last summer. It will be a terrible stroke to his good old mother, I fear it is him, let me know. Neither have I heard from James yet. If you have heard, write me. Has Billy Whitmire returned to his regiment yet- I would be glad if he could get into my company. Remember me to Uncle Whitmire & Aunt Edna, Sallie, and Fannie and all. Also, to your father and mother and all the rest. I would like to attend Jimmie Martin's wedding but cannot hope to be there. Write often.*

*Your affectionate husband*
*L. Williams*

Leonard knew well that James and the gritty men of Stonewall's Brigade were camped just a few minutes ride down the Telegraph Road near Moss Neck below Fredericksburg. How he wished to visit his dear brother, but picket duty, the daily posting of guards, and a mountain of requisition forms prevented him from getting away for even an hour. Also, Burnside's army was beginning to show signs of stirring in the hopes of capitalizing on the mild winter weather. Later, he wished he had risked the consequences of stealing away to share a cup of rye coffee with James, as it would prove to be six months until he would receive word of any kind concerning his health and well being.

Meanwhile, the present state of the Army of the Potomac was at an all time low. No less than four generals in the 6th Corps went directly to Lincoln with complaints about Burnside's generalship. McClellan's allies were lobbying for his immediate return with total control over the army. Joe Hooker called on Washington's influential in order to gain support for himself. Nearly one hundred hungry and disgruntled soldiers a day deserted in January and thousands more feigned sickness. Discipline was replaced by corruption, and camps smelled to high heaven from sanitary deficiencies. There were short rations and short tempers on the other bank of the Rappahannock too, but in the 2nd South Carolina Cavalry camp, Leonard sat contentedly beneath a bare pin oak with a full belly and an empty sheet of paper.

*January 9, 1863*

*If the clothes are not made and Will Thompson is at home, I wish you would get him to bring the cloth. There are tailors in the regiment that can make them up for me. All are [                    ]. Mrs. Ketchum's lad stands the service finely and is a capital soldier- always prompt and ready for any kind of service. Tell Mrs. Williams all her sons are in fine health and spirits. Lieuts. Perry and Stokes are both quite well & so indeed are all. The health of my company was never better- no news in last night's paper except the purpose of the French Emperor to recognize the Confederacy. This may, however, prove as fallacious as the past. Our hopes are the strength and constancy of our armies.*

*I have just arisen from an excellent breakfast. We purchased yesterday a side of pickled pork, which gave enough grease for making biscuits, frying steak & made an excellent bill of fare. Beef steak- and gravy mush & nice biscuits & rye coffee with sugar. We got sugar from the commissary, the first we have had since last summer. I want no better. I wish you may be able to do as well. I frequently feel grieved at the idea of the poor fare you are subjected to. Keep the cows and the* *calves out of the yard and soon get someone to put out fruit trees in the yard & other trees whenever you feel proper. Don't mind the expense of $25 or $30. Keep everything out of the yard. Let the grass and trees have a fair chance to grow. You had better dispose of the calves. Keep the pig about the stables. Has Harvey Gaillard called on you yet? I am glad Mr. Whitmire has a new house.*

*Remember me to Mary Susan and Lizzie and ask them to tell my dear friend, Allen, to write to me. I see Mr. Gaines frequently. He is quite well and contented. My respects to Mrs. Parker and family and to Carlisle. Tell him to send me a few lines. Everything quiet this morning. It is still fair and cold and cold does not hurt if it does not rain. Tell the servants I think of them often. Kiss baby and tell her her papa wants to see her very much. Write often my dear Anna and bear up under the adversities of the times. I hope and trust the dawn of better times are at hand.*

*Your husband,*
*L. Williams*

General Ambrose Burnside also hoped and trusted for the dawn of better times when he boldly moved his army just eleven days later on January 20. The unusually dry winter made an attack practicable, and if his forces could cross the Rappahannock and storm Lee's exposed flank, the Rebels would be forced to come out from behind their fortifications. On flat ground, not far from the heights where his army had been decimated, Burnside believed his much larger force could exact their revenge. But this time it appeared that God himself had conspired against the luckless general as the skies opened precisely when Burnside began his march. For two straight days it rained in icy torrents, transforming a once promising venture into a hopeless embarrassment.

From the hills along the Rappahannock, Leonard and Ruby watched the befuddled bluecoats as their caissons and supply wagons became swamped in the half-frozen mud. Wheels were stuck up to their axles, infuriated men were buried above their knees, horses and mules slipped, struggled to get upright, only to fall again. Some of the Confederate pickets jeered them and quickly fashioned homemade signs that read "This way to Richmond!" In the mud, the Army of the Potomac had sunk to rock bottom literally and figuratively. Two days later, Burnside terminated his doomed operation, and four days after that,

*182*

an exasperated Abraham Lincoln terminated the ill-fated, mutton chopper's command. "Fighting Joe" Hooker was selected to replace Burnside, becoming the fourth commander to step into the Virginia ring against Robert E. Lee.

With the bumbling Burnside still covered in equal measures of mud and shame and playing out his final days as commander, Leonard thought it an opportune time to put in for his first leave.

> *Camp Near Stephensburg*
> *Culpepper County, Va.*
> *January 23, 1863*

*My Dear Anna,*

> *It has been two weeks since I have written you. Since then we have made two moves and I have been on picket three days. I have, therefore, had but little leisure to write. We will probably remain in our present quarters for a few weeks. We have built chimneys to our tents and are quite comfortable. The last few days we have had rain and cold weather. It is still cloudy but warmer. This is the 1st rainy spell we have had for months. Our scouts report that Genl. Slocum's moving from Occoquan towards Fredericksburg & also that Milroy is moving from Winchester to the same point to reinforce Burnside. I presume Burnside will make another battle at or near Fredericksburg and general order was recd here a few days ago permitting two soldiers from each company to apply for a furlough. I took occasion to send in my application for a leave of absence for 30 days. They all went forwarded but came back endorsed "furloughs suspended at present", I judge on account of the enemy's late movements...*

The Old Captain remembered clearly how he bitterly clutched that rejection notice, stared into the sky, then ripped it to shreds. Four words had dashed his dream of returning home, *"furloughs suspended at present."* Unknowingly the Old Captain had crumpled the letter he was in the midst of reading thinking it for a moment to be that heart breaking order denying him his furlough. Back then he learned to never to get his hopes too high, but he had been so certain that after over a year and a half of riding and shooting he'd finally be able to spend a few hard-earned weeks with Anna and Carrie. But his faith had taught him and Anna that the Lord does indeed work in mysterious ways. When He deems it his will to leave one prayer unanswered, He often makes up for it by providing a bit of good fortune elsewhere. That was precisely the case when a magnificent mount appeared in camp just as old Ruby and his aching packhorse were running out of strength and forage. The January 23 letter continued.

*Last week a citizen near here brought in here a fine mare to sell. Asked six hundred dollars for her. She was a beautiful animal, clay bank color and young. No one having money enough to buy her, some of the boys concluded to get up a raffle for her. I took a chance and gave one of my men ten dollars to go down and throw for me. I never thought that much more about it till I heard I had won her. You must not think I have turned a gambler. I raffled for her as anyone would for a fine picture or a piece of sculpture. I have been offered 500 dollars cash but I think I will keep her to rest my old veteran charges.*

*We have a scout of 15 men across the river near Bacon Race who are a terror to the Yankees. They have caught a great many prisoners. Three of my men are with them, one of them Calhoun Sparks with one other. In one of their excursions they took five Yankees. They have brought and sent in some 30 or 40 Yankees. We have nothing new. The health of the regiment is very good. We are in a country thoroughly stripped of foliage. Our horses are in very poor condition and many have died. I keep mine in pretty good order and buy for them whenever I can and have to pay $3 per bu. for corn.*

The very sight of the name "Calhoun Sparks" caused the old veteran's heart to jump. None came any bolder. Few were as brave. A fellow Greenvillian, Sparks was born to scout and fight...even when he was forbidden to. When Sergeant Mickler of the Iron Scouts was at Calhoun's side he always instructed him, "Mind, I am going on a running, not a fighting trip this afternoon, and you well know what an open country this is."

Never was a man more perfectly named. His eyes had a special spark. He sparked infectious laughter with his tales of eluding the Yankees and making off with their brandy and whiskey. He created sparks whenever and wherever he rode. He was, in effect, the very spark that lit the fuse of Company K. Leonard admired the sergeant so much that he hated to send him out on those uncertain scouts, but to send out scared young privates without him would have been unforgivable. Every time Calhoun would return from such excursions, Leonard would inevitably be the first to meet him and later one of the first at his side by the campfire. They had promised each other on more than one occasion that when the war was over and they had returned to Greenville, they'd get together on Leonard's porch and share a whiskey and a red-hot tale or two. But this was a prayer that God, for a reason only comprehensible to Him, chose not to answer.

An eggnog or two, a new strong mare, and a bond of fellowship with his fellow soldiers made January bearable for Captain Leonard Williams. Thanks to a bit of lottery luck, Ruby could now rest her aching back while the young mare forded the cold streams and climbed their slippery banks. Ruby hated picketing. Her master hated it more. It was a lonely, boring, isolated proposition. Ride out hungry. Stop. Look. Ride a few miles farther. Stop. Look around some more. His eyes get heavy. A snake startles the horse. Bugs crawl in his boot. He wonders if he's lost. Does he follow that ridge or that railroad bed? Wasn't he at this ford just a few minutes ago? As he finds his bearings, rainwater overflows his hat brim then rushes down the back of his neck chilling him to the bone. He shivers. The horse shakes. His gut reminds him that he's had nothing to eat. In the muggy summer, locusts would drone him to sleep in the saddle then a nasty mosquito would prick him awake as if a needle stabbed him. But in the winter there was nothing. The only sound was the hypnotic clopping of hooves accompanied by the rhythmic snapping of twigs or the repeating hoot of an old barn owl. Now and then he'd break the monotony by filling his canteen along the Rapidan or quietly tapping in a new horseshoe so as not to alert the enemy. He knew it was vital and necessary but there was no drearier duty on the face of the earth. It was tough for a young man, tougher for a man who hoped to see 40 the next winter. The Captain could have shirked it all together or at least cut it down some because, after all, it was he that assigned the work in the first place. But he didn't and years later it would be the one exercise he remembered most often... because he did it so often.

The only good part of picket duty was when it was over. The anticipation of a leftover piece of hard tack, a warm bowl of rice, or perhaps even that elusive slice of bacon always made him pick up the pace as he neared camp. He knew whether or not such delights awaited him well before he got there by the aroma of the cooking fires drifting out to meet him. First off, he'd hook the new mare to the picket line tied between two birches, and then toss her some hay if any was to be found.   Next, he'd report to Major Butler with any intelligence his ride had discovered.  A peek into the pot or the frying pan followed. He ate, then he wrote.

*January 25th*

*I recd yours of the 16th last night and was glad to learn you were all well.  I think corn is cheaper than rice at present prices.  I wish I could get home to supply you for another year.  Corn is cheaper down the country.  I will see if I can't get you 25 bu. sent up from Newberry. At present, until I can make other arrangements, send to Major Alexander at the mill.  Send an order each time without bothering Mr. Whitmire with it and also arrange with the butcher to call at the house and select for yourself.  Find out from him the price and quantity each time and settle every month.  Provisions, I think, will still be higher and such things as peas, beans, Irish potatoes, dried fruit & c, you ought to buy 2 or 3 bu. of each, especially Irish potatoes if you can get good ones.*

*I wish you had a good cow now.  The time will soon be at hand when they can do well grazing in the spring and summer.  They need but little feeding.  Sell your calf.  It will be more trouble than it's worth. I see it is no use to you to raise pigs.  You ought not to keep a pig longer than one year then get another.  You can raise one hog with but little expense and it would help you out wonderfully.  You had better sell yours and invest proceeds in pork.  Don't get another sow pig, they do not grow as large and fat as the male.  You can raise 300 lbs of pork from the kitchen and the garden.  It behooves everyone to study thrift.*

*If you have not had the overcoat cut out, turn it back to Mr. Whitmire, the color is objectionable.  The Yankees wear black and blue overcoats. The only objection to my Yankee overcoat is that it's blue and when I go out on a scout or are near them, I have to take it off.  The black is liable to the same objection.  Gray is the color, but if it is already made, send it on with the other clothes.  It will be warmer than the one I have.  I have but one pair pantaloons and they are about worn out.  I am glad to hear that my new suit is coming.  I will endeavor to have someone in Richmond to bring them on as soon as they arrive.  I could not make out the name of your cousin who was kind enough to send*

186

*baby the present. My respects to all. Write often. I enclose a short note to Maj. Alexander which you will send him.*

*Your affectionate husband*
*L. Williams*

Once in a while, blue was the color of choice. On one dark night in early 1863, Isaac Curtis, Lee's famous scout, and Bolick, one of Butler's scouts, dressed themselves as Federal officers and rode brazenly by enemy pickets right into the camp of the 8th Illinois Cavalry. The two rode to within 150 yards of General George Meade's headquarters, rudely poked five men awake, and whispered to them to remain silent. They ordered the half-asleep men to saddle their horses, claiming they were needed for a secret mission of sorts, and after blankets and saddles were in place, they soon passed the Yankee pickets on their way back to Confederate lines. Ultimately realizing the ruse, one of the bamboozled Federals said to Curtis, "Ain't we prisoners?" and just as he said it, put spurs to his horse and galloped into the black night. The others were told if they ran, they would be shot. The two "Yankees for a night" returned with four prisoners and their horses. Not a single shot was fired in a bold display of sheer nerve.

The willpower of all the soldiers and their horses was tested severely throughout the following weeks when a series of cold fronts blew in over the Blue Ridge Mountains leaving the men knee-deep in snow from three consecutive storms. New Year's Day eggnog and fair weather were just fond memories. Weak tea and strong winds were now the order of the day. The wear and tear was visible on the faces of the men of the 2nd South Carolina Cavalry. Rib bones were visible on Ruby and the packhorse. Only the new mare seemed fit for duty. The horses couldn't survive much longer on the barren, snow-covered ground that lay between the Rapidan and the Rappahannock, and the cold was wearing down the troopers as well. Boredom ruled the previous winter. Discomfort and homesickness took hold now.

*Camp Near Stephensburg, Va.*
*February 5, 1863*

*My Dear Anna,*
*I recd both your letters of the 22ⁿᵈ and the 25ᵗʰ this morning by Dr. Williams & Will Thompson who arrived in camps this morning. Will*

*left his trunk with my clothes in it from Richmond. He could not get the overcoat in his trunk and therefore, left it. The one I have is pretty good and will do me sometime yet. You need not send it til I give you notice. Our brigade will be relieved of duty here in a few days. We will go somewhere (not yet known) to recruit our horses, probably near Charlottesville. After we move, I will send for my trunk. It is now very cold and snowing. This is the 3rd snow we have had in the last ten days. The first one 8 or 10 in. deep and this bids to be still deeper. We are very comfortable, however, in our tent to which there is a good chimney. It is bad for outdoor work. I had my time of it the last 4 weeks out during the snow but on account of the snow I established my headqrs. at a house nearby...*

Single digit temperatures brought frostbite and lowered resistance to the fever, dysentery, and cholera. Sickness, as always, preyed on the men as Dr. Taylor labored from morning until dusk in his poorly equipped field hospital. If not too busy, he'd also make rounds at night, visiting tents and some of the nearby farmhouses where the most critical patients were sometimes taken to be quarantined or just to be provided a soft, snug bed for their last days. On a few chilly evenings, the Captain rode out to one of those farmhouses to see to young Pressly Gaines, son of one of Leonard's esteemed friends back in Greenville. Unfortunately, the very capable Dr. Taylor was not his surgeon since Gaines was from another regiment. There was little the old physician could have done anyway. As the temperatures fell, Pressly's fever rose, and with each of Leonard's visits, he had drifted farther away from the battlefields and closer to his final resting place. In the February 5 letter, Leonard told Anna about the end.

*I regret to have to tell you that Pressly Gaines is dead. He died last Tuesday morning a week ago. His brother wrote to Lizzie and I suppose before this time, she has received the sad intelligence. I would also have written her had I known where to direct the letter. Tell Lizzie he recd more attention than usually falls to the lot of a soldier. He was at a comfortable house in a warm room with his brother with him. His brother came to me a few days before his death and told me he was suffering with a rising in his ear and asked me to get him an instrument to enable him to wash it. I obtained one from our surgeon. I was the same day put on duty as officer of the day and could not go to see him till the following night. When I got there he was wandering but his pulse was steady. I did not apprehend he was near so bad. Next day I went back and found him dead. I did not see his surgeon and did not learn what was the matter. I think it was pneumonia. I have his watch and other personal effects, hoping to be able to send them to Lizzie by one of Capt. Westfield's men who is entitled to a discharge...*

The Old Captain stopped for a moment as his eyes found their way over to his hotel bed. It was a four-poster, larger but in many ways similar to the one in which Pressly Gaines died. He pictured him there resting again, eyes shut, peace etched upon his face. In some ways he thought Pressly was one of the lucky ones because the battles that loomed ahead at the time would be grim and brutal affairs. He would not march out to Chancellorsville. He would not be swept up in the shooting and slashing at Brandy Station. He would never lay his eyes on Little Round Top. Heaven's gate beckoned him. Devil's Den awaited many more. Had the Old Captain known back then what he knew now, when he gazed down tearfully at the freckled face of young Pressly Gaines for the last time, he would have deemed his death merciful.

Leonard and his fellow cavalrymen would have to press on through the winter and the coming bloody summer. All he could do was fight hard, pray hard, and keep intact that tenuous, fraying lifeline back home to Anna and Carrie. His February letter ended with advice on managing affairs at home: all he could do now to help his family.

*There is nothing new in camps. All my men are well and in good spirits. Have had no difficulty for many months. All are getting on well. I am glad to see you looking forward to provide for the future. It would give me the greatest satisfaction to see you thrifty and take advantage of all the favorable stages of the market to lay in supplies. To do this, you have to inquire and know what everything is selling at: Maj. Alexander will furnish you with meal and flour. I feel badly at your being so illy provided for in the way of meat, salt, flour & c, especially your want of a good cow. The first opportunity I get I will send you money and continue, if I am spared, to send you all that I can for another year. Tell Mr. Whitmire to keep a sharp lookout after the Charleston market, now that the blockade is raised and if he sees cargoes of goods advertised he had better attend to them.*

*I wrote you in my last to speak to Mr. Cline about the fences, also your aunts. I had not heard of the death of Capt. Wallace. I would like very much to own Sancho. If you see the property advertised, clip it out and enclose it in a letter to me. If I could manage to buy him, I would like to do so. I wish you could have him now to work in the yard and garden, go to the mill, attend to the cows, & c. Do try to get the yard fenced. The high prices of provisions, I have no doubt, will continue and increase and it will be most difficult at best to get even the necessaries of life. It is necessary to think and study how to make your little means accomplish most. It will soon be time to prepare your garden. I am still in the enjoyment of good health. My love to all. Tell baby her papa wants to see her and that she must kiss her mamma for him. Willie Thompson says she is a fine, healthy looking child and looks very dainty. Write soon.*

*Your husband,*
*L. Williams*

Forty-five days would pass until he wrote to Anna again, the longest gap between his letters so far. This time the reason wasn't illness, a lengthy raid behind enemy lines, or a rash of skirmishes. There was no need to write because his commanding officers and perhaps God himself had finally deemed it allowable for him to be granted a 30-day leave. Leonard was going home. Once again, he found himself on a train puffing away on his pipe, but this time he wasn't bound for Richmond and the cavalry camp of instruction, he was headed for the Greenville depot. He would be met by Anna and Carrie. Big Ned would toss his bag on the back of the wagon and in a few minutes, he'd find himself back on Augusta Street. Would Anna leap into his arms? Would Carrie even remember him? Was his small farm now tangled in weeds and debt? He really didn't care. He just wanted to get there.

By horseback, wagon, and rail, he had finally arrived back in the red clay, South Carolina hills. As the iron horse expelled its last smoke-filled belches, Leonard emptied his pipe and peered out the window. He scanned the platform nervously sorting through the faces. Some he recognized. Some he didn't.

All wore faces as anxious as his. Where were they? Had they not received his telegraph? Then he saw his old wagon, but it sat unoccupied, attended only by his old gelding. A moment later, seated on a bench off by themselves, he saw Anna searching the windows of the train and holding Carrie, who seemed transfixed by the huge black machine that had just steamed in. In an instant, the Captain grabbed his bag and was down the steps where Ned was waiting for him with his broad black shoulders and a broader white smile. Ned was now technically a free man for the President had said so with his proclamation, but in the deep South those words did not translate into action. In any case, Ned and the others would not be able to easily cut the ties that bound them to the family. The Captain's word meant more to him than Lincoln's, and Ned had to be at that depot. Leonard knew he would be. As Ned made his way to the wagon with his master's frayed carpetbag, Leonard walked as if in a trance over to the two solitary figures on the bench, his eyes straying from Anna's just once for a peek at the tiny face tucked inside her bonnet. Little was said but much was felt as they all embraced for the first time in over twenty months. On the ride home, neither Anna nor Leonard felt a solitary bump from the old rig. They were riding on a soft, sweet dream…the dream that this day had finally come to pass.

Weeks that had dragged along in wintry northern Virginia now sped by in the warmth of family in his upcountry home. He met with Mr. Whitmire and tended to the inventory and bookkeeping of their mercantile store. He made arrangements for Anna's provisions the best he could. He and Ned walked the property and inspected the out buildings and the condition of the livestock and garden. They sold the pig and bought a calf.

It was decided that they would visit Anna's family in Columbia. The evening before their departure, the Captain rode up Augusta Street with a few surprises in the back of the wagon and hid them in the barn. He gave them out the next morning. For big Ned there was a new pair of shoes. For Maum Fannie there was a new cotton housedress, apron, and money to buy a few treats for Steve, Clough, Bill, Nan, and Lucy. For little Carrie a new straw doll and bonnet. She held the doll in her lap as she and her parents rode off for the depot.

In Columbia they called on the Lavals, which meant another late night brandy with the Major. This time the topic of discussion was not Leonard's engagement to Anna but the engagements between Lee and the enemy. The Major demanded details and his son-in-law provided them. Leonard grimly recounted instances of privates vomiting at the sight of dead comrades, defecating in their trousers as minie balls whistled over their heads, and sobbing like babies in fetid trenches. He spoke somberly of his ride across the killing fields of Second Manassas and of the carnage at Sharpsburg. He reenacted the rescue of Corporal McClanahan, stuck in a ditch, under his horse, with the Yankees closing fast. With a flash of his invisible saber, he depicted the decapitation of that Hessian in the Yorktown retreat. It was both appalling and cathartic at the same time as he rendered his eyewitness testimony on subjects such as disemboweling, severed limbs, and eyes blown from their sockets. In the midst of these sobering accounts, the Major exchanged brandy for whisky. Even the battle-hardened and decorated Major Laval had never experienced such horrors. They spoke until well past midnight, then after a final toast to departed brother Ephraim, both retired for the night. Tired and unburdened, the Captain fell into a deep sleep while the old Major stared up at a black ceiling, his haunted mind transforming it into a grim canvass of blood and death.

Anna would never know of such things nor would she ever inquire about them. The Captain never once even alluded to them while in her presence. Instead he spoke to her softly and reassuringly just as he did the morning he left to return to his regiment. After kissing his beloved Carrie and instructing her to take proper care of her new doll, Leonard escorted Anna out on to the Major's side porch. From the front yard, a young black man, a boy really, named Middleton, watched them sit close together on the white porch swing. He grew curious as he saw the officer hand his young love something shiny before wiping away her tears and kissing her farewell. A few moments later the Major had climbed into his carriage, wooden leg and all, in order to drive the Captain and the young black man to the station.

The wide-eyed country boy wanted to see the war. Now he would. A day earlier, just a few blocks away from the Planters Hotel in which the Old Captain now sat, the young captain had enlisted Middleton for what he knew would be a trying spring campaign. On the ride up to Richmond, the curious boy had many questions but the first was about what the "Massa" had given his wife on the porch. The captain filled his pipe, and as he sparked it up he simply informed him that it was a gold locket with a note inside. For some reason, Leonard knew he could trust his new servant so he shared with him that he had forgotten his and Anna's anniversary and had hoped that the note would atone for his lapse. By the time they reached the snow covered village of Staunton, the young servant had become "Mid" and Massa was now "Cap'n."

The Old Captain put down his letter and reached into his pocket. There he found his watch with a gold locket attached to the chain. The locket was now empty. The note it once contained was in the right hand of his beloved wife who now rested at Christ Church Cemetery back in Greenville. Like that locket, she still remained at his side forty years later.

The watch reminded him to pick up the pace a bit if he was to finish the letters before the reunion march, as did the sudden burst of a cannon blast. Loaded with plenty of powder but no projectile, it was fired from the square by a local Columbia battery testing the gun that would signal the start of the festivities. He quickly poured himself a new cup of coffee and began his next letter.

*Stanton, Va.*
*March 22, 1863*

*My Dear Anna,*

*Although tired and sleepy, having a comfortable room and fire, I take the opportunity to write you a few lines, not knowing when again I may have another chance. We lost one day on the road to Richmond. It commenced snowing on us Thursday night and continued all day on Friday. The whole face of the country was covered from 10 to 12 inches deep. We spent our night in Richmond and today came to this place, a distance of about 140 miles. I got in company with Lieut. Varner of our regiment immediately today. I overtook Capts. Clark and Screven plus 2 or 3 Lieuts. and they are now all here and none of us know where our regiment is. Some of them have been here a week. So I have lost nothing by my stay in Columbia. I hear tonight our regt is on the move for a point about 15 miles distant from here. I will probably remain here tomorrow in order to ascertain definitely where to find the regiment.*

*I have not had much time to brood over my loneliness since leaving you. I can scarcely realize that I was with you almost a month. The time seems to have sped by so rapidly yet I am thankful that I was permitted to be with you even for so short a time. I have gotten entirely over my cold. My eyes are also well and have so far saved my trunk and other baggage. I will write you a long letter when I get to camp but the regiment being on the move, I cannot say when I will be settled. It may, therefore, be a week or more before I can write again. Direct your letters to Richmond. They will be forwarded from that place. Remember me to your father and mother and the girls and Wm. and tell him I was disappointed in not seeing him at the depot. Tell baby her papa wants to see her and she must kiss mother for him. I have no news to write and being fatigued with constant travel, you must excuse this hasty and short letter.*

*Your affectionate husband*
*L. Williams*

The furlough resuscitated the Captain. It raised his spirits and strengthened his resolve. New Union Commander Joe Hooker was doing the same for his Army of the Potomac. He sent corrupt quartermasters packing, upgraded rations, and cleaned up the camps and hospitals. Ignored furloughs were now granted, and when the men returned they were given new insignia badges, which instilled pride in their corps. As a result, morale returned, sickness declined, and desertions dropped. Hooker also addressed the needs of his cavalry by reorganizing them into a separate corps. Now the Northern riders could operate independently and seek out and destroy the likes of Wade Hampton, M. C. Butler, and even their chief nemesis, Jeb Stuart himself. In 1862, the Confederate cavalry had embarrassed their blue counterparts. Now, Hooker gave his cavalrymen the organization and the means to turn the tide in the coming campaign. This did not bode well for one Captain Leonard Williams. The cavalry superiority they had enjoyed in the past was soon to be over.

As Hooker was sipping his whiskey and fashioning his attack plans, the men of the 2nd South Carolina Cavalry were drinking from their canteens on the way down to southern Virginia. They had been sent to just above the North Carolina border in order to provide their mounts with much needed forage. Unfortunately for Ruby, even the journey down to those lush fields was a hard one so the Captain rode only the new mare now. Not only did the packhorse have more to carry because of the extra provisions the Captain had added from home, the colt had Ruby tied to his pommel as well. Mid seemed to fare the best, keeping up on foot while playing his harmonica without a murmur of complaint.

*Nelson County, Va.*
*March 31, 1863*

*My Dear Anna*

*I reached Staunton on the 22ⁿᵈ, next day started in company with Lieut. Varner on foot to Greenville to intercept the regiment hearing it was to pass through that place. After waiting 2 days they got within ten miles of me when my horses were sent. I joined the regiment on the 25ᵗʰ. Had I known that the regiment was moving, I might have remained with you another week without impropriety. I am now fully reinaugurated into camp life. Day before yesterday we crossed the Blue Ridge from Augusta into Nelson County. We will remain in this camp probably a week having plenty of horse feed. For that length of time we are under orders to feed towards Halifax County which borders on N. C., which will, I presume occupy some 3 or 4 weeks. Our object is to recruit our horses- being ordered towards N. C., I think it is intended for us to operate in that state this spring and summer. I do not expect to find a more agreeable country or people but I am pleased that we have an opportunity to see more of the country. I am now pretty well acquainted with eastern and middle Va. and would like to see more of the old north state.*

Crossing the border into the Tarheel State, though a tempting possibility, was out of the question. If Lee was to advance in the coming spring, the cavalry would be vital to him and must remain within two days ride. The cavalry would also be indispensable in monitoring Hooker's moves against Richmond and in masking the counter punches of Lee. For the next six weeks, however, conditions were such that Leonard and the 2nd South Carolina Cavalry could remain in southern Virginia to round up as many fresh horses as they could to replace those that suffered from greasy heel, sore feet, diseases of the mouth and tongue, and overall malnutrition. But there were never enough fresh horses and the old mounts were stuffed with as much hay, oats and forage as they could hold. Horseshoes were changed, cuts were stitched up, and the company vet sought to remedy diseases ranging from glanders and farcy to distemper and hoof rot. For nearly two years, these poor, worn down, taken-for-granted creatures had carried as much as 220 pounds of gear, a 30 to 50 pound saddle and the weight of their demanding masters day after day. This time of rest was well deserved and well timed because the coming months would be full of exhausting picketing, dusty rides, and desperate charges. It would be a brutal ordeal for Union horses as well but with one crucial difference. The North had a growing supply of horses and an efficient system of remounts to keep its troopers in the saddle. The South did not. Southern cavalrymen had to provide and maintain their own mounts. It was critical, therefore, for them to care for their equine partners as vigilantly as they would a fellow soldier.

Leonard wasn't much of a horse doctor, but he did have some good, old-fashioned horse sense. He knew that his lightweight McClellan saddle and the good fortune of having a spare mount and packhorse had extended Ruby's endurance. He walked alongside her on marches in order to save her aching back whenever time was not of the essence. He spent his own money on hay when none was issued, purchased forage whenever he came across it, and scoured the mess tent garbage for anything that could tide her over. He was devoted to her for personal and professional reasons, and Ruby never failed to respond to his small kindnesses. He admired her stubbornness when she had pulled the plow. He witnessed first hand how her confidence grew during their rigorous training at Ashland. But more importantly, he had seen her courage and obedience in the heat of battle rise to a level that matched that of any mount in his regiment, including Butler's "Benchlegs" and Hampton's "Butler."

He knew her as well as he had known any man. Now he realized that despite a month of leisure and comparative abundance, Ruby's improvement was almost imperceptible. He had hoped that with each and every pile of hay she nudged her nose into she would become more like her old self. Leonard's horse sense told him to be patient. Mid also did all he could for Ruby, which was mainly to keep her brushed and contented. Little by little Ruby's appetite and health returned. Leonard also worried about things at home and continued his March 31 letter.

> *The people here say we will have one more snow. There are as yet few signs of vegetation. Fruit trees have not yet begun to blossom. You must tell me about baby. I am now more interested in her now than ever. Tell me what she says and does and if she still loves her grand pop and mother. I wish you could get your and her likenesses taken in Columbia before you leave and send them by Sergt. Benson who is at home on furlough. He will start back about the 12th April. Also send*

*me my pistol belt. I intended to divide my funds with you in Columbia, at least to share with you a little bit but I entirely forgot it. Write to Mr. Whitmire for some. You will need more than you have to get the pictures. How long will you be in Columbia? Although I would be glad for you to stay a month or two in Columbia, I am anxious for you to get home again.*

*I want to hear how your garden is doing and about the cows, pigs, trees and grass. Tell me whether the bacon is hung up and whether the corn has been sent up. I paid Mr. Whitmire for 30 bu. A part I bought at Abbeville. He said he would send it up as soon as it came. It is shelled corn and you had better perhaps get 2 barrels and [      ] and have it put in your storeroom like the peas.*

*On account of the snows and hard weather, my horses have not improved any. The mare had fallen off a good deal but since I had been back they are improving and doing well. My boy Middleton is doing very well. I think he will make a very handy fellow in camp. The health of the co. and regt. is very good. I am very anxious to get a letter from you. Write to me often. My love to all.*

*Your affectionate husband*
*L. Williams*

As the spring of '63 neared, tensions simmered north and south of the Mason Dixon Line. Union papers were rife with instances of looting and rioting ignited by the draft. Northerners who employed blacks had their businesses burnt to the ground. Copperheads like Ohio Democrat Clement Vallandigham were offering up fiery, anti-Lincoln, "end the war now" diatribes and gaining support with every incendiary speech. On the military side, the specter of over a thousand dead and frozen bodies from the Union fiasco at Fredericksburg not only meant a dismal Christmas, it created a lingering pessimism regarding the coming campaigns. That pessimism continued as April and the cold Spring rains arrived in the west. Grant couldn't find a few yards of dry land to stand on let alone a few acres for his mired army. His plans to capture Vicksburg, control the Mississippi River and divide the Confederacy were on hold and stuck in the mud. Unable to reach Vicksburg, Grant reached for the bottle. Closer to Washington, even the most optimistic of Lincoln supporters doubted if Hooker had the stuff in him that McDowell, McClellan, Pope, and Burnside had all lacked—the guts and guile to crush Lee and his out-manned yet rugged Army of Northern Virginia.

Down in Dixie, things were almost as dreary. Men up to the age of 45 had been ordered to forsake farming and start soldiering. Plantations had no masters and production declined. Belles who once tied bonnet bows with dainty fingers as they dressed for grand balls now weeded, dug, and planted with blistered hands. The drought from the previous summer left parched, cracked ground, and families were unable to sustain themselves. Inflation and the blockade made even the bare essentials almost impossible to procure. Absentee fathers, sons, and brothers weighed heavily on the hearts of their families back home.

On the battlefield, however, President Jefferson Davis' brilliant commander had masterminded a string of recent victories and in doing so, had become far more than a gifted general. Lee was now the very emblem of Southern dignity, courage, and resolve. The gray bearded, blue eyed, fifty-six year old had boldly implemented his offensive/defensive strategy to perfection against "those people" as he called them, and with Old Pete and steady Stonewall at his side, the stoic general was cautiously buoyant. In April of '63 he wrote to his wife stating that "If we can baffle them in their various designs this year, next fall there will be a great change in public opinion at the North. The Republicans will be destroyed & I think the friends of peace will become so strong as that the next administration will go in on that basis. We have only therefore to resist manfully...our success will be certain."

Captain Leonard Williams was not as optimistic as his commanding generals. Letters from Anna were either not being written or were not being forwarded from Richmond down to Nelson County. Instead of heartwarming accounts of Carrie's latest achievements, the only news coming out of Greenville was an alarming rumor brought back by soldiers returning from furloughs. Smallpox had invaded the upcountry.

> *Nelson County Va.*
> *April 10, 1863*

*My Dear Anna*

*I have been looking most anxiously for a letter from you for several days but none has yet come. It has been over 3 weeks since I have left you. I hope I may get one this evening. I have thought more about you and baby and have been more desirous to see you than before going home. I have been wondering if baby has forgotten me, having been with so many people just before leaving and seeing so many people in Columbia. She is more likely to forget me than if I had left her at home. How long do you expect to remain in Columbia? Have you and Mary Susan made your arrangements for a visit in Edgefield? I would be glad if you would spend a week with Uncle Ephraim and William Andrews and Nanny. They would be glad to see you. I have been a little uneasy about the smallpox in Greenville. Clough, Bill and Lucy, I think, ought to be vaccinated and if the disease spreads, all ought to be. They ought to be kept in the yard as much as possible.*

*I'm anxious to hear how your garden is going, but I do not expect you will be at home before the 25th. But when you get home you must tell me about it, whether the potatoes have come up well, about the cabbage, plants, peas & c. Every foot of the garden must be planted. There is a part of a bag of guano that ought to be spread over a square. The cabbages will be ready to transplant before May. If you can get a load of manure, or 2 or 3 loads, it would be well to get it for the cabbages. I forgot to call and pay Mr. Robt. Greenfield for the use of his wagon. I wish you would ask Mr. Whitmire to see him and pay for it. I believe that is the only unpaid matter I left. I want to hear too, how the old cow is doing, whether she still increases in the quantity of milk and also how the young cow is doing and how the pigs get on. You cannot now be at a loss of interesting topics to write me about. Mr. Cox, I believe, comes to town every month. Ask Henry or Mr. Whitmire to inquire of him about Steve and Nan...*

Three days prior to writing that letter, Charleston Harbor was shelled furiously by Federal gunboats. But Anna's hometown was still safe for the present, as was Vicksburg, the "Gibraltar of the West."

*It has given us great pleasure to hear of the repulse and defeat of the Yankee gunboats at Charleston, but have yet learned none of the particulars of the attack. I have been with the regt. over two weeks and since joining it, have crossed the Blue Ridge from Augusta into Nelson County. We are feeding along the county in the direction of Halifax County. We are, today, merely bivouacking, having moved today some*

*16 miles. Tomorrow we will move a short distance to get a better campground. It is likely we will be in this neighborhood two weeks. The impression at present at HQ's is that we will be sent back about the 1ˢᵗ May in the valley to operate against Milroy's forces, now near Winchester. We left a very pleasant community near our last camp. Soldiers had never been here before. We were treated most hospitably. At dress parade, our camp shone with all the beauty of all the belles of the co. The band which now plays will, I presume, have its share in attracting the ladies and citizens to witness the dress parades.*

*I am now entirely rid of cold, sore throat and cough and am enjoying fine health. I have become accustomed to the hard ground again. The weather now is beautiful but has been very chilly. Yesterday the ground was frozen. Today is the first spring like day we have had. There are but a few signs of vegetation yet. The forests still look as bleak as winter. I expect in Columbia the trees have all begun to leaf. The farmers say the spring here is very backward.*

*I am very pleased with my boy, Middleton. He cooks well and is a very good hostler and is quick, cheerful and good-natured. It has been nearly a month since I left Greenville and although I wrote to Mr. Whitmire from Staunton at the same time I wrote you, I have heard nothing from him. We are at present leading a very quiet life. Our mornings are occupied by dress parade and dismounted drills. The evening is used for visiting, walking, reading & c. This is a mountainous country with fine valleys and the people all in very comfortable circumstances and generally hospitable. I took tea twice with an old gentleman near our last camp who was the impersonation of hospitality. I almost felt akin to him. His wife was a Williams and the name of one of his sons was Floyd and one of his daughters was Fanny. He insisted I was a relation of Genl. Marion. His own name is Whitehead and all the boys agree in pronouncing him a real Whitehead. Tell me how Uncle Whitmire's health is getting. Remember me to your father and mother and the girls and all. Write soon and often and tell me all about baby and tell her papa wants to see his baby.*

*Your affectionate husband*
*L. Williams*

Seventeen days later, on April 27, "the greatest army on the planet" as Fighting Joe called it, started to move and the first volley was launched by the feisty Hooker himself. "May God have mercy on General Lee, for I will have none!" he proclaimed. Hooker's plan was a three-phrased one. First, General George Stoneman would lead 10,000 supremely saddled cavalrymen above and to the left of Lee to raid supply lines and break his communications. Next, Hooker would march 70,000 infantrymen north up the Rappahannock to cross at fords beyond Lee's left flank, while leaving 40,000 more behind at Fredericksburg to keep the Confederates occupied. To his credit, these movements were made flawlessly, without casualty and on time. "Our enemy must ingloriously fly," declared Hooker, "or come out from behind his defenses and give us battle on our own ground, where certain destruction awaits him."

The Army of Northern Virginia rarely flew. Lee had no intention of hiding, and he seemed to always find a way to transform the enemy's ground into his. Hooker was correct in one sense, however; "certain destruction" did await one of them. Before the Army of the Potomac even reached their attack positions, Lee had already deduced that the main body located near the road junction and large mansion at Chancellorsville was the real threat. He massed the majority of his forces there, leaving only 10,000 men under Jubal Early to face the 40,000 in Fredericksburg. It was a risk, but as always, Lee never flinched in his bold course of action.

South of all this maneuvering and gamesmanship was Capt. Leonard Williams and the 2nd S.C. Cavalry, ordered to remain in Nelson County until they had enough healthy horses to make them again the reliable screeners, raiders and scouts they had been in months past. But for the present, the number of strong mounts was still insufficient and many remain hobbled from disease and lack of feed. The Captain was also hobbled, seriously ill from a cold, and while recuperating, he wrote a long letter to Anna trying to stay in touch with his family and affairs at home.

> *New Market*
> *Nelson County*
> *April 29, 1863*

*My Dear Anna*
> *I am at present in the little town of New Market on the James River and the regiment about a mile distant. I am at the residence of Dr.*

*Peters with whom I have been staying 2 or 3 days. I had a most violent cold together with a derangement of my liver which together made me very sick for a day or two. The Dr. advised me to leave camp for a few days. Since I have been here I have been improving constantly and will, I hope, be quite well again in a few days.*

*I am glad you are again at home. I recd this morning the letter you sent by Sergt. Benson and had been looking many days for it before it came. I recd both your first letters by the same mail so that until today you may say, I have heard but once from you since I left Columbia on the 19th of March and being all the time on the line of the RR where we have been getting daily mails. I am glad your mother's with you and hope she may spend 2 or 3 months with you. I hope the Major may find leisure to run up and take a little respite from his office. I do not know how he stands the confinement and monotony of office life so well. Prevail on him to spend 2 or 3 weeks with you this summer.*

*I am sorry Sumner made the blunder he did in the plants. He ought to refund you the money or give you the plants next fall or winter. I think you ought to inform him of the mistake he made and consequently of the worthlessness of the plants. You ought not to have taken them out of the depot at all. He is bound to furnish you another supply but he will need no other impulse than simply to be informed on the subject. He will do what is right.*

*I am sadly disappointed in the cow. I saw her milked. She gave ½ gal. and not more than half the milk was taken from her. There is miserable mismanagement. I am afraid Fannie is becoming worthless. If the cow had been properly fed and milked, she would have been giving a gallon at least at a milking. You had, perhaps, better put Lucy to milking again. I directed Ned to give the cows peas and meal in about equal quantity. I mean before the peas are boiled, after they are boiled the peas are nearly doubled in bulk. I wish you would see to it when Ned cannot attend to it. They ought to be fed, milked, and turned out to graze in the morning, a little after sunrise. I am much disappointed. I hoped you would have butter and milk enough for the place and some to share with one or two very poor families near you. The family at the corner of the lot are I know, but poorly supplied, they would be troublesome if you were to tolerate intimacy. But if you had* buttermilk to share, it would be doing them a charity to send them a pitcher full occasionally. The husband of one of them is in the army and the other lady is a widow. I would keep them at a distance. I do not know much about them.

If the fodder has not yet been put away, I think you had better quit feeding it to the cows. I expect by this time the grass affords pretty good picking for the cows. I think you had better dispose of the calf as soon as you can. I hope they will both improve, for without milk and butter, your vegetables will not be as valuable. Green peas and Irish potatoes need nothing more than butter and salt. You did not tell me about the potatoes, whether they had come up or not or cabbage or tomato plants nor about the peas and beans. What is the prospect for the garden? With a good garden, plenty of butter and milk, you can defy the blockade another year. I think you had better have the grass and clover removed from about the roots of the little trees in the yard, say for about 2½ ft. round and spread manure from the wood pile around then over the ground from where the turf has been removed. Also, throw some on the hedge, it begins to need some stimulant. It was a very fortunate hit when you bought rice. You bought it for something less than half what it is selling now. Did you get up the half barrel from the store out of which you were using?

It will take nearly all of my salary to support me. I am paying $1.37 per ½ pound for bacon, flour 20 cts. per lb., meal $6.00 per bu. and everything else especially high. I don't think however, these prices will last a great while. I have no army news. I am expecting every day orders for active duty. I am getting tired of this lazy life. We have been in the mountain districts to where there has been but little interest.

The season of the year's now coming when your strength begins to fail. Remember the Dr.'s advice. Rise early in the morning, take the fresh outdoor air and sunshine. Sunshine is as important as pure air. I fear poultry raising will be a great annoyance to you but if so, you can soon eat out your stock. I am still troubled with your neighbor's poultry. I have some directions for Ned but I will give them on a separate piece of paper which you will read to him. I am glad Uncle Whitmire is again in health. Remember me to them all. You said nothing about the small pox. Has it disappeared? I wish you would inquire after Bill. If

*you think he is not properly cared for, you had better take him away.*
*Did Mr. Feaster call on you? Remember me to your aunts and also to*
*your mother. Tell baby papa wants to see and kiss his baby.*

*My dear Anna, you must write oftener to me. I have been away-*
*tomorrow will be six weeks. You have written me 3 letters and those*
*six weeks seem almost like six months. Don't wait to send letters by*
*hand. I am nearly well and will, I think, be able to return to camp*
*tomorrow. Write me all the news and tell me all about baby.*

*Your affectionate husband*
*L. Williams*

As the Old Captain read on, he had wished that he'd been riding alongside Jeb Stuart instead of lying in bed suffering from that second attack of jaundice. Jeb and the boys were in the midst of important screening duty riding between Stonewall and the enemy. Jackson's men, including the 14th S. C. V. I and one James Williams, were on the move. The night before, while seated on a couple of rickety old cracker boxes by a small fire, Jackson and Lee had decided on yet another risk-it-all flanking maneuver. Stuart had informed them that Hooker's left flank, like McClellan's a year earlier, was "in the air" and could be surprised and overrun. Stuart's intelligence, Lee's guts, and Stonewall's reliability added up to "certain destruction" for General Hooker. This was high stakes generalship on the grandest scale. Early was still outnumbered 4 to 1 back in Fredericksburg. Lee's immediate army, minus Jackson's 30,000, was now at the wrong end of 5 to 1 odds. If Stonewall's movement was discovered, Lee's bold gambit would end in disaster. Word did reach Hooker concerning Stonewall's actions, but instead of crushing Lee's stripped force that now faced him, "Fighting Joe" hesitated. He believed Jackson to be in retreat, perhaps "ingloriously flying," oblivious to the fate that would soon befall his naked right flank at precisely 5:15 in the evening as his men turned their attention to what was in their dinner pots.

Suddenly, Jackson's three divisions, two miles wide, exploded from the woods in a howling, rebel yelling hurricane. Thousands of birds swept up into the sky as 30,000 gray clad troops tore into the shocked encampments of the Union XI Corps in a swirl of gunfire and chaos. For several hours, Jackson's and A.P. Hill's seasoned veterans drove the enemy's flank back while Lee simultaneously smashed Hooker's front. Lee finished the job the next day as

Hooker watched from the front porch of the Chancellor Mansion his army crumble. Suddenly, a shell struck one of the porch pillars, splitting it and knocking a chunk of wood hard against the stunned general. For about an hour he maintained his command, but then became too disoriented to continue and was helped to a bed in the rear of the burning Chancellor house.

For Lee, Sunday's grand victory was earned at a terrible price. As the final, haphazard shots echoed in the silence of that previous evening, Dorsey Pender's Tarheels had drawn a bead on what they determined to be a party of Union horsemen headed toward them at dusk. It was difficult to see but their first volley killed two unknown men. The second volley wounded a third causing his horse to bolt into the bushes jerking the rider out of his saddle and hurling him onto the hard ground. The horse was Little Sorrel. The rider was General Thomas Jonathan Jackson. He lay between the lines on the edge of a road. General A. P. Hill rushed forward with a group of men to carry Jackson back to safety, but as they attempted to do so, Union artillery began pounding their escape route with shrapnel. One litter bearer was hit and the rest of the party dropped the wounded General's stretcher and ran for cover. A second detachment was organized but again another man was struck. In the process, Jackson's litter tilted and he fell to the ground in agony. Finally, Jackson was transported to a field hospital and at midnight his left arm was amputated at the shoulder. The next day, Lee put the finishing touches on his masterpiece but he was filled with gloom over the man he called his right arm. A week later, on May 10, Jackson, was on the brink of death. Deliriously, he called out once more for A. P. Hill to come up, the last order he gave on the Chancellorsville battlefield, and then uttered his final peaceful words. "No, no," he murmured, "let us pass over the river, and rest under the shade of the trees." The man who thought it unrighteous to fight on Sunday died on a Sunday. He would fight no more. Many a brandy and many a whisky were hoisted in the memory of their stoic warrior in the old, worn hat. Stonewall's death was a heavy blow to all. The Captain recorded the general's loss in his next letter home.

*1 ½ Miles from Gordonsville, Va.*
*May 11, 1863*

*My Dear Anna*
*The last time I wrote to you I was at Dr. Peter's at New Market,*
*Nelson County. I stayed with him 6 days and was never treated more*

*attentively. Were the regiment left though, I would have been glad to remain with his family longer and not being quite well, still I joined it and have been marching with it ever since. I am improving but still not perfectly. We are on our way to Orange County and from there we have no knowledge where the regiment will be ordered. I was very glad to receive your 4th letter by Joel Ketchum. Just think of it, 4 letters in 42 days and I expect it will be several days before I get another. You used to write me every week and sometimes oftener and now not oftener than once in 10 or 12 days.*

*I have heard of but few of the casualties of the fight at Fredericksburg. I hear Billy Whitmire is wounded but I understand not severely. I hope it is slight. I have heard nothing from James. His regt. was hotly engaged and suffered severely but I cannot hear whether he escaped or not. Our great victory, perhaps the greatest of the war, was purchased at immense cost. If other valuable lives have not been lost, the death of Genl. Jackson makes it a sad victory. He was the favorite of the army and country. I trust that God will endow some other man to take his place. I see Lincoln has called out 500,000 more men but I do not think his army will be in any better condition if he can carry out his draft than it was before the fight at Fredericksburg. So many of the present army will go out of service soon.*

*I am greatly disappointed in the white cow.*

Here the Old Captain abruptly stopped reading. Beloved General Jackson had died. A decisive victory had been won in Chancellorsville. He had expressed his remorse over the fallen general and he had shared the news about Lee's great victory with Anna. Yet even in the face of great historical events it was Anna's face and that white cow that concerned him then. The Old Captain realized that back then, even though he was making history, there was no time to linger on sadness or celebrate defeat. He couldn't save Jackson. Battles would be won and lost with or without him. In war, both death and victory were fleeting. His family and farm were not. He returned to his May letter.

*You speak of buying more peas. I think you will not need any more. I bought 22 bu. and directed Ned to use 1 bu. peas plus 1 bu. of meal per week for them which would last 20 weeks or there about, or if that was not enough to feed more, say 1 ½ bu. each of peas and corn. At that rate, it would last 3 months and over. I expect you had better use all your milk to make butter and buttermilk for all. I mentioned in my last that you had better have the grass removed from around the trees in the yard and chip manure spread around them. I am glad your garden looks well.*

*I have no news. Why did you not tell me the names with which rumor has been busy, especially the one in conjunction with Billy. I am as ignorant as possible. I learned Billy Whitmire's wound is trifling, being wounded in the hand. I wish you would send me a list of the casualties from our papers. I have heard almost nothing. Speak to Mr. Whitmire and let him begin in time to buy clothing for the servants. Our brigade was so much scattered and so far off we could not make a strike at Stoneman's cavalry. The other brigades were engaged more or less at Fredericksburg, consequently, the raiders were unmolested. As soon as they heard of Hooker's defeat, they ran for dear life. I am annoyed at their escape but circumstances saved them. It was a brilliant achievement of Forrest's near Rome, Georgia. Give my love to all. Have your aunts moved their negroes up to Greenville? If they have not, it is but little use to move. They had as well to stay with you. Remember me to all. Kiss baby for her papa. Write soon.*

*Your affectionate husband*
*L. Williams*

Post Chancellorsville Dixie was a time and a place for great reveling. Lee's Army of Northern Virginia had won its most decisive victory of the war against a force that outnumbered them better than two to one. Despite the fact that with each passing day the South was losing food, funds and soldiers, the victory at Chancellorsville had buoyed their spirits. Conversely, up north, the fallout from the defeat was nearly equal to that of Fredericksburg back in December. "My God! My God!" lamented Lincoln, "What will the country say?" In Lee's tent and President Davis' cabinet, the glory was diluted with a sense of gloom. The tragic and senseless death of Stonewall Jackson from friendly fire created a palpable sense of despair that permeated every conversation. For Lee, worse even than the hurt in the heart created by the loss of Jackson was the realization that the deaths of so many men had really amounted to nothing. No ground was gained. No upper hand was achieved. No knockout blow was delivered. The 17,000 union casualties amounted to roughly fifteen-percent of Hooker's army. Thirteen thousand Confederate casualties, however, represented nearly a quarter of Lee's. Lincoln had many more lined up to fill the ranks. Davis did not. Out west, Grant was nearly at Vicksburg's door. Soon, Lincoln, Davis, Hooker, and Lee would realize that Chancellorsville was nothing more than a prelude to seven straight months of brutal warfare in the eastern theatre.

For the 2nd South Carolina Cavalry, soldiering was becoming more like a ride on an out-of-control carousel, riding round and round, from skirmish to battle, never resting, always fighting. In the beginning the brass ring to be grasped was a resounding victory that would win the war. Now the regiment merely hoped for an end to the infernal spinning, grinding, wheel of war…win or lose. Captain Williams was about to get on that cruel carousel. Homesick, weak and sick of war, he had a deep sense of foreboding as he climbed aboard.

*Camp Near Gordonsville, Va.*
*May 14, 1863*

*My Dear Anna*

*It is just two months today since I left Greenville and have been on the line of Rroads and have had almost daily mails and yet I have recd but 4 letters from you. I have scarcely ever been so low spirited as far as the last month, but I have been unwell for nearly that length of time, although I am up and doing my duty whenever called on. I have but a poor appetite, but it is improving a little and I hope I will soon be strong again. It seems to me the last two months have hung more heavily than any four months previously and I have been more dispirited at my separation from you than ever before and I have looked with more eagerness for letters.*

*Notwithstanding the great victory at Fredericksburg, the prospect is most gloomy. The Yankee people are being deceived into the belief that they were not badly whipped and represent that the Confederate prisoners in longer numbers are taking the oath of allegiance to the U. S. and Lincoln is calling for 500,000 more men. The mouths of the Peace Party are closed by the fear and uncertainty of imprisonment. From the present signs, I can see no prospect of an early peace. It is not in human wisdom or strength unless directed from on high that we are to look for deliverance. God will punish us until He sees fit to withhold his chastening rod and in His good time will relieve us from our accumulated troubles.*

*I wish I could write you a more cheerful letter. I am frequently prevented from writing for lack of materials and although I wrote you 2 days ago, I write again not knowing how soon we may move or when again I may have an opportunity. I almost feel like my visit home was unfortunate for me. It may be owing to my increased anxiety to hear from you that I imagine you do not write me as often as you used to.*

*The death of Genl. Jackson has cast a gloom over all reflecting men. I fear we will never have his like again. He was most highly endowed with every requisite for a commander and had the confidence and admiration of all. I have seen no list of the casualties in the S. C. regiments. Do send me a paper with the lists. We do not know when we will move nor on what service. A great deal of the cavalry are concentrating in this vicinity. I understand seven brigades. The Yankees, I hear, have twelve brigades. Stoneman's raid was a fruitless one. They did but little damage. I suppose their object was to hinder the retreat of Genl. Lee after Hooker dislodged him as he expected to do. They retreated in all haste after hearing of Hooker's failure.*

*Ask Mr. Whitmire to call on G. E. Elford and pay him for his paper 6 months and also prepay the postage for the same length of time and have it sent to me. I very rarely see a S. C. paper. I expect in a few days to get another detachment home for horses. If so, Will Thompson will be among them. I wish you would make me 2 cotton shirts (colored), something like your dresses and 2 pair drawers (coarse). I have lost my cotton drawers and one pair socks. The weather is getting too warm for my woolens and also get me a peck of dried peaches, if you can. I cannot buy cloth or shirts out here, else I would not bother you with them. If no other convenience offers, you can box them and send by Mr. Barnwell. My love to all.*

*Your affectionate husband*
*L. Williams*

The Old Captain winced at the tone of his grumbling words home, but moments later, he'd soon realize that Anna wasn't the sole target of his woe and worry. Thinking it merely another letter to her, he opened the next envelope without looking at the addressee. The old man sat up as he examined the salutation. It was written to his brother Henry, too old for conscription, who had remained back in South Carolina. Anna must have saved it along with hers. She even took the time to carefully insert it amongst hers in the correct chronological order as it was written on May 16. In comparison to Anna's, this one was perhaps even darker and more brooding, but to borrow a phrase from his letter to Henry, *"even in its desolation it was beautiful. It smiled in its tears."*

*Bivouac Near Culpepper, Va.*
*May 16, 1863*

*Dear Henry*

*I received your favor through the hand of Ct. Lanneau, since then, we have been on the move. I take this, the first opportunity to write. We are back again on the Rappahannock and will picquet the lines on the river. It has been two months since I left home and they have apparently been longer than twice that period before. The privation of the companionship of wife, baby, and friends bear more heavily on me than ever before. I need not say I long to be with them again. I have been unwell for 2 or 3 weeks but am now, I think, about well again. I am reduced a few lbs. in flesh.*

*Our regiment has been for 2 months in Nelson Co. recruiting horses. We are still poorly supplied with good horses. The men who went back home brought back very good horses. Horses are very high here, from $450 to $800 for good to first rate horses. Horses that were bought at Greenville for $300 were appraised from $450 to $600. I need another good saddle horse and if you can find a first rate one, I am willing to pay $500 for such a one. Col. Butler is trying to get off another squad of men for horses. If so, I could get a horse brought on. Please look out for one for me and if the detail gets off, I will notify you immediately. Mr. Whitmire will advance the money and I will send it to him. I do not care for $50 or $100 if you can get 1 horse.*

*In the march, we passed through Albemarle Co. It is a rich and beautiful country and is yet unpolluted by the enemy. The wheat is fine everywhere and the farmers have put in much heavier crops than usual.*

*Of corn, Nelson Co. also is rich and productive. The people, wherever I have been, are making every effort to make large crops of bread stuffs. Culpeper, I think, has been more severely ravaged by the Yankees than any county I have seen. For miles and miles, the country is depopulated, fine mansions are standing untenanted and the fencing of the plantations are all destroyed. Yet in its desolation it is beautiful. It smiles even in its tears. The number of fields everywhere, though unfenced, are covered over with the finest clover and timothy.*

*At present, since we have been in this country, our horses have been well grazed and it is well, for it is impossible to get hay and only 8 lbs. of corn is allowed per day. Lieut. Stokes has been in a week with this squad. Perry is not yet in. I'm looking for him every day. I would not be surprised at any time to hear of another attack on Charleston. May the Lord grant us another triumph. I have yet seen no list of the casualties from the S. C, regts. At Fredericksburg, I hear McGowan's Brigade suffered severely. I have not heard whether James was hurt or not. If you get a paper with the lists, cut them out and send them to me in a letter.*

*Our victories at Charleston, though a bloodless one, and the last at the wilderness and Fredericksburg, overwhelming and disastrous as it was to the Yankees, do not seem to have produced the despondency at the North as the first victory at Fredericksburg did. They still threaten vengeance and the war spirit seems to be on the increase, especially with the government. I think it is doubtful whether Lincoln can raise 500,000 men. If he does, no man can predict when the war will end. He will no doubt raise enough to take the place of the regiments whose term of service is about to expire. If he does no more, their army will still be inferior to the present one.*

*Although the enemy have been baffled almost without interruption for the last 6 months, our prospects for peace are as distant apparently and uncertain as ever indeed. The prospect seems to be gloomier than ever. I believe Lincoln will succeed in suppressing public discussion of his war measures. The peace advocates will be afraid to open their mouths. I am anxious to see the progress and result of Vallandigham's trial. Its issue will seal the fate of the Peace Party.*

*Do write soon. I look with anxiety for every mail hoping to get letters. You have no idea what a pleasure and relaxation from the dullness of camp a letter gives. Tell Anna I have recd no letter from her since the 28th last month and many have recd letters of the 7th and 8th. Just remember me to Cousin Frances and all my friends. You did not tell me whether you had moved or what you were doing. Write often.*

*Your affectionate brother*
*L. Williams*

The carousel had spun Leonard round once more to the banks of the Rappahannock. Soon, it would achieve maximum entropy, hurling him, James, and his mounted comrades into the very vortex of war. James had survived the swirling maelstrom that was Chancellorsville. He and the 14th S.C.V.I. had endured Stonewall's 26 mile flanking march, withstood a Federal assault right up to and over their works, then marched victoriously past the Chancellor House on Sunday in pursuit of Hooker's retreating army. McGowan's brigade suffered 452 casualties. The 14th had 8 killed and 137 wounded in action. Leonard had no way of knowing that James had escaped unscathed.

Stonewall's death meant that Lee had to reorganize his command. He did so by creating three corps of three infantry divisions each. "The Old Warhorse," James Longstreet, retained command of the First Corps. Richard S. Ewell, out of action since losing his leg at Second Manassas, had returned and was given the Second Corps. Stonewall's subordinate, Lieutenant General A.P. Hill, led the Third. Jeb Stuart, with Wade Hampton never too far away, continued to oversee the cavalry, which was now massing near Culpeper Courthouse. The Captain wondered what this sudden concentration of men and horses was all about. For now, only Lee and his corps commanders had to know. It was enough to know that things were going fairly well at home, letters from Anna were arriving, and Spring was here again.

*Camp Near Culpepper, Va.*
*May 19, 1863*

*My Dear Anna*

*I am well again and have a good appetite. Your last letter of the 11th which I recd on the 16th lifted me out of the blues. The last letter I sent you was a mirror of my feelings-gloomy and quarrelsome, which was attributable to my indisposition. I hope you will excuse it. I did not stand in need of your nursing as much as your company. If I get very sick or have a long spell of sickness or I get wounded, I will send for you. We are now occupying the outposts along the Rappahannock- our regiment - the same post we had last winter.*

*I am glad to hear your garden promises well. I would like so much to be at home this season of the year. Do not allow the pigs to be stunted- have them fed enough to keep them fat and growing. I think you may make enough bacon to do you next year with good luck. I should think you could get young frying chickens now and some beef will be brought in. Don't deny yourself such things. Get Mr. Whitmire to buy them for you.*

*My heavy woolen shirts and drawers are getting too warm and I get not anything suitable here. I priced yesterday a common white shirt as Bates' indifferently made. The price was $6. My boy, Middleton, is also out of clothes. Try to get me two home spun shirts, checked or any good color. Make the sleeves a little fuller than the woolen ones and also 2 pair of Knaburgs plus 1 pair socks for myself. I want for Mid 2 coarse colored shirts- 2 pair coppuas or colored pants. If you can get any Linsey get him a round jacket. Have them cut about Ned's size. He's not quite as tall as Ned but I want them large enough. Also send me the pair of cassimere pants I was looking at and spoke of bringing. Put them in the carpetbag. Sergt. Beattie will bring them or Corpl. McClanahan. Don't put anything else but the clothes in it for fear of making it too heavy. I dislike to bother you so much. You will have 3 or 4 weeks to get the clothes up. I fear the greatest difficulty will be in finding suitable cloth. Any kind of coarse checked or striped or colored cotton goods will do for Mid's pants. Get the goods, let it cost what it may, for I cannot get any here.*

*I was delighted with your long letter and good accounts you gave about everything almost. I am sorry to hear of Auntie's disposition. Hope she may soon be well again. I feel under great obligations to her for staying with you and assisting you in so many ways. I feel, while she is with you, you are always well cared for. It makes me more contented while away so long. Remember me to Mrs. Earle and thank her for the present of fruit. I believed I asked you to get Mr. Whitmire to pay Robert Greenfield for a day's hauling. Did Auntie send Alex Greenfield's papers to his wife?*

*I was deceived in the white cow but I think she will come out when the grass comes out more. I think you can bring the red cow to one gallon at a milking. She has improved wonderfully. Keep up their feed and feed well for 3 or 4 weeks yet. Then I think they will do with less. I feel the poultry yard is too small for the chicken to do well and I expect they might be let out into the yard 2 or 3 hours a day without injuring anything. If Mr. Whitmire ever gets any wheat bran, get some to mix with the peas. I expect it will be difficult to get anymore peas. When they give out you must use meal and whatever can be gleaned from the garden. Maj. Alex. might let you have a bu. of wheat bran every week or two.*

*There are 4 or 5 brigades of cav. in the co. More than half the population are exiled and more than half the farms desolated. There is nothing, therefore, to be had to live on but flour and bacon. We have enough, however, of this and we ought not to complain. I have no news. The enemy are on the other side of the river, quiet at present. Write soon. Give my love to your mother and aunts. You told me there was a report of Wm. marrying. Who is the lady? Remember me to Uncle and Nath and all the family. Kiss baby for me.*

*Your affectionate husband*
*L. Williams*

After Chancellorsville, Lee had three courses of action open to him: march west to save Vicksburg, move south to defend Richmond, or go down to the gulf to campaign near New Orleans. Jefferson Davis considered the risks and merits of all three options, but instead he chose a fourth championed by Lee himself. The Army of Northern Virginia would invade Pennsylvania. Lee had no visions of conquering the North; he merely wished to feed his army from the Union table and let Virginians sow their crops in peace. A resounding victory on Union soil would amplify the voices of the Peace Party and perhaps win European favor. Lee's army had won in the Seven Days Battles, Second Manassas, Fredericksburg, and Chancellorsville, and he was certain that success in the enemy's heartland would shatter the will of the Union citizenry once and for all. It was time to take the war north.

Lee began massing his forces at Culpeper, and by June 5 two infantry corps under Longstreet and Ewell had arrived. Six miles northeast, holding the line along the Rappahannock, was Jeb Stuart with no less than 8,000 Confederate horsemen. Their purpose was twofold: keep the location of Lee's forces a secret and when the march down into the Shenandoah Valley was ordered, act as a screen between Hooker's vast army and Lee's smaller invasion force. Stuart knew the vital role his troopers would play in Lee's bold campaign, and he drilled them daily across the rolling swales of timothy and clover at Brandy Station. It was open country, nothing like the swamps around Richmond or the brier-filled, overgrown wilderness near Chancellorsville. At Brandy Station, 8,000 horses and riders could gallop unfettered and at full speed with ample room to parade, wheel, and charge.

Years later, the Old Captain recalled those grand reviews with a blend of pride and contempt. To be sure, the sight of so many magnificent horses and men was as breathtaking a scene as he or the war had ever witnessed. Stuart's Chief of Staff, Major Henry B. McClellan, recalled it vividly.

*Eight thousand cavalry passed under the eye of their commander, in column of squadrons, first at a walk, and then at the charge, while the guns of the artillery battalion, on the hill opposite the stand, gave forth fire and smoke, and seemed almost to convert the pageant into real warfare. It was a brilliant day, and the thirst for the pomp and circumstance of war was fully satisfied.*

But it was not warfare, and the Captain wondered how the stressed horses and fatigued men would respond when it was time for the real thing. These were not the concerns of the flamboyant Stuart as he sat, plumes in full array, near the reviewing stand. Another cavalryman wrote:

*...it was observed that General Stuart's personal charms never showed to better advantage than on that day. Young, gay, and handsome, dressed out in his newest uniform, his polished sword flashing in the sunlight, mounted on his favorite bay mare in gaudiest trappings, his long black plume waving in response to the kisses of the summer breeze, he was superb in every movement, and the personification of grace and gallantry combined.*

One taxing review would have been enough, but Stuart demanded another the next day on June 8. The Captain had pressed his young mare into service for the first, but upon hearing that General Lee himself would be gracing the reviewing stand this time, he saddled up Ruby. To be sure, she no longer possessed the strength and agility she had brought to the war, but she had earned the right, by virtue of her dedication and reliability, to strut her stuff in front of the finest General that had ever commanded a field. Besides, Lee's own horse, Traveler, had aged a bit too. The General would understand. That morning, Mid fed, groomed, and readied Ruby for her command performance while the Captain took a moment to write Anna about the war, weather, and economy.

> *Camp Near Culpeper*
> *June 8, 1863*
>
> *I recd yours on the 26th and the 4th inst. Since then we have been moving and changing camps. On last Friday, Genl. Stuart had another grand division review. Today he has another. I think it probable the army is about to advance. A large body of infantry are already near here. In what direction I do not know, or whether it is the intention to invade or merely advance our lines to draw Hooker away from his entrenchments at Fredericksburg. We are changing our lines and Hooker must change his. We have many rumors from Vicksburg of a most cheering character, but they lack official confirmation. There is no doubt Grant's army has been severely cut up by Kirby Smith. If so, affairs are in a most satisfactory condition out there, notwithstanding Hooker's bombastic assurance to his army and people that the enemy (we) were badly injured and his own loss much lighter than ours. That fact is patent that he was badly whipped and his army knows it. I think our prospect is brightening if Grant's army can be destroyed and demoralized, and thirty or forty thousand troops sent from Vicksburg to support Bragg. I think Rosecrans might be dislodged from his position and Tennessee cleared of Yankees.*
>
> *There has been but little rain for the last month and crops are beginning to suffer. I hope the seasons have been favorable for wheat. From the accounts in the papers, it bids fair to yield well. The critical time for corn is the latter part of June and July. Are the gardens needing rain? How high are the Irish Potatoes? Are they blooming? I expect*

*you are using green peas. Tell me about your tomatoes, beans, onions, squashes & c individually so that I can take a look at the whole garden. Are the young pigs fat? Do they look like they would make porking by next February or 1ˢᵗ March? Does Ned find difficulty in getting them up at night? How does he get on making manure, with hogs, cows penned every night, he ought to save enough to make the garden perfectly rich for the next crop and some to share for the yard to improve trees and grass.*

*Labor is too low in Greenville for the times. I am willing for Ned to work at the usual rates but $1 is not enough considering the price of provisions. Day laborers here get 2 ½ to $5 per day for the farm work. The old rate of hire was 75 cts. per day. Now provisions are 5 prices and also clothing. To show you allowance of bacon ½ lb. today, 182 ½ lbs., 8 oz., 145.60 (bread at present prices 52.00, clothing, hats and shoes 75.00, 5.00). The total is 272.60. Tax is not counted. Loss for rainy days and sickness counted. Doctor bills & c. A good hand ought to get if he is fed at home, $1.50 or $2.00 per day. $1 per day will not support a hand at present prices. As long as he can be employed profitably at home, don't let him hire unless at $1.50 or $2.00 per day. Ask Mr. Whitmire what laborers are worth. Next time I get home I would like to provide him with a horse and wagon and plow. He could use them to do all the work at home to make wages besides.*

*It is remarkably cool, almost enough so for frost. It has been so a week, but last night colder. I hope Auntie is well by this time. I am sorry to hear you also have a cough. I think it is very well you have Clough out in the country but he is in bad hands as he will be allowed to do as he pleases. If they get sick, you had better have them brought home. Remember me to your mother and Auntie and all. Kiss baby for me. Write me. If you examine, you will find you have not written every week. I am nearly out of a hat. If there are any good felt hats in Greenville or Columbia, I wish you would get one for me. Get your father to look for one in Columbia, if none in Greenville and send it with my clothes. Get the money to pay for it from Mr. Whitmire-all my letters are full of wants, but when I get a hat and the clothes you are making, I think I can do well for a year without more.*

*Your affectionate husband*
*L. Williams*

That evening, after Lee's review, all troopers were ordered to prepare their gear and horses for the long ride up to Pennsylvania, which was to begin promptly the next day on June 9. Little did they know that just across the river, Major General Alfred Pleasonton was planning a surprise dawn attack with 10,000 seasoned cavalrymen eager to prove they were now the equal of their Southern counterparts who had so outperformed them throughout the war's first two years. The Union plan was three–pronged. Brigadier General John Buford's 5,500 cavalrymen would quietly cross at Beverly's Ford east of Brandy Station. From the southeast, Brigadier General David M. Gregg's 2,800 would cross down river at Kelly's Ford as would Alfred Napoleon Alexander Duffie's 1,900, who would then proceed to Stevensburg and attack Stuart's forces from directly south. If all three commanders could attack in unison, Jeb's unsuspecting, parade-fatigued cavalry could be destroyed and Lee's position and numbers would be discovered.

At 4:30 in the morning, Buford's men splashed across the Rappahannock initiating what would become the largest cavalry battle ever fought in the Western Hemisphere. Twenty thousand blue and gray uniformed men, 17,000 of them on horseback, would range back and forth across the flowing fields of Brandy Station for 14 dramatic and bloody hours in a series of charges and countercharges the likes of which North America had never seen before or since. Fortunately for Stuart, General William E. "Grumble" Jones, perhaps the best outpost commander in the entire army, was posted in front of Buford. Grumble was true to his name that morning when he and his men had to fight for their very lives in long johns and on empty stomachs. But fight them they did, delaying Buford just long enough and alerting Stuart just in time to gather his stunned and shocked riders together.

From his headquarters atop Fleetwood Hill, Stuart soon grasped the gravity of the situation and rode to the sound of the guns. For the rest of the harrowing day, he would gallop over the undulating, fenceless fields of Culpeper County shifting his cavalrymen from one emergency to another. Hundreds of Union and Confederate troopers were gunned down or slashed to death. Sabers rattled. Cannons roared. Stuart's headquarters were overrun. Nearly the entire Southern cavalry, which had just paraded so splendidly the day before, was at the brink of extinction. Buford knew it and pressed on with Gregg joining him later. Stuart knew it also and desperately deployed and re-deployed his men in order to hold the field. Duffie's 1,900 men, overdue from Stevensburg, could make the difference and make Buford the victor. Where were they?

They were poised right in front of Captain Leonard Williams and a handful of Confederate cavalrymen who had been instructed to head toward Stevensburg earlier that morning. Major Thomas J. Lipscomb, 2nd South Carolina Cavalry, had given the actual order. "The Second South Carolina Cavalry, commanded by Colonel M. C. Butler, left camp on the morning of June 9th, with 220 men. After sending 30 men, commanded by Captain [L] Williams, to picket at Carrico's Mills, he was to hold his command as a reserve at Brandy Station." Now, Leonard's meager two and a half dozen men supported by the small 4th Virginia regiment were staring at Duffie's entire division of Union cavalry. Outnumbered by nearly 10 to 1 and 8 artillery pieces to 1, they needed a miracle.

In the vicinity was Wade Hampton's younger brother Lt. Col. Frank Hampton with 20 men, who also had been ordered to do what he could to hold Duffie until Butler could deploy the rest of his men racing to the scene. Meanwhile, Williams and his unit were already in the thick of it and between two of Duffie's regiments. As Leonard chanced upon the road just traveled by Duffie's column, he hoped to cut through the woods toward the battle now raging at Brandy. But it was too late, his men were cut off on all sides, so he calmly waited in the thick trees until support might help extricate them from their predicament. He had, however, managed to send off a courier to Butler and Wade Hampton with details of their dire circumstances. A few minutes later, Frank Hampton finally arrived with 36 men. Hampton almost immediately encountered the tip of Duffie's column and boldly charged. Rather than stand and crush the few Confederates attacking them, Duffie's men inexplicably retired and awaited further orders.

Each minute was now critical. Butler needed every spare second to set his defenses on Hansborough's Ridge, the perfect place to conceal his numbers. Every minute that passed with Duffie not on the main battlefield alongside Gregg in the assault on Stuart was critical. Frank Hampton needed time to consider his options with 1,900 of the enemy waiting just down the road. Colonel Williams Wickham's 4th Virginia Cavalry was racing the clock in order to get up in time to reinforce Butler. Leonard's heart pumped furiously as he and his men fidgeted nervously in the woods. Surrounded, he and his fellow South Carolinians wondered if they'd ever escape. For Captain Williams, the minutes seemed like hours.

Suddenly, Frank Hampton ran out of time. Just as he was about to close back and unite with the 4th Virginia, Wickham's men emerged from the tight woods in an awkward attack position. They had to instantly wheel to the right by fours, and while in the midst of the maneuver, were discovered by the enemy who immediately charged. Frank Hampton's scratch force was instantly overrun. Stuart's aide, Major Henry McClellan later wrote that, "In a moment they were swept to the side of the road, and the full force of the charge fell upon the Fourth Virginia. Colonel Hampton, while engaging one of the enemy with his sabre, was shot through the body by another, and was mortally wounded." In Wade Hampton's autobiography, the death of his younger brother is grimly described. "His big, handsome face was slashed terribly by a saber," and as his wounded horse ran off, so did Wickham's men. While panic apparently possessed the 4th Virginia Regiment, it did not take hold of Leonard Williams and his small unit attached to it. Neither retreat or attack was an option. His meager force was separated from Butler's, and it would have meant annihilation had he attacked Duffie's column on his own. Leonard was no fool and he was damned if he would throw his men away in some useless charge here. He stood fast and wisely held his force in reserve.

Having split the 4th Virginia in half and sent them running in disorder, Duffie then turned his attention to Butler's 200 on nearby Hansborough's Ridge and began shelling them with his horse artillery. The specific targets of their bombardment were the only two figures still on horseback up on the ridge, M. C. Butler and his loyal scout Captain Will Farley. Butler recollected what happened next.

> *Our horses were facing in opposite directions, mine facing the enemy. A twelve –pound shell from the enemy's gun on the hill (we had evidently been located by a field glass), struck the ground about thirty steps from our position in the open field, ricocheted and passed through my right leg above the ankle, through Farley's horse, and took off his right leg at the knee. My horse bounded in the air and threw me, saddle and all, flat on my back in the road, when the poor fellow moved off with his entrails hanging out toward the clover field where he had been grazing in the early morning, and died there, as I was afterwards informed. Farley's horse dropped in the road, terribly lacerated, and Farley fell with his head on the horse's side...Farley's horse was struggling in the last agonies and I was afraid would injure him with*

*his hoofs. I therefore requested the gentleman present to move him on the other side of the road, and it was done. With that splendid chivalric nature in which he much excelled he said, 'Gentleman, return to Colonel Butler's assistance...he requires your attention more than I do.' His leg was taken off as smoothly as if it had been cut with a saw right at the knee joint. Mine was shattered above the ankle and dangled by the skin and the cavalry boots that I wore. After its mission of destruction had been thus accomplished, the shell dropped near Farley's horse.*

Lieutenant John T. Rhett was one of the men who tended to Farley at the side of the road. He bore witness to an everlasting, defining display of quiet courage and heroism.

*We went to Captain Farley...He was very cool, in fact pleasant and smiling, though evidently in great pain. Just as we were about to send him away, he called me to him. And pointing to the leg that had been cut off by the ball, and which was lying near by, he asked me to bring it to him. I did so. He took it, pressed it to his bosom as one would a child, and said smiling, 'It is an old friend, gentlemen, and I do not wish to part from it.' Chestnut and myself shook hands with him, bidding him good-by, and expressing the hope that we should soon again see him. He said, 'Goodbye gentlemen, and forever. I know my condition, and we will not meet again. I thank you for your kindness. It is a pleasure to me that I have fallen into the hands of good Carolinians at my last moment.' Courteously, even smilingly, he nodded his head to us as the men bore him away. He died within a few hours. I have never seen a man whose demeanor, in the face of certain, painful, and quick death, was so superb. I have never encountered anything so brave from first to last.*

With young Hampton dead and Butler gravely wounded, command of the 2nd South Carolina Cavalry fell to Major Thomas J. Lipscomb, the very officer who had ordered Captain Williams and his 20 men down to Stevensburg that morning. Lipscomb rallied his men, but just as Duffie was about to launch a deadly counterassault, the Federal commander received urgent orders to hightail it up to the main Brandy Station battlefield in order to join the ebbing fight.

Duffie left the 3rd Pennsylvania Cavalry behind to keep the Confederates in check, but in effect it was he that had been held in check just long enough. The 2nd South Carolina Cavalry had single-handedly halted an entire division of cavalry in its tracks. A few hours later, Butler was taken to a farmhouse owned by a Mrs. Fitzhugh, and there his leg was successfully amputated at five o'clock in the evening.

Thanks in large degree to a late afternoon charge by Wade Hampton's hard-riding Carolinians, Stuart held the Brandy Station field, but he and his once invincible cavalrymen had lost much of their luster. The cool cavalier, who twice led daring raids around entire armies, had been caught completely off guard. Federal commander John Buford had outgeneraled him in many respects in the battle, and his mounted bluecoats proved that they were now the equal of the Confederates. One trooper of the 8th New York wrote, "The rebels were going to have a review of their cavalry that day, but our boys reviewed them." Stuart's own aide, Major Henry McClellan, admitted, "This battle...made the Federal Cavalry. The fact is that up to June 9th, 1863, the Confederate cavalry did have its own way...and the record of their success becomes almost monotonous...But after that time we held our ground only by hard fighting." The days of Confederate cavalry domination were over. In time, the Federal cavalry, with the likes of Phil Sheridan, John Buford, David Gregg, and even a young George Armstrong Custer, would overwhelm them with more and more capable riders and healthy horses.

After the war, the Old Captain engaged in plenty of spirited porch debates concerning the near disaster at Brandy Station. He commended Stuart's actions on the day of battle, but at the same time questioned why he had so many riders parading and so few watching the other side of the Rappahannock. On one particular summer evening on the old wraparound porch, with cigars and without the ladies, the Old Captain consumed a few more brandies than he required, and offered up this scenario concerning June 9, 1863. At Brandy Station and in all battles, he began, the "what ifs," "might haves," and "not quites" ultimately determine the outcome. What if his 20 men, Frank Hampton's 36, and later Butler's 200 weren't sent south to Stevensburg? What if Duffie's 1,900 had ridden up unchecked and joined with Gregg's and Buford's divisions instead of not quite getting there? Would their numbers have turned the tide? Might Stuart's entire cavalry have been swept off the plain? What if Lee's infantry had to come out of hiding to assist? Almost certainly the Gettysburg Campaign would have been reconsidered. Surely, Jeb Stuart wouldn't have had the craving to atone for his near defeat and scathing reviews in the Southern papers by taking risks on the advance north. Finally, he proclaimed that Gettysburg was really lost at Brandy. The events of that day proved they were now vulnerable and because of Buford's daring at dawn, Lee's invasion began one day late. Was the 24-hour delay critical? He answered his own question as he poured his final brandy of the night. Most assuredly it was. One single day difference meant that the two armies would not have met...how...when...or where they did and thus, not only Gettysburg, but the very course of history was changed forever.

Two days after the great cavalry affair, he wrote of his narrow escape and the grit of Butler's South Carolinians.

*Camp Near Brandy Station*
*June 11, 1863*

*My Dear Anna,*

*As I do not know when I can have another opportunity, I take the present leisure hour to write you a short letter. We have now on hand 3 days cooked rations with the intention probably of an advanced movement. Genl. Robt. Lee's army is near here. Before yesterday, the 9th, we had the most general cavalry fight that has been made during the war. Nearly all of our forces and perhaps 15,000 Yankee cavalry were engaged. We were waked up by the booming of cannon in the direction of the Rappahannock Bridge. We were moved off as early as possible towards the scene of action and halted at Brandy Station to be held as a reserve and was immediately ordered to take my squadron to Carico's Mill and watch all the roads leading from Kelly Ford to that point. I had just established my vidette position and was moving forward towards another road leading into the same road as a point higher up and ascertained that a squadron of Yankees had already passed by towards Stephensburg. I galloped back to my videttes to put them on alert. When a regiment and then a brigade of Yankees came in sight and drew up in battle line, I attracted their attention. They threw out their skirmishers the length of a mile in front of me. They advanced briskly. I kept out my videttes and placed my squadron back across the stream, dismounted the men to hold them in check as long as possible.*

*In the meantime, gave Col. Butler and Genl. Hampton intelligence of the situation of affairs. All my couriers got through safely, but when I began to fall back from the mile, I discovered that a Yankee regiment was in front of me, the rear vidette, having been, I suppose, captured. I was thus completely cut off, a brigade in my rear, a regiment on the road in my front and neither more than 500 yards from me. On my right the artillery fight was going on and knew nothing of the situation. I had, therefore, but one alleviation. I had but 30 men. I turned the column into the woods and endeavored to head there and get to Brandy. On nearing the place, I halted the column and went towards the road to reconnoiter and found they had passed upon and heard 2 or 3 consecutive charges. I then endeavored to get out on the road that leads from Brandy to Stephensburg. On hearing it again, halted to examine. Seeing no Yankees, I ordered the column forward, but we had been discovered and the whole regiment charged down like an avalanche, but were discovered in time to wheel about and get back in the woods. I discovered that I was encompassed on all sides and then carried my squadron back into the densest wood I could find with the intention of remaining till night and then running the gauntlet through their lines. But by 3 ock my videttes reported that the enemy had been driven back and that we held Brandy and Stephensburg. It was universally supposed we had been captured. I attribute our safety to a divine providence.*

*I had the misfortune to lose one of my own, Jno Ligon, and one of Company D whom I left behind to guard my rear with instructions to keep 150 yards behind. I selected Ligon for his soldierly qualities and experience and regret very much his loss. I have every reason, however, to believe he is a prisoner. Our regt. & the 4ᵗʰ Virginia were opposed to the force that advanced by way of Stephensburg, which was no less than 6 or 7 regiments. Our regiment did not number more than two hundred men. Two squadrons were dismounted as sharpshooters and my squadron on piquet. There were, therefore, only 2 small squadrons, numbering in all about 60 men in front to resist a brigade supported by a small Virginia regiment. They also had 8 pieces of artillery and we only 1 small piece and by some oversight or by mismanagement, our small force was turned to the right about in order to move them off.*

*Too late the consequence as the enemy were on them at once. When they broke in disorder, the Virginia regiment, although unassailed, broke. I do not blame the men for it. It would have been disastrous to meet the enemy. The officers ought to have drawn them out of the way. There was a blunder in not sending a stronger force to Stephensburg.*

*One regiment of this small command was detached from the brigade. Genl. Hampton, with his brigade, was near Brandy and I have no doubt rescued the day. He and his brigade distinguished themselves and made the most brilliant of charges and saved our artillery and Stuart's headquarters. This country is under obligation to Hampton and his brigade. Our victory was decisive, drove the enemy across the river before night, our loss estimated at 700 and among them it was our misfortune to lose our gallant and high-toned Lieut. Col. Hampton. Col. Butler was severely wounded in the ankle, which had to be amputated, the loss of privates trifling, some 15 or 20 missing. It was stated by prisoners that thirty-five-thousand Yankees crossed over. There was also a brigade of infantry. There must have been at least 15,000 engaged. Our forces, not over 6,000 or 7,000.*

The Old Captain opened the next envelope and checked his trusty pocket watch. It read 10:30 A.M. At that precise time, on the morning after the battle, the Confederate dead were being buried where they fell on the rolling plains of Brandy Station. Stuart ordered the dreadful work to be done quickly. Lee's army was heading north.

# CHAPTER ELEVEN
## A MYSTICAL BELIEF

*Fear not, I am with you;*
*be not dismayed, I am your God.*
*I will strengthen you, and help you,*
*and uphold you with my right hand of justice.*
*Yes, all shall be put to shame and disgrace*
*who vent their anger against you;*
*Those shall perish and come to naught who offer resistance.*
*...They shall be as nothing at all who do battle with you.*
Isaiah 41:10

On the misty morning of Sunday, June 21, a petite and pious twenty-four year old mother and her squirming two and a half year old sat side by side on the end of a hard pine pew in the last row of the Greenville's Second Presbyterian Church. On that Sabbath, fifty-six year old General Robert E. Lee sat in a hard saddle atop Traveler and alongside James Longstreet, in front of the column heading north along the Blue Ridge. Thirty-nine year old Captain Leonard Williams found himself on his young mare comparing damp but new cotton shirts with Mid, who was leading Ruby as they sloshed their way up the muddy Upperville Turnpike. Anna prayed for Leonard and for the little wiggler next to her to behave. Lee prayed for divine guidance and good fortune ahead. Leonard prayed for the health and well being of his family and each man of Company K.

The mission of Stuart's Cavalry after Brandy Station was to screen Ewell's 2nd Corps, guard his supply wagons, and keep Pleasonton's Union Cavalry from capturing any mountain passes as Lee's army pressed on toward Pennsylvania. On this Sunday morning, the rains had ceased and the sky had cleared, but lightning struck just as the Confederates cleared the mountain village of Upperville. Vincent's Brigade, over 1,500 strong and supported by artillery and three brigades of Gregg's Cavalry, hit Stuart's force and after hours of fierce fighting, the Confederates were in peril. At stake was the secrecy of Lee's movement and the lives of the 2nd South Carolina troopers. On the top of a nearby ridge overlooking the action, Wade Hampton watched the scene unfold. He knew he was in trouble. In addition to being severely outnumbered, his cumbersome, old-fashioned muzzle-loaders were no match for the Union's state of the art, repeating Spencer Rifles. He ordered Cobb Legion Colonel P. M. B. Young to fall back to the next crest, but just as the order was given, a large gun from Hart's Battery blew up. The ammunition exploded, blowing the cannon from its carriage and stampeding the horses. "Well," observed Hampton soberly, "I am afraid Hart has lost a gun this time." The retiring brigade had no choice but to abandon the piece, one of Hampton's prized Blakely's— the only gun Hart ever lost in battle.

For ten hours, sharp fighting raged as Hampton's men were caught up in a deadly pattern of falling back, regrouping, holding on, then retreating once more. Men were shot and slashed. One was Angus P. Brown of the 1st South Carolina, who lay by a bridge wounded in the leg and hand. Federal troopers tried to run him over but their horses, more humane than their riders, could not be forced to trample him. If the rest of the riders were to survive as well, someone needed to dramatically alter the course of battle. Not surprisingly, Wade Hampton did so. The nearest regiment to him was the 1st North Carolina. He sped up alongside them, rose to his stirrups and hoisted his giant saber. "First North Carolina, follow me!" he thundered, and galloped directly at the enemy columns. The Tarheels cheered and raced off behind him. Other units formed and charged. "Give it to them!" Hampton yelled.

The young mare responded instantly to Leonard's sharp spur as the 2nd Cavalry followed up the North Carolinians in three separate charges. Adjutant James Moore of the 2nd South Carolina was nearly lost forever in one of the assaults.

> *As I reached the ditch, I nearly rode upon a Federal dragoon, who was lying in the grass with a terrible saber wound in his head. He was lying face down, and raised his head and groaned as if the blood was smothering him. I started to dismount to turn him over on his back. Just at that moment two balls struck my horse, one barely missing my knee, the other striking him behind the left ear. He fell dead and rolled over on me with my right leg under him. I tried in vain to draw my leg out from under my horse, and then I realized that, lying hidden by the tall grass, I was liable to be trampled to death by the horses of our own men, when they advanced to the charge...The regiment had seen my horse go down with me, and thought we were both killed...Major*

> *Lipscomb...sent three men, who raised my horse off me and dragged me out from under him.*

Two troopers from Leonard's company were not as fortunate. Private Jaudon was struck in the head by a minie ball, and Private F. Y. Salmons received a horrible wound, the entire side of his face ripped away by a shell fragment. Finally, Gregg was driven back with heavy losses, including 80 men taken prisoner. The Confederates retired to Ashby's Gap and held it. Hampton's daring and decisiveness carried the day and Stuart's report deemed his efforts "brilliant." Upperville was the third and most deadly of three cavalry clashes in the mountain passes. As a result of the cavalry fights in Aldie, Middleburg, and Upperville, Stuart lost 510 in killed, wounded, and missing, while Union Colonel J. I. Gregg reported an even greater loss of 827.

Later that Sunday evening, Anna reminded Carrie about appropriate behavior while in church. Lee instructed his subordinates in camp that he would not tolerate theft, pillaging, or any form of insensitivity toward the local citizenry as they advanced closer to enemy soil. Leonard, as usual, directed Anna to write more often.

*Camp on Shenandoah*
*June 24, 1863*

*My Dear Anna,*

> *With the prospect of getting a letter to Winchester today, I write you a brief note to say that I am well. We have been fighting and marching constantly since we left Brandy. We had a most terrific day's work of it on the 21st. The fight commenced at 8 ock and lasted until 6 in the evening. During the whole day, we were compelled to fall back pressed and flanked by at least 3 to 1. Our brigade lost a good many men, mostly in prisoners. The Yankees, I think, suffered most in killed and wounded. I had 2 men severely, but I think not dangerously wounded, F.Y. Salmons and Jaudon, the 1st by a shell and the latter by a miniball, both in the face. Joel Ketchum, slightly wounded in the leg, and also Lieut. Perry, bruised on the leg by a spent ball, the latter two wounds very slight. Several were shot through the clothes and had their sabers struck. We, however, held the gap and next day or in the night the enemy retreated.*

228

*We are within 20 miles of Winchester and have orders to be ready at a minutes notice. Genl. Lee's combinations are so complicated we cannot unravel them. The papers will give you an account of our late successes in this quarter. Ewell is following in the footsteps of his lamented predecessor. We hear nothing late from Vicksburg. I trust things are going on well there.*

*It has been 2 weeks since I have had an opportunity to write you and it has been nearly that long since I have heard from you. The facilities for the mail will be, I expect, for some time, very poor, but write often. I will get them all. My company enjoys good health. My love to all and tell me all about baby-as I will be so far away you must write oftener. I hope your mother is still with you.*

> *Your affectionate husband*
> *L. Williams*

Leonard's supper consisted of some hardtack and two green apples, a king's fare in comparison to what was being consumed inside the crumbling, besieged fortress of Vicksburg that night. Soldiers were surviving on quarter rations. By June, almost half were on the sick list, many suffering from typhus and scurvy. Skinned rats and tough mule meat appeared in the markets. Dogs and cats were eaten almost gratefully. Living under siege drove soldiers to the brink of insanity. The hearts of Southerners were heavy and Sunday evening prayers were offered up for the starving and suffering at the hand of the merciless Ulysses S. Grant. Very soon, however, Dixie's eyes turned north to the Army of Northern Virginia. Vicksburg was simply too appalling to think about. Lee's glorious second invasion, however, filled them with hope. If Vicksburg was destined to fall, Lee would surely succeed in his plan to occupy Harrisburg, destroy Washington's communications, and occupy Philadelphia. It was a bold undertaking that fueled Southern hopes so much so that many deemed the campaign not only brilliant but certain to succeed. Washington would shake with fear and Lincoln's cabinet and citizenry would learn what invasion really meant. With Philadelphia captured, the Confederacy would dictate the terms.

Just west of the Blue Ridge rolled a sea of gray. General A.P. Hill's corps with Gen. Richard Anderson, Maj. Gen. Henry Heth, and Maj. Gen. William Pender as division commanders led the way. Ewell's corps with Maj. Gen. Jubal Early, Maj. Gen. Robert Rodes, and Maj. Gen. Edward Johnson as division commanders followed. Bringing up the rear was Longstreet's First Corps with Gen. Lafayette McLaws, Gen. John Bell Hood, and Maj. Gen. George Pickett as division commanders. Seventy-five thousand men were now heading north through Stonewall Jackson's former stomping grounds without him. The sight of this grand assemblage of veterans marching up the Shenandoah Valley was breathtaking. The Union army confronting them was even more so. Deep blue companies of 100 men merged to form regiments of about 1,000. They in turn grew to become brigades consisting of 2,500. The brigades formed divisions numbering about 6,000. Finally, the divisions, three or more together, formed five corps. The grand, brass-buckled, Federal army on route to battle Robert E. Lee's three corps numbered over 100,000. The men, horses, and artillery moved in on different roads that were separated by several miles, with the total force stretching out some 7 miles long.

As the rebels moved into Pennsylvania and the Army of the Potomac crossed its namesake on June 25, the course of events was dramatically changed by Jeb Stuart. Lee had given his cavalry commander discretionary orders to shadow Hooker's force, following the route he deemed most wise to later link up with the main Confederate army, and provide the numbers, location, and specifics concerning the enemy. By June 28, Hooker had been replaced by General George Meade, and Stuart was nowhere to be found. While Lee groped his way blindly north, unaware that Meade's entire army was in hot pursuit, Stuart had decided to ride around the enemy for a third time, put a scare into Washington, and launch a raid of his own. Stuart did manage to capture 125 supply wagons, but it was reconnaissance, not ammunition, that Lee so sorely needed. Circumnavigating a briskly marching 5 by 7-mile force proved to be impossible and by June 30, Stuart's plumes were far away and Lee's feathers were ruffled. His heart palpitations were now coupled with a most inopportune bout of diarrhea, but it was the absence of Stuart and knowledge of the enemy's disposition that caused Lee the most distress.

Captain Williams was on edge as well. His duty was dangerous and exhausting. Worse, he was behind enemy lines and separated from his regiment. Doubt and grave concern stirred within him. On the eve of the epic battle of Gettysburg, he wrote a stress-filled letter home.

> *Camp 5 miles N. of Chambersburg, Pa.*
> *June 30, 1863*

*My Dear Anna,*

*Hearing of a probability of getting a letter through today, I write you a short note to say I am quite well. I have been in Pa. three days. The people seem tolerably indifferent about the invasion. They seem, most of them, careless about it, except those whose property is taken for use of the army. We know nothing of the movement and purpose of Genl. Lee. It is reported that our army (Genl. Ewell's) having occupied Carlisle, proceeded to Harrisburg, and took possession of that place. Private property is respected, the most stringent orders are enforced against plundering, forage and provisions are paid for. Everything is flourishing here, no visible evidence that they are engaged in a gigantic war. Farms and villages are very neat and pretty and the aggregate wealth is considerable, but I think no great wealth among individuals. There is a commonness in the appearance of all the men and women I have seen. I have seen none above mediocrity in intellect or personal appearance.*

*I think Genl. Lee's army can go through the W. S. or wherever Genl. Lee may wish to carry it. It's a fine army of veterans in excellent discipline and health and unbounded confidence in themselves and officers. May God grant us a successful and fortunate issue. I do not think Hooker is near us yet but suppose he is on his way. I am, at present, unpleasantly situated. I was left, my own horses having lost their shoes, with some 50 men to have their horses shod and the brigade went back towards Warrenton, I supposed only for a day or two. The trains were ordered forward. I was to wait orders to report to the regiment. I have recd none and have heard nothing from the brigade since. I am looking now every hour for them. I dislike very much to be separated from the regiment. Our horses are faring finely as much corn and clover as they can eat. If we could have a week's rest, they would get in capital condition.*

*I have been on very important duty since getting into this state, being in charge of a squadron, guarding a heavy ordnance train, which was in the rear. At one time, for 36 hours, I was on my horse without a wink of sleep. I have spent 2 nights here and have rested and am ready again. Col. Black's here and is in command of the division (or that portion who came on as we did to get horses shod). Write as usual. I may get your letters and it will be a great satisfaction to hear from you. Tell Ned I have no objection to his request but must spend but 2 nights in the week from home. I will write to you as often as I have opportunity. My love to all.*

*Your affectionate husband*
*L. Williams*

As the Old Captain placed the letter in the neat pile of those already read, he recalled with renewed distress that the last days of June were perhaps his edgiest of the entire war. While respecting the enemy, he had never feared them, but like any soldier he feared the unknown. He knew that he, along with the superior half of Lee's cavalry force, were far from where they should have been. Not knowing where the main body was, including his youngest brother whom he hadn't heard from since the past winter, shrouded him in worry and helplessness. The proverbial, double-edged sword had been driven deep in Leonard's gut. There was no infantry to protect his company while in turn, his cavalrymen had left Lee's infantry blindfolded. Surprisingly, the numbers say that throughout the course of the war, Stuart spent only 28 days raiding, but in the waning days of June, even a few days would cost him dearly.

On the 30th of June, Stuart, bogged down by his captured trains, neared Hanover, Pennsylvania, where he was delayed by a spirited full day engagement with the Wolverines of George Custer's brigade. Stuart, the legendary cavalier, was beaten and nearly captured by his dashing blond haired opponent. Worse, the battle slowed Stuart's men and forced them even further out of their way to the north. Two days later, Custer confronted Stuart, Hampton, and Captain William's worn down riders again at Hunterstown. Stuart, with the help of Hampton's South Carolinians, prevailed, but he was forced to detour yet again from the battle now roaring below him in Gettysburg.

Since June 9 at Brandy Station until July 2 when they finally reached Gettysburg half dead in their saddles, Leonard and the exhausted men of Stuart's Cavalry had either marched or fought every single day in that punishing 24 day span. Finally, after a nightlong spirit-breaking 30-mile march, Stuart limped into Lee's Headquarters. His commander recognized the mixture of distress, fatigue, and regret etched across his tardy subordinate's face. Lee noted Stuart's torn uniform, which he had always endeavored to keep in first-rate order. He studied the general's parched lips, raw hands, and spent horse. Stuart averted his eyes. He could not look his commander in the face. He knew he had let Lee down and left him blind in the face of the enemy. Lee also turned away and his anger quickly faded. Moving to the maps on a knotty kitchen table, he turned his attention to the Federal army stretching fishhook fashion from Culp's Hill across the top of Cemetery Ridge.

Barely possessing the strength to even grip the reins, Captain Williams had wearily ridden into camp with the rest of the Legion. A moment's rest and a cool drink of water beckoned, but there was no time for that. He left Ruby and the packhorse with Mid then rode at a full gallop toward the mass of soldiers gathering behind Seminary Ridge. It was Longstreet's Division making last minute preparations for an overdue attack on the Union left flank. He found a gruff First Lieutenant who curtly pointed him toward the hastily erected hospital tents in the rear.

The smell led the way and by the time he had found his destination, the stench was overpowering. Already, the dead and wounded had overflowed the tents and spilled out on to the surrounding grounds. Wails of pain and cursing cries engulfed the place. Rebel yells had become muffled whimpers. Like huge, ghastly carrion birds, surgeons hovered briefly over one wound, then moved on to another. Blue flies feasted on the dying, and mosquitoes tormented the living. The unmistakable odor of foul bandages, sweat, urine, and vomit hung in the humid July air. Sawed off arms and legs were heaped in a grotesque pile. Maggots would come. Gangrene was lurking. Infection was waiting. Death was already here. But the one he was searching for, yet hoping not to find, was nowhere to be found.

Could James have survived yesterday's bloody advance unscathed? If so, it would have been nothing short of a miracle. The morning before, he and the 14th South Carolina Volunteer Infantry had marched at first light toward Gettysburg. Lee had ordered a concentration of all his forces at Gettysburg because the twelve roads and turnpikes converging there made it the logical place for his divisions to mass. John Buford, the astute Union Cavalry commander who had nearly captured Stuart's entire cavalry a few weeks earlier at Brandy, recognized the geographic significance of Gettysburg at once and had posted his outnumbered force on high ground anticipating the enemy advance that he knew would come. Confederate Major General Henry Heth encountered him first. A skirmish was sparked and the mighty battle was on. Artillery fired away. Union General John Reynolds, born and raised in nearby

Lancaster, raced to the scene with his infantry and the tough Iron Brigade. An hour later, Reynolds lay dead, drilled through the skull by a single shot from a sharpshooter. Around him lay many of the Union infantry, dead or dying. But the line held.

James and the seasoned 14th would have made their old commander Stonewall Jackson proud that morning. Now, under A.P. Hill, the South Carolinians double-quicked it up past Heth's and Pettigrew's fought-out brigades. In the advance, W. D. Pender received a wound from which he would die seventeen days later. Still, they rolled ever forward driving the Federals back to, into, and eventually clear through town. They did so at a terrible cost as James' superior, Colonel Abner Perrin of McGowan's Brigade, wrote after the battle.

> *We...moved forward...and as soon as the brigade commenced ascending the hill in front, we were met by a furious storm of musketry and shells from the enemy's batteries to the left of the road near Gettysburg...The brigade received the enemy's fire without faltering; rushed up the hill at a charge, driving the enemy without difficulty to their last position at Gettysburg. We continued the charge without opposition, except from the artillery, which maintained a most galling fire upon us, until we got within 200 yards from a grove near the college, the brigade received the most destructive fire of musketry I have ever been exposed to. We continued to press forward, however, without firing, until we reached the edge of the grove. Here the Fourteenth Regiment was staggered for a moment by the severity and destructiveness of the enemy's musketry. It looked as though this regiment was entirely destroyed. I here found myself without support either on the right or the left...This gave the enemy an enfilading fire upon the Fourteenth. This regiment, under the lead of Lieutenant Colonel Brown and Major E. Croft, most gallantly stood its ground.*

Hour by hour, both sides furiously poured thousands upon thousands of men into and around the town of Gettysburg. Neither Lee nor Meade had intended to fight here and neither commander had reached the field. When Lee arrived later on in the afternoon, his eyes almost immediately found the high ground that the enemy occupied. It was good ground, easily defended like the heights Lee employed to slaughter Burnside's men back in December at Fredericksburg. It was known as Cemetery Hill in these parts, an apt name. He studied the hills that rose before him once more. There was envy in Lee's eyes.

Back in the hospital tent, the eyes of Captain Leonard Williams settled on those of First Sergeant James Williams. For seven months he had longed to peer into them …but anywhere but here. There, third from the end, nearly lost in the second to the last row of the wounded, he rested. The older brother took a mental inventory, hurriedly scanning the younger. He looked down at an empty face, drawn and pale. Though his eyes were welling up, James resolutely refused to allow his tears to escape. His lips were parched and powder-blackened. Blood had spattered his gray cap and crimson dots were interspersed between his brown freckles. Curiously, only one muddied brogan lay next to the strewn hay that served as his bed. As James slowly removed the brown blanket that covered him from the waist down, the Captain realized why. His right foot had been blown nearly completely off, leaving behind nothing but a bloody bit of his heel. Tendons and sinew had been clumsily wrapped in dirty cotton. Amputation was unavoidable. James knew it. Leonard knew it.

James fitfully sipped from his brother's canteen then spoke of the horror of the day before. He informed Leonard that Dick Ewell had hesitated and failed to drive the Federal right flank off the hills, and that Old Pete Longstreet was now preparing to storm their left. It hurt James to talk and what he said pained Leonard. Then, the Captain reached into his saddlebag and found the daguerreotype of Anna and Carrie and knelt down beside his fallen 33-year old brother. James managed to summon up a half smile. An hour later, the Captain kissed him farewell and rode off to inspect his exhausted company and inquire if Doctor Taylor might kindly see to James' amputation. The respected physician had performed this duty so capably just weeks before for Colonel Butler, but now Doc Taylor was already off seeing to more wounded than he could ever hope to save.

That evening, the dead and soon to be dead lay hidden among the boulders in Devil's Den, strewn across a Wheat Field and a Peach Orchard, and in between the rocky crags of Little Round Top. Although Longstreet's tardy assault had come within a whisker of succeeding, the valor of Joshua Chamberlain's 20th Maine had held the high ground just long enough for last minute reinforcements to maintain possession of the heights Lee so sorely coveted. That night, as Leonard slept, James prayed, and even more down in Vicksburg died of starvation, Robert E. Lee pondered his options for July 3, Gettysburg's fateful and final day. The outcome of the war hung in the balance. More than ever, Southerners clung to their unshakeable "mystical belief."

The South as a whole held fast to the belief that God, and only the Almighty alone, would decide the war. If He deemed the South and its cause righteous, He would grant them deliverance and a crowning victory. In the heart of churchgoing Dixie, right made right, and no matter how many men, cannons, bullets and generals Lincoln hurled against them, the fighting spirit of the natural born Southern soldier would overcome all odds. This axiom had already been proven true at Manassas, Fredericksburg, and Chancellorsville. Surely, it would earn them glory yet again at Gettysburg. Adding to this confidence was the mystical belief that the war was in reality, a second, purifying revolution that the founding fathers had foreseen and made allowances for in the Constitution. Finally, while the Confederacy might be short on men, rations and money, the soldiers and people had a never-ending supply of faith in the quiet man they considered the finest general to ever walk the earth. Lee was more than the equal of Alexander the Great, William the Conqueror, or Napoleon. He was David incarnate. If a handful of smooth stones could slay the mighty Goliath and make David ruler of a new kingdom, then certainly Lee's shining array of 75,000 would slay Lincoln's heathen force and make the South overseers of a new democratic country. In early July, God made up his mind.

The morning of July 3, 1863 was picture perfect. Bright red Mackintosh apples hung in the sun-drenched orchards of Adams County. At seven minutes after one in the afternoon, basket loads of the red fruit crashed to the hard ground, shook from their branches by a barrage of artillery fire from James Longstreet's 150 belching guns. The ungodly noise rumbled across the mountains and rattled windows as far away as Pittsburgh. The aftershock nearly hurled Leonard from his saddle when a startled Ruby reared up upon hearing the nearby blasts. The old girl had heard the crash of cannon before, but nothing like the deafening roar that echoed from Seminary Ridge.

Out to the fields of the Rummel Farm three miles east the guns thundered. Here Stuart, with four brigades including Wade Hampton's, had been ordered that morning as part of Lee's final day battle plan. They were to guard Lee's left flank, then turn the Union right in the event the Confederate infantry captured Cemetery Ridge. That horrific cannon fire would be sustained for hours, the objective being to soften up the Union center, which would hopefully enable a three o'clock charge aimed at the middle of the Federal stronghold to succeed. Ewell had failed to turn the right the first day. Longstreet had fallen just short of turning the left on the second day. Today, over Longstreet's strong protest, Lee would attack Meade dead center in his heart. As General George Pickett readied his and two of Hill's divisions for what would soon become the single most heroic and hopeless charge ever attempted in the entire war, four brigades of Stuart's cavalry were fighting for their very lives a few miles away. None fought more tenaciously than Wade Hampton himself.

Still dazed and smarting from a nasty head wound suffered the day before at Hunterstown, Hampton rode forward with his saber drawn. Captain William Miller of the Third Pennsylvania watching from the edge of the woods recorded a stirring account of what happened next. "Row upon row of galloping horses bore down, flags and guidons fluttering, sabers flashing. Loud rose the rebel yell, challenging the sudden roar of Gregg's artillery that fired into the squadrons. Yankee carbines barked forth volley after volley…Shell and shrapnel ripped lanes in the riders, who rode on without faltering."

Brigadier General David Gregg's division and Brigadier General George Custer's brigade were here to accomplish what they had failed to do at Brandy Station. Stuart and Hampton recognized a fire in the enemy the likes of which they'd never witnessed before. Beneath the sweltering July sun, the two bitter foes raced headlong into one another and for an instant, the resulting collision nearly drowned out Longstreet's artillery barrage going on near Little Round Top. Hampton's biographer Manly Wade Wellman would later write:

> *Columnhead drove into columnhead at a gallop. The sound of the impact was like the crash of falling timbers. Arms, legs, ribs were broken in that multiple collision. Riders flew from their saddles and horses somersaulted head over heels. Then gray troopers and blue were where they had ridden so hard to be, within saber-length of each other. Steel rang in scores of simultaneous duels, superseding the crackle of gunfire. Oaths, shouts, in accents of Virginia, Carolina, Michigan and Pennsylvania filled the air. The squadrons behind Hampton's had not long to wait for action on their own account, for Gregg hurled men upon them from either flank. The quality of the fighting was more desperate than that of Brandy Station. A color-sergeant of Fitz Lee's collided with a Federal captain who tried to snatch his flag. Jabbing*

> *with the spike-tipped staff as with a lance, the sergeant broke his foe's*
> *jaw and hurled him senseless to earth. A Virginian and a Pennsylvanian*
> *sabered each other dreadfully, then clinched, rolled from their saddles,*
> *and died tearing at each other's throats. That evening, burial parties*
> *had trouble in dragging their bodies apart.*

At one point Hampton was separated from the rest of his force and hemmed against a fence. Blue riders swirled around him. He shot one with his revolver as others sliced at him with their swords. One stroke reopened the head wound from the day before and blurred his vision. But Hampton remained saddled and rode to the assistance of one of his troopers. Again he was struck in the head, but an instant later, he scored with his own heavy sword, splitting his attacker's skull down to the chin. Blood-splashed and dazed, he now faced even more Federal riders who were closing in. "General, General, they are too many for us," panted First North Carolina Sgt. Nat Price. "For God's sake, leap your horse over the fence; I'll die before they take you…" Hampton reached deep inside him. Blinded with blood and on the brink of exhaustion, he spurred Butler toward the rail fence and escape. The great horse cleared the top rail easily, but as if stuck in a deadly freeze frame, a sharp piece of shrapnel tore into Hampton's side, just as he was at the crest of his jump. Gravely injured, and too weak to ride, Hampton was carried to safety. His skull was fractured and blood gushed from his many wounds, but before retiring from the field, he ordered Colonel Baker to take command and urged his men to fight on.

It was a brutal, wild fight. Even with cavalry gloves, Captain Leonard Williams' pistol was nearly too hot to hold. His four preloaded spare cylinders were long emptied. His cartridge belt held but a solitary round. His bruised right arm ached from wielding a saber that was getting heavier by the second. A red streak appeared on the flank of the young mare. It was a nasty cut but fortunately not a mortal one. He dismounted. The fighting was hand-to-hand now. Sabers cut through the thick July air. Pistols released their deadly loads. He fired his final round then fought solely with fists and sword. For several grueling minutes, neither side yielded an inch. Finally, the Federal cavalry broke and both parties withdrew to their original lines. Scattered over the fields adjacent to the Rummel barn where horses had lazily grazed just hours before, 181 of Stuart's cavalrymen lay dead. Stuart, Fitz Lee, Hampton, and Leonard Williams's company had done all they could, but it wasn't enough to overtake Gregg's force and gain access to the Federal rear as Lee had hoped. This meant there would be no support from the cavalry later in the day, should Lee's direct assault on Meade's center succeed.

Finally, with their ammunition all but gone, Longstreet's guns stood silent. For two hours, they had hurled shells at the Federals sheltered in shallow trenches reinforced with fence rails but nearly every round had sailed harmlessly over the heads of the enemy, which remained full of heart and ammunition. At three o'clock, two armies divided by culture, ideology, politics, and sheer hatred faced each other across three-quarters of a mile of ground that sloped up from Seminary Ridge toward Cemetery Hill. Lee surveyed his army, a veteran assembly of men who had never been this far north and so close to their finest victory. Opposite Lee stood anxious George Meade. Commanding for only six days, he was now the new general of a new army. The old army was used to being whipped, but on the march up to Pennsylvania, it had grown in confidence and was now brimming with enthusiasm. It was an army tired of losing and determined to atone for Fredericksburg. Most of all, it was an army defending Northern ground now, and one that believed it could win.

As Leonard tended to the mare's wound back in the safety of Cress Woods, two shadowed figures were conversing in the shade of Seminary Ridge three miles east back on the main battlefield. One was James Longstreet, struggling to look the other in the eye. Thirty-eight year old George Pickett, a classmate of George McClellan's at West Point and a Mexican War veteran, paced impatiently. Longstreet sought to delay. The mustached and goateed Pickett sought glory. "General, shall I advance?" asked Pickett. There was no answer. Again he asked. Longstreet, unable to bring himself to give an order for what he believed to be a useless slaughter, and with face turned away, bowed his head. Pickett answered himself. "I am going to move forward sir." At three in the afternoon, as Lee sat anxiously atop Traveler, Longstreet galloped out to the guns only to find that Alexander, his chief of artillery, had little ammunition left.

"Stop Pickett immediately and replenish your ammunition," he ordered.

"There is no ammunition with which to replenish," answered Alexander, "and besides, if we wait for that we will lose all the effect of the fire we have had."

"I don't want to make this attack," answered Longstreet. "I would stop it now but that General Lee ordered it and expects it to go on. I don't see how it can succeed."

What was to become remembered as "Pickett's Charge," became the single most celebrated, analyzed, and debated operation of the war. The grand advance was both hopeless and heroic, and for precisely those reasons, it shined the brightest in the minds of soldiers long after the war and historians who delve into the conflict today. Fourteen thousand men, nine full brigades, rifles gleaming in the simmering July sun, marched forward, sweeping up the slope, across walls and fences, toward a sea of blue and immortality. Ahead and to the right, cannon. Ahead and to the left, cannon. Straight ahead, an endless supply of dug-in troops and more cannon. Into a deadly crossfire, with no hope of succeeding, they marched. Pickett led three brigades on the right. James Johnson Pettigrew led three more in the center. Isaac Ridgeway Trimble led the final three on the left. With parade ground precision and spreading nearly a mile across, the three divisions steadily advanced. When a section of men was obliterated by an artillery shell, the companies closed ranks, maintained the lines and kept moving forward. Shot, shell, and canister tore through the gray mass as if the gates of hell had been opened and evil itself had been unleashed against them. Still, the lines and their spirit remained unbroken. Virginians were beheaded. Mississippians mauled. Alabamans hurled into the air like rag dolls. Carolinians shot right between the eyes. Two of Pickett's three generals were killed. Fifteen regimental commanders were killed or wounded.

Still, Lee clung to that mystical belief that had both sustained him and paved the way for previous successes. He believed that somehow this audacious charge would divide the Federals, Longstreet would then follow it up as Stuart's cavalry harassed the enemy from the rear, resulting in another miraculous, God-granted victory. For an instant, it appeared that Lee's bold attack just might carry the day. Around 3:30 PM, July 3, General Lewis A. Armistead breached the Union line at the Angle along with about 300 adrenaline-driven Virginians and Tennesseeans, the high tide of the rebellion. Incredibly, a tiny swatch of gray could be seen clearly through Lee's field glasses piercing the great blue canvas. Armistead himself raised his hat on the tip of his sword as a guide for the troops at the stone wall on Cemetery Ridge. Momentum was theirs and defeat was unthinkable. Then, with his hand on a Union cannon, Armistead was mortally wounded. The handful of rebels fighting beside him were soon cut down or captured. Pickett's Charge was over.

Three brigades were dispatched to cover the retreat as the remnants of what were once three grand divisions drifted back to the shadows of Seminary Ridge. In thirty minutes, less than half of those who marched out staggered back dazed and defeated. "It's all my fault," said Lee as he rode among his men. "It is I who have lost this fight, and you must help me out of it the best way you can. All good men must rally."

Lee's men did manage to hastily form some semblance of a line, but no counterattack was ordered by Meade, who was satisfied with merely holding the high ground after three bloody days. After their resounding defeat on enemy soil, Robert E. Lee and his band of overachievers were no longer invincible. Lincoln breathed a sigh of relief. A day later, Grant captured Vicksburg thus splitting the South in two. It was the beginning of the end for the Army of Northern Virginia, the Confederacy, and ultimately the war itself. Three weeks after the disaster at Gettysburg, Chief of Confederate Ordnance, Josiah Gorgas, summed up the South's dire straits best:

> *One brief month ago we were apparently at the point of success. Lee was in Pennsylvania, threatening Harrisburg, and even Philadelphia. Vicksburg seemed to laugh all Grant's efforts to scorn...Port Hudson had beaten off Banks' force...Now the picture is just as sombre [sic] as it was bright then...It seems incredible that human power could effect such a change in so brief a space. Yesterday we rode on the pinnacle of success-today absolute ruin seems to be our portion. The Confederacy totters to its destruction.*

In a torrential downpour, a seventeen-mile long procession of wailing wounded wobbled south in crowded, unsprung, uncovered wagons. Through the storm they marched grimly through the mud. Orders were strict. Those who could not keep up were to be left on the roadside and the columns were not to stop until they reached the Potomac. Men moaned. Some even prayed to die. Many had their prayers answered.

Of the 88,000 men fielded by Meade at Gettysburg, 3,155 were killed, nearly 15,000 more were wounded and 5,365 were unaccounted for. Of the 75,000 men of the Army of Northern Virginia, 3,903 were killed, nearly 19,000 more were wounded and 5,425 were missing in action and most likely in enemy hands. The combined casualty count at Gettysburg was a staggering 51,112.

Thousands of soldiers and hundreds of horses were left where they fell, and it was the sad task of volunteers and medical personnel to deal with the death, despair, disfigurement, and disease that lingered for weeks around the small, shell-riddled town.

Sophronia Bucklin, a volunteer nurse on her first visit to the fields of Gettysburg, wrote this disturbing account of the aftermath:

> *I visited the battleground...when the evidences of the horrid carnage...lay on every hand in fearful sights. Battered canteens, cartridge boxes, torn knapsacks, muskets twisted by cannon shot and shell, rusted tin cups, pieces of rent uniforms, caps, belts perforated with shot, and heaps of death's leaden hail, marked the spots where men were stricken down in solid ranks...right above my head, at one place, so close that it touched me, hung a sleeve of faded army blue- a dead hand protruding from the worn and blackened cuff- I could not but feel a momentary shudder. Boots, with a foot and leg putrifying within lay beside the pathway, and ghastly heads, too-over the exposed skulls of which insects crawled-while great worms bored through the rotting eyeballs. Astride a tree sat a bloody horror, with head and limbs severed by shells, the birds having banquetted on it, while the tattered uniform, stained with gore, fluttered dismally in the summer air. Whole bodies were flattened against the rocks, smashed into a shapeless mass, as though thrown there by a giant hand, an awful sight in their battered and decaying condition. The freshly turned earth on every hand denoted the pits, from many of which legs were thrust above the scant covering, and arms and hands were lifted up as though pleading to be assigned enough earth to keep them from the glare of the sky.*

One of those left behind was James, unable to be transported to safety with his retreating army. Now a Yankee doctor would tend to his post-amputation care, and the Union command would decide if James was to be hospitalized, exchanged, or even imprisoned. He was first and foremost in the thoughts of a soaked and beleaguered Captain Leonard Williams as he sloshed toward Cashtown, protecting the wagon train of "Lee's Miserables." Finally, he and his beaten comrades reached the Potomac only to find it in freshet from the steady rains. With Meade believed to be in hot pursuit, engineers hastily began erecting a patchwork bridge of planks, scows, and barges to enable them to cross the swollen river. It made for an anxious wait. While the workers were busy jury-rigging the contraption that would ultimately save the defeated rebels, Leonard Williams quickly fashioned some words home to Greenville just eight days after Pickett's ill-fated charge.

*Washington Co., Md.*
*July 11, 1863*

*My Dear Wife,*
*I take the present moment to drop you a few lines to let you know that I am well…*

Never had nineteen precious words been more longed for and eagerly prayed for by Anna Olivia Laval Williams. She would not now have to scour the death lists, bow her head when asked of her husband's condition, or endure the sudden bursts of tears that would cascade down her ashen cheeks unbidden. She paused just long enough to whisper to little Carrie and inform Maum Fannie that daddy and "Massa Wimms" had somehow ridden away from Gettysburg unscathed. Relieved, she read on.

*I have been mercifully protected in the many fights and skirmishes we have been engaged in. For the last month, we have been in constant service without a day's rest, for over a month, many whole days and nights together in the saddle without sleep. I write now in hearing of our skirmishes and write now without having time to give you any of the details, merely to let you know I am safe and all my company except 3 or 4 wounded in the fight at Upperville of which I told you in my last letter.*
*My brother James was badly wounded in the foot, which had to be amputated, merely to save his heel. I saw him next day and was with him an hour, but being on the march to the battlefield, I could not stay longer with him. My duty called me off several miles so I could not see him again nor have I heard from him since.*
*We have lost heavily in the Gettysburg fights. We are still in Md. and expect another large battle. Our soldiers believed they worsted*

*the enemy. They drove them several miles but failed to dislodge them from a mountain, which gives the enemy the plea to claim victory. They acknowledge a loss of 30,000 men, ours, I understand is not more than 12,000. I have not heard from you in a month- my love to all. Write often, the next few days will, I think, decide the issue of the campaign- when at leisure if my life is spared, I will give you an account of all I have seen and experienced. The Butler Guards suffered pretty severely. Alex Whitman was wounded. Tell Uncle Adam he is doing well. I saw Wm. a day or two ago.*

*Your affectionate husband*
*L. Williams*

For the next few weeks, the soldiers and citizens alike were busy dealing with the horrid results of the great battle. Horse carcasses were covered with bullet-splintered fence rails and incinerated across the fields of Gettysburg. Thousands of shallow graves were dug by men now numb to the sight and smell of death. Wade Hampton made his way back to South Carolina to recuperate from his three latest wounds while M. C. Butler learned how to mount and dismount with his new cork foot. Leonard and the men of Co. K picketed vigilantly, their tired eyes peeled for an assault that never came. Mid cleaned the mare's wound, brushed Ruby, and cleaned her pebble-laden shoes with his hoof pick. Hopefully, James would gain strength in an enemy field hospital, thankful that gangrene, like Meade, had not attacked. President Lincoln sat forlorn in the White House lamenting that his new general did not press his advantage and crush the enemy once and for all. Lee mentally replayed the critical battle over and over pondering whether he would have prevailed had Stonewall been there to spearhead the assault on the first day. James Longstreet still seethed over the order to send three divisions to slaughter. A stunned George Pickett was still dealing with the cold reality that three of his brigades had been erased in just thirty minutes. In the west, Grant was enjoying one of his fat cigars and victory at Vicksburg, herding the thin defenders into prison camps.

The Old Captain opened the next letter. This one wasn't from him to Anna but from an aunt in Charleston, who like the South itself, wondered how much more she and her niece could endure.

*July 14, 1863*
*Tuesday*

*Dear Annie*

*Yours of the 24ᵗʰ was received. It came about a week before I got back from W. Martin's, where I had been for something over three weeks. I got back to Jimmy's on Wed. the 8ᵗʰ. One week tomorrow your letter was sent down to me by the boy who came for me. But as I started a few hours after I received it, and three letters to write and my things to pack up, I did not have time to read your letter until after I got here. I was exceedingly glad to hear from you once more and to hear you're all well again. I had concluded that you were tired of the correspondence and did not wonder at it for it is but dry and uninteresting letters that I can write. I hardly expected you to answer it before [          ] and Wm. went away. For I know that every moment of your time would be occupied with him and after he left I concluded you did not feel like writing, not knowing at what moment sad, sad tidings might be brought to you, I could not blame you if you did not write. Under the circumstances, you may know then that I value your letters very highly. Situated as you are with your mind harnessed about your heart's treasure, not knowing at one moment sad, sad tidings might be brought you, I could not blame you if you do not write. Under the circumstances, you may know that I value your letters very highly. God grant his protection and mercy on him who is dear to you and us all on your account as well as his own. You must indeed have been very much surprised, as well as overjoyed at his sudden and unexpected visit, but alas, it was too soon over and he is gone again. Oh! that our dear father in heaven may offer him the return to his home again to his loving wife and darling child. I am so glad she took up with him at once and evinced such marks of affection for him. It must have been gratifying to you both and I think it very uncommon that she should have done it for she had no recollection of him. It reflects great credit on your training, together with a loving little heart. Kiss the dear creature for me. And I know she will know nothing of the ugly, old aunt out here. You say she recollects life and I fear she will forget us all before she sees us again. What a memory she must have. I should not have thought it possible for her to recollect us. She saw so little of us.*

*May she be spared to you is the prayer of my heart.*

*I hope you hear often from Captain Wms. He is in a perilous situation now. Oh, this miserable, cruel war. Will it ever end? You must have been very uneasy about Miss Susan. What could have given her such a spell? I am glad, indeed, to hear that she has recovered. I hope she will take good care of herself. Indeed Annie she has been a good aunt to you. I don't know what you would do without her. Give my kind love to her and tell baby to kiss her for me. You are indeed favored in having your aunts all so near you. It would afford me great pleasure to visit you all this summer but the times are too precarious and too hard to boot to go travelling. Even the charges on the road have increased. The fare you [      ] is as good as anything we have, and beside that, I hope you know my visit would not be influenced by what you could give me to eat. I have no doubt we live as poor as the next one. Sugar, tea, coffee, we have given up long ago, and often we have not a candle in the house and have to use light wood. As to the present time, I can't even buy a tallow candle in the neighborhood. The times are truly awful.*

*Sis is home and went down to John Martin's so as to be there when Sis's vacation took place. We came home from there together. The vacation took place on Wednesday, the 1st and she came home on the Thursday the 2nd. On the following Wednesday, we left for Jimmy's. It will keep me busy some to prepare for her school again, for she has come home in a mood pretty mean. How am I to fix her up, these times, heaven only knows. I do not think her improved in anything. Jimmy thinks her somewhat into her music, but considering the time she has been at it, I do not think her improved much. I liked Mrs. Eliza's teaching better than any she has had since. I'm sure she improved further under her than any other and I know her fingering was prettier. I believe that could she have been kept under Mrs. Eliza, her improvement would have been another thing to what it is. She still has the old dislike to practicing and the old song of I can't play. She has spoken frequently about your not answering her letter and I know would be proud of a letter from you. If you write her, you can give her a few hints about improvements. She loves you dearly, I believe, for she is all the time talking about you and Dumpy and says she loves you both dearly. She* *was quite disappointed when she came home and found I had given up all idea of going to Greenville. She sends much love and many kisses to you and Dumpy. Also, her love to Miss Susan, Mrs. Eliza, and Matt. I am glad your mother went home with you. It was pleasant for both of you and I hope her health will be improved by it. I am glad you have a fine garden. We have a tolerable one, and I think, with you, that with a plenty of vegetables, we can't starve. I love vegetables of every kind and corn dodgers too – so I can't starve if, we can get a plenty of that, but corn at $3.50 per bushel is dear eating, even if it is corn dodgers.*

*And now Annie dear, what do you think of Vicksburg? Don't you feel like crying? Is it not disturbing? Oh, the thousands of lives that that villain Lincoln has butchered. May he meet with his doom, and now, alas! our own city, our own beloved home is attacked in earnest and God, our father, only knows what will be the result. Oh, that he would make bare his arm in our defense for none but He can save us. Oh Annie, if our city falls, what will become of us. May the good God save us from such a calamity. Jimmy and Nettie gain in love to you and thank you very much for your kind invitation but see no hope of leaving home this summer. Nettie says she would like very much to see the mountains and her mountain cousin. I am in such terror and consternation that I have no heart for anything life gives me again in love to all. I hope I have convinced you that I am not offended.*

*Yours very truly*

*L. M.*

From July 8 to 11, Captain Williams and his ever-shrinking company fought most often dismounted in a series of vicious skirmishes against Generals Buford and Kilpatrick in dusty hamlets named Boonsboro, Beaver Creek, Funkstown, and on the Sharpsburg front. Both sides claimed victory although neither gained any ground or reconnaissance of significance. Eventually, the 2nd S. C. Cavalry manned a picket line from Falling Waters to Hedgesville. For seven straight days, the Federals demonstrated near Hedgesville, forcing back Baker's Brigade. Sharp cavalry skirmishes were fought daily while the Confederate infantry was tearing up the Baltimore and Ohio Railroad. In Martinsburg, keeping watch as those rails were being ripped up was a healthy but hungry captain. That night, with the sound of gunfire growing louder and closer by the minute, he sat by a crackling fire. There was no coffee to warm or food to cook, but its light served him well as his pencil raced across a piece of crumpled and torn paper.

> *Camp Near Martinsburg, Va.*
> *July 19, 1863*

*My Dear Anna*

> *I again have a little leisure to write and an opportunity to send to Winchester. I wrote you from Md. a few days ago. Our army is now on this side concentrated near Winchester. We crossed back without any loss of importance. Our work still continues of the most constant and fatiguing character. I, however, stand it as well as the best. Have had almost uninterrupted health, although we have not had a day's rest in over a month and have slept in wet clothes and on a wet blanket half the time.*

> *This has been, by far, the most laborious campaign of the war. We hear the sadness of the fall of Vicksburg, Port Hudson, and the probable fall of Charleston. The times are indeed gloomy but my motto is never despair. I hope everyone will cherish our state motto, Dum spiro spero. I have recd letters from Henry, William and Jenny Clary, and several others since I left Brandy, but none from you. It has been over a month since I have heard from you. Everybody gets letters from home.*

> *James, I understand, was left in the enemy's hands. I expect he was not able to be moved. I am very anxious about the result. It would have been better, I expect, to have taken off his foot entirely. He will have a hard time in the hands of the unsympathizing. I have not leisure to give you any act. of the campaign in Pa. Must wait til we get a little respite from duty. I have been mercifully protected so far and all my command, except one, who has been missing several days. Miller and Ligon have been exchanged and will soon join me. The horse detail are looked for every day. My love to all.*

> *Your affectionate husband*
> *L. Williams*

By the end of July, Captain Williams and his men had helped oversee the movement of Ewell's Division from Gettysburg back to Virginia, where they now occupied the same position they held after the first invasion of

Pennsylvania, south of the Potomac in and around Brandy Station and Culpeper. General Meade had hoped to cut Lee off from Richmond, but like his predecessors had failed to move quickly and decisively enough. Mercifully, the Gettysburg campaign was over at last.

Back at the Planters Hotel, the Old Captain put aside the letters and reflected for a moment upon the seven blood-filled, work-filled, sorrow-filled weeks that followed Brandy Station. He sighed a deep sigh and stretched his legs. Then he ventured down the hotel stairs to the front desk and requested a fresh pot of coffee, four slices of rye toast, and a healthy dab of orange marmalade. Despite his advanced age and a stiffness in his legs, he spilled neither drop or crumb as he carefully made his way back up the steep staircase. Well supplied and limbered up, he opened the next letter, a lengthy, insightful summation of his history-making journey back from Gettysburg.

*Camp near Culpepper, Va.*
*July 29, 1863*

*My Dear Anna*

*After a vigorous campaign of 40 days into the states of Pa. and Md., we find ourselves again in the camps from which we started. We reached here yesterday evening under the most drenching rain I have seen and had to repeat what I had often done, sleep in a wet blanket. Today, ourselves and horses are resting, and hope we may have several days of rest as it is much needed. The cavalry has done much work and fighting laterally than any other branch of the service. I have written 2 or 3 times but so hurriedly, I could give you no details.*

*I told you that on the 23rd, I was separated from the regiment to get my own and other horses shod. Two days after the 12 hours fight at Upperville, of which I told you, the brigade went back toward Warrenton and crossed the river near Washington and took a large train of wagons and sutler stores. I regretted very much being separated from my command. After crossing the river at Williamsport, I had command of over 300 men from Hampton's Brigade and guarded the ordnance train of 30 wagons and also our division train from that point til we reached Chambersburg, Pa. – which was a work of very great anxiety to me as the ordnance was indispensable and 2 regiments of Yankee cavalry even reported to be advancing to attack them. At Chambersburg, I was superceded in my Colonelcy by Maj. Screven.*

*From there we proceeded to Fayetteville and thence to Gettysburg, when the bloodiest fight of the war was made. It lasted 3 days. We were on the right wing when I had constant employment in scouting, picketing and fighting. In the meantime, our brigade was on the left and had 2 days fight and was victorious! On the right on the 3$^{rd}$, the enemy endeavored to flank us. Capt. Nesbit, of the 1$^{st}$ Regt. and myself, each with about 50 men, were dismounted with rifles and opposed them and held them in check until a regiment of infantry came to our relief. We led their sharpshooters into the woods when it was in position and they succeeded in killing and capturing over 200 of them. As soon as the infantry relieved us, I took a position on the right on a hill where I could see the Yankees advancing which they did at the double quick, but were soon hurled back in rapid flight. The Yankee army evacuated his position several hours before Genl. Lee did.*

*Our army then fell back to Hagerstown, Md. and offered him battle for the 3 days which he declined. The cavalry were engaged all the time and drew them on to within ¾ of a mile of Genl. Lee's lines. The campaign in Pa., though not a success, did not result disastrously. The enemy were severely punished and lost much more heavily than we. Our army was withdrawn across the river and over the mountains without any loss. Our loss in killed, wounded and prisoners are put down at 20,000, the enemy's at 40,000, which I think is nearly correct. I regret our failure to rout and destroy Hooker's army. In that event, we could have occupied the state of Pa. and supplied our army with everything.*

*It is a very fine farming country and everything abundant: the population are mostly Dutch and many of them speak no other language. They seem to be a thrifty sort of people. They live in good houses, mostly brick and rock. You sometimes see a fine 3 story large brick dwelling that looks to be the abode of wealth and refinement and the female inmates barefooted and carelessly dressed. The population, though apparently comfortable, are poor. I do not know whether our cause has been improved any by the invasion.*

*James was wounded as I told you in my last letter and had to suffer amputation of his foot, and was left in the hands of the enemy. I have heard nothing from him. His wound was very severe and I have fears for the result.*

*I recd yesterday all your letters by Beattie and Thompson, the only letters I have had from you since the 12th June. I hope your garden will do well. I think you had better give the potatoes time to grow and not use them for a time. Tell Ned to bring up the pigs as fast as possible as it will be our dependance for bacon another year. I think you ought to use all the butter you can. Make and spare nothing but the buttermilk. I gave my consent to Ned's marrying with the consideration he was stay from home but 2 nights in the week. Tell Mr. Whitmire to watch the wheat market and whenever he thinks advisable, buy wheat bran for your cows from the Maj. I do not think the cow ought to be let into the yard at all.*

*The fall of Vicksburg and Pt. Hudson and the failure of our army to occupy Pa. has emboldened the Yankee's very much and it will perhaps enable them to recruit their armies without difficulty. There is nothing, however, in these misfortunes to dishearten us. Our prospect is gloomy enough but I have an abiding faith that all will be well with us whenever God in His wisdom hath chastened us enough for our sins. I regret to tell you that many of our soldiers behaved badly in Pa. and they copied after the Yankees and plundered and destroyed private property and many instances wandering. I hoped our men would have respected private property and acted honorably. I have stood the trip pretty well and I have had good health but loss of sleep and labor has reduced me about 10 lbs. I am now resting finely. Write often. My love to all.*

*Your affectionate husband,*
*L. Williams*

*"I have an abiding faith that all will be well with us whenever God in His wisdom hath chastened us enough for our sins."* The Old Captain read that haunting line again and yet again. He wondered how after such a resounding defeat, with rations dwindling, horses breaking down, the blockade nearly impenetrable, and one brother dead and another wounded, he was still able to possess even an ounce of this abiding faith. But somehow he did and so did those who would continue to fight alongside him. Incredibly, even after defeat up in Pennsylvania and the surrender down in Vicksburg, Dixie's almost mystical

belief in Lee, its brave soldiers, and God's divine providence, while shaken, did not crumble. There was still a heart to persevere by the citizenry and a will to fight in the troops, but things had changed. For Captain Leonard Williams and the 2nd S. C. Cavalry, the fighting would now be mostly defensive. Lee's depleted army would never again be the mobile, attacking entity it had been.

Such was the case on August 1, exactly a month after the first shots at Gettysburg were fired. Over the same broad, fenceless fields where the grand cavalry fight had taken place earlier at Brandy Station, Union forces again splashed across the Rappahannock's Beverly Ford. This time, however, the 2nd S. C. Cavalry wasn't south of the main battle, it was front and center with Maj. Thomas E. Screven commanding. Corporal E. Prioleau Henderson of Company B described the action that day.

> On the 1<sup>st</sup> day of August, the enemy crossed at the railroad bridge and Beverley's Ford, driving in our pickets, and following in close pursuit, and were nearly in our camps before we were aware of their approach...we were compelled to fall back before the overwhelming numbers opposed to us. We fell back toward Culpeper C. H., where we knew we could find assistance... "Load, fire and fall back", was the routine of the mounted skirmishers, for several miles, regiment after regiment taking turn to charge an entire brigade of the enemy, and checking them at that, the mounted skirmishers several different times joining the regiments in the charge...When we arrived in sight of Culpeper C.H., Gen. Longstreet, who was stationed just beyond it, sent out a force of infantry to assist us-the first I saw of them...We...had just halted in a thick piece of woods, waiting, and glad to wait too, to see what the next move of the enemy would be, when here came part of a regiment of infantry to our support, and, by the way, they were South Carolina infantry at that. Their first greeting to us was, "Get out of the way, Cavalry, and let the Infants get at them." About the time they commenced forming, the Yankee Cavalry, not dreaming there was infantry in their front, made a dashing charge upon them, and to our surprise, the infantry broke and retreated as fast, or faster, than the cavalry had ever done. Now was our time to get even with them, and the mounted skirmishers yelled to the Infantry to "Get out of the way and let the cavalry get at them." It did not take many minutes to drive

*the enemy back, faster than they came, ably supported by the infantry, and we never left them until we had driven them across the Rappahannock River, killing and capturing a great many. By sunset the last of them were on the north side of the river.*

The enemy was driven back, the cavalrymen regrouped, but Leonard Williams was dazed and bleeding. In the fierce hand-to-hand action, he had been hit twice by the same bullet, first in the shoulder then the neck. Fortunately a thrust of the Captain's saber forced his attacker's second shot to miss. The encounter lasted but a few seconds and then it was over. His blade bore a streak of red and blood trickled down his neck as he trotted back into camp. Doctor Taylor quickly tended to him, relieved that the bullet had traveled cleanly through and out without striking any arteries. It was easy work for the old physician who gave each wound a good rinsing and a cotton dressing. By the next morning, the Captain's shoulder had stiffened up a bit and his neck wound needed a new bandage. Doc Taylor saw to him after breakfast and a bit later, Leonard found a soft place to rest and write a letter to inform Anna of his face-to-face encounter with the enemy.

> *Camp Near Culpepper, Va.*
> *August 2, 1863*
>
> *My Dear Wife*
> *Yesterday we had another of the most desperate fights of the war for the number engaged. The Yankees crossed the Rappahannock in large force, 1 or 2 divisions of cavalry and 1 of infantry. Our brigade met them. The entire brigade did not number more than 800 men. We were opposed, I judge, to 5 times our number. The fight lasted from 12 ock till near night, we lost a good many men and wounded. I recd a flesh wound in the lower part of the neck and shoulder from a pistol shot. The wound is slight and I hope to be well in 10 days or 2 weeks. I recd the shot in a hand to hand encounter. I used my saber on him to some purpose though he got away. I regret to tell you Lieut. Williams recd a wound from which he died this morning. Will Thompson recd a slight wound in the little finger. Cunningham and Day each slightly wounded by a shell, Holloway, a serious wound in the side. Cooley and Thornburg also recd slight wounds. My company also had 3 horses*

*killed and four wounded. My company probably suffered more than any other in the regt. I regret the death of Lieut. Williams; he was a good officer, brave soldier and a gentleman. Campbell Williams and Stephen Smith were taken prisoners while in attendance for Lieut. Williams. The wounds of my men are so slight none of them but Holloway have been sent to the hospital.*

*I am with the regiment but Dr. Taylor advises me to go to a house for a few days which I think I will do tomorrow. I write hurriedly, will give you a longer letter in a few days. You need not be uneasy about my wound. I think it will heal up in the course of 2 weeks at farthest. All my men behaved well in the fight. A good many not engaged, some detailed, some sick and others had disabled horses. I have a company of fighting boys. They have proved themselves on many occasion.*

*I have recd no letter from you by mail since the 12th last June. I think you certainly write else I would be very discontented. Do write oftener, direct 2 Regt. S. C. Cav., Hampton's Brigade, Richmond. My love to all. Kiss baby for me. I sincerely sympathize with Mrs. Williams and her family. Pierce, I have no doubt, was the favorite of the family. His death will bring deep sorrow upon them. Remember me to your father and mother and all the family.*

...

Six days later, on August 8, 1863, from Lee's new headquarters near Orange Courthouse, an envelope left camp bound for Richmond. Inside it was the resignation of the commander of the Army of Northern Virginia. President Jefferson Davis, of course, rejected it on the spot. Instead, he hoped that both his general and army might be rejuvenated by General Order No. 76, which he had issued a few weeks earlier.

*After long and trying marches, endured with the fortitude that has ever characterized the soldiers of the Army of Northern Virginia, you have penetrated the country of our enemies, and recalled to the defense of their own soil those who were engaged in the invasion of ours. You have fought a fierce and sanguinary battle, which, if not attended with the success that has hitherto crowned your efforts, was marked by the same heroic spirit that has commanded the respect of your enemies, the gratitude of your country, and the admiration of mankind. Once more you are called to meet the enemy from which you have owned on so many fields a mane that will never die. Once more the eyes of our countrymen, are turned upon you, and again do wives and sisters, fathers, mothers, and helpless children lean for defense, on your strong arms and brave hearts. Let every soldier remember that on his courage and fidelity depends all that makes life worth having- the freedom of his country, the honor of his people, and the security of his home. Let each heart grow strong in the remembrance of your glorious past, and in the thought of the estimable blessing for which we contend, and invoking the assistance of that Divine Power which has so signally blessed our former efforts let us go forth in confidence to secure the peace and safety of your country. Soldiers! Your enemy is before you! Win from him honors worthy of your righteous cause- worthy of your comrades dead on so many illustrious fields.*

As fall approached, with Gettysburg and two and a half years of fierce fighting behind them, the Confederates clung ever tighter to their flagstaffs, rifles, sabers and most importantly, their mystical belief.

# CHAPTER TWELVE
# THE RIVERDANCE OF FALL

*And the third angel*
*poured out his vial upon the rivers*
*and fountains of waters,*
*and they became blood.*

Revelation 16:4

The faster winter would arrive, the better. The humid, pollen-filled air of summer always made it more difficult for Anna. The upcountry heat exacerbated her frailties and more than doubled her visits to the doctor, who hoped she was merely asthmatic but increasingly began to sense that she may have tuberculosis or perhaps some chronic respiratory disease. Maum Fannie always kept one eye on the stove and the other on the lady of the house during those muggiest of dog days at the foot of the Piedmont. Carrie would be three in a few months and was beginning to become a handful. It would not serve Anna well to chase her impish little daughter around the house in the summer sun.

The summer heat was baking Leonard too. His face was red. His lips were cracked. Each day, his checkered bandana was soaked through by noon. His floppy felt hat now had a dark and permanent sweat ring. All spring and summer, from Chancellorsville to Gettysburg, he had ridden, marched and fought. His backside was bruised and his once shiny boots now sported holes. His uniform was barely a uniform at all now. To be sure his faded captain's bars were still there, but his coat was stained with coffee and dirt, and his pants were torn and ragged. Soon enough he would trade the summer campaigning for winter complaining. He had a lot to complain about. Mid too, who had been hit hard with dysentery throughout the Gettysburg Campaign, would gladly trade those stomach-cramping, rainy, summer marches for a touch of frost. With many more hot skirmishes looming ahead, Mid checked the mare's wound while a local physician saw to Leonard's. On August 8, 1863, the very day that Lee sent his quickly rejected resignation letter to Jefferson Davis, Leonard wrote to Anna, describing his wound and his present situation as well as trying to offer what counsel and help he could to his weakening wife.

*Near Gordonsville, Va.*
*August 8ᵗʰ, 1863*

*My Dear Anna*

*I am at present with Dr. Cowherd about 2 miles from Gordonsville. I am most comfortably situated with everything I need at my command. The Dr. and his family are very pleasant, sociable and hospitable people. I feel perfectly at home. My wound is healing rapidly. The bruise has nearly disappeared and I expect to go to my regiment in 4 or 5 days. The brigade is still near Culpeper. I was advised to come this way across the Rapidan and I was obliged to come this far before I could get accommodation and feed my horses, which I am recruiting. Genl. Lee's army is near here about Orange C. H.*

*From where the ball entered to where it came out is only about 2 or 3 inches. My arm was raised giving a thrust when I was shot, the ball entering on the upper part of my shoulder where it joins the neck. He was on my right side. It was a narrow escape but the wound was slight. But for the irritation in riding and moving about and the danger of bringing on inflammation and fever, I have continued my duty. But the surgeon advised me to go to a private house, which I thought advisable. I will, however, be with them if nothing unforeseen prevents in a few days. I feel restless when away from my command when there is work to be done. I do not look for another battle for several weeks. I do not know where Genl. Lee proposes to make a stand, probably at the Rapidan River and maybe again along the Rappahannock.*

The close call with the enemy bullet made the Captain even more anxious to guide and instruct his wife on all that needed to be done.

*I have recd no letter from you later than the 3ʳᵈ last month. I expect, however, there must be letters for me at the regiment. My clothes, Beattie left at Richmond. As soon as we get settled, I will send for them. Did you get a hat for me? I was unable to get anything in Pa. The stores were all closed and the goods moved and hid out before we got there. I am living delightfully here. Beans, cucumbers, onions, tomatoes, squashes, potatoes & c and plenty of milk and butter. I saw the Dr. sell beeves to the army yesterday and a cow the size of your white cow, he* *recd $175 for.*

*I think you had better dsy your white cow towards the latter part of Sept. or the 1ˢᵗ Oct. Fatten her and have her killed. You can use one while fresh and pickle the balance. The hogs will not make bacon enough without help. Tell Ned to give good attention to the hogs. I think by next Feb. they will make pretty good sized hogs which together with the beef will make enough meat to do you. It will be almost impossible to buy, bacon is selling at Richmond at $1.75 per lb. If the red cow has a calf, with good care and plenty of feeding, she will give you plenty of milk, at least 3 gal. per day. I think you would do well to buy 8 or 10 gal. of homemade molasses if it can be bought at $3 or $4 per gall. You ought also to buy 2 or 3 bushels dried fruit. Ask Mr. Whitmire to buy you 2 or 3 bags flour and when he thinks the prices are as low as they will be, to get enough to do you. Let a part be wheat as it will keep longer than flour. How are the potatoes doing? Save as many for winter use as you can and also cabbages if you have enough. Now is the time to sow turnips. Put in all the spare ground, they make excellent cow feed when cut up and boiled with meal among them. If you can, get wheat bran for the cows. Also, have all the beans that have dried gathered.*

*Now is the time to show your thrift and economy. I want to send my mare home this winter for Ned to plough and also to work in a 1horse wagon. If I can get one, it will enable him to earn more and keep more constantly employed. I bought another horse to send with her but I lost her in less than a week, she got loose and strayed off. I have never heard from her since. I paid only $125 for her but she was worth $400. I may yet get her but I hardly expect it. I expect she was taken up and sold.*

*You told me you expected company this summer without telling me who you expected. I wrote you on the 3ʳᵈ giving you the casualties in my company. None of the wounds were serious except Lieut. Williams' of which he died next day and Holloway's. He was shot in the side, was doing well when he went to the hospital. The weather's been very warm for the past 10 days and it has rained almost every day. I suppose you have heard of the death of Capt. Pulliam, wounded at Gettysburg. I've heard nothing from James. Kiss baby for me and tell me all about*

*her. How is Whitfield and Billy Whitmire? I fear Charleston will fall,
am much anxious to hear about it. Write soon and direct as usual. It
has been nearly 2 months since I have recd a letter by mail from you.
My love to all.*

*Your affectionate husband
L. Williams*

In the four months after Gettysburg, prices rose over 70 percent throughout the South. Indeed, as her husband had instructed her, Anna would have to master the art of thrift and economy. Maum Fannie had long since found ways to fashion meals from nothing and to create subsequent dishes from the leftovers. Mr. Whitmire too was of vital assistance as he watched for bargains on foodstuffs and supplies. For Leonard, rations became sparse as he and his famished company rode over barren ground past evacuated houses. Company K was smaller now. Too few recruits had mustered in to fill the empty spaces since the Pennsylvania invasion. Desertion and disease increased while ammunition stocks dwindled. Perhaps worst of all for the long run, there was a scarcity of capable officers.

Neither Lee nor Meade seemed willing to hurl their vast armies against one another in August, yet both knew there would be some deadly fall skirmishing before bad weather dispatched both blue and gray to winter quarters. To best face the coming fall battles, Lee again reconfigured his cavalry. Wade Hampton and Fitz Lee were both promoted to Major General and placed in command of the two divisions under Stuart. Their promotions coupled with the transfer of Jones and Robertson left openings for five brigadiers. Two of these were Lawrence Baker and Matthew Butler, both of whom were recovering from serious wounds. Thomas Lafayette Rosser, a bold youngster who had been one of Fitz Lee's colonels, became Hampton's third brigadier. For now the freshly appointed Rosser was the only general officer present for active duty. Two new brigadiers' commissions soon followed. James B. Gordon would substitute for Baker and Pierce Young would temporarily fill Butler's position. Young's regiments included most of Hampton's old veterans, the 1st and 2nd South Carolina, and the Cobb, Phillips and the Jeff Davis Legions. Leonard Williams would now take his orders from the raw but ready Young. Until Hampton could sufficiently recover from his trio of Gettysburg wounds, Stuart often took personal command of the division.

M.C. Butler, the South Carolinian; Pierce Young, the Georgian; and Tom Rosser, the Virginian, were the hard riding horsemen Leonard would go to battle with in the coming fall. Each was six feet tall and all three were noted for their hard drinking, hard language and hard fighting. Each had distinguished himself on the field, extricated his men from tight spots, led gallant charges, and now bore the battle scars to prove it. Despite being over a decade older than the three saucy, twenty eight-year olds, Captain Williams respected them and obeyed their orders with alacrity. As Lee and Meade parried for position, Stuart's cavalry was once again called on to screen the movements of Lee and report back with the dispositions of the enemy. Having let Lee down in the days leading up to Gettysburg, Stuart was determined to perform these functions with West Point precision. Thus began the "riverdance," splashing across the Rappahannock, crossing then cutting back over the fords of the Rapidan, racing up the Robinson, re-scouting the Rapidan then settling back once again along the banks of the Rappahannock for the winter. Captain Williams was now healed up well enough to join in that dance, and he wrote Anna to tell her that he was again fit for duty, and again question her on affairs back home.

> *Clifton, Orange Co., Va.*
> *August 13th, 1863*

*My Dear Anna,*

*I have been here since the 5th enjoying the quiet of a retired country residence and all the luxuries of the seasons, dispensed with a most hospitable hand, the course of life I was subjected to for the 2 months previous, enables me to appreciate to its full value. I shall, however, bid adieu to these comforts day after tomorrow to report for duty. My shoulder is nearly well. All the soreness and bruise has disappeared and is healing rapidly. Dr. Cowherd has a beautiful place. Just in front about 200 yards runs the RR parallel with his house about 300 yards farther, the public highway and a few hundred yards beyond this, a range of mountains are running parallel and in full view. He has his large barns, fine cattle, horses, fine orchards, ice house and many other appendages of comfort and independence to which the denizen of towns is a stranger, the picture of which has always dazzled all the feeling of cupidity in my nature. The Dr. is an army surgeon and is now at home on sick leave. He will return in a few days, so I'm anxious to return to* the regiment to get letters. *I know I must have several waiting for me.*

*It is believed Genl. Hampton is promoted to Maj. Genl, and Gen Hood is Lieut. Genl. over all the cavalry. I'm very pleased with the arrangement. Stewart is a cool, brave man, as I had the opportunity to see in the last fight, but I do not believe he has the capacity to manage in all the details to the greatest advantage the entire cavalry. Our cavalry force has to be increased, I understand they are raising a cavalry regt. in Greenville for home defenses. Who have they elected col.? I think if the enemy should take Charleston and Savannah, Greenville would be safe from incursions. You are, I think, in the safest locality I know of.*

*I see in the papers some intimations of despondency among the people in certain quarters. I am sorry that such is the case. I want to see our people and army hopeful and defiant to the last. The Yankees have gained no advantage anywhere except Vicksburg and I doubt whether that will be of any advantage to them or not. A great many soldiers are returning under the president's proclamation of pardon.*

*Tell me about baby, her amusements, her progress in learning & c and also about yourself. How do you stand this warm weather and how does your garden keep up? Are the potatoes doing any better? How does the bacon hold out? How many pieces have you yet? Do you get enough milk? Is it probable the cow will have a calf? If she does, I think by bestowing all the feed for 2 cows on her, she will give you more milk and butter than you could get from the 2. Tell Ned to give the hogs all the slop and waste from the kitchen to the pigs and keep them growing as fast as he can. Also tell him to save all the litter about the lot and yard for his manure heap, to gather all he possibly can to make the garden perfectly rich. By clearing up the lot every day or two, he can save a great deal. When he gets the present receptacle full, he must dig another. I want him to save enough to cover the entire garden 2 in. thick. With rich ground, much is added to the pleasure and profit of gardening. I am very anxious to hear from you. Do write soon. My love to Auntie and all.*

*Your affectionate husband*
*L. Williams*

Regulations allowed for officers to utilize local residences for recuperation while the enlisted men remained in the camps, sleeping on the ground under their ragged tents, nursing their wounds as best they could. Leonard always felt guilty about this inequity between the ranks and kept his stays at places like the Cowherd's short, but he did appreciate and relish the ability to bathe during his recuperation. Icy creek water and dirty, sweat-drenched cloths simply could not match a clean basin, fresh towel and a new bar of lye soap. Knowing well that hard, dusty riding lay ahead, the Captain personally gave Ruby a fine bath too before leaving the Cowherd house. He had saved his bar of lye and found a bucket near the well. Ruby stood contentedly as Leonard scrubbed her from the tips of her ears down to her hooves. Mid did likewise for the young mare, paying careful attention to her wound that was now nearly invisible. Even the old packhorse never looked better. The Captain's sparkling mounts were the exception in the Confederate Cavalry in the summer of '63. Charles Adams, a dedicated and deeply caring groom in the 1st Massachusetts Cavalry, wrote home to his mother lamenting the abuse and hardship that horses on both sides had endured after two and a half years of service.

> *The horse is, in active campaign, saddled on an average about fifteen hours out of the twenty four. His feed is nominally ten pounds of grain a day, and, in reality, he averages about eight pounds. He has no hay and only such other feed as he can pick up during halts. The usual water he drinks is brook water, so muddy by the passage of the column as to be the color of chocolate. Of course, sore backs are our greatest trouble. Backs soon get feverish under the saddle and the first day's march swells them; after that day by day the trouble grows. No care can stop it. Every night after a march, no matter how late it may be or tired or hungry I am, if permission is given to unsaddle, I examine all the horses' backs myself and see that everything is done for them that can be done, and yet with every care, the marching of the last four weeks disabled ten of my horses...Imagine a horse with his withers swollen to three times the natural size, and with a volcanic, running sore pouring matter down each side, and you have a case with which every cavalry officer is daily called upon to deal, and you imagine a horse which still has to be ridden until he lays down in sheer suffering under the saddle...The air of Virginia is literally burdened today with*

*the stench of dead horses, federal and confederate. You pass them on
every road and find them in every field, while from their carrions you
can follow the march of every army that moves...We marched over a
road made pestilent by the dead horses of the vanished rebels. Poor
Brutes! How it would astonish and terrify you and all the others with
your sleek, well-fed animals, to see the weak, gaunt, rough animals,
with each rib visible and hipbones starting through the flesh, on which
these 'daring cavalry raids' were executed. It would knock romance
out of you.*

Without enough salt, food, and water, and with diseased horses circulating
among the healthy, the Captain was indeed fortunate to have three reasonably
healthy animals in tow as he made his way back over the familiar fields of
Brandy Station toward camp. A week after rejoining his unit, he wrote Anna
that he was back in the saddle.

> *Camp Near Brandy Station*
> *Culpeper Co., Va.*
> *August 18, 1863*

*My Dear Anna*
> *I am with my regiment and find all well but a great many absent, 3
on sick leave furlough, four wounded, and about 10 now at home for
horses. The enemy are perfectly still. They have made no advance
since 1ˢᵗ inst. I suppose they are recruiting and filling up their ranks.
Our company is also filling up. Absentees are coming in rapidly. I
think the army will soon be reinstated to its former efficiency.*
> *I wrote you on the 13ᵗʰ hoping to get you into the habit of writing
oftener. I write again today. I recd when I came into camp only one
letter of the 28ᵗʰ July and since then one dated 9ᵗʰ Aug. You need not
apprehend any miscarriage of letters if you direct 2ⁿᵈ Regt. S. C. Cav.
Hampton's Brigade, Richmond. They always know at Richmond where
the brigade is. I wrote you one or two letters while in Pa.- which I
suppose you never recd. I have no news. I hear fighting is going on in
Charleston. I have hopes Charleston will stand against all their attacks
even if Fort Sumpter is reduced. I trust batteries more formidable will
still be encountered on the land. I hear yellow fever is prevailing in*

*Vicksburg. If so, the Yankees will have to evacuate. I recd my carpetbag with my shirts and drawers and socks today. I have not yet tried them on. I like the shirts very much. The socks came in good time as I had on my last pair. I wish you would make me a couple of pocket Hdkchfs., small size out of such cloth as my shirts or a little thinner if you can get it, and also a towel and send them by Willis Benson, who is now at home for a horse. I gave $1.00 yesterday for ½ yard or nabings for a towel.*

A day after he had started this letter, Leonard finished it with some sobering observations as well as expressions of his interest and pleasure in receiving news from home.

*August 19ᵗʰ*

*I would telegraph you the casualties of battles but the telegraph agents will not send any messages for individuals, especially the details of fights for several days after they occur, being monopolized by the government. I wrote to Mrs. Williams the next day after the death of her son. I suppose you have seen a published list of the casualties of the fight of the 1ˢᵗ inst. I see it published in the Richmond papers. I regret very much to see the spirit of avarice abroad in the land. I am disgusted. I hope there is Christian benevolence enough yet to provide for the poor. It is amazing that while half the male population are periling their lives daily, and subjected to as many privations and hardships as have ever fallen to the lot of any people, with the families of many of them distressed and reduced to a scanty substance on account of their absence and while the whole country is in mourning for fellow relations and friends and while the enemy are threatening us with more unrelenting fury and fiendishness than ever, that in the face of this, so many of our people at home should think of nothing else but gain.*

*I am always delighted with your accounts of your occupations at home, of garden, yard & c and above all of baby's smartness, what she does and says. I have no doubt she is a very smart child and I want to see her and you more than I ever have if my life is spared. I don't think I can stay away so long again but will do my best to get home again next winter. The weather is much pleasanter, nights cool enough. Have*

*you sown turnips yet? Keep a good lookout and be on time. Write*
*soon. Remember me to all my friends.*

> *Your affectionate husband*
> *L. Williams*

*P. S. My wound is nearly healed up. I suffer no inconvenience from it.*

The Old Captain rose slowly and made his way over to the gray uniform hanging patiently on the brass closet hook. His eyes focused on the right shoulder as his arthritic fingers caressed the precise stitching a few inches down and over the three captain's bars on his collar. Like a jeweler examining a fine diamond, he inspected Anna's repair work and found not a single flaw. She had mended the bullet hole from the inside in such a manner that the puncture point was nearly invisible even forty years later. The old man sighed as he imagined her tiny, china white fingers tending to his rent uniform. The hole in his shoulder had long since healed. The hole in his heart never would. As he returned to his shrinking pile of letters, he concluded that Anna's handy work was the equal of Doctor Taylor's, who had done some remarkable patchwork himself that first night in August.

August and early September picketing along the Rapidan was joy riding. Watching, not fighting, was the order of the day. With both sides still licking their wounds from Gettysburg, recruiting horses, and filling ranks, there was plenty of idle time for card playing and reading. There were spirited camp meetings and loud revivals. The camp newspaper, *The Rapid Ann*, written in pen and pencil by the soldiers was full of gossip and humor. One of the editions that was circulating around contained a clever revision of *Hardee's Tactics* called "The Tactics of Kissing."

> *Recruit is placed in front of the piece. First motion-Bend the right knee; straighten the left; bring the head on the level with the face of the piece; at the same time extend the arms, and clasp the cheeks of the piece firmly in both hands. Second motion-Bend the body slightly forward; pucker the mouth, and apply the lips smartly to the muzzle mouldings. Third motion-Break off promptly on both legs, to escape the jarring or injury should the piece recoil.*

Pickets along the Rapidan during that quiet period became quite cordial but fearing that conversation with the enemy might result in unintentional communication of military significance, the Confederate command determined to put an end to it.  One afternoon, John Gordon rode out to one of his Confederate posts to see if any such forbidden meetings were taking place.  As the general rode up, he noticed his men suspiciously running about.

"What's the matter here? What's all this confusion about?" he asked.

"Nothing at all, sir.  It's all right here General."

As the general turned his horse around, he looked back over his shoulder and noticed that the high weeds by the creek seemed to be moving rather strangely.  Immediately, Gordon trotted back over to his men and ordered them to cut the weeds down.   What he found among those shaking reeds was a shaking, half-naked Yankee.

"Where do you belong?" he asked.

"Over yonder," pointing to the Union side of the stream.

"And what are you doing here, sir?"

"Well, General, I didn't think it was any harm to come over and see the boys just a little while."

"What boys?"

"These Johnnies."

"Don't you know, sir, that there is a war going on in this country?"

"Yes, General, but we are not fighting now."

Assuring him to strictly obey, the general ordered the visitor to stand at attention.

"I am going to teach you, sir, that we are at war.  You have no rights here except as a prisoner of war, and I am going to have you marched to Richmond, and put in prison."

"Wait a minute, General, interposed Gordon's men.  "Don't send this man to prison.  We invited him over here, and we promised to protect him, and if you send him away it will just ruin our honor."

Nearly biting the lip hidden under his beard, the General turned to the Yankee visitor, and said:

"Now, sir, if I permit you to go back to your own side, will you solemnly promise on the honor of a soldier, that—"

"Yes, sir," interrupted the swimmer, as he hopped over the weeds and into the river and swam furiously back to his own side of the river.

Captain Williams too reminded his men that fraternization with the enemy would not be tolerated. He posted such an order alongside the picket assignments for the next day, then he employed that same pencil for a letter home to Ned, his trusted servant who was recently married.

> *Camp Near Brandy Station*
> *Culpepper Co., Va.*
> *August 22, 1863*

*To My Much Esteemed Servant Ned:*

*Mr. Whitmire, Uncle Adam, your mistress and everybody who writes, agree on giving me a good account of your fidelity and care of everything with which you are entrusted. I do not know of anything that gives me greater pleasure, especially as I have entrusted everything to your care. There is no telling how long this war will last, or how long it will be my duty, if my life is spared, to stay from home. It may be 2 or 3 years, and every year provisions have been scarce and higher and I think times will still grow worse and people who have no farms will find it hard to get enough provisions to live on. Now what I have to propose is that you go farming. If you can rent 35 or 40 acres of land-I mean good land-I would not want you to work a poor place. I will send you a good horse. The reason why I speak of this early is to give you time to get in a small wheat crop (we cannot afford to pay 50 a barrel for flour). I would like for you to get a place where you could raise 3 or 4 hogs and keep 2 or 3 head of cattle. I want you, if you approve my plan, to take time and look out for 25 or 40 acres of rich land.*

*I am told Mr. Lewis Rodgers has a large plantation and has been in the habit of renting out a good portion of it and that the land is good and particularly a place belonging to his daughter, Mrs. Smith, formerly Mrs. Yeargan, about 35 or 40 acres and also Esq. McBee has a piece of good land near the factory which he has been renting to Mr. Moore and there may be other good land that could be rented in the neighborhood. I would rather get a place in that neighborhood where you are acquainted than anywhere else and if Mr. Rodgers has good land to rent, I would prefer you to get land from him because I hear his man is a faithful fellow and he could and would take an oversight of your fencing, fields & c when you might wish to be away.*

*What I would propose is this for you, to put in about 6 or 7 acres of wheat this fall and at the proper time, about 4 acres of oats and the latter part of March, I will send my man, Middleton, that I have with me with a horse to help you make a crop. Let him stay with you til the middle of August. He has been raised at the plow. You and he could plant and cultivate the 20 acres of corn. You could make enough corn and wheat and bacon to support us and perhaps fatten a beef in the summer and fall and make corn enough to recruit my worn down horses. The only thing I dislike about it is that it will keep you away from home more than I like, but your constant attention will not be needed til about the 1st May and then Mid will be with you, so that you can go up to Greenville once a week, after you get the corn crop gathered. You can stay there most of your time, say from the 1st Nov. at least half your time if you can get land that will make ordinary year's 10 bu wheat and 20 bu corn per acre. I would not want to work land that would yield much less and would prefer bottom land for cover that would yield much more if it can be had. I want you to look out at once and let me know if you can rent a place, what sort of land it is and what price of rent in money and what you think the land will make, what kind of fencing & c.*

*Get your Miss Anna to write to me and also what you think is best, whether to farm or whether you could do better to run a one horse wagon in town. Do jobs of plowing occasionally and tend to the garden, other matters about home.*

...

As Leonard was divining ways for Ned to help his fellow servants and the Williams clan withstand the privations of war, Anna's parents were in far more dire straits back in Charleston. Both Charleston and Fort Sumter were in the midst of a merciless Federal shelling launched from Morris Island that had begun back on August 17. For the span of an entire week, the venerable old Laval House was shook to its very foundation as were Anna's parents. Day after day, the Major, his wife, and the servants sequestered themselves in the back of the house, as the shells fell on the town. Finally, on August 23, Charleston Harbor fell silent once more, and word reached the Lavals that the garrison manning Fort Sumter had held out. Like their pressed predecessors in

Vicksburg, the small force defending nearby Fort Wagner would have to endure another Union siege, but for the time being, the Captain's in-laws and dear old Charleston were safe.

In the coming weeks, affairs would change like the autumn leaves at Charleston, in Tennessee, Georgia, and along the Rapidan. For Captain Williams and the Confederate cavalry, the trees would soon be awash in color, but the shades he remembered most were the weary blue eyes peering from powder blackened faces, the red speckled caps, the dull butternut uniforms, and blue-gray skies. He knew that in the coming days a moment to write home would be impossible to find, so the Captain wasn't about to waste one. There was much he wanted to say to his hard-pressed wife both on running the farm and on the state of the war.

*Camp Near Brandy Station, Va.*
*August 27, 1863*

*My Dear Anna*

*I was made glad by the receipt of your letter of the 13th, which came to hand on the 19th. Don't you think you made a mistake in measuring your potatoes? If you made the 25 bu, it was a good crop and very valuable. I wish I had 2 or 3 bu of them. We get a mess now and they are $3 per peck and they are delightful. I think you are equal to a Dutch housewife. It is no doubt a pleasant sight in these times to see your heaps of potatoes, bags of beans, dried fruit, tomatoes, okra, and strings of red pepper, your milk pans and butter bowls. I do not like the idea of your doing without flour. Tell Mr. Whitmire to send you up a barrel. If he has none, send to Maj. Alexander. You must keep up your supply of milk and butter, you must not let them diminish. If necessary, feed your cows better. I am glad you have learned the art of making loaf bread. They make it to perfection in this state. You must also get beef. Okra soup cannot be good unless boiled with beef.*

*I am delighted with the accounts you give of baby. I hope you can succeed in teaching her unselfishness and kindness. I imagine her temper is a good deal like mine, it needs a good deal of care. Teach her in all cases to submit to your decision when you command, exact obedience; self- denial is a most important lesson. How are your aunts, mother and Eliza getting on housekeeping; how are they satisfied? I* hope they are well pleased. I would be glad if your sisters would spend a few months with you. They would make you forget your loneliness and keep up your spirits and then you can go down with them and spend Christmas and then I will take you up home when I go on furlough. How do you like the arrangement? If it meets with Genl. Lee's and many other inferior officer's approval, you may look for me. It is 3 weeks today since the last battle. My wound, I think, will be quite well in another week. I am not suffering any at all from it now but it is not quite healed.

You have no idea how fine I feel with my new shirt, drawers and socks. The shirts are very handsome and all fit well. I wish I had my woolens safely deposited somewhere for winter. Our chaplain, Manning Brown, preached 2 sermons yesterday or last day. He is doing good in the regiment. I can see a change since his arrival. I like him very much. He has not been with us long. Several have joined the church. He preaches every Sunday and has prayer meetings once a week. They are well attended. I hope that our people yesterday throughout the Confederacy, lifted up their hearts and souls in solemn and earnest prayer to God to grant us success and an early termination to this wicked war. I hope your health is better than it has been usual with you in the summer. My own health and that of my company is very good. Tell Mr. Thompson Will is quite well and just came in from picket. They are all very well and in good spirits and have none of the gloomy apprehensions some seem to have at home. I enclose a letter to Ned, which you will please read to him. I want him to take a day or two and go down to Mr. Rodger's and see if he can rent a good piece of land. If he can get it, he can make more than you will want, plenty of flour, corn, peas, bacon and cow feed. I will leave the thing to his judgment after consulting Henry. It would do to postpone it till winter but for the fact wheat ought to be sown in October. I wish everybody would raise enough provisions to do them and then there could be no extortion. Government could get its supplies at its own price. We are now perfectly quiet and likely to remain so for several weeks. I feel, somehow, that Charleston will not be taken. I have strong hopes of its successfully withstanding every assault. My love to all.

Your affectionate husband,
L. Williams

270

Yesterday's Sunday morning sermon offered up by Chaplain Brown centered upon God's wisdom and mercy, and the Captain was moved as much by the messenger as the message. Like the other chaplains he wore an untrimmed officer's frock. But unlike the fire eating, hell and brimstoners who had invaded the camps so many times before him, Brown spoke not of the wages of sin but of God's tender mercy to long suffering soldiers who hadn't been paid in over two months. The flock assembled before him had already looked death in the eye and experienced hell first hand in the corpse-filled trenches and on the scarred battlefields of Virginia, Maryland, and Pennsylvania. Chaplain Brown had seen it all too. He touched only briefly on the hard war and their hard duty, then recited a reassuring passage from Isaiah to comfort the men. The preacher did not have to remind Captain Williams and the men of Company K that they were truly Christian soldiers marching on to war, and that only an abiding faith in God would sustain them. As the chaplain blessed them, thus concluding his heartening service, young and old alike whispered prayers of their own. The Captain paused to thank God that the bullet that had struck him had not done so a few inches lower, or to the right, lest his heart would have been pierced or his skull shattered. He prayed that brother Ephraim was seated at God's right hand, brother James was in caring hands, and that his dear wife and daughter had enough to eat. All left the campfire knowing they'd soon meet the enemy and possibly their maker.

September had arrived. Eyes would soon turn toward the armies massing around Lookout Mountain in Tennessee, and in a couple of weeks, Captain Williams would face the single most harrowing day in his military career. For the present, however, it was a time for writing and not for fighting. There was much on his mind- the safety of his family, the irregular mail service, the lack of supplies and letters from home and, of course, the progress of the war.

> *Camp Near Brandy Station, Va.*
> *September 5, 1863*
> *I recd your last letter of the 24th on the 2nd inst. and was sorry to learn that you were unwell. Your ride was too far for one not used to riding, especially in the hot sun. I wish to buy you a horse sometime this winter to send to you by Mid next March if I can buy a good saddle horse. The mare started today but she recd a kick which lamed her and I have some fear she may have to be left on the road. I am sorry she*

*will not suit you for riding, her gaits are rough. I sent her to Ned to work in the wagon and plow. I have a great deal of leisure lately, but now I expect work will begin. Day before yesterday, we were out on a scout day and night but without doing anything and today a review.*

*You are mistaken about your letters not coming through. I think I have recd them all. I recd yours of the 1ˢᵗ, 9ᵗʰ and 13ᵗʰ and 24ᵗʰ last month between the last 2, I had an interval of 11 days and would have been very uneasy about you (for I looked for your letter 5 or 6 days before it came), had not Will Thompson told me he had recd letters of the 14ᵗʰ and 19ᵗʰ and that you was well. I then began to blame Mr. Whitmire or Uncle Adam for neglect in mailing. It may be still they were somewhat at fault for though dated 24ᵗʰ, it did not reach me til the 2ⁿᵈ this month. I can't help but quarrel a little. I believe I wrote you 5 or 6 letters during the time you wrote me 3 or 4 and I have been on the point of writing frequently but put it off waiting to hear from you.*

*Did Henry get the letter I wrote him asking his opinion in regard to trying to farm a little next year? I wrote him explaining at length my opinions and plans and asked his views on the subject. I will be glad to hear from him on the subject. I wish you would tell Ned to fatten the mare. She is very poor having no corn for several months. He must get corn fodder. He must get her in good working order as soon as possible.*

*We have at present the company of W. P. Price, who is our guest. He has been with us 2 or 3 days. We find his company very agreeable and hope he will stay 2 or 3 days longer. He is here to distribute clothing & c to our regiment or to such as are in need. Shoes are badly needed, several being barefooted. As to clothing, they are doing well. I, myself, will need nothing except perhaps a pair of pants for a year unless I should lose my clothing. I am, however, much in want of a decent hat. I am now wearing a wool hat of the commonest kind looking pretty seedy, such as Steve used to wear. If you can get a good soft felt hat in Columbia, Perry's boy, Wiley, will bring it to me. I expect it will cost $30. Here they cost a good deal more than in Richmond. I can't get there to buy one.*

*Mid is doing well. He was sick in Md. and Pa. pretty bad off. He is now very well. It will take a great deal to winter both cows but if you think it best to keep both, do so, but don't let them get as low down as last winter. I have been interrupted so often, that darkness prevents me from writing more. The mail leaves in the morning very soon. If I have time I will finish in the morning.*

After a piece of hard tack and half a tin cup of rye coffee, he did indeed have a few minutes to add on to the letter the next morning.

*September 6th*
*Everything is still quiet along our lines. We are looking with deepest anxiety towards Charleston. I understand some of our most intelligent citizens in Charleston consider the fall of Charleston inevitable, but the telegrams encourage me to hope all will yet be well. The issues of the operations in Tenn. are fraught with great benefits or damage to our cause. I hope for the best. I have no sickness in the company. All are fit for duty. Tell baby her papa wants to see her and hear her talk and that she must be a good baby and go to Sunday school. Remember me to all and do write oftener.*

*Your affectionate husband*
*L. Williams*

On September 8, two days after he had sent his letter home, Confederate defenders evacuated Fort Wagner and barely managed to maintain hold of Fort Sumter by narrowly repulsing 400 Federal marines and sailors. Charleston was teetering on the brink, and the Lavals would soon have to flee to Columbia. Out in Tennessee, prospects were darker still as Rosecrans sneaked his Union army through a series of gaps in Lookout Mountain, threatened Braxton Bragg's supply and communication line to Atlanta, and occupied Chattanooga without firing a single shot. Lee had no choice but to dispatch Longstreet and 12,000 of his sorely needed men from the Army of Northern Virginia to the western theatre to help even the odds.

Back home, Anna was running desperately low on everything from corn to corsets. Even the unshakable Maum Fannie found herself in tears alone in the empty root cellar. Through it all, Carrie blissfully wore the same clothes and the same innocent smile every day. Leonard fared well enough except for his empty tobacco pouch and the tattered, ratty creation atop his head that he believed to be a hat. He almost lost the head that it sat upon a few days later.

On September 13, Meade's army, supported by a large cavalry force, advanced toward Culpeper County. A battle soon heated up around the courthouse and as Stuart watched from the distance, three guns of Thompson's Battery were in the midst of being captured by the Federals. Saving those guns was impossible so Thompson ordered his men to save themselves and their horses, but he turned to face the oncoming Federal force charging his position. The Union officer who now possessed the three prizes, was fifty yards ahead of his troopers when Thompson suddenly galloped toward him with his Colt blazing. Both men were firing at each other until one of Thompson's bullets hit the Federal officer, who fell dead from his horse. The now riderless horse continued to gallop toward Thompson who quickly snared the reins and raced down the streets of Culpeper. Although he lost three guns, Thompson had at least gained a prime new mount. Captain Williams and his gritty company helped fight off the pursuing riders until the Confederates had safely reached their defenses at Rapidan Station. After dashing across yet another moonlit river to safety, Leonard sat between his dear friend Calhoun Sparks and a weary Mid staring into a boiling tin pot containing something that looked and smelled like his sorry hat. Whatever it was, there were no leftovers for Ruby who was already fast asleep. Two days later, Leonard wrote a quick letter home to describe the fight.

> *Raccoon Ford*
> *Orange Co., Va.*
> *September 15, 1863*

*My Dear Anna,*

*We were in another severe fight on the 13th. We were again compelled to fall back before overwhelming numbers. We are now on the south side of the Rapidan. We had but few casualties in our regiment. Sergt. Beattie was severely wounded in the head near the temple. Our surgeon thinks he will get well though his wound is a bad one. I had no other casualty in my company except the wounding of a few horses. I sent Mr. Beattie a telegram yesterday and hope he will come on to see his son. The enemy have made a general advance. The river separates the two armies. Whether Meade intends to cross the river to give us battle, will be determined I presume, in a few days. The enemy are said to be in heavy force. Of this, I know nothing but they certainly have a very large cavalry force, perhaps treble ours. We have heard nothing from Charleston or Tenn. for 3 or 4 days. We are listening with the intensest anxiety. There is a mere rumor in camp that a collision has taken place between Bragg and Rosecrans and that we have badly beaten them. God grant it may be so. I do humbly trust our army in Charleston may hold out in its gallant resistance and utterly baffle and discomfit the enemy. Our army here is reduced by the withdrawal of Longstreet's corps for western service; notwithstanding, I believe our army is sanguine of its ability to whip the enemy if he gives battle.*

*I recd your letter of the 2nd Sept. but being constantly on duty since, have not had an opportunity to write earlier. Today, our regiment is resting. There is no sickness in my company. Write soon. Have you heard from James lately or from Robert? Kiss baby for me. My love to all. The mail is waiting for me so I must close.*

*Your affectionate husband*
*L. Williams*

The rumors were inaccurate. Captain Williams had been right. Bragg had retreated without a fight in Chattanooga and the Captain was accurate in his estimate of the number of Pleasonton's cavalry pursuing them in Virginia. General Judson Kilpatrick, General John Buford, and Colonel Thomas C. Devin led about 7,500 well-armed, strongly mounted troopers, while Jeb Stuart rode with only 2,500. Not only were the Confederates outnumbered three to one, M.C. Butler was still recuperating from his leg wound, and shot-up Wade Hampton would not be able to rejoin them until November. In precisely one week, these two cavalry forces would collide just north of the Rapidan. Out in Tennessee, two huge armies were already engaged in a bloody, pitched battle along the Chickamauga.

In what would prove to be the Confederates' last major victory in the west, General James Longstreet's eight brigades made the difference and nearly destroyed Rosecrans' entire army. That night, rescue workers tripped over corpses while searching for the wounded, guided only by their tapers and the chilling sounds of muffled groans. At the Battle of Chickamauga, Confederate General Braxton Bragg lost 20,000 killed, wounded, and missing, more than thirty percent of his effectives. Ten Confederate generals had been killed or wounded, including Hood who narrowly survived amputation of a leg. As Rosecrans reorganized his force behind his fortifications at Chattanooga, many Southerners questioned why Bragg had not finished the job when he had the advantage.

Like the very winds of war, Leonard had some questions swirling through his mind of a more immediate nature. What was to become of his in-laws in besieged Charleston? Where was Meade headed? What was Lee contemplating? Did his young mare arrive in Greenville yet? How long could Anna persevere? Where was brother James? On the very night that Bragg and Longstreet were drawing up their victorious attack plan, Leonard was jotting down a litany of concerns to his distant wife.

*Camp Near Orange C. H., Va.*
*September 19, 1963*

*My Dear Anna*

*I wrote you a hasty note while in battle line last Monday, the day after the fight and retreat to the Rapidan. We have since been pretty actively employed picqueting and some skirmishing. Today everything is quiet. I think it is very uncertain whether Meade intends to advance or not. The loss of Tennessee to the Confederacy is a very serious one, as it deprives us of the vast resources of that state for army supplies. The consequence; that government will be compelled to draw more heavily upon other states. If Charleston should fall, it will throw a great many people into the interior and upper portions of the state, the refugees from Tenn. too must find a home in some part of the country not yet overrun. I, therefore, apprehend a great many difficulties in procuring food for the army and people. I am sorry for the unfortunate who have to fly from their home and take up their abode amongst strangers, many of them, too, I have no doubt, with slender means. I'm sorry that you have not the means of accommodating some of them. They are entitled to our sympathy and aid.*

*Just as soon as new corn begins to come into market, get Mr. Whitmire to buy you 50 or 60 bu. I expect the mare will reach home in a few days. She was quite poor and I expect the trip home will reduce her still more. It is time to begin to feed the hogs more freely. I understand bacon is selling for $1.50 a lb. in Greenville. It is therefore* *important to urge their growth as fast as possible. I hope Mr. Whitmire has supplied you with flour. Now is the time to buy country molasses. Buy enough to do a year if they can be had. It's bad your potatoes are rotting. I am glad you have learned to make good light bread as it dispenses with a very scarce and costly ingredient (lard). The Virginians make a capital meal with dried fruit, light bread, butter and milk, but I have never seen anyone come up to the Virginians in making bread.*

*I wrote you that Sergt. Beattie was severely wounded. The wound, I am glad to say, is not as serious as was at first thought to be. The Dr. thinks he will get well. Gibbs of my company was sent out with another man on a scout on Monday and have not yet been heard from. I fear he is a prisoner. I understand Smith and Campbell Williams, who were taken on the 1st August are held with 20 other South Carolinians as hostages for the rendition of the negroe prisoners taken at Charleston and now in Gov. Bonham's hands. Have you heard anything more from James? I have heard nothing more than you told me. Has William Mitts left for the war yet? The times are more gloomy now than I have known them. We will no doubt have much suffering, both in the army and among our people at home, and the prospect of a peace indefinite. It may last another year or two.*

*How is Aunt Polly Feltz since the death of John? Remember me to her if you have an opportunity. I know that Whitfield's strength was insufficient for the hardships of a soldier. I regret his death very much. He ought to have had a place in some of the departments where there would have been no exposure. Where is Nathan Whitmire? I have not heard from him in a great while. I have not recd a letter from you in 10 days but I look for one tonight. You need not be afraid of repetition. Your letters are always full of interest. I will be glad to hear from you every 4 or 5 days at least til you catch up. We have nothing new in camp. The health of our regiment is very good. Have you sold my suit of clothes yet? I understand jeans is selling at from $10 to $12 per yd. I have no overcoat but will try to get one here. My love to all. Write soon.*

> *Your affectionate husband*
> *L. Williams*

Three days later, on September 22, Stuart's Cavalry was marching north up the turnpike from Liberty Mills above the Rapidan. Leonard and the 2nd South Carolina guarded the rear of that column. Ruby seemed more fidgety than usual and with good reason. At the same time, General John Buford was on a reconnaissance, heading south and parallel to the turnpike. Buford was searching for passable fords across the Rapidan, and in order to cover more ground he had divided his cavalry division almost equally into three parts as they headed south. Buford took 2,500 troopers and headed down the old Blue Ridge Turnpike. To his right Kilpatrick led a column of about 2,500, while Colonel Thomas C. Devin guided 2,500 men on the left. Buford's troopers were on a collision course with Stuart's 2,500 riders. Neither commander knew the whereabouts of the other until a scout raced back to Stuart informing him that Buford was just minutes away and closing fast. Although outnumbered three to one, and unaware that Buford had split his force into three deadly prongs, Stuart had two distinct advantages. First, he possessed six guns capably managed by the battle-tested artillerists of Chew's Battery. Second, he had infantry support only a half an hour away, under the command of General Isaac Trimble. Stuart instantly dispatched a courier to inform Trimble to come on the double quick. At around 10 A. M., Buford and Stuart, familiar foes who had squared off at Brandy Station, near Gettysburg, and in skirmishes before and after, collided again at Schifflet's Corner.

As the battle heated up, Leonard and Ruby ultimately found themselves in the front of the column as lead riders continually peeled back to reload and reform. Not far from Buford himself, the Captain formed his 45-man squadron smartly and ordered the first of many charges on a day that would indeed be the most dangerous and demanding he'd ever face. Stirrup to stirrup he fought with pistol and saber. His tender right shoulder ached from the gunshot wound just seven weeks earlier. He struggled to wield his saber that was getting heavier by the moment. He felt every day of his 39 years as he toiled under the blazing sun, often times being assaulted by two and three bluecoats at a time. "About Wheel! Charge! Fall back! Reform!" He screamed the orders, gripped the reins, and spurred gallant Ruby to the limit. Both his Colt pistols empty, Leonard reined up to reload. His hands were sweaty and shaking; his vision blurred with the swirl and smoke of battle. Buford's men were closing fast on his tiny squadron. Calhoun Sparks was fighting like Hampton himself with the force of ten men. Young Corporal McClanahan, whom the Captain had saved a year ago by pulling him out from under his horse, fired away by his side. Chambers full now, the Captain ordered yet another charge.

"Fall back!" shouted Stuart. Leonard and his squadron wheeled around with Buford hot on their tails. Stuart's six guns on the nearby knoll began firing into the heart of Buford's advancing horde. Moments later, Leonard's squadron formed to spearhead yet another charge when they came under heavy fire. Kilpatrick's 2,500 men had outflanked the Confederates to the southwest and were now fighting dismounted behind a tall, five rail pioneer fence. Stuart ordered the men of the 2nd S. C. to hold at all costs, but now they would have only three guns instead of six supporting them. The others had been turned in the direction of the new threat from Kilpatrick.

Suddenly, the quiet village of Jack's Shop, named for a well-respected blacksmith who resided there, was the site of a grand cavalry spectacle. The harried crew of Chew's Battery found themselves ramrodding for all they were worth, firing north and south simultaneously as charges were launched in unison in both directions from the hill. The Confederates were caught in a classic crossfire. Those facing Buford were picked off by Kilpatrick's men behind the fence. Those charging Kilpatrick were drilled between the shoulder blades by Buford's sharpshooters. Leonard Williams wasn't the only one who stole a furtive look west toward the safe mountain passes of the Blue Ridge. Those magnificent mountains rose just minutes away from the clashing sword and the whizzing bullets. They had hidden Stonewall's men before. They had screened Lee's army on its way to Gettysburg. They looked damned tempting right now as the situation went from bad to worse.

To the north was the stern Kentuckian, John Buford. To the south was the irascible Judson Kilpatrick. In the middle of these two forces, Stuart suddenly realized that Colonel Devin was riding to the sounds of the guns with 2,500 more men. Jeb was trapped. None could escape and all six guns would certainly be lost. With each passing second, Stuart's men were being pressed back around the overworked cannons on the knoll. Two were blasting away at Buford. Two were raining volleys down on Kilpatrick's dismounted force behind the fence. And now two more were aimed toward Devin's galloping reinforcements. Stuart's men looked to him.

With Trimble's infantry unwilling or unable to come to his rescue, Stuart's only slim hope now was to break out, splitting Kilpatrick like the Red Sea, and leading an all out race for the Rapidan and the cover of Trimble's tardy infantry.

Leonard's task was to lead one final, near suicidal charge into Buford's sea of blue as the rest of Stuart's troopers charged Kilpatrick. With one final spur of Ruby, the Captain shouted "About Wheel!" and his squadron leaped forward. At the same time, Stuart's riders soared over the five rail fence in front of them and divided Kilpatrick's stunned men in a few spots just wide and long enough for his men to cut their way to freedom. Chew's Battery clattered right behind them with all six guns in tow.

Chaos ruled as the Confederate cavalrymen raced down the turnpike toward Liberty Mills in disorganized clusters, screaming their unnerving Rebel Yell. In one of those desperate groups was Calhoun Sparks, McClanahan, and a dust-covered Captain Leonard Williams, each riding at breakneck speed, firing away over their shoulders as they sped south down the turnpike past Old Jack's blacksmith shop toward the Rapidan. Buford's bluecoats followed but not at a full gallop. They couldn't risk stumbling blindly into a body of infantry that may be waiting around the next bend to enfilade them or blast them directly in their faces. The Yankees' hesitant pursuit now allowed Stuart's force to escape.

Somehow, at around 5 o'clock in the evening, after seven hours of insane fighting, Leonard Williams found himself in one piece next to six still smoking pieces of artillery. Outnumbered and surrounded, Stuart had incredibly saved his men and his guns and added to his reputation as perhaps the finest cavalry commander of them all. To Jeb, his escape against all odds was just in a day's work, and he never bothered to make a report concerning his miracle at Jack's Shop. He did, however, deem it of the utmost importance to personally commend one man and one squadron for their unsurpassed valor and courage that day. Stuart rode over to Leonard, who was sharing a tin cup of cool Rapidan water with Corporal McClanahan. The dashing figure dismounted and the humble Captain rose to salute him. Stuart returned the gesture then shook Leonard's hand. The cool commander proclaimed that he had witnessed more cavalry charges than anyone on the continent, but none quite as bold as the one Williams led late that day at Jack's Shop. The Captain blushed. McClanahan grinned. The general galloped off.

Stuart's demeanor and that of his men in the battle of Jack's Shop, dispelled all rumor that the cavalry had lost confidence in their commander as a result of his tardiness and defeat at Gettysburg. John Buford and his riders had fought admirably that day as well. To be sure, a golden opportunity to capture Stuart and his guns had slipped through his fingers, but Buford's mission was reconnaissance, not an all out attack. In any case, everyone had certainly done their duty and performed well. The same can be said for Ruby. The old girl was tractable and fearless. For hours on end, without a sip of water, she carried her master in and out of danger. She galloped as swiftly late in the afternoon as in the morn, racing full tilt on weary legs with a sore back down the turnpike to Liberty Mills. She still glistened with sweat as Mid unsaddled her. Carefully, he led her down to the banks of the Rapidan for a long overdue drink. Streamlets of blood trickled down both her flanks from the Captain's spurs, but Mid knew that in a day or two she'd be back in first rate shape. Now, with her nose immersed in the cool Rapidan, Ruby simply drank her fill. It was reward enough for her.

Moments later, as the Captain watched Mid tend to Ruby, Calhoun Sparks ambled over to congratulate his tired friend on his late afternoon charge, and to remark on the stylishness of the Captain's new hat, that he had captured in the fighting. Later Leonard would write Anna a detailed account of the action, and about the hat.

*North of Rapidan*
*Orange Co., Va.*
*September 25, 1863*

*My Dear Anna,*

*Since my last we have gone through the ordeal of another day's fight against great odds. Information was recd that the Yankees were moving beyond our left flank in heavy force towards Charlottesville with the view of destroying the RR and other property. We were moved at daylight day before and about 11 ock met them. We had our usual luck to fight and retire before superior numbers. The position we first held was so obstructed that we were liable to be flanked and indeed we were at one time almost encompassed. After 3 or 4 hours of fighting, we fell back to a better position, where the enemy refused to attack us. The next day, yesterday, being reinforced, we drove them back across the Robinson River. They were completely baffled in their purposes. We took about a hundred prisoners and we lost 40 or 50 prisoners. Our regiment lost 4 killed and some 8 or 10 wounded in the company. Jos. Knotts was severely wounded in the neck. He is, however, doing very well.*

*The enemy got round us which made it necessary to fall back. At the same time two charges were made, one to the front, and the other to the rear while we were retiring. The enemy were pressing us severely with their sharpshooters. I was ordered to charge them. With my squadron, it was a dashing charge and a success. We drove the enemy into the woods and gave the brigade time to move off, at the same time the Philips Legion made a brilliant charge to the front and routed them. These two charges enabled us to draw off in a better position of safety. I regret losing two capital men in the charge belonging to Company D (Capt. Hydrick). This company with mine constitutes the 3rd Squadron, which I have the honor to command. My squadron behaved gallantly and recd the commendations of our col. and also Col. Gordon Comdg. and everyone who witnessed it.*

*After two days incessant marching and fighting, we succeeded in thwarting the enemy and driving him back across the river. The Richmond papers erroneously state our loss at much greater than it was. I presume our loss is less than about 100 in all killed, wounded and prisoners. The enemy lost that many prisoners and no doubt many in killed and wounded. The enemy are now beyond Robinson River which empties into the Rapidan near Rapidan Station.*

*Our army here is in high spirits on account of the great victory at Chickamauga. From the last dispatches, Rosecrans is cut off from his supplies at Chattanooga and that he will now have to give battle. I do hope our advantages are not overstated and that something still better may grow out of the situation.*

*I lost my old hat in the charge, which the enemy captured. I had the good fortune to borrow a cap on the field, which I am still wearing, waiting for the arrival of Sergt. Benson. The weather is quite chilly, have had 2 frosts.*

The next day Leonard added a postscript that revealed both the dwindling strength of the unit, and his growing concern for his extended family.

*September 26th*
*We are quite well. Health of our regiment has never been better. The regiment now has only about 125 men for duty. About 200 of them*

*are at home for horses and a good many here are without any. I have 5 men now in hospitals from severe wounds but I think they are all doing well. Have you seen no account of James yet in the papers? I am uneasy about him. Have you heard from Robert? I recd both your last letters of the 11ᵗʰ and the 17ᵗʰ at the same time. Was glad to hear you were all getting on so well and remember me to friends and write soon.*

*Your affectionate husband*
*L. Williams*

The fall days were shorter and their shadows longer. As October's chilly gales whipped through camp, the Captain got wind of two pieces of heartening news. The young mare had somehow survived her journey and had made it all the way back to Greenville, and raising his spirits even more, Leonard learned that brother James had not been left solely in enemy hands. The chaplain of the 14th South Carolina Volunteer Infantry had remained behind at Gettysburg to preside over the spiritual needs of James and what was left of his regiment, decimated during the first day of that horrific battle. Perhaps it was fortunate that Federal physicians had presided over his aftercare. Morphine and chloroform were all but gone from Confederate field hospitals as a result of the now unbreakable naval blockade. Leonard pictured his younger brother recovering in a Union hospital and was relieved that he would soon be paroled back to South Carolina. The Captain had also swapped his pocket mirror for a substantial quantity of cherry tobacco, and as wreaths and curls of blue smoke danced above him, he began a long letter home, secure in the knowledge that James had to fight no more.

*Camp between Robinson and Rapidan River*
*October 1, 1863*

*My Dear Anna*
*We are enjoying a brief repose, in consideration of the arduous duty gone through with, but I do not know at what moment it may be broken into. I recd yours of the 24ᵗʰ, 2 days ago and was glad to hear you were all well. I am very much pleased, of course, with the accounts you give of baby. But few children enjoy so good and uninterrupted health. I am glad to hear of her activity and sprightliness. Teach her*

*that your will must be her law and to fear to do anything displeasing to you. Children very soon learn to distinguish between right and wrong.*

*It is said that Meade has sent 2 corps of his army west to reinforce Rosecrans. If it be so, I presume Meade will not venture an advance. It seems to me that our authorities ought to strengthen Bragg to enable him to meet the accumulating forces of Rosecrans. Our victory is not complete while the enemy are allowed to fortify and occupy Chattanooga. I had hoped that they would have been dislodged before this time. I hope, however, that their source of communication and supplies with Nashville is cut off, Longstreet being said to occupy Lookout Mountain, which commands the river and RR.*

*I visited yesterday McGowan's Brigade and saw a good many of my acquaintances. I heard that the chaplain of the 14th Regiment, who remained at Gettysburg with the wounded, in a letter about 3 weeks ago, reported that James was doing very well. I suppose that, as he will never be fit for field duty, he will be exchanged as soon as he is well enough.*

*I wrote Mr. Whitmire 2 or 3 days ago and asked to buy 10 bu more wheat and if you could not take care of it for him, to store it upstairs until you needed it. It will take some 5 or 6 barrels of flour to do you. I also asked him to buy as much homemade molasses as you thought you would need and also 2 gall. for myself. I never cared too much for molasses at home but now there is nothing I am fonder of. I also asked him to provide you corn and cow feed. You must try to keep your cows up and in good milking condition this winter.*

*You must have fodder provided for the mare. Corn will not do without fodder or hay. The mare's leg was only swollen when she left. I expect, however, rest and plenty of feed will soon bring her out. She has endured the severest hardships. I wish you would have the mare tried in a wagon to see if she will work and try it before she gets rested well. She will be easier broke to work than when she gets fat and also ask Henry to buy me a one horse wagon and harness. Even if it costs 200 or 300 get a good one. Perhaps it will be as well to get one from Gower, Cox, Markley & Co. With a one horse wagon Ned ought to make $3 per day. I wrote to Henry some time ago to try to hire Steve and Nan next year to Mr. Cox. He might get Bill in with them. He is old* enough to begin to learn how to work. I requested him to bargain for corn in place of money for their hire. I would be glad if a support could be made next year without applying to Mr. Whitmire as I have no doubt his business will be small. It would be at any rate, precarious, and if the business should cease altogether, I would like to get underway a system of employment for Ned, Steve and Nan as would under ordinary circumstances, ensure a good supply of provisions.

You need not think for a moment, my dear Anna, that your affectionate entreaties are obtrusive or distasteful. On the other hand I recd them with deep emotions and hope I am profited by them. I am glad to see religion taking deep root in our army. Revivals are taking place, I believe, in all the regiments. Our regiment is much changed in the last few months, which I think is due to the religious feeling in the regiment. The health of my company and regiment is very good and the army seems to be in good condition.

I am disgusted with the Charleston Mercury in its abuse of President Davis. He says the army and people have lost confidence in him; as far as the army is concerned, it is untrue. I have never seen anyone who did not have full confidence in the wisdom and purposes of Mr. Davis and I believe the Army of Northern Virginia would now give Mr. Davis a unanimous vote for the presidency if a reelection was now to take place. The course of the Mercury, if it had influence, is calculated to do a great amount of mischief.

I hear the Yankees are fortifying at the warm springs on the French Broad, about 90 miles from Greenville. The passes over the mountains are easily held and I hope the state troops may be stationed at the gap to prevent any incursion. I do not apprehend a thing of the kind, at least while things are in the present attitude.

My horse holds out most remarkably. I have rode her in every campaign and excursion since I have been in the war and she has never failed. She is now getting in good order and I would not take a thousand dollars for her. Now remember me to Auntie and all and tell baby her papa is glad she is a good baby and goes to Sunday school and loves mother. Write soon.

Your affectionate husband
L. Williams

285

*P.S. If your potatoes are rotting, you had better get Mr. Whitmire to dispose of a part of them. You did not tell me about your onion crop. Now the weather is getting cold, you ought to have a bbl of crout made. It will keep til next spring until early greens come.*

A week later, General Lee considered it the opportune time to attempt to turn the Union right flank and interpose his stubborn Confederate army between Meade and Washington in what would be called his Bristoe Campaign. Lee hoped to reverse the momentum the North had generated since Gettysburg, and as always, Stuart's Cavalry would play a prominent role in covering his movements around Culpeper County. The riverdance continued with a recrossing of the Rapidan. Leonard and the horsemen of Company K were sent out on a reconnaissance mission toward Catlett's Station.

Meanwhile, Lomax had discovered a large body of Federals and their well-stocked, half-mile long wagon train near Warrenton Junction. Stuart hoped to secure its contents for his half-starved riders as he raced toward the wagons. He gazed on the coveted prize through his field glasses. There they were, wagons loaded with meat, fodder, and ammunition. Behind them were caissons, ambulances, and supply wagons brimming with everything from cabbages to carbines. But as he panned his field glasses to the left, Stuart's expression suddenly changed from anticipation to frustration. Just beyond the wagons, he spied a moving cloud of dust rising from the trees, the sure sign of Federal infantry on the move. There could be no raid.

At dusk, Stuart rearranged his columns, bringing up his artillery and alerting his cavalry as the Federal columns moved closer. He then ordered his outnumbered force up on a wooded ridge where they were to remain silent while the Federals passed by. Protected by the trees, Leonard and his company dismounted, laying down and holding the reins in their nervous hands. In less than an hour, Stuart's silent men were surrounded by bluecoats. So close was the enemy that Leonard and Mid could overhear the Yankees laughing and playing cards around their campfires.

That night, Stuart's sentries captured a few stunned Union soldiers who had ventured up the ridge in search of firewood. Eyeing the prisoners, the resourceful general settled on an idea as to how to yet again save his trapped guns and men. Corporal E. Proileau Henderson, of the Beaufort District Troop, recalled both their prickly situation and the manner in which Stuart hoped to rectify it.

> *Soon after we captured the prisoners...Gen. Stuart made several of his Virginia troopers, who knew every foot of the country, don the knapsacks of the wood-hunters, and started them afoot to Warrenton C. H., through the Yankee lines, bearing this message for Gen. R. E. Lee. 'I am completely surrounded by the enemy, will you please send some of your people to help me out.' What a night it was. It seemed to me it was forty-eight hours long. No saddles taken off, and worse than that, nothing to eat. It was worse than fighting. As I heard one of the men say, when the order was extended that no matches were to be struck; 'What, all night without a smoke; I would rather fight all night, than to be deprived of smoking my pipe.' Just after daybreak the next morning... we heard musketry in the direction of New Baltimore, and we knew that Gen. Lee had sent a force to 'help us out.' Gen. Stuart had his artillery ready, the pieces loaded with grape and canister. He immediately ordered them to 'open fire' on the nearest camp of the enemy, and if you ever saw men run and leave their cooking in a hurry, it was that body of Yankees. I am sorry to say that we did not have time to get any of their breakfast, for Gen. Stuart ordered a charge through their lines...and we soon joined our infantry in safety.*

A few days later, the Captain and his messmates were sharing a pan full of poached eggs Mid had come across in a rickety old hen house nearby. "That old farmer will never even miss 'em," chuckled Calhoun. Afterwards, the Captain lit the pipe he had to forego a few nights earlier. Soon he was filling yet another page with thoughts home to dear Anna and Carrie. As always, his concerns for the family were foremost on his mind, even in the midst of war.

> *Camp between Robinson and Rapidan*
> *October 8, 1863*

*My Dear Anna*
> *I recd yours of the 1ˢᵗ inst. through Mr. Montgomery. I was glad to hear of your continued health. I am glad too that your sisters are with you. A part of my programme is commenced. They can stay with you til December and then you can go home with them. This part is all very*

*easy and practicable but there comes the uncertain part of the proposition, my meeting you in Columbia and spending Christmas with the Major and thence home for a whole month. Here is the difficulty. It depends on what the enemy may be doing, upon the weather, the pleasure of Col. Lipscomb, Genls. Butler, Hampton, Stuart and Lee. I shall, not withstanding, make an effort about the 20th December, if everything is quiet to get a leave of absence. I would like very much to be at home now to look out for a piece of land for Ned but apart from this I think Jan. is the best time for me to be at home.*

*I expect Mr. Westfield will work Genl. Easley's land again. I do not know anything about Mrs. Loveland's place but I expect it is a pretty good place. I hardly know what to advise. I would say, however, that if Mrs. Loveland has a field of 8 acres or such a matter of land, and well fenced, that if it is suited for wheat, that I would like to get it and have it sown at once. It will take only a couple of weeks or thereabouts to prepare the land and sow and will require no more labor until it ripens. Let the corn land alone til I get home. It will be time enough then to bargain for corn land. Tell Ned to go to Mrs. Loveland's, and see if she has a field of 8 or 10 acres of wheat land and well fenced to engage it and then proceed to prepare the ground as soon as possible. Ask Mr. Whitmire to get seed wheat of a good kind. Tell Ned if he gets the land to prepare it well to sow and put in the wheat carefully. It ought to be grown this month.*

*Since the fight at Jack's Shop, we have been comfortably well. I was on picket yesterday. The enemy are thick on the other side of the river but have no indication of their intentions to advance. We hear their drums and bugles every day. I recd a letter from Robert last night. He is in good health. He is detached on the Engineer Corps and working on the fortifications. Tell Julia and Susan they must stay with you til I get home. Remember me to all and write soon.*

*Your affectionate husband*
*L. Williams*

In the absence of their fallen leader, Colonel Pierce Young presently commanded Butler's Brigade during Lee's Bristoe Campaign, and on October 10, the brigade marched out to Woodville on the Sperryville Turnpike.

Riverdancing yet again, Stuart then led Young's Brigade across the Robinson at Russell's Ford toward James City. The enemy's picket at Russell's Ford was driven back to Bethsaida Church, where the 120th New York Infantry and part of Kilpatrick's cavalry waited in reserve. While Gordon's Brigade attracted the Federal's attention in front, Stuart led Young's command through the woods to the right and rear. Williams was part of Young's force, but unlike Jack's Shop, it was the 1st S. C. Cavalry that led the decisive charge this time, routing the Union riders. Young's Brigade alone captured 87 prisoners.

After aiding in the prisoner round up, Leonard and his men then headed for James City, two and a half miles away, where Kilpatrick's Cavalry, supported by infantry and six guns, were mounted on a knoll north of town. Having successfully screened the army, Stuart wisely chose to hold his position rather than attack. A bit later, another Confederate general was not so shrewd. On October 13, the usually steady General A. P. Hill, a native of Culpeper County, stumbled into a Federal trap at Bristoe Station. The year before, Stonewall's Brigade captured wagonloads of Pope's supplies there before the Second Battle of Bull Run and brother James had shared in the good fortune. But this time providence was not on the Confederate side as Hill lost 1,300 in captured and killed at Bristoe. Lee's advance was halted.

Six days later, Leonard and his cavalrymen sprung a trap of their own a few miles away near Buckland Mills. Stuart once again found himself with Kilpatrick in front of him, but 27-year old Major General Fitz Lee, nephew of General Robert E. Lee, had an idea. Stuart listened then nodded approvingly. Lee's plan called for Stuart to withdraw from Kilpatrick along the Warrenton Turnpike in the hopes that the enemy would follow in pursuit. In concert with Stuart's retrograde movement, Lee would come up and press Kilpatrick from the rear. At the sound of the first gun, Stuart would wheel his column around and charge Kilpatrick. The Union force would then be trapped. What transpired came to be known as the "Buckland Races."

When Lee's cannon opened fire, Stuart's men sprung into action. The division wheeled about and charged headlong into Davie's brigade, while Gordon's brigade covered the road. Pierce Young, along with Leonard's company, charged one flank, while Tom Rosser's troopers charged the other. The sudden Confederate attack shattered the Federal lines. Routed in front and rear, Kilpatrick's men broke and galloped off for their lives. Leonard and his fellow South Carolinians spurred their horses, yelling like madmen as they raced after the bluecoats. The chase continued for nearly five miles but Young's men were unable to get near enough to hit the fleeing Yankees, although they rode like hell to do so.

As the memories came back to him now, the Old Captain again began to pace about his room back at the Planter's Hotel. In his mind, he raced once more through the woods near Buckland. What a race it was. Ducking to avoid a low hanging black oak branch, he lost the hat he had picked up at Jack's Shop, then Ruby threw a shoe somewhere between a leap of a stream and a soar over a rail fence. An impatient Pierce Young yelled for everyone to put their spurs to their mounts. Leonard shouted the order back to his squadron of riders. Ruby, reaching deep inside her, found the stamina to maintain her lead in the mad dash. Dust flew in the air as did a flock of startled crows. Sabers clattered and pistol shots cracked. Rebel yells echoed through the gnarled woods and across trampled corn fields as Young's brigade launched a final, all out sprint toward Broad Run to cut off the surprised Federals. The hard charging Confederates bagged hundreds of trapped bluecoats, as well as General George Custer's headquarters wagon, baggage and papers. But the blond haired Custer, who had thwarted them near Gettysburg, disappeared on the other side of the stream, a hair before Young's men arrived at the scene.

The Old Captain sniffed and crinkled his nose at the thought of letting Custer get away. He returned to his chair, quickly reading the letter that detailed his account of James City, A. P. Hill's failed attack, and of course, the exhilaration of the famed Buckland Races. He had so much to share with his distant wife that he had not written his usual "My Dear Anna" and, as he had at Buckland Mills, cut right to the chase.

*Bivouac near Hazel River*
*Culpeper Co., Va.*
*October 22, 1863*

*We have just concluded another arduous campaign of 2 weeks. Genl. Lee has made another failure. His plans, I have no doubt, were well conceived but it is said owing to Genl. Hill's slow marches, the enemy had time to affect a timely retreat. I hear Genl. Hill is under arrest. If Genl. Hill had been up on time, Genl. Lee could have forced them into a general engagement. Genl. Lee has been forced to fall back again on account of supplies for the army and the whole country from the Rappahannock to the Potomac is in unbroken waste- the people have all fled from their homes and the Yankees have burned a great many places. Fencing has been destroyed for miles and miles, not a corn stalk can be seen, "nor a rose left on the stalk to tell where the garden had been". The enemy were driven into their fortifications near Centreville. The cavalry went around to their rear and felt and found out their position.*

*It was the fortune of our regiment to be engaged in only two of the many fights. Our cavalry was engaged in both advancing and falling back. The first, in Culpepper, we came into the fight about 5 ½ ock in the evening. We drove the enemy from the field without any loss on our part except 2 or 3 wounded. The Yankee cavalry have been whipped and driven back in every fight. In the last fight at Buckland, 6 miles beyond Warrenton, we retreated leisurely til about 4 ½ ock and then turned on them. Our brigade was sent around to flank them but Stuart pressed them so severely that he routed them and drove them back in the utmost confusion and with such rapidity, our brigade could not reach the point of attack before they were driven beyond it. We, therefore, missed the exciting mele. We captured 350 prisoners. Killed and wounded, I suppose, from one hundred to one hundred and fifty. It was the completest rout of the war. In the several engagements, our cavalry has made the capture of 1,200 or 1,500 prisoners. Our army is now on the south side of the Rappahannock.*

*The campaign was a very trying one. The troops were much distressed for want of provisions- several days without a mouthful to eat and at no time with half enough. Yet it was borne without a murmur. I lost one of my men, John Green, in the first fight at James City. He was acting courier for Genl. Gordon- he was the son of Mr. Pleasant Green, who you remember came to see me at my home. He was a brave and good soldier and if his life would have been spared would have made a useful citizen. He was killed instantly by a shell. I regret his loss very much.*

*We had a large mail yesterday but nothing for me. I have not recd a letter from you in nearly 3 weeks. In my haste I forgot to mention that the hat, hdkfs., and towel came safely to hand. The hat is very handsome and fits nicely- the hdkfs. were also very acceptable as I had been without one for months. The tobacco bag was also a beautiful present, universally admired, give Miss Sallie my compliments and thanks for the elegant present. Did you get my last letter of the 8th or 10th? I advise to get 8 or 10 acres of land and have it sown in wheat and wait til I get home to select land for corn.*

*I understand Genl. Butler has been assigned to S. C. for duty and that he has applied to the War Department for the transfer of our regiment to his command. I would be pleased in the change in some respects but would fear to be kept there during the summer. I have no doubt it would be easier to get home. I think campaigning is about over here this winter. I fear our victory in Tennessee will eventuate in no permanent advantage. We hear that Longstreet has been placed in command of Bragg's army. The health of our army is fine. I have no sickness at all in my company. How is the mare doing? Has she got well? Tell Ned to give her plenty of feed. Has Henry bought a wagon yet? Write soon and give me all the news.*

> *Your affectionate husband*
> *L. Williams*

At the close of the Bristoe Campaign, the Confederates were again encamped on the Rappahannock along the Orange and Alexandria Railroad bed back in old Culpeper County. It would be weeks before Federal engineers could repair the torn up tracks and bent rails enabling Meade to supply his army. Holding the line of the "Nile of the East" once more, Leonard rode the familiar picket line, assigned guard duty, and looked for letters from Anna everyday. He also kept his eye out for a young colt to replace the mare he had sent back home and scanned the week-old Richmond papers for developments in Tennessee and Charleston. Always, he searched for nourishing forage for Ruby. Rations were still short.

One morning while mounting up for morning patrol, his pants suddenly slid down. He reached into his knapsack, fished around for his bowie knife, then cut a new notch in his belt a full inch and a half. As he trotted out toward the nearest Rappahannock ford, he estimated that from Upperville to Buckland Mills he had lost close to twenty pounds. Winter was approaching and he knew his body had little on reserve to draw upon. He shivered now as Ruby splashed along the river. A few minutes later, he spied a Union picket from one of

Buford's Brigades mirroring his duties from the other side. Leonard calmly reined up as did his counterpart. The blue clad sergeant studied the lean rider perched atop his bony, red-maned mount across from him. Leonard looked longingly at the fine black steed effortlessly supporting his well-fed master. Neither man said a word. After a lingering pause, each moved off, like the destiny of their respective armies, in opposite directions.

As Leonard and a handful of riders from his squadron neared their Stevensburg encampment, they rode past the exact location where Butler lost his foot and young Frank Hampton his life. An hour later, the thin, worn down Captain reached for his stubby, worn down pencil. The news he wrote reflected the season and his mood.

*Camp Near Stephensburg, Va.*
*October 26, 1863*

*My Dear Anna*

*We are again in camp, near the spot we occupied last winter. We may remain here a month or longer. As I mentioned in my last, I think active operations are over fore the winter. Our duties will consist of picketing, scouting & c. Our brigade is picketing the same fords on the Rappahannock it did last winter. I am enjoying rest which I appreciate highly. Our last campaign was as severe and trying as any we have ever had. Had it not been that we found Yankee crackers in their deserted camps, we would have suffered from hunger. In 13 days we drew rations for only 5. The men lived on persimmons, acorns and parched corn.*

*I am very sorry to hear the mare would not work. She is very gentle. I think she can be broke. Send her to Mr. Poole, I think he can make her work, if not, get her fat and in good keeping so that I can trade her for a good workhorse.*

*There is considerable excitement in the regiment on account of a prospect of exchanging with Aiken's Regt. and getting to S. C. I, for my part, am not so elated. I dread the malarias of the low country. I am willing, however, to try it, in fact, would be rather glad. I would certainly be able to see you oftener and direct business at home much better. I hear the governor has called into service every man up to 60 years of age. If so, Mr. Whitmire will have to go. I hope it is not the case.*

*What have you done with my overcoat and suit of clothes made for me last winter? I learned jeans is selling at Greenville for $8 and $10 per yd. If so, you ought to be able to get a good price for the suit and will try to get government cloth for an overcoat. If you cannot sell the clothes, keep them. I can dispose of them here. I am glad Wm. has undertaken to buy corn for you. Ask him to buy you 50 bushels. If I get home I will get more. How are the hogs doing? You must keep the cows up. With plenty of milk and butter a good start is made towards a living. He may be able to buy you a few bu. of wheat. Since the mare refuses to work or if she cannot be broken to the plow, I do not know how Ned can put in the wheat. Ask Henry to assist in breaking the mare. I am satisfied with proper effort she can be made to work.*

*The Yankees have taken off all the negroes from this county. It is said they are turned off the cars with nothing to eat and nowhere to get shelter. They are crying and begging in Alexandria to be brought back to their masters. The last time they went back, they nearly stripped the county of negroes.*

*Do you know anything of the probability of James getting paroled or exchanged; I will be glad to hear of his getting home. How large are your turnips? If you have a good crop, by washing them well and cutting them up or boiling, they will help out the cow feed very much. Write soon. My respects to all and kiss baby.*

> *Your affectionate husband*
> *L. Williams*

On the icy morning of November 5, the Captain's thoughts were far away as he tossed some more tinder on the fire. It was Carrie's birthday, the third she would celebrate without her father. Certainly Maum Fannie would fashion together something resembling a cake for her, even if there were no candles within a hundred miles from Greenville to place on top of it. Mid thought it sad indeed that even the South's very youngest had to make sacrifices. "Lil Carrie aint got one tallow candle to help brighten up these dark days," he lamented.

There was little time to ponder sacrifices or circumstances for the Captain or the men of the 2nd S. C. Cavalry. There was to be a full review that afternoon. Mid meticulously brushed Ruby, smoothed out her saddle blanket, cleaned out her shoes, and tightened her tack. The Captain put a shine on his saber and loaded both revolvers and his short rifle. Mid then fussed with his master's wrinkled and stained uniform and put a hasty spit shine on his cavalry boots. There could be no imperfections to catch the eye of the general about to inspect them. A half an hour later, the columns were formed for the review, but it was a less grand and far different one than what Stuart had orchestrated five months earlier at Brandy. The ranks were thinner now, as were the men and their horses. Suddenly, a bugle blew and the men came to attention. Standing before them was the great man himself, General Robert E. "Bobby" Lee, mounted on Traveler. Man and horse were only ten yards away from Captain Leonard Williams and Ruby.

Leonard seized the moment to study the man, who while leading them never slept or ate any better than the lowest private. His eyes outsparkled the three stars on each collar. They were wise eyes that had seen victory far more than defeat. Young privates peered into those eyes for future success. Leonard marveled at how those eyes had seen them through so much already. In turn, the general looked into the faces of the men. He saw beyond the worn uniforms and gaunt mounts; he seemed to look deep into their hearts. To Leonard, the general appeared every bit the gentle warrior who once stooped to pick up and care for a stunned bird as shells burst and bullets whizzed by him. He seemed to be the true, living masterpiece of military art in its highest form. He possessed the rare requisites of leadership, the wisdom to strike boldly, and the strength to suffer stoically.

But now, on this bitter cold, overcast winter afternoon, the Captain wondered how much more his near 57-year old commander could endure. The esteemed general pondered the same question about his hungry cavalrymen. As the veteran West Pointer concluded his inspection of the final column, Leonard sensed that he would never again look directly into the eyes of Robert Edward Lee, the very face of their noble, lost cause, in whom power and mercy mingled in full measure. The review ended and the men were dismissed, returning to camp. The Captain hung up his saber and unbuttoned his jacket. He now had time to write home. As always, he was concerned about how things were being managed there, and he wanted to tell Anna that he had just seen Lee.

*Camp Near Stephensburg, Va.*
*November 6, 1863*

*My Dear Anna*

*I have been so much engaged for the last week that I have had no opportunity at all to write and this morning I have time only to write a few hurried lines. I recd yours and Mr. Whitmire's letter of the 25th and Henry's of the 26th all by the same mail. I was glad to hear you was all well. If the mare cannot be broken to the plow, I do not know what is to be done about the wheat. I have considerable confidence, however, that she can be broken. As to seed wheat, it seems to me that 8 or 10 bu might be bought at Greenville. Col. Irvine or Mr. Gilreath, I have no doubt, could furnish it. I wish Mr. Whitmire would see to it at once as now is the time for sowing and if the mare will not work, Ned must go into the country and hire a plow horse for putting in the wheat. If the mare is made fat in case she refuses to work, I can trade her well. She is worth $1,000. Begin now to feed the hogs well. It will take a good deal of corn but it is cheaper than to buy bacon.*

*I intend if nothing prevents to send Mid and a horse home next March to make a crop of corn. I expect in the course of the next month to make special application for a leave of absence for the purpose of starting a farm. It is absolutely necessary. I will take $500 to buy full feed even for the milk cows. I heard last night something of the mare I lost 6 months ago. As soon as I get breakfast, I am going to look for her. I may, however, have a ride for nothing. I bought another horse a week or two ago that I think a great deal of. He is rather thin, but I expect to stable him this winter a month or two. I think he will be a $1,500 horse when in good order.*

*Yesterday the cavalry were reviewed by Genl. Robert E. Lee. The army is in good condition. The cavalry fully established itself in the last campaign in the confidence of the infantry. The review was witnessed by thousands of them in their holiday clothes. We are well. Write soon. I do not think the Yankees will attempt to raid so far as Greenville this winter. Next spring, if the Yankees still hold east Tenn., I think they may make an attempt. A few hundred men on the French Broad can hold as many thousand in check. My respects to all.*

*Your affectionate husband*
*L. Williams*

Two days after Lee departed, another great soldier finally returned. On

November 3, General Wade Hampton reported for duty and five days later, he found himself back on the field near Stevensburg where the cavalry were going into action. His men cheered him so loudly that they nearly drowned out the sounds of gunfire going on nearby. That skirmishing was coming from Parker's Store where Stuart had taken Rosser's Brigade headlong into a swarm of Yankee cavalry. Hampton quickly led his cheering men to the sound of battle. Recognizing instantly that the Federals were driving Jeb and Rosser back, a rejuvenated Hampton bellowed out his patented "Charge!" The men sliced into the Federal column, Hampton leading the way. The South Carolinians, heartened at the sight of their fellow countryman up front where Wade always had been and always should be, would have followed him through the very gates of Hell. In a few minutes it was all over and the Rebels recrossed the Rapidan to safety. Yet, while Leonard had joined in another success on the field, he seemed to be losing the battle back on the home front.

*Camp near Orange C. H., Va.*
*November 13th, 1863*

*My Dear Anna,*

*I recd yours of the 2nd yesterday. I regretted very much to learn that my favorite scheme of farming has been defeated. It is so difficult to buy even seed wheat after a plentiful harvest, you can well imagine the difficulty of ever getting any more flour. All this I was apprised of and, therefore, the more solicitous to grow wheat. I would gladly have paid $12 per bu for seed rather than have failed and I have no doubt wheat will sell for $15 before next crop and will in all probability be the ruling price of next crop, besides the straw is very valuable for winter food for cows. I will try to see to it that I get corn land. In truth I see no other way of getting along. The prices will advance, I have no doubt, in all the necessities of life and what is now considered exorbitant will be regarded as reasonable. Tell Ned to take good care of the mare. Feed and curry well. If she can be put in as fine condition as when I first saw her, she will bring $1,500. I will trade her for a good workhorse, that is, if she cannot be broken.*

*I am sorry to hear that a regiment of soldiers are to be quartered in Greenville. There are always, more or less, in every regiment, those that will not respect private rights. A thousand men can soon eat out everything in Greenville. They will contribute to raise prices and the country people will soon learn to go to the soldiers and sell their produce, who are always ready to pay any price for what they need.*

*Our army has fallen back from the Rappahannock to the Rapidan. The Yankees have moved forward to Culpepper. Our regiment and brigade had a fight on Sunday, the 8th. It was severe but of short duration. No one in my company was hurt. I had but a few of them with me. Lieut. Stokes had a detachment on a scout at the time, 2 of my squadron wounded, but not very seriously.*

*If Mr. Mitts comes to Greenville, you must write to Mary and ask her to come see you while he is there. I intend, if things become quiet, to ask for a leave of absence to go home about the 15th of next month. I do not know what the prospect of success will be but I see nothing to hinder at present unless the enemy continues to threaten and advance. All the officers are expecting to go home. Some of them will be disappointed. I hope you will get shoes made soon for the servants if they are not already shod. The winter has been very cold. We had one snow and some very good days. It is now pleasant enough but cold. I have bought me an overcoat, jeans somewhat worn but nearly new for $50 (cheap enough) and also a Yankee overcoat for Mid. If you have not sold my suit, keep it. I wish you could get a heavy suit for Ned. He must be warmly clothed to work out during the winter.*

*A captain's uniform with boots and hat will cost now $650. Our currency is miserably depreciated, the highest prices of provisions, clothing and everything else is attributable more to that than to the spirit of speculation and extortion and if the congress and the state legislatures would do something to retire the redundant currency and to establish confidence in our money, everything would soon be adjusted. Laws against extortion and fixing maximum prices always will work in injury. Mankind are not worse now than formerly. They hold their commodities at a high price because they have but little confidence in Confederate money and look forward to a time when it will be more than worthless. They are acting on the principle of self preservation. The people are not responsible for the high prices. It is the government. The financial business of the country has been mismanaged.*

*Tell Wm. Mitts he must write. I've written him once or twice but have not heard from him. The prospect of an early termination of the war is a gloomy now as it has ever been. We should begin to make up our minds for a long war and base our calculations and shape our course accordingly. The country is destined to experience still deeper distress in every point of view, refugees, villagers, city people, and now producers generally will find the difficulty of procuring supplies increased month by month during the war. People who cultivate the soil, as long as they are unmolested by armies, friendly and hostile, will get on very well. I felt but little interest in our congressional election. In fact, had no preferences. Why were you pleased with the result? I will write Mr. Whitmire soon. I have no news. Our lines are the same as before the advance. Write soon. My love to all.*

*Yours affectionately*
*L. Williams*

Three days later, on November 16, two men with deep affection for their country but with disparate views as to how to preserve it, were on horseback. One was a 2nd S.C. Cavalry captain who was trotting up a rutted road toward Orange Courthouse to hear testimony in a court-martial hearing. The other was the 16th President of the United States who was riding in a military parade out toward the Gettysburg National Cemetery. At the courthouse, Leonard and six other officers sat at a long pine table awaiting the first witness called to address the tribunal. At the cemetery, the President sat shivering on a crowded platform awaiting the finish of Edward Everett's two-hour long speech. The Captain paid careful attention to the accounts given by both sides in the cases he was to render judgment. As Leonard lit his pipe and perused the evidence before him, a reluctant President rose from his seat, put on his spectacles and reached for a few sheets of folded paper tucked inside his overcoat. Lincoln spoke in a squeaky voice and three minutes later, he returned to his seat. Leonard rose from his after having disposed of over a dozen cases ranging from insubordination to failure to obey orders. Later that same day, after Lincoln had delivered what he considered a rather disappointing speech at Gettysburg, one of the 200,000 who fought there offered up a few humble words home.

*Camp near Orange, Va.*
*November 19, 1863*

*My Dear Anna*

*I recd yours of the 10ᵗʰ a few days ago and was glad to hear you were all well and also that an effort was still being made to get wheat sown. I have no doubt the mare could be made to work but I think she ought to be worked in a 2 or 4 horse wagon sometime before she is tried in shalfs. She might be entirely ruined by putting her in shalfs before she is accustomed to harness and has learned how to draw. I have allowed my hopes to run to fast and I fear I have raised your expectations too much in the matter of getting home this winter. I had hoped to be able to spend Christmas with you but the leaves of absence are stopped for the present and it may be that none will be granted before Jan. or Feb. next.*

*The weather is now delightful and the roads good and everything favorable for military operations. The weather so far has been favorable but citizens predict a severe winter. I have been told that snows in this section frequently are so deep as to cover all the fences, that is some 5 or 6 ft. deep. The travelling is out of the question at such times. Everything at present is quiet along the Rapidan. Genl. Hampton went on a scout nearly as far as Shippensburg, returned last night, brought back some 40 prisoners, 60 horses and a few wagons. The enemy are making no demonstration of an advance as I can hear of.*

*I have been attending Court Marshal at Orange several days this week and will, perhaps, have to go for several days as a witness. Orange, though full of wagons and soldiers, looks like a deserted village. There are at least 40 or 50 sutler stores in the town with paper, ink, tobacco, cakes & c. They're making fortunes out of the soldiers and poor hungry privates will go in and call for cakes and cider and the lunch will cost him a week's wages. Apples sell at $4 per doz. and cheese at $4 per lb., butter, same price. Our money is of little value.*

*I would be very glad to get home about Christmas, I believe more so than I was last year. I, however, still think I can get home sometime this winter. Corn is selling at Richmond for $18 per bu. and flour at $13 per bbl. If I could get home about the 20ᵗʰ Dec., I could lay in stock to a better advantage than later; provisions will be much dearer next than they were this past summer.*

The next day Leonard added a note to this letter.

*The mail is about starting. I will only add that we are still quiet in camp and in the enjoyment of good health. The weather continues fine, warmer than usual. Tell Mr. Whitmire he must write to me soon and also ask him to save me the molasses I wrote to him about and also get me a bu. of dried peaches and apples each. We can buy nothing in this country. Homemade molasses sells at $6 per qt. and scarce at that. All in my company quite well. Write soon. Tell Ned he must begin in time to make the garden rich. I want when the season suits to have the garden walks on each side sodded with blue grass to prevent washing. Write soon.*

*Yours affectionately*
*L. Williams*

Leonard continued to sit on the court-martial for the next damp and dreary week, while his regiment scouted Louisa County in a desperate search for fodder. The land proved to be as barren and stripped as Culpeper and Madison. Soon the order came down for the foragers of the 2nd S. C. Cavalry to return to camp and the gavel came down adjourning the court martial. The Army of the Potomac was stirring.

On November 26, General George Meade launched his Mine Run Campaign. His objective was to turn the tables and flank of Lee. Federal engineers had finally succeeded in rebuilding the Orange and Alexandria Railroad, so Meade's army crossed the Rapidan at Germanna and Ely's Fords in the direction of Orange Court House on a straight line for the Confederate encampments. Lee rolled up his sleeves, but it was Hampton, as usual, who hit them first.

Hampton's Division, supported by the advance of Hill's Corps, halted a Federal advance on November 27 outside of New Hope Church. Early helped push them back further on the left, but as his men approached Locust Grove, they encountered a force too large to confront. Believing that Meade was on the brink of an all out attack, Lee withdrew to a strong position west of Mine Run where he dug in. On the next morning, Meade's army advanced to the Confederate position, but instead of attacking, the Federals entrenched themselves as well. For four days the armies faced each other, then on the night of December 1, Meade evacuated his position and crossed back across the Rapidan. If Grant had been commanding the Army of the Potomac, he would have dug his spurs deep into his fine colt "Cincinnati" and thrust his army full bore into the outnumbered Confederates until he had driven them back to Richmond. Meade, however, timidly turned "Baldy" around and backed away. At the start of this brief Union campaign, Leonard posted guard duty and one letter.

*Orange C. H., Va.*
*November 26, 1863*

*My Dear Anna*

*I am at present in attendance on Ct. Marshal at this place and lodging together with 5 or 6 other officers with the family of refugees for a day or two. The regiment had moved into Louisa County on the Central RR near Toliesville. We moved there for the purpose of feeding but have found the country as destitute of forage or corn as can be conceived. Our cavalry is destined to play out this winter unless we are moved back and distributed over the county. As to getting back to S. C., the idea is now abandoned. If horses could be fed, I would prefer staying in this country.*

*I am very much disappointed about starting the farm. It is too late now to sow. Wheat ought to be sown in October. Mr. Arthur offered his place very low; if the land is of any account I would rather pay $20 per acre for good land than to pay a part of the crop. For instance, if the land will yield 20 bu. corn per acre, the 3rd which is the usual rent would be 6 1/3 bu. at $5 per bu. would be over $30 per acre. I would a great deal prefer to pay money for rent than a portion of the crop. If I understand your figures, Mr. Arthur agreed to let the land for $3 per acre which is perhaps 8 or 10 times cheaper than part of the crop. As the matter has been so mismanaged, you had better not do anything til I get home.*

*As I have said before, provisions will be so expensive next year that I will be compelled to farm. I have no doubt the amount of provisions of the plainest kind necessary for support will cost $4,000 per year. Two hands on a farm can make a crop that would sell for more than this. Flour is selling at Richmond and other places for $130 per bbl and will probably go higher. If we could have had wheat sown,* it would have secured you plenty of flour. The bran, straw & c would have wintered your cows in a great measure. The neglect cannot be mended now, however, but I endeavored to impress Henry and Mr. Whitmire with its importance last August and September in time to make every arrangement. It may have been impracticable, but I think I could have arranged everything in two days. If no bargain for land has been made, let it alone till I get home.

Our country will, I fear, be reduced to great distress this next year. Our area of cultivated land, as well as number of laborers, are diminishing. One year ago, provisions were a great deal lower than now and a year hence I predict there will be quite as great an advance. I do not know what the people are doing. I do not think they are half working. If they would trade less and work more, the country would do much better off. The army is now suffering for their turnips and cabbages, Irish potatoes & c. There might have been enough of these provisions made to have supplied the army had an effort been made and that too without injury to the grain crop. One hand in this country, if he had devoted his labors to vegetables, could have realized $10,000. For instance, cabbage sells for $1 to $1.50 per head, potatoes, $10 per bu, onions, $3 per doz., turnips, $5 per bu, apples, $3 per lb., and everything proportionately high, chickens, $3 a piece, eggs, $2.50 per doz. A hungry man can eat $3 worth of sweet potatoes at one meal.

I am now writing in the presence of 4 young ladies who are sewing. They are showing me their homemade dresses. They pay $30 a bunch for no. 12 cotton yarn and $50 cts. per yd. for weaving. Their dye stuffs are the same as yours (copperas and barks), common 4/4 shirting sells here at $3.50 per yd. I write you this hurried letter not knowing when I may have another opportunity. I expect by this time you are in Columbia – remember me to all. I do not know when I shall make application for a leave of absence but I hope to get off before you leave for home. I shall direct this to you at Columbia. Write me as soon as you get there and write often. This morning is a bright, cold freezing morning and looks like shady weather.

Yours affectionately
L. Williams

The Captain's farm campaign and Meade's Mine Run Campaign had both resulted in failure. Leonard knew his failed venture meant increased dependence on others, no hedge against inflation, and growling stomachs. Meade knew that his retreat meant rebuke from the War Department, his possible dismissal, and growling from a frustrated president. The riverdance between the two parrying armies was beginning to wind down, however, and soon both blue and gray would settle uncomfortably into winter quarters. Many on both sides hoped that perhaps this would be the last winter they'd have to endure in this bloody ordeal. December had arrived and with it would come drifts of snow and waves of interminable boredom. For now though, the spirits of the Army of Northern Virginia and its overworked cavalry were bright. Just outside Fredericksburg, the site of their splendid rout the winter before, the rebels steadfastly huddled by their campfires, warmed by the fact that they had stared down Meade and firmly stood their ground. The Old Captain paused in his reading, his thoughts drifting back to that cold winter of '63. It seemed ironical now how he had continued to have a positive, hopeful outlook back then. He opened the next letter. Several of the words were unreadable now, like holes in his logic then.

> *Camp near Fredericksburg, Va.*
> *Louisa County*
> *December, 1863*

*My Dear Anna*

*It has been[          ] since I wrote you from Orange Court House. I was there attending Court Marshal but upon the advance of the enemy the court was adjourned. I joined my regiment and only returned to camp a day or two ago after two weeks service. The enemy brought over their entire army and advanced to Mine Run on the south side of which our army was in position. The two armies confronted each other for 2 days. In momentary expectation of general conflict, our brigade in consequence of the wooded ground on the extreme right, was dismounted to fight on foot. Genl. Meade, I presume, thought Genl. Lee would retire before him, but when he found himself confronted [          ] he had only left the river some 10 or 12 miles. The moral effect of his backing down and retreat will, I think, be as injurious to his army as a defeat. Our men were buoyant and sanguine of victory and had Meade made an attack, it would, I believe, have been a disastrous day for him. The Yankees are now mostly beyond Culpepper. Our brigade is still picketing on the Rapidan, though it is back some 30 miles. It moved here for forage. Tomorrow it will move again to Guinea Station on the Fredericksburg RR.*

*Several officers have sent up their applications for leave [     ]. I found both your last letters and also one from Mr. Whitmire. I was glad to hear that you had at length succeeded in getting wheat land but I fear it is too late to do well. I judge by this time you are in Columbia. I hope you may enjoy your visit. Did baby know her grandfather? I know she will be pleased with everything you did. You did not tell me whether Auntie was with you or not. I suppose, however, she is.*

*We are living well at this time, though at a high price, butter at $5 per lb., sorghum, molasses at $16 [     ]. It is raining heavily this morning after a night's rain, not withstanding, we move at 10 ock. The health of the company is prime, no sickness at all. My men have no tents yet. They have to lay out in all kinds of weather. I hope before long to get tents or flies. While you are in Columbia, you can write often and send me a paper now and then. Remember me to the Maj., and all the family.*

*Your affectionate husband*
*L. Williams*

Like Abraham Lincoln, Union Brigadier General John Buford was born in Kentucky and reared in Illinois. After receiving a wound in the Second Battle of Bull Run, the 36-year old cavalry commander returned in mighty fashion. In June, he had come within a whisker of overrunning Stuart's entire force in a well-conceived surprise attack at Brandy Station. At Gettysburg, it can be argued that he in effect chose the field for the battle, and in his stubborn resistance of Heth's forces at the dawn of battle, he contributed greatly to the grandest Union victory of the war. Leonard had witnessed Buford's talent and toughness firsthand at Jack's Shop, and like Jeb Stuart himself, the Captain considered this wise and gritty nemesis to be the North's finest cavalryman. He was like a shark, ever moving, ever sniffing the scent, and with Buford there was always blood swirling in the water. Here was a worthy leader and adversary, and for those reasons both North and South paused for a moment upon learning that on

December 16 John Buford had died of typhoid fever in Washington. On that day he was posthumously awarded the well-deserved commission of major-general. Not having the steely eyes of Buford staring back at them through their field glasses any more fostered a feeling of relief in the Confederate cavalrymen, who knew that the Union had indeed lost a gifted soldier.

John Buford passed away at the young age of thirty-seven. On December 15, the day before his death, Leonard Williams reached the milestone of forty years. He did so with only the usual complaints, a bit of a backache and an aching for a letter from Anna.

*Camp near Fredericksburg, Va.*
*December 17, 1863*

*My Dear Anna*

*I have not heard from you since the 2nd inst. Since my last we have moved again and are now on the Fredericksburg Road and picketing on the Rappahannock. It is probable the brigade is settled, perhaps for the winter, and as soon as the weather clears up, will begin to build chimneys and other protections against the inclement weather. The fall and winter so far have been favorable beyond precedent, but little rain and but few days of cold weather. There is now a prospect of continued bad weather. Some of the applications for leave of absence by officers of the regiment have been returned disapproved. I thought at the time they were premature.*

*I had hoped to spend this Christmas with you. This pleasure, however, must be deferred til another one comes. I shall too be debarred the pleasure of celebrating with you your birthday which occurs on the 30th, but whether it is your 25th or 30th I have no certain information and all the data which I have yet been able to accumulate on the subject, by reference to the records of schoolbooks, by consultation with friend Carlisle, and other less reliable sources, have been insufficient to direct me to any more definite conclusion. By the by, the 15th just passed was my own birthday, but I have told you too often, it is hardly necessary to repeat that it was my 40th, a time that only precedes the beginning of old age by a few years. But barring a little rheumatism which exposure and hardships occasionally visits me with, I feel no approaches of that venerable period in a man's life. But as you are almost as buoyant as*

*20 years ago, and with prospects and hopes (but for the shadows of war) as bright and ambitious as ever, which you remember is to be a "country squire" with enough of worldly comforts to enable me to enjoy that dignity with becoming placidity and to go to town twice a year to buy whatever our position and little vanities may suggest, for instance, a silk gown and a beaver hat & c.*

*I think both armies will be quiet for the next 3 months. The roads are so bad as to prevent wagon trains and artillery from moving. We have no news. I've been suffering with a pain in my back for several days but now am nearly rid of it. Remember me in the kindest terms to the Major and all the family. Write soon and often.*

*Your affectionate husband*
*L. Williams*

In late December, the soldier becomes the builder instead of the destroyer. Guns are set aside and axes are taken up. It is time to erect permanent winter quarters. Captain is now foreman. Private is laborer. The horse is transformed into hauler of timber. Each company helps in the laying out what will become the mess, latrine, and cabin areas. The sound of axes wielded by grunting men is followed by the crash of old oaks and pines. Next the logs are cut, notched, and fitted together. Many men slip and fall in the snow while carrying the logs to the cabin site. The top log is placed and the structure is nearly complete. A roof is made of split oak pieces and if one has the desire, chimneys and porches are added later. To keep out the winter wind, each crevice of the cabin is filled with a mixture of water and clay. Planks serve as bunks, and straw borrowed from sleeping farmers provides the mattress. The work is hard but a fiddle and an occasional pull on the jug lighten the load a bit.

While the work may not have been performed with the same energy or enthusiasm as it was two winters earlier and tents far outnumbered cabins, the required task was completed nonetheless by the depleted men of the 2nd South Carolina. The Captain did his fair share of chopping while Ruby and the pack mule dragged pine logs back to their camp near Hamilton's Crossing. Mid did his share of the heavy work, cooked, and played his harmonica. With a light snow beginning to fall, the Captain finished up a letter from Anna detailing her journey from Greenville, through his boyhood town of Newberry, to Columbia. Then he dug into one of Mid's gravy-drenched biscuits and wrote his final letter of 1863. The letter became a litany of personal and general loses, a grim reflection of the times.

*Camp near Hamilton's Crossing*
*December 23, 1863*

*My Dear Anna,*

*I recd your letter written from Wm. Mitts, and also on yesterday one from you at Columbia. I am very glad you paid my relations a visit on your way to Columbia. You speak in high terms of your visit and the people around my old homestead. But were they anything else but hospitable and kind they would be recreant to the spirit of former times. The neighborhood, however, is much changed. Fifteen or 20 years ago, there lived in that vicinity a generation of men, the like of whom can hardly be found in any section of the country. There was John Suber, the plain and unostentatious gentleman, my father's friend, surrounded with wealth and dispensed all the kindnesses of neighbor and friend. On the other side, was my old friend, Geo. Mitts, the patron of boys, who always delighted to have around him a throng of young people and to make them happy. And then there was the eccentric John Mason in whom there was no guile or shadow of deceit and George Speake, one of the most amiable of men, full of sincerity, truth and good sense, respected by all men, and Davis Martin and William Rook, men of distinctive characters and great worth. These were my father's neighbors in my boyhood days against any one of whom I never heard him make an accusation or a disparaging remark. They lived together without fear or feud, no lawsuit or arbitration ever disturbed their friendly intercourse. But they have all passed away and their places occupied by their descendants.*

*I was not appraised before I recd your letter that William Mitts intended to sell his land and move to a village. I think it is a bad notion to sell his land. If he moves to a village he ought still to have a farm to support his family. I think it is an injudicious move at the present time. A great many already in towns ought to leave for the country. Christmas is already at hand, and for the first time I find myself without the ability to celebrate the day with a stew or eggnog. Brandy is selling at $25 a qt., sugar $4 per lb., and eggs $3 per dozen. We are in a country where* *there is nothing to buy. We cannot even get a tolerable dinner. It is snowing this morning, but not so cold as it has been, but I am quite snug. I have a chimney to my tent, which makes it just as comfortable as a close room.*

*I am now writing by a blazing fire. I'm very sorry to hear of your father's suffering from rheumatism and hope he may soon be well to enjoy your company. The accident of the death of your brother's little boy is truly distressing. I sympathize with you all. The death of young Blackburn is saddening. He was a most amiable boy of high promise. He is the 5th son to die all about grown. Write me where to direct a letter to James. Is he in Ohio or Baltimore? I have heard nothing direct from him yet and then only what you have told me.*

*You mentioned William Mitts had promised you 300 bu corn. That is more than you need. You've already 100 bu, another hundred will be enough, but take the flour he offered. You mentioned in your letter at home that Ned would commence sowing wheat. Has he sown? Mr. Whitmire wrote me that he could get on his business without Uncle Adam, which I have no doubt is so. I dislike giving the old man up. I fear he will find it very hard to make a living if turned off. How long do you expect to stay in Columbia? I hope I may be able to get off before you return home, but at present they are giving no furloughs. Remember me to all the home folks. Tell me about baby. I have no news to tell you. We are at present very quiet with no apprehensions of any move soon. There's a rumor that the Yankees got into our recruiting camp in Beaufort County and captured some of our men and horses but have learned no particulars. I had some 4 or 5 men there. A few days ago a man from Co. D started to Madison County on business and was murdered on the way about 12 miles from our camp. Supposed to have been done by robbers. No clue to the facts yet as ascertained. Write soon. Remember me to William and his family.*

*Your affectionate husband*
*L. Williams*


On this cold Christmas Eve night, the Captain sat alone staring at the glowing embers of a crackling fire. For the third straight year, far from Anna and little Carrie, he would have no Christmas. As the campfire sparks flitted around him, he imagined Maum Fannie singing one of her hymns as she sliced up a few sweet potatoes she had saved for her pie. Little Carrie was standing on her toes and peeking out the window hoping to snatch a quick glance at St. Nick. Anna was humming as she sewed. A weathered daguerreotype of him as a shy, young schoolteacher from Newberry sat on the table beside her.

The Captain tossed another thick pine log into the fire. The Old Captain placed the final letter of 1863 on top of his neatly stacked pile.

**Fortunes Begin to Reverse and War Nears End**

# 1864-65

Wilmington N.C.
Feb 11th 1865

My Dear Anna

I have had three
days of perfect quiet in camp
but in a few miles of the roaring
artillery, the yankees shell our
[...] every day, & occasionally
at Anderson's. I believe they
have made no progress since
the capture of Fisher. I will
probably go out again to-morrow
will therefore write to-day
[...] are listening with deep anxi-
ty to hear the news from our
[...] near Branchville, a general
sadly needed in S.C. I wish the
President would place Dick Taylor
in command of all our forces in
S.C. & Ga. if I am correctly informed we have troops enough
at Charleston Branchville & Augusta
[...] to chastise Sherman, our
forces ought to be concentrated
[...] thrown first on one & then another
of Sherman's columns. It seems to
me he ought to be whipped.

Letter reporting Sherman at Charleston

312

# CHAPTER THIRTEEN
## DEAD CALM

*The earth is utterly laid waste, utterly stripped...*
*The earth mourns and fades,*
*the world languishes and fades...and few men are left.*
*...all joy has disappeared and cheer has left the land.*

Isaiah 24:3

Point Lookout, Maryland, was a splendid vacation spot where the idle rich came to frolic in the Chesapeake, listen to the bands, and watch the seagulls soar. That was before the war. After the Battle of Gettysburg, the peninsular ground in St. Mary's County was hastily converted into the Union's largest and bleakest prison camp. Fifty- two thousand Confederates would ultimately limp through its doors. Fourteen thousand would die there. At the dark center of that desolate camp was the Hammond General Hospital, a facility that popular author Charles Dickens might have chosen for one of his grim settings. It was overcrowded with morphine-addicted sick and wounded, yet reeked of institutional sterility and loneliness.

Staring out of one of its cracked windows, down on to the vast yard of prisoners was a gaunt first lieutenant who had lost his right foot in the first day's fight in Gettysburg. What he saw sickened him. Once proud fighters now roamed aimlessly about the grounds looking for crumbs while a few more rooted through the trash for peelings. Rations were irregular and virtually inedible. Malnutrition and scurvy invaded the dank hallways as did malaria, typhus, and small pox. Prisoners were tormented by rats and gratefully ate those they could catch. Raw fish and dead seagulls that washed up on the shore filled their empty bellies. Lice and fleas were bunkmates, and chronic diarrhea sent prisoners scurrying to putrid latrines. When the clothes they arrived in finally fall apart, blankets and rags became their only recourse. Those not assigned to the hospital ward were housed in tattered old Federal Sibley tents, which provided little shelter from the sweltering sun or icy Point winds. High tide meant flooded tents and nearby marshes brought mosquitoes. Worst of all was the "deadline," a no man's land located about ten feet from the fourteen-foot wall. Any prisoner sighted in that dead zone, even to sneak a look through the fence, was shot. Prisoners were also executed in their sleep, merely for crying out in pain. Point Lookout was the Andersonville of the North.

The crippled Confederate looked beyond the yard and out on the dead calm bay. He had once endured the marathon marches of Stonewall's Brigade. Now, after six months of the cruelest incarceration, he wondered how much more he could endure. On the worse days, James wished he could be where brother Ephraim already was. Slowly, he made his way over to his hard, blanket-less cot with the aid of a homemade walking stick. He rested but a moment. The sooner the once hard- fighting South Carolinian became accustomed to his lost leg, the sooner he might be exchanged and furloughed back home. He eyed the long dark hallway that lay before him. He reached for his cane. Miles to the south, just below Fredericksburg, his older brother, also thinking of home, reached for his pen.

*Camp near Hamilton's Crossing*
*January 5, 1864*

*My Dear Anna*

*I am in receipt of both your last letters of the 23rd and 31st. I have been unwell for several days and had to take medicine. I am now feeling a good deal better and I was glad to hear that your father was getting better and the rest of you well. I did not intend to impress you with the opinion that I did not expect to get home at all this winter. I think I probably will. I have sent up my application. It will be some 10 or 12 days, probably, before it is heard from. I may get off in 2 weeks, if not, I shall continue to apply as long as there may be any chance. I have as good claims as anyone and I shall press them. I think it is important for me to get home this winter, not only as gratification to myself, but to provide as far as I can, ways and means of getting along another year of high prices and scarcity, to ascertain how my affairs stand, and to stimulate Mr. Whitmire into a little more energy and boldness and also to get a farm to raise provisions on.*

*The taxes will be so high this year that it will require more industry than usual to meet them. You told me William Mitts has sold one of his places but did not say which one and also that he agreed to let you have corn cheaper than the market price, but did not mention the price;*

*nor do I know what land you procured to sow in wheat. Neither Mr. Whitmire nor Henry have written to me. I believe neither one of them would wait 6 weeks to get an opportunity to send by hand. I presume they think I ought to know or guess everything. I have been looking for a letter from both of them for 10 days but they are both waiting, I have no doubt, to send them by Charlie Lanneau next week.*

*I forgot to mention that they are giving furloughs for 21 days only, it will allow but 13 days at home, hardly enough to justify the expense of travelling back and forward. I have asked for 30 days but if granted at all, I fear it will be cut down to 21 days. I will write you again in a few days and can tell you when you may look for me. I think I will certainly get off this month, or if not, next month. I am very anxious to see you and baby. Do you think she will know me? If I had my choice, I would prefer to wait till February as it would give you a longer visit in Columbia, but all the officers in my company wish to get home and only one can leave at a time. They gave me the preference.*

*There has been a very cold spell of weather and some sleet, but today it has cleared off and the ice has melted. So far, we have had less snow and cold weather than usual. The ground has not yet become covered with snow. Last year, before this time, there were several snowstorms. There has also been but little rain. I never knew a milder season so far. Remember me to your brother and ask him to go up with us and spend a few days. He never has made us a visit. He, no doubt, can leave his office a few days. I have no news, haven't seen a newspaper this year. All my men are very comfortable. They have built themselves shelters and put chimneys to them. The government has furnished no tents, they use small flies captured from the Yankees. If my application is honored, you may prepare to go home about the 20th. I wish to spend a day or two with your father or longer, if I get 30 days. Do write oftener. I get no letters except business letters from no one else. Send my love to all.*

*Your affectionate husband*
*L. Williams*

Each misty morning, the Captain looked for the mail courier in the hopes that he would be bearing either a letter from Anna or a response to his application for leave. Most days, the courier's battered bag contained nothing for him. Crestfallen, he'd untie Ruby and gallop out to the picket line. Fortunately, crusty Calhoun Sparks had just returned from a three-week leave in Greenville and had informed the Captain that he had much to tell him about their mutual friends back home. He promised that as soon as he returned from his scouting duties, he'd bring Leonard up to date about the goings on back in the up country. But Calhoun was two days overdue. The scouting party had run into trouble.

Sparks, Sergeant Mickler, and E. Prioleau Henderson had trotted up to the house of Widow Burdine where they hoped to rest a moment. As the three began to tie up their horses, the widow's niece ran out and informed them that there were Yankees hiding in the basement. Henderson described what happened next.

> *Sergt. Mickler had left Sparks to hold the three horses, and he with the other scout rushed down to the cellar. Just as he unfastened the hasp, and raising the door, placed his foot on the first step to descend, the Yankee officers fired, shattering the Sergeant's leg just below the knee. He was dragged back by his comrade, the door closed and the hasp hooked, and assisted out to his horse...Just as Sergt. Sparks wheeled his horse from the house, to follow Mickler and his companion, the Yankees fired the second time, through the cellar window (of glass), killing the brave sergeant instantly.*

The body of Leonard's close friend and one of Hampton's best scouts was buried at a nearby church. His brother, Pierce Sparks, later dug up Calhoun's remains and solemnly transported them home. News of his death arrived in Greenville long before his pine box.

> *Camp near Hamilton's Crossing*
> *January 20, 1864*
>
> *My Dear Anna,*
>
> *I have heard nothing of my application and probably will not before the 15th. Am tolerably sanguine but prepared for a refusal just so I would have you not be surprised in either issue. I have been suffering from the worst attack of dysentery I've had during the war for 10 days and am looking worse. I am now, I think, getting well. The wear and*

*tear of the past year shows on me more than you will expect to see. We are in a country where there is no provisions to be bought. We live on what the command may furnish us, simply meat and bread without any vegetables or milk, rather worse off in this respect than we have ever been before.*

*I had the misfortune to lose one of my most valuable men a few days ago, Calhoun Sparks. He was killed in the enemy's lines while on a scout. He was one of the bravest and coolest men I ever saw, was the most reliable scout in the regiment. My company has recruited a good deal this summer and fall. I was last spring, reduced to about 50 men, now my roll numbers 65 men. It is very cold and clear but the ground covered with snow. Do write soon and remember me to all the family.*

*Your affectionate husband*
*L. Williams*

Dead calm. That was the only way to describe it. Trees stripped of their leaves now stood like lone sentries. Farmland had long since become a wasteland of shredded corn stalks and ruined fields. Not even Calhoun could have brightened their surroundings. Both armies sat motionless. Winter had frozen them stiff. Unloaded rifles were stacked. Half rations were eaten in silence. Cannons rested unattended save for the occasional icicle clinging to their cold barrels. Officers trickled away on leave. The hustle and bustle of campaigning had come to a frozen halt as did the Rapidan, now nearly solid and silent. There was an overwhelming presence of absence. Prince William County had become a snow covered no man's land, and no man was left untouched by the cold grasp of winter.

On February 13, Leonard and Mid trudged out of one wasteland to make their way down to another. The Captain's leave had been granted but, as he had feared, it had indeed been reduced to a precious 21 days. Four days down and four days back meant that he would have less than two weeks to spend in Greenville.

Ned again waited at the depot, but this time he barely recognized the unshaven, near skeleton of a man that stepped off the train. On the way out to Augusta Street, few words were spoken as they passed by what appeared to be a family of refugees, an infantry private absent without leave, and two barefooted strangers. The upcountry never looked more down. Some of the fences that once encircled thriving estates were fallen down with neither nails nor hands to repair them. In the year to come, the fences would disappear altogether with only their ashes left behind in fireplaces. Outbuildings were deteriorating. Livestock was bone thin. Weeds ran rampant as did inflation and discontent. Soon, civility itself would be on the brink of collapse. A few slaves had already run for the Piedmont hills. Many more would follow. Others like Ned would remain with their mistresses to the end to defend the only life they'd ever known. As the wagon creaked along, Ned muttered that it couldn't get much worse. The Captain said nothing but knew that it would. Mid was just grateful to have shoes and to be riding rather than marching.

As he approached his own property, the Captain thought it looked better than most but nothing like it used to. Anna and the house servants had done their best with what little they had. Ned reined up on the gelding. Instantly, the Captain's eyes shifted down from his worn out roof to the angel that had just appeared beneath it. Anna stood on the wraparound porch as Carrie raced down the muddy front path to greet the three returnees. Her father swept her up, smothered her in kisses and counted each and every freckle on her face as he made his way up to the steps. Handing Carrie to Ned, he grasped Anna's thin, china white hand. He caressed her hair then wiped away a tear. After a long embrace, soon all were in the kitchen as Maum Fannie fashioned a hearty meal out of some turnip greens, a handful of Irish potatoes, and a few pieces of salt pork. Anna, as usual, ate like a bird, stealing furtive glances between bites at the man now thirty pounds lighter seated across from her. Carrie, growing almost before their very eyes, cleaned her plate. Mid and Ned made sure there were no leftovers.

The next day, the Captain examined the land being rented for the crop and studied the books down at the mercantile with his business partner, Mr. Whitmire. The land was good enough, but the accounts were dwindling. Most of his attention, however, was devoted to Anna. She was thinner than ever now, more pensive, and seemingly growing closer to God with each passing day. She felt unswervingly that the Lord alone could save her, Carrie, and her war-weary husband. She read scripture and prayed for His mercy whenever she found a respite from managing the house.

Leonard and Anna prayed together the morning he left, and as he donned his mended winter coat, she secretly tucked a volume of bible verses into his carpetbag. Inside that bible was a pressed yellow jasmine. Then, as they had done so on the last visit home, each held the other tight in the hopes that they would do so again after the war. Bonnet-less with eyes full of tears, Carrie kissed her papa over and over goodbye. She had remembered him. She missed him already. Soon, Ned and Mid rolled up in the wagon, and with a wink of the eye and a tip of the hat, the Captain was on his way. Dead calm descended once again upon the abandoned household until Maum Fannie could be heard singing and rattling pans in the kitchen… but sadly… not quite loudly enough to drown out the whimpers of a three year old.

Two days later in Columbia, the Captain shared a hasty brandy with Major Laval before returning to the frozen front. He knew that the bottle his father-in-law sent along would be heartily welcomed by the cavalrymen of Company K. He did not know that by next February, Columbia would be in flames.

*Camp near Hamilton's Crossing, Va.*
*February 5, 1864*

*My Dear Anna*

    *I arrived in camp this morning, had a very pleasant trip without accident or hindrance and find all well. I lost nothing on the way and plenty of provisions to last all the way through and afford a lunch to several after reaching camp and the bottle came through safe also and has been discussed. After enjoying myself so pleasantly at home, the camp looks dreary enough, but I shall get used to it again very soon. It seems almost like a dream that I have been home, my stay was so brief and pleasant. I can scarcely realize it but I am thankful that I enjoyed the privilege of seeing you again and finding you all well and trust that the time may not be far distant when I may return to you, when the rude alarms of war shall be heard no more, when we shall have peace and hope and happiness doubly appreciated by the trials and sufferings of the past.*

    *In the meantime, my dear Anna, bear up bravely and courageously under whatever remains for us to endure. I pray that the Lord may give you strength and courage to sustain you in all adversities. On Monday night I slept soundly and dreamed continually of you and baby. I am glad you have good friends and neighbors around you. I feel that they will sympathize with and assist you if you should ever need their help. I shall cherish and hold dear the recollections of my visit home, not only on the account of unalloyed satisfaction of home but of the kindness and attentions of neighbors.*

*There are many things I didn't have time to tell you about and there are some things I did not explain to Ned as fully as I had wished. In regard to the farm, it is in the first place indispensable to have a wagon to carry corn and fodder for the mare, plows & c and provisions for Ned to the farm to last while he may be there, say 3 or 4 days. He can then bring in a load of wood twice a week, which will be about enough to supply you. Let Ned take enough provisions to last him while he is to be away, say 1/2 pound bacon, 1 1/2 to 2 lbs. meal per day and whatever vegetables you have. He ought to be plowing now. He must devise the best plan he can for getting utensils and horse feed hauled to the farm until he can get his wagon. Tell Mr. Whitmire I must have one and get it as soon as possible. Inquire of Mr. Whitmire how long meat ought to lie in salt before it should be hung up and when it has been in salt long enough, have it hung up.*

*I regretted that I could not stay a night in Columbia with your father. I called a moment to tell them goodbye. They were all well. I want Ned, in addition to the corn ground, to get from Esq. Watson, 2 acres of good land to put in sugar cane and Irish potatoes. I will however, write to Esq. Watson on the subject. It was quite cold yesterday, but today, the 5ᵗʰ, it is warm and pleasant but somewhat cooler than it was in Greenville. It is a fine time for plowing and I hope Ned will improve it though he has great disadvantages for getting to his work without a wagon. Find out how Ned feeds the cows and hogs and have them fed as early as he fed them and in the same quantity and see that they are penned every evening and turned out early in the morning. I hope that the sow has no accident, you may have pork for next year. You may have more pork for next year than you have this year. Do write often. Tell baby her papa is back again in camp and thinks a great deal about her and that she must love her mother and obey her and be a good child. Remember me to Auntie and all. Tell me how you are getting on. I will write soon to Mr. Whitmire.*

*Your affectionate husband*
*L. Williams*

Back on January 19, as the Captain watched Ned turn the soil in the hopes of a fine corn crop, Robert E. Lee turned 57. In a letter home to his wife, the stoic general shared the same sentiments about the upcoming campaign as his long-suffering army, "if victorious, we have everything to hope for in the future. If defeated, nothing will be left for us to live for." Hopes for a Southern resurgence were pinned on two Northern issues. First, the three-year enlistments of many Federal soldiers would be up in 1864. If they couldn't be convinced to remain in the field, Lee's outnumbered veterans just might have a fighting chance. Second, Lincoln would be up for reelection in November. If he could be defeated by a Democratic Peace Party candidate, then perhaps a compromise could be settled upon that would end the war. On these two uncertain possibilities did the future of Jefferson Davis, Lee's Armies, the beleaguered Southern citizenry, and the entire Confederacy rest. For the present, however, Lee could hope for little more than an occasional full ration as he endured the trials of winter, not much better off than his coughing men and hungry horses. On the other side of the Rapidan, General George Meade and his men rested comfortably and ate plentifully in their government supplied winter quarters. The Yankees were in hibernation; nonetheless, Leonard and Ruby still took their turn riding the lines on blustery nights.

*Camp near Hamilton's Crossing*
*February 12, 1864*

*My Dear Anna*

*I returned last night into camp from 5 days piquet. Lt. Perry leaves directly for home so will have time to write you only a few lines. This leaves me quite well. I got well of the cough before reaching here. My memory dwells with delight upon my pleasant visit home. My regret only is that I could not stay another week with you and attend better to some little matters. I expect to let Mid go home about the 20ᵗʰ March to stay a month or two. He can assist Ned in his crop, hauling wood & c, which will allow him more time at home. Tell Ned I am anxious to have the oats sown and also an acre of Irish potatoes planted this month or as soon after as possible. Mid will be at home to assist in planting corn and giving it and the potatoes one working. I sent by Lieut. Perry, which he will hand you, a $50 note not to keep but to spend. I hope you have the corn housed and all the shattered corn* *saved for the hogs. I have not yet recd a letter from you. Do write soon and often at least for a month or two till I get back into my old habits again. I was very sorry I could not spend a night with your father in Columbia. I have nothing of news to write you. Remember me to all.*

*Yours affectionately*
*L. Williams*

Clothing issues had dwindled and rations were sparse. General Lee himself ate meat but twice a week. Soldiers huddled by fires stirring their cush. In previous winter quarters, eager privates joyously tossed snowballs at one another; now they realized that many of the targets of their icy projectiles were dead. So were family members back home, unable to overcome disease and hardship. More than one soldier now clutched a fading picture of a dead mother, father, wife or child. The spirit of innocent enthusiasm was long gone. They had read newspaper accounts of the horror at Shiloh. They had seen first hand the Bloody Lane at Sharpsburg. They had barely escaped the killing fields of Gettysburg. For the soldiers on either side of the Rapidan, it was unimaginable that the coming spring would be the bloodiest of them all.

Leonard thought often of Brother Ephraim and inquired everyday as to the whereabouts of James. He missed the mischievous Calhoun. He stared at his only picture of Anna and Carrie. He read Bible verses to Mid. He wrote home.

*Camp near Hamilton's Crossing, Va.*
*February 15, 1864*

*My Dear Anna*

*I thought you were joking when you told me you did not intend to write to me for a good while but I find you were in real earnest. This is the third letter since my return to camp and none from you today. I felt disappointed. We have had up to this time most beautiful weather but it is now snowing and I look for continued bad weather. My horses are very poor and the falling weather will be very trying to them. I cannot buy a bundle of fodder or grass for them at all in this country. They subsist entirely on clover.*

*I am reading the little volume you put in my carpetbag. I shall read it over and over again and shall be more diligent in reading the scriptures hoping to be impressed with a right conception of the fearlessness of sin and the necessity of turning away from it. The little book (I think it is the one) was sent to me by some unknown person many years ago, but I neglected to read it. I can almost appreciate the beauty of the holy life, what a comfort and happiness Christianity imparts to the believer! It is worth all things else.*

*Everything has indicated the commencement of active operations. We have been under marching orders for a week with cooked rations on hand, but this snow and the bad roads that will follow, will put a stop to them. I must think there is a great deal of winter yet ahead of us. We are very comfortably protected with shelters. If our horses were as well off I would be glad.*

*Tell Mrs. Thompson Will is well off with a snug warm tent and is very well. All the boys are well. Lieut. Stokes, I expect, will start for home with a detachment to buy fresh horses in a couple of weeks. I believe I will send Mid with him and when he gets home I wish him to stay a month or six weeks to help Ned plant his corn and give him a good start. Has Mr. Whitmire bought a wagon yet and has Ned commenced to plowing? In this bad weather, your cows will need a good deal of feeding and I fear the shucks are gone by this time. Get Mr. Whitmire to buy you another load. Try to keep them up through March, after that time, they will require but little feeding. You ought to have your wheat ground. I fear it will make but indifferent flour. Keep all the bran till your cow has a calf and in the meantime, buy if you can, 5 or 6 bu. more. Try Maj. Alexander for a bushel now and then, I would like for you to feed the old cow while if so, she will give you more milk than you can use and make butter enough for your use. I am rather afraid to keep the sow in the same lot with the cows. I think probably she had better be fed outside the lot but have the other 2 fed and kept up at night. Good luck with the sow and our prospect for hogs next winter. Let me know when you hang up your meat and how it looks. Ask Ned whether he thinks best to keep the sow outside or put in your chicken enclosure. It might be fastened up so as to keep her from getting into the yard. Have you had the walks filled up in the upper side of the garden? Ask Ned if he has selected a field and let me know when he begins to sow oats.*

*You will have your hands full to tell about baby, the farm, garden, cows, hogs & c. With such subjects I would never be at a loss. Do write oftener, say twice a week.*

*Yours affectionately*
*L. Williams*

As Lee ruminated in his drafty headquarters, 136,000 Union soldiers re-enlisted. Had he known, his salt and pepper beard would have turned entirely white on the spot. Lured by a $400 federal bounty, a thirty-day furlough, and a special chevron to wear on their sleeves, most stayed put. Still, 100,000 chose not to return and the enemy was weakened to a degree in that inferior conscripts and substitutes had to be mustered in out of necessity. Nevertheless, the final numbers meant Lee would battle a force over one and a half times the size of his in the coming May clashes. But that was all still to come, too far down the road to worry about now. In frigid February, Lee's only concern was the suffering of his men and horses. "You must sometimes cast your thoughts on the Army of Northern Virginia," he told a relative, "and never forget it in your prayers. It is preparing for a great struggle, but I pray and trust that the great God, mighty to deliver, will spread over it His almighty arms, and drive its enemies before it." The Captain and his wife shared the same hope as the winds of war and March approached.

*Hamilton's Crossing, Va.*
*Camp 2nd S. C. Cav.*
*February 26, 1864*

*My Dear Anna*

*I recd today yours of the 19th, was glad to hear you were all improved and getting on as usual. Today there is a high wind, the severity of the cold has much moderated. For the last few days it has been like March weather. The roads are very fine and there seems to be nothing in the way to prevent active military operations, but as far as we can hear, the enemy are quiet. A great many of our officers are now at home on furlough and the rest only waiting the return of the absent to get off themselves. I wish I was in their place looking forward to a furlough in a few weeks, instead of having to look back at ours, already enjoyed. But this is not without its pleasures. It is a pleasure to review the few happy days I had at home, to think how well you treated me, how well my inner man was provided for. I think I have never faired so well in my life. I was not allowed to know there was any blockade at all. We are getting on here pretty much as usual, living scantily but enjoying fine health. I am, again, used to the simple fare and I expect it is better for us than more luxurious living.*

*Your poultry are repaying you well. I only wish you had proper facilities for raising chickens. It is a nice recreation to attend to them. The poultry yard, garden, & cows require a daily amt. of outdoor exercise and sunshine, which is of great importance to health. About this time your meat ought to be hung up to dry and after it is dried sufficiently, if you think proper, it might be removed to your storeroom. It will be safer to do so. It will not do for Ned to ride the mare to Mr. Watson's and back home at night. It is too far. It will be harder on her than the work if the wagon is not finished. Ned must get someone to haul to Mr. Watson enough corn and fodder to last a month or until the wagon can be repaired. Mr. Whitmire will haul it out for him and Mr. Watson will find a safe place for him to keep it so he can ride out Monday morning, and if his work requires it, and there is no work at home to prevent, he can stay till Saturday night. If he chooses and his work is not punishing he might come home Wednesday evening, but it is best to stay the week generally and be at home enough to work the garden. While he is gone you will have to look after the feeding of the cows and hogs.*

The Old Captain turned the page to discover that he had added to the letter the next day. Evidently, Clough was shirking his duties and that could not be tolerated.

*February 27*

*I expect it will be best to get the harness Mr. Painter has for sale if they are in sound condition and will fit the mare, as it is cheap as they can be bought. Does Mr. Watson want Clough; if so, send him by all means unless someone wants him that lives at a greater distance, anyhow, you had better send him with Ned. To keep him out of mischief, Ned can put him to some sort of work and tell Ned to frail him and make him do whatever he puts him to. Make him afraid of him and if*

*Ned would do it, I would as soon put him out for he will be a great help in many things. Tell Ned if no one takes him, he must take him out in hand, make him obedient to him and learn him to work. If Ned was to set to work to train him, he could make him worth his living this year and valuable to him next. He is large enough to use the hoe, he must not stay at home. He would keep you annoyed the year around and get into habits that would be hard to break him of. I understand from your letter your father has sold out all of his houses in Charleston. Have no doubt under the circumstances, it was a good trade. The city and Confederate taxes are so high. What did he get for his homes? Whenever Ned plows your garden, have him to plow your aunt's and her boy can help Ned when he gathers his wheat and oats. Remember me to all and continue writing twice a week.*

*Yours affectionately*
*L. Williams*

On February 28, the dead calm was momentarily interrupted when Union General Judson Kilpatrick, along with 4,000 troopers, crossed the Rapidan bound for Richmond. This winter, it would not be Stuart or Hampton, but the Yankees who did the raiding. Their aim was the seizure of Richmond and the release of captured Federals at Belle Isle. The raid was personally approved by Lincoln, and if successful it might prove disastrous for the Confederacy. Ulric Dahlgren, a fine rider despite the loss of a leg, led 500 of Kilpatrick's best cavalrymen to attack Richmond from the south, while Kilpatrick and 1,500 men under George Custer attacked from the north. Union and Confederate cavalry units soon clashed. General Lee's son Custis halted Kilpatrick's advance with his artillery, while Wade Hampton and 306 mounted men rode all night through sleet toward Kilpatrick's camp. Hampton ordered 100 of his troopers to dismount and the rest to split up and ride on either flank. None were to speak until the Federal camp was reached. Then, Hampton said, "All the yells that throats could furnish were to be poured forth for dear life."

Kilpatrick's sentries spotted the gray figures moving toward their lines and fired nervously from the edge of camp but instead of answering that fire, Hampton rushed the defenders, sending the enemy flying and capturing many more while they were still sleeping. The surprise attack was flawlessly executed and brought great rewards as Hampton's hungry men feasted on the food left over in the Federal kettles.

In the early morning, Kilpatrick fled toward the safety of Williamsburg. Dahlgren attempted to head for Tunstall's Station, hoping Kilpatrick would be waiting there at the rendezvous point. Three hundred of his men fighting like hell actually got there, but most were trapped near Walkerstown. Dahlgren was killed and the remainder of his men were captured. Later, a courier informed Hampton that papers found on Dahlgren's body contained orders for the burning of Richmond and the assassination of Jefferson Davis and his cabinet. Robert E. Lee sent copies of these writings to Meade, who along with Kilpatrick, denied any knowledge of such plans. Shortly after, Kilpatrick was ordered west to serve under Sherman.

Hampton had scratched together his force and raced out so hurriedly to cut off the Yankee raiders that some of his units were not engaged, the 2nd S. C. Cavalry included. They had formed up and ridden out as quickly as possible but Kilpatrick's force had already passed by them. As Leonard trotted back into camp, his mind was still racing. A night raid against a larger force was risky business, and despite missing Kilpatrick's force, the adrenaline was still flowing. He tied up Ruby, put a pot of coffee on the fire, and stoked up his pipe. It took a while to boil, just long enough for his disappointment over the failed raid to subside.

Home was on his mind now and he thought of Anna. If not for darkness and a lack of a pencil he would have written her a letter right then. An hour later, he was fast asleep dreaming of her. A few days later, he had plenty of time and sunlight to write a long letter home. There was much on his mind and the excitement of night action had energized him.

> *Camp 2ⁿᵈ S.C. Cav.*
> *Hamilton's Crossing, Va.*
> *March 5, 1864*

*My Dear Anna*

*I have recd two letters from you since I have written, one last Monday and the other yesterday. We have been on the move the entire week. On Monday morning, a courier brought intelligence that Kilpatrick with 4,000 or 5,000 men had passed Spottsylvania C. H. about 8 miles from our camp at 2ock in the morning. Our brigade went out to meet him on his return provided he should come back the* same route. He was too far ahead to overtake him and our mounted force was so small it would have been useless to undertake it. Came back into camp, next day, heard he was returning by the same route, went out and back again. The enemy made several demonstrations on the fords and crossed over once but were beaten back. We were so situated as to be able to get any number of rumors but nothing authentic. During the week, we struck tents and repitched them 4 or 5 times. It has been a week of great excitement and uncertainty but now as far as I know, everything is again quiet.

I am very sorry to hear of Mr. Whitmire's illness. Tell him for me he must not expose himself so much. He must stay at home in bad weather and when he does not feel well, to stay at home and let business alone. I feel he may not recover in time to invest in bonds for the payment of our taxes. It is highly important to do so before April, as our money can be used at par in payment of taxes if put into bonds by the 1st of April. I'm very glad that you attended yourself to getting the wagon repaired. I wish, if Mr. Whitmire is not well enough, you would ask Mr. Gower for his bill so that it may be settled at once. I do not wish to have them charged at present rates and then have to pay in new currency but would like you to have the bill paid as soon as the work is done. It will not do for Ned to come in oftener than twice a week and one of the times Saturday evening. The travelling is worse on the mare than the plowing. To go and return that distance every day would kill any horse in a short time. Now that he has a wagon, let him take out with him 3 days rations for himself and horse and when he returns bring back a small load of wood. It will not do to load too heavy after plowing all day. The distance being so great, there would be too much time lost in travelling there and back to say nothing of the injury to the mare. Tell Ned to send me word whenever you write about what work he is doing, if he has sown oats, and if he is breaking up the land for corn. I wrote Mr. Watson some time ago to select out a spot of good ground for an Irish potato patch. Ask Ned if he has a piece yet and what he thinks of it.

I'm very glad you have a prospect for milk and butter. Have your wheat ground, say a small quantity of the poorest so that if the flour is not good, you can have it chopped up for your cow and if it makes good *flour have it all ground so that you can have bran and shorts for the cow. She ought to be well fed on meal once a day (as you cannot get peas) and once on a good quantity of bran. Wheat straw is a very poor feed for a milk cow, give her in the morning a feed of meal and a bundle of fodder, at night bran if you have it and plenty of straw. Feed abundantly and she will give plenty of milk and repay twofold. It may be after things settle down in the spring, you can get peas. I requested Mr. Whitmire to call on Mr. Burgess and pay off the note I gave him for Ned. I made the note payable in current funds. I asked him if he refused to take money, to hand it to a lawyer and get him to make tender of payment. The note is about due now. I collected between $800 and $900 when I was at home and deposited with Mr. Whitmire for the purpose. I have some fears of Burgess not acting fairly and want the matter attended to in time. Let me know how Mr. Whitmire is getting and whether he will be able to attend to it. I'm sorry Mr. Whitmire's health is getting so impaired. He must take better care of himself.*

*Lieut. Stokes is looking every day for his furlough. I will send Mid with him. He will not, however, get home under two weeks. What kind of tires is Mr. Gower putting on the wagon? Are they old ones and likely to last 2 or 3 years or are they entirely new? Ned can tell you about it. I send by Mid a small bundle of cast steel and axes, which I bought at Fredericksburg, which Mr. Whitmire can exchange for iron to keep the farming implements in order. They are cheap in Fredericksburg and very costly at Greenville, perhaps 7 or 8 times dearer. I proposed if I'm not mistaken in this way to pay for the repairs on the wagon. I wish you would remember when the axes come, you would have Ned to get timber suitable for helves and when he is at leisure on rainy days, make handles for the axes (there are 4 of them). Grind them and put them in the store for Mr. Whitmire to exchange for lard, bacon, flour, peas or corn or whatever you need. The cast steel, he can sell to the blacksmiths, there is only about 20 lbs. of it but I hear it is worth $25 per lb. in Greenville. However, it will be time enough to talk about this hereafter.*

*Does the meat seem to have taken salt well? You had better use the joints first as they are the more liable to spoil. Have you enough*

*Irish potatoes left to plant another acre or so at Mr. Watson's? If not, try to secure enough good ones. Perhaps you had as well buy one or two bus. of N. C. potatoes anyhow, as they are better for planting than ours and eat those you have. I'm very anxious if rich land can be got to have 1 or 1 ½ acres planted as Mid will be at home 6 or 8 weeks. Ned can easily manage the crop. I also want enough sugar cane planted to make molasses enough.*

*I have recd all your letters. It takes them generally 6 or 7 days to come. I feel prosy enough after the week's excitement and bother and have written you a letter on material affairs entirely which more than likely you are tired of as they furnish the staple of so many of my letters. I am always happy to get your letters and am glad you can find time to write twice a week. I wrote a week or two ago to your brother but treated him so badly in not writing to him earlier, I would not be surprised if he, too, were to take his time. My love to Auntie and all. Tell me about baby.*

> *Yours affectionately*
> *L. Williams*

Four days later, on March 9, President Abraham Lincoln made a fateful decision that in essence would win the war. He commissioned Ulysses Simpson Grant as a lieutenant general and placed him in command of all Union armies. The soon to be 42-year old Ohioan had previously failed as a farmer, real estate inspector, merchant and clerk. His tenure at West Point was less than brilliant, but as a lieutenant in the Mexican War he had led his men with distinction. He entered the war as a mere drill instructor of a tiny Illinois militia company, but by 1864 he had come to be regarded as a stern winner. He certainly didn't look like one. His muddy pants were haphazardly crammed into his worn old cavalry boots; his coat buttons were only sometimes fastened and his thick black beard was rarely trimmed. A stubby stogie was permanently tucked between his tight lips. While other officers surrounded themselves with an elaborate staff and housed themselves in the best estates they could find, Grant's only baggage was a flask and a ratty toothbrush. His careless appearance, however, belied his sharp, straight-line thinking and uncompromising approach to battle. For Grant, war was neither art nor science. It was a grim business where men died. He recognized this from the start and more importantly, he had the iron will to accept it. The Army of the Potomac had a new master, even though Meade was technically still the commander, and Grant grasped immediately that his enemy had fewer men, inferior weapons, less funds, and meager provisions. He could afford to lose men. Lee could not.

Encamped on the flowing fields of Brandy Station where the grand cavalry fight had raged nine months earlier to the day, the Army of the Potomac had a new commander and a new spirit. No longer would the Army of the Potomac let Lee do the dictating. There would be no more falling back as the focus shifted from the capture of Richmond to the annihilation of its defenders. Grant's aim was the destruction of the two armies that opposed him, Joseph E. Johnston's gritty Army of Tennessee and Lee's proud Army of Northern Virginia. To that end, Lincoln's decisive new chief placed tough fighters like himself in key roles. First, 44-year old fellow Ohioan, General William Tecumseh Sherman, was given command of all troops in the west and the order to move toward Atlanta and crush Johnston's army in the process. Next, Grant placed scrappy, five-feet, four-inch tall Phil Sheridan in charge of his splendid 10,000 man cavalry and counted on "Little Phil" to seek out and crush Jeb Stuart's 4,500 poorly mounted riders. At the start of 1863, the North was no match for Generals Lee, Jackson and Stuart. Now, in the spring of 1864, Grant, Sherman, and Sheridan would emerge as the Union's unconquerable triumvirate.

Grant's promotion and the fact that over 130,000 Yankees had re-enlisted were as of yet unknown to Leonard. Buoyed by rumors that many of the enemy had instead high-tailed it for home, that his depleted 2nd South Carolina Cavalry might be transferred back to the Palmetto State, and the knowledge that Kilpatrick's recent raid had ended in yet another resounding Union defeat, the Captain wrote a brief but optimistic letter home.

*Hamilton's Crossing, Va.*
*March 12, 1864*

*My Dear Anna*

*I was very glad to hear from you yesterday. Your letter of the 3rd came to hand. I had the day before recd one from Henry who told me you had been quite unwell. I was therefore, uneasy, until I recd your letter. I returned day before yesterday from five days picketing which explains my not writing earlier. Our duty is now very heavy but we will probably be relieved in a few days. I do not know where we will go but we must have time to recruit our horses. Some are in hopes of being sent to S. C. but where we will go nothing is known with certainty. Lt. Perry returned yesterday. Several of my company went home yesterday on furlough. I bought some cloth yesterday from the Qr. Master for pants. The cloth you spoke of to make me a suit, keep till next winter. I hope Mr. Whitmire is well and has attended to the business I requested him to look after. Let me know how he is getting. I want Mr. Burgess paid at once. I have nothing new at all. Lt. Stokes left for home on Wednesday, Mid went with him. He will stop at Richard Clary's, William Mitts' and Robert's. I was absent on picket when he left and did not, therefore, have an opportunity to write by him to any of them. He will not, probably, get to Greenville before the 1st April or thereabout.*

*There is a rumor that Kilpatrick has carried his command transports to Washington. If so, we are done with raiding for a while. His raid was the greatest failure they ever made. He lost, I suppose, a fifth of his command. Everything this year has been prosperous with us. Our armies are strengthening rapidly. I understand only about 40,000 of the Yankees have reinstated. They will have to fill up their armies with new levies. I think our cause looks much brighter, though we hear very little about peace yet, in either congress or newspapers.*

*I recd Mr. Watson's letter also. He says Ned is doing very well. Are you acquainted with Mr. Watson? He is a very nice, intelligent old gentleman. I stopped here to eat breakfast and have had a cup of good Rio coffee furnished by the commissary, but the mail is starting so that I stopped my breakfast to finish rather abruptly. My love to Auntie and all. I hope you are all quite well before this time. I am quite very well and the health of all good. Kiss baby and write often.*

*Yours affectionately*
*L. Williams*

For now the dead calm persisted. Winter was soon to melt away, but not before unleashing ice storms that locked men and horses stiff in their tracks. Nearly all Confederate officers and soldiers had returned from the comforts of home only to find their camps around Fredericksburg more dreary and desolate than ever. There was little meat to be had and even less to be seen on their emaciated mounts. Boredom and inactivity dulled them. Racked more and more by heart-related pain in his chest, arms, and back, Lee seemed to be aging by the hour. The grim task of facing Grant in the coming weeks, however, did not paralyze him. If there was a weak point in the Northern sword and a hidden strength in the Southern shield, the Confederate commander knew he had to find them. Unfazed by the seemingly insurmountable odds, Lee began to devise a plan of action that would enable his 65,000 dedicated disciples to somehow withstand the 120,000-man killing machine that Grant would unleash the moment the skies and roads cleared.

The Captain meanwhile tended to smaller issues. He had to cook for himself now that Mid was in transit back to Greenville to assist Ned in the cornfield. Each day he vainly searched for fodder as Ruby's condition continued to worsen, and borrowed other horses for picket duty to rest her. On picket, he ran down his mental list of worries— James' dire circumstances, Ned's broken wagon, Clough's disobedience, unpaid tax bills, inflation, the blockade, Anna's health, Carrie's development, the morale of Company K— these were the demons that swirled around him on the ides of March.

> *Camp 2ⁿᵈ S. C. Cav.*
> *Hamilton's Crossing, Va.*
> *March 15, 1864*

*My Dear Anna*

> *I was disappointed today in not receiving a letter from you. Our brigade is about to be relieved and instead of going back to Richmond, is now believed we are to go into Essex County. It is impossible that this brigade can be ready for efficient duty under 2 months and I fear we are going into a scarce country. It is a long way from any RR. Mail facilities will be bad. We here a good deal of cannonading today, a distance we cannot tell where it is. I expect operations will be commenced very early. If Meade does not take the initiative, I expect General Lee will. All movements of the army up to this time have been failures. I see by the papers the exchange of prisoners has been resumed. I hope James may soon get home, he has certainly had a dreary time. I was very glad our authorities took a stand not to negotiate with Butler. I hope all our men may be in their respective regiments again very soon.*

> *I saw Col. Black a few days ago. I called on him, he was just from*

*home. He always inquires about your father and William. I like him much better than I did previously. I expect Mid got as far as Richard Clary's yesterday. He will stay at Robert's a week or so. I gave him directions to get home by or before the 1st April. I am getting along very well without him and if he can make himself useful at home 2 or 3 months, I may let him stay. Probably I ought to plant more corn. I will see about it. You had as probably let Bill work with Ned and if you can put Clough out anywhere, do it. Henry promised to find a place for him. He is a great nuisance to you. I would be glad if you could put him out for a year or two.*

*I have a pair of shoes for Mid. I wish I had an opportunity to send them to him. I did not have an opportunity to charge Mid with a lecture on his behavior while he was away. Tell him I expect to hear by Mr. Watson, by Mr. Whitmire, yourself and everybody that he conducts himself well, attends faithfully to his business, not to idle away his time, to keep good company and not to go out anywhere without getting a pass from you stating where he is to go, to keep out of all difficulties and make a good name for himself. Tell him if he behaves well, he will always have friends and be respected. Tell him I put great confidence in him. Read this part of the letter to him. Everybody speaks well of Ned's industry and attention to business. Tell Mid I want to hear a like good report of him.*

*You did not tell me whether, since Ned had commenced repairing the wagon, he stayed at Mr. Watson's for several days or not. I want him to stay 3 days at a time if it is too severe on the mare after working all day to travel home at night and too much time lost travelling. Do you know whether Mr. Whitmire has paid Burgess? I have not heard from him yet. I hope he is well by this time. How is your cow and hogs doing and also your garden? This morning, the 16th, is quite cold, considerable ice. Tell Ned to send me word when he commences to plant corn and also let me know how much ground he has sown in oats and if he has finished and also if he has found any piece of land suitable for potatoes. Mr. Watson wrote me that he could furnish suitable land for sugar cane. Do write soon. I was in hopes we would get to Richmond then I could hear oftener from you. My love to all.*

*Yours affectionately*
*L. Williams*

If an army "marches upon its stomach", then the cavalry advances upon its horses' bellies. In March of 1864, the mounts of the 2nd South Carolina Cavalry were in no condition to bear their masters anywhere. Earlier in the war, overuse and disease were the culprits. Now it was a shortage of fodder. Madison, Culpeper, Albemarle, and Prince William Counties simply had nothing more to give. All of Northern Virginia had become a desiccated, empty shell, picked clean by thousands of soldiers and horses. The Union could replace hobbled mounts with a steady supply of strong stock from their massive stables around Washington. The Confederate cavalrymen, who had supplied their own since the outset, had no such recourse. Some had been fortunate enough to return from the home front with a fresh mount on occasion, and daring raids had garnered Union horses from time to time. Confederate farriers and a handful of skilled veterinary surgeons had done their best to provide shoes, stitches, and medicine when available, but now their equine ranks had reached rock bottom. Newspaper accounts revealed that affairs were even worse out west during the siege at Knoxville when shoes were stripped from dead horses and mules that the Union had tossed into the river.

Back in 1861, when Wade Hampton first formed the Legion, Leonard had selected Ruby for her strength and resolve before the plow. Three years later, she wore the scars of fifty stitches from blackthorns, prickly brambles, and the spur. She had lost as many pounds from Manassas to Dahlgren's raid, yet safely bore her master through it all. Mid knew more about horse doctoring than the Captain, but even Mid's knowing, black hands could do little now.

Although he had not received his $90 dollars a month pay for long stretches of time, Leonard never hesitated to spend whatever he could scrape together of his own for fodder. Twice he took the packhorse up to the ghost town of Fredericksburg in search of hay or oats. Both times he returned empty handed. Like the other mounts, Ruby used to stomp her hooves and snort impatiently to be fed. Now, she stood silently, waiting not for food but for death in an eerie dead calm.

Wade Hampton could no longer overlook the deplorable condition of the regiment's mounts, nor could he in good conscience order the scant and scrawny veterans of the 2nd S. C. to endure much more. At its height, Company K numbered more than 140. Now, Captain Williams commanded less than 50. Hampton needed at least two full, fresh regiments from Carolina and the weakened 2nd needed to be relieved of duty in barren Virginia. In a letter to his older brother Henry, the Captain informed him of the wretched state of their horses and the likelihood of a transfer out of the Old Dominion down to the South Carolina coast.

> *Camp 2nd Reg. S. C. Cav.*
> *Hamilton's Crossing, Va.*
> *March 18, 1864*

*Dear Henry*

*Your letter long looked for, came to hand a few days ago. I was very glad to hear from you. I have no news of any importance to write but it is probable we will move from here very soon, having been relieved from duty and I write simply because I have an opportunity. Our regiment has been doing duty here all the winter. Our horses are worn down principally from starvation. We have not more than 40 or 50 mounted men here. Most of the horses have been sent to Nelson and Augusta Counties to recruit but I understand their condition is no better than those here. A great many have died. There is at present a rumor and general impression that the 1st and 2nd regiment will be ordered to S. C. and 2 or 3 fresh regiments brought out here in our stead. I think myself, the thing very probable. We will, at any rate, be moved somewhere to recruit. Our company are filling up and if allowed time to recruit and remount, we will be in condition for the field again in the summer if not before.*

*I have some fears of sickness on the coast but I understand some Virginia regiments have stood the climate without sickness and do not desire to be removed. If allowed to encamp in the pine country, I suppose healthy localities can be found. We have been at all time in the healthiest sections of Va. and a great part of the time in and at the foot of the mountains.*

*A great council of war has been held in Washington and if the papers are to be believed, the grand aim of the enemy is to take Richmond by marching 3 columns and concentrating on the city. Grant advises the concentration of 250,000 men. If so, the campaigning of the west and southwest will be minor affairs and the great bulk of both armies will be assembled in Virginia. The star of Grant is now in the ascendant and his opinions will have more weight with the Yankee*

*War Department than any other man's- and I think it probable that their whole available energy will be directed against Richmond this spring. Our papers are again discussing the probabilities of French recognition. I am of the opinion that during the summer, France will recognize us as a political necessity to ensure success in her Mexican schemes.*

*The weather is at present rather cold, have had ice several mornings but have had the mildest winter known for many years. Have had but little snow or rain, the health of the army is prime, rations of meat scarce, but plenty of cornmeal. The men are getting very well satisfied with cornbread. Everything is quiet along our lines at present, though scouts tell us the 5th Yankee Corps are under orders to move but has not been found out what movement is intended.*

*I have given Mid a furlough and if he does well I will let him stay at home 2 months. Let me know if he gets indolent and lazy or gets into bad company or habits. If he does, I will bring him away immediately. I wish you would examine the wagon and tell me what kind of tires are on it and how long it will last and if you know, what charge for repairing. I am in good health and also my company. I have no news. Remember me to all and write whenever you can find time and inclination.*

> *Yours truly*
> *L. Williams*

The next day, he shared with the Anna the news of returning to South Carolina, even if the company's position would be over two hundred miles away from her down in the low country on the Atlantic coast.

> *Camp 2nd S. C. Cav.*
> *Hamilton's Crossing, Va.*
> *March 19, 1864*

*My Dear Anna*

*I recd your letter of the 11th only today. I had begun to get uneasy as I knew you had been sick. It had been 8 days since receiving any from you and I feared you were prevented by sickness from writing. We are at length relieved from duty and start tomorrow at 8 ock for a station midway between here and Richmond. We have not yet recd orders but it is known that orders have been issued by the Sec. of War to send our regiment and the 1st South Carolina. I expect we will start for S. C. about the 1st April. Everybody is jubilant at the prospect and many sent off telegrams to their wives to look for them early in April. I fear the change of climate but am pleased at the prospect of fattening our horses and mounting all the regiment and getting in good condition for service once more and I am also pleased with the prospect of getting home this spring for a few days and then of having you with me. I do not know whether we will be put on duty immediately or in camps to recruit our horses. If the latter, I suppose Columbia will be the place and then you can kill two birds with one stone. Let us be stationed wherever it may be. I will wish you to spend a month or two with me, I judge there will be no difficulty to get boarding or hire rooms. You must, therefore, make up your mind and make arrangements to pay me a visit; all the officers are calculating to have their families with them. I do not look forward to hard work but expect plenty of leisure; unless we have a great deal more to do than the cavalry now, there we will consider it merely recreation. Maj. Screven from Beaufort assures me that camps can be selected where it is perfectly healthy and I understand the Va. Regiments on the coast have had good health and do not desire to be moved. I am therefore hopeful and wonderfully pleased with the idea of having you in the wars with me. I would like very much to have my company detached for service in Greenville, but I cannot hope for such good luck. At any rate, I think we will be stationed somewhere on the RR for 50 or 60 days to recruit, which will be almost as good as a furlough, however, it will be time enough to make arrangements. Hereafter, I think I can make some smug arrangement to have you and baby with me, at least a month or two.*

*Do as you want about the white washing & c as it can be done so cheaply. You need not fear being tedious telling me about things at home. You said nothing about your garden or pigs. I fear I have offended Mr. Whitmire in some way as he does not write to me. If I did, it was unintentional and I am sure I am certainly satisfied with his management. Tell me when Ned expects to be planting corn. Mid, I expect, will be there to help him about the 1st next month. How does the mare look? When did Ned get harness? Are the harness good and what does Ned think of the wagon? I hope to share with you this year the products of your garden. Write soon and direct as usual. I am glad to hear Mr. Whitmire is well again.*

*Yours affectionately*
*L. Williams*

The location from where the next letter was sent read "Chesterfield Station, Va." Ironically, his last Virginia camp was not far from his first. Chesterfield was due north of Richmond on the railroad, a short ride from Ashland where he and Ruby were first put through the rigors of cavalry instruction back in 1861. Both had learned well and served well. But now it was time to regroup. Both were worn down. As Ruby buried her nose deep in her second pail of oats, her first sustained feeding in weeks, Leonard buried himself in another letter home.

*Chesterfield, Station, Va.*
*March 24, 1864*

*My Dear Anna*

*Perhaps this is the last letter I may ever write you from Old Virginia and dear to me by many associations. I feel somewhat sad at the thought of leaving my comrades in arms behind who are just as much entitled to a respite from the toils and privations of war as we are. We have borne the heat and burden of the day for nearly 3 years and now we go home to recruit our shattered strength and I am sorry the whole brigade is not going with us. I feel that the war, if it should end in another year, is already over with us. I do not apprehend any fighting on the coast of S. C. unless the Yankees raid into the country but there is another enemy I fear, the malaria of the lowlands.*

*The boys are very much elevated with the idea of getting home. One third of the regiment will go through with the horses, the rest of us will go by RR. We will start, I think, next Monday 28th, and will probably be in Columbia about the 2nd or 3rd of April. I do not know the program yet, but I suppose a good many will be furloughed a few days. I may get home for a week and I hope so, and then if the regiment is quartered in Columbia for 3 or 4 weeks, you can go down.*

*We had a few nights ago, a snow of 10 or 12 in. in depth, the ground still covered. I have not recd any letter from you in a week. Why have you abandoned your promise? I write by firelight. I will write you next if nothing happens from Columbia. I have no news. We are all in good health. I am in high hopes of the war closing in another 12 ms. Our prospects are very bright at present. My love to all.*

*Yours affectionately*
*L. Williams*

The next morning, news of Mid's safe arrival in Greenville came in the form of a letter bearing the distinct scent of lilies of the valley. Leonard sniffed the envelope for a while then raced through the words. There was still time before the courier would take the morning's mail so he quickly added a few sentences to the letter he had scrawled by campfire light the night before.

*Friday Morning*
*March 25th*

*Since writing the above, the letters of the 7th and 17th have come to hand. I am glad Mid has reached home. Tell him to go ahead with his work and assist Ned as he may direct and get all things in good condition by the time I get home. I miss Mid very much. I am glad the wagon is in use. The price no higher than I expected. The cow will repay you for all the food you give her. Do not stint her. Have your potatoes come up yet? I have not heard from Mr. Whitmire. I am taking the neglect patiently until I can learn the cause. I think it probable I can get home for a week after getting to Columbia, but not certain of it. I will send my horses through. They are so poor, I fear one of them may have to be left. Write to me in Columbia to the care of your father to reach there 1st April.*

*Yours*
*L W*

The state house bells chimed twelve times back at the Planter's Hotel. The Old Captain's hearing wasn't what it used to be, but the booming old carillon nearly blasted him out of his wing chair. It was indeed high noon as he placed his final letter written from war torn Virginia with those already read. He still had two hours to conclude his dwindling stack before he would don his old uniform and assemble on Lady Street for the long awaited final march. He took a moment to rekindle his pipe and examine the scene from his window. Violinists, trumpeters, bass and snare drummers were gathering. Tiny hands clutched taut strings knotted around ripe red balloons. Parents munched peanuts. Veterans traded salty tales. The reviewing stands were filling up. Old soldiers on young stallions would soon pass before them. The Old Captain would be one of them...but not for two hours. He tapped out his pipe then reached back into the last twelve months of the war.

# CHAPTER FOURTEEN
## EXILED IN HIS HOME STATE

*...the Lord does not spare the young men,*
*and their orphans and widows he does not pity.*
*At the wrath of the Lord of hosts the land quakes,*
*and the people are like fuel for fire;*
*No man spares his brother,*
*Each devours the flesh of his neighbor.*
Isaiah 10:16

She wondered if the Easter Sunday service at Greenville's Second Presbyterian Church would ever end. Wedged tightly between her father and mother, exploration was difficult and escape impossible. She knew it would take days for the pudgy, spectacled man in the black robe to finish reading that entire thick black book. Carrie needed a savior right now. Finally, after four interminable verses of the recessional hymn and a pat on the head from the preacher, Carrie found herself in the repaired wagon bound for freedom and Augusta Street.

The wagon stopped at the Bailey's, who were hosting a simple Easter brunch next door. Anna watched the little Bailey boys chasing Carrie around the blossoming magnolias and listened to the conversation heating up between Mr. Whitmire, Judge Bailey and the Captain. She could only make out smatterings from the far end of the veranda but what little she could discern painted a bleak future indeed. Later, Maum Fannie was stitching up Carrie's torn Easter dress while Anna packed up her husband's carpetbag. Out in the barn, the Captain huddled with Ned and Mid, instructing both to tend zealously to the crop and the garden. At dusk, Leonard was off for Columbia to call on the Laval's, who fortunately lived close to the 2nd South Carolina's camp near the railroad. Yet again, another visit home was over and the Captain returned to his duties. He wondered if the routine would ever end. At least he was back in South Carolina and nearer his family, and his letters now were even more concerned with affairs at home.

*Columbia, S. C.*
*Sunday Evening*

*342*

*April 24, 1864*

*My Dear Anna*

*When I reached here I found your mother quite sick and low spirited with cold, the glands about the jaw very much swoolen. A blister applied the day I arrived here gave her a good deal of relief. Yesterday I could see she was better and today a great deal improved, so much that she is sitting up and much more cheerful. I think she will be well in a few days. Susan is sick with cold and sore throat but is better. Your father is well again. On finding your mother sick, I wished that you and Auntie had come with me and I learned that they had written for Auntie and Aunt Motte to come down so I shall look for them on Monday. I will leave you very lonesome if I stay here two weeks longer. You must come down anyhow for a week or so and if your Aunt Motte does not come, I think you might come with Auntie but I expect your aunts down Monday but I should be gladder to see you and Auntie.*

*If you come, it would probably be best to take your meat down, put it in bags and send it to the store for Mr. Whitmire to take care of until you return. Give out enough to last till your return and tell Ned to come home every night while you are away. I do not know how long we will stay here. It may not be a week or it may be 2 or 3 weeks. I will let you know as soon as I can ascertain. I have been as low spirited as usual on leaving you and I humbly trust this may be the last year of our separation. I took dinner here today, stayed with William last night, have been here nearly all the time, have been to camp only once. If we are not ordered away soon, I must have you here. Will write you again in a day or two- you need not be alarmed about your mother. She is now doing well. I have not been well. Came down with a headache and relaxed by the warm weather. I now feel much better. Write soon.*

*Yours affectionately*
*L. Williams*

The next day, Leonard scanned the Columbia papers and came across some shocking news. General Grant was contemplating calling a halt to all prisoner exchanges. If he did so, the Southern armies would lose a critical means of restoring their losses, and the Confederacy would have to call on their already overburdened commissaries to scrape together a means of feeding Union prisoners. Worst of all, brother James would remain locked up for the duration of the war. Grant's grim contemplations also might mean a death sentence for Northerners housed in hellholes like Andersonville. Leonard prayed the same verdict wouldn't be the fate of his poor brother, although he had heard the Yankee prisons were notorious for their high death rates. While James hobbled about on his cane and an empty stomach up on Point Lookout, Leonard spent his final week in Columbia caring for Anna's mother and ailing sisters.

*Columbia, S. C.*
*April 26, 1864*

*My Dear Anna*

*I have just finished supper. Auntie is here. Had a pleasant trip and is cleared of headache. Had I had known your Aunt Motte was not coming down, I would by all means, have insisted on your coming with Auntie and did look a little for you this evening. I am glad to report your mother is still improving. Susan is again up after a day or two confinement in bed. Julia is now sick with some fever, but I hope she may have no longer a spell than Susan had. I was sorry to hear you had a very bad cold. We have recd no orders yet and cannot tell how long we may yet remain here but hope we will not be removed for some 10 days yet. I would be glad if you would come down on Friday, if you are not suffering too much with cold. Auntie asked me to caution you about wrapping up yourself and baby, especially before day. I think probably you had better leave out enough bacon to last at home till your return and send the balance in bags to Mr. Whitmire till you return and have Ned come home and stay on the premises at night while you are away. This he can do for a week without any disadvantage. I shall look for you on Friday evening. I have not been quite well for several days but now feel quite well. I want to see you and baby most as much as ever. You must borrow enough money from Mr. Whitmire to pay your expenses. It is growing late and I must go into camp tonight so I continue briefly and hurriedly. If anything should prevent your coming, write.*

*Yours affectionately*
*L. Williams*

Moments after Leonard had tucked the envelope in his shirt pocket for later mailing, Auntie marched into the parlor with a suggestion as to where to hide that bacon. It seemed a minor notion really, but bacon was a commodity not to be parted from. Besides, he wished to change the arrangements he had made at his last meeting with Anna. Minutes later, a final paragraph was added and the envelope resealed.

> *Ask Mr. Whitmire to put the bacon under the counter. He can lend you 3 or 4 bags so that if anyone should ever enter the store by night, they would not find it, or if you think best, you can put it in your garret. The last suggestion Auntie makes. It is probably as good a plan as any. Do as you think proper, either plan will do. Preserve enough to last, say for 2 weeks, for if we are permitted to stay here that long, I would like you to stay til I leave. I think probably you had not come til Saturday. I shall be at the depot Saturday for you. This will give you more time and give Ned 2 nights at home to begin with.*
>
> *Yours affectionately*<br>*L W*

The following day, on April 27, Grant turned forty-two and spent his birthday putting the finishing touches on his spring campaign that would destroy Lee's army once and for all. Miraculously, three days later, James was exchanged at City Point, Virginia. His brutal eight months of incarceration were over, and on May 5 he headed home. In 1861, when the war was young and hearts were high, three healthy men in their prime marched off to war. Now, in 1864, with the fiercest and bloodiest campaign of the entire war just eight days away, only the eldest of the Williams trio was left to fight.

On May 4, 1864, Grant's blue coats swarmed across the Rapidan. Like their commander, they were determined to smash their enemy in the open field. But something else equally as formidable as Lee's army lay between them and the Confederate capital. It was known simply as "The Wilderness," a tangled maze of dense timber and underbrush twenty miles west of Fredericksburg. If Grant would pick the fight, then Lee would pick the ring. It was on the outskirts of this Virginia wilderness where Lee and Jackson had flanked and flattened Hooker at Chancellorsville, perhaps another shining victory could be found in its gnarled darkness. Grant knew that Lee would take his Confederates there.

Lee knew that Grant knew, but Lee also realized it was his only chance. Few roads entered the wilderness so Grant's 120,000 men and his train of 4,000 supply wagons would have difficulty in massing. Union cavalry couldn't fight there, and their deadly artillery could not be brought into action at all. Grant's army would be cannon-lacking, rider-poor, and smaller, but when the two generals confronted one another there on May 5, neither could foresee just how unforgiving the terrain would be.

The roads were rutted, narrow, and surrounded by dense tangles of second growth pine, chinkapin and scrubby oak. The cruel nature of the ground, however, was no match for the actual fighting in that frightful place. The underbrush covering the Wilderness floor became a terrible tinderbox as wind, crisp leaves, rifle sparks, and shells sparked a deadly blaze. Wounded men were caged and cooked. Cartridge boxes attached to their belts exploded. Horace Porter, an aide to Grant, witnessed this incineration of men. "Forest fires raged...;the dead were roasted...; the wounded...dragged themselves along, with their torn and mangled limbs..., to escape...the flames... It was as though...hell itself had usurped the place of the earth."

Federal gunner Frank Wilkeson recalled a soldier with two broken legs staring down the inferno with his loaded carbine by his side. "I knew he meant to kill himself in case of fire— knew it as surely as though I could read his thoughts." Yet another of Grant's men remembered the victim's "shrieks, cries, and groans, loud, piercing, penetrating" that vied with gunfire as the flames raced closer to the anguished men. "There was no hope of rescue...After the battle, men remembered seeing trees with streaks on their blackened trunks— the marks of desperately wounded men trying to pull themselves upward, out of the way of horrible death."

Years before, as a youth hunting small animals, the mere sight of blood made Grant ill. Now, numbed by the skewered bodies that choked the woods, Grant robotically chain smoked twenty cigars and unleashed a second attack the next day. The grim result was over 26,000 casualties in the God forsaken, gloom of the Wilderness. One soldier remembered that as the wounded wailed, the eerie screeches of the whippoorwills competed with their groans. "These birds seemed to mock at our grief and laugh at the groans of the dying." One of those that lay dreadfully wounded was General James Longstreet, whose men had arrived just in time on the second day to turn the tide for the Confederates. Like Stonewall before him, and less than two miles from where

Jackson fell, Longstreet fell victim to friendly fire. Darkness was the culprit for Jackson. The dense woods befell Longstreet as a ball ripped through his throat and stopped in his shoulder. As he was propped up against a tree, blood bubbled from his mouth, yet somehow he managed to gurgle the order to fight on before he was transported behind the lines. Five months would pass before "Old Pete" could return to action.

The brutal two days ended with Grant thwarted and Lee's army badly cut up. The Federals' 17, 666 casualties were terrible but could be replenished. Lee's 7,500 were gone forever. Previously, Union generals had licked their wounds and retreated with their battered Army of the Potomac back across the river. Not this time. Grant advanced. While the Army of Northern Virginia was stunned, their commander was not. Lee knew Grant would press on and he knew where he was headed. On May 7, both generals raced toward Spotsylvania Court House, a key crossroads above Richmond, while out in Tennessee, Sherman began his push toward Atlanta. On the same day, far from the tormented tangle of the Wilderness, one Confederate Captain found himself in a different kind of hell, the malarial bogs and pine-barrens north east of Charleston on South Carolina's coast. The low country was a wilderness of its own.

*Georgetown, S. C.*
*May 7, 1864*

*My Dear Anna*

*I am very anxious to hear from you all and especially how your mother and Julia are. I hope you have not become sick. Do let me hear from you soon, direct to me at this place. I arrived in Charleston at 3 ock Monday and left on the N. E. RR next day at 12 ock, got off at Kingstree and there made 3 easy days' marches to this town, through the most barren and monotonous country I ever saw. The country for miles along the road without a habitation or even a hillock, but the trip was not without interest on account of ancient associations. We passed near Indian Town, crossed the Black River, camped on Black Mingo and are now on the Sampit in sight of Winyaw Bay. Georgetown is almost deserted. I was glad to see that Charleston had suffered so little from the shells of the Yankees. I noticed grass growing in the East Bay and Meeting Streets. I passed through Anson to take a view of your old homestead. It looks exceedingly lonesome. I thought of the happiness that once had its abode there and of the hard lot of the refugee.*

*We are to be stationed 9 miles below this place at Camp Jackson and will be put on duty tomorrow. In my next, I will tell you something about the situation. We had a frost at Kingstree on Wednesday morning. I dread to hear the consequences in the up country. I fear corn is killed and will have to be uprooted, tell me about it and when you heard from home. In writing to me, you had better omit the designation of the regiment list. It might be sent to Col. Lipscomb, but address me as directed in the care of Capt. McFie. I have no news but from rumor. I expect a conflict in Virginia has begun. May God prosper our arms. We can get Charleston papers on the 2nd day after publication and letters from Greenville in 3 days. It is 40 miles to Kingstree, the nearest RR depot. This is the most out of the way place I have ever been in. Do write soon and often and let me know how you all are. My love to all the family. Kiss baby for me.*

*Your affectionate husband*
*L. Williams*

The next day, on May 8, a skirmish erupted at Spotsylvania that would spiral into twelve straight days of sheer slaughter. Behind the strongest field works of the war consisting of an elaborate array of fences, earthworks, trenches and felled trees, the Confederates seemed impenetrable. Grant did not hesitate. He poured in men to both flank and smash the defenders head on, and near the west face of a rebel salient known as the "Mule Shoe" he almost did. "I propose to fight it out on this line if it takes all summer," Grant declared as the carnage continued. Day after day, Grant probed for weakness while Lee skillfully formed and reformed his lines.

For the next week, the Confederates held a new line that would come to be called the infamous "Bloody Angle." For eighteen hours in soaking rain, some of the war's most brutal fighting raged along a portion of Confederate trench line only three hundred yards long. Both sides fought like madmen. The assaulting Federals leaped walls, fired point blank into the masses, then fixed bayonets. When rifles were empty, reloaded ones were tossed up to men who were then bayoneted themselves. So furious was the action that at one point an oak tree nearly two feet thick was felled by minie balls. Grimly, Lee's men watched one wounded Federal lying in front of their trench. For two days, he vainly endeavored to cave in his own skull with the butt of his musket. Finally, on the third day his persistence paid off. Blood mixed with rain, filling trenches with a crimson ooze. In the end, the Bloody Angle overflowed with corpses and Grant's burial squad found 150 dead Southerners in a trench covering just 200 square feet. They were buried where they fell when the parapet was pushed on top of them.

Between May 5 and May 12, the Union suffered 32,000 casualties, the highest total by far of any single week in the war. At Spotsylvania, Grant's losses were again far greater than those of the ragged Rebels, but his war of attrition was gutting the ever-shrinking army he was hell bent on destroying. Lee's brave boys had withstood two heavy heart punches in the Wilderness and at Spotsylvania, but Grant knew that if he kept up the pressure, their legs would inevitably buckle. Marveling in Lee's genius in the Wilderness but unaware of the toll it took on his old comrades, Leonard took pen in hand once more. The Captain's words were tempered with hope as word spread through camp that the new Union commander had mimicked his predecessors by retreating in disgrace after defeat. Little did he know that Grant's resolute army had marched south to chew up Lee's soldiers in the Spotsylvania meat grinder.

> *Camp Jackson*
> *Near Georgetown*
> *May 9, 1864*

*My Dear Anna*

*We have reached our destination 9 miles below Georgetown. Our camp is on the western side of Winyaw Bay. The whole country is a barren pine land except the rice fields on the rivers with no settlements to be seen in a half a day's ride. I am told that on the Santee 5 or 6 miles distant, there are some plantations and farmhouses. These are mostly abandoned. I do not suppose a lb. of bacon or a peck of meal could be bought in 10 miles of this place. This situation is particular hard for officers with servants. They can get but one ration, our living is pretty scant, indeed, hardly half enough, but getting a large allowance of corn, we make hominy. I hope to get on pretty well soon as fish are abundant and game of all kinds. I will write to Mr. Whitmire today to buy my mess some 40 or 50 lbs. of bacon, flour & c to be sent by Sergt. Benson who has been detailed to bring supplies for the company. We* are camped in the pinewoods, the weather is quite warm, but a good breeze blowing during the hottest part of the day. I was told in Charleston that we were coming to the Egypt of S. C., but I find it rather a desert. Georgetown, I have no doubt, has been a very pleasant place, but now scarcely a person to be seen. Many of the rice plantations have been abandoned.

We heard of the commencement of the battle on the Rappahannock and today there is a rumor that the battle has been fought and that our army is again victorious and that the enemy are in full retreat having lost several thousand prisoners. Though the news is not all together reliable, I am ready to believe it and rejoice over it! If it be so and the victory presumed to be a rout, and the Yankees driven back across the river, I think their last trump has been played and their hopes of success utterly extinguished. I shall be anxious to see full accounts of the fight. Please send me a few of the Columbia papers. It takes 2 days for the Charleston papers to reach here.

I had no idea so much of our state was valueless for farming. Since traveling to this point, I hold the upper country in much higher estimation and I think if I am to get through this war, will be content to spend the rest of my life in Greenville District. I hope your mother and Julia are well by this time. I think your mother would be greatly benefited by spending a few months with you in Greenville, the change, I am sure, would be beneficial. I hope you are well and strong again. I would like to hear from Greenville, how they are getting on at home and on the farm and how the cow is doing, the hogs, the garden & c. When do you expect to go home? Write soon and tell me everything, how baby is getting on and how the sick have got. Remember me to all in the family and to your brothers. I saw Billy Whitmire in Charleston. He and Nath were well. I did not see Robert. I heard he was to start to Dalton last Monday. The army around Charleston is now very small. This place is reckoned healthy. Last summer and fall there were about 300 troops here and in the vicinity. They had some sickness but no deaths. I hope for the best. Write soon.

> Yours affectionately
> L. Williams

While the most ferocious fighting of the entire Civil War shook the ground around Spotsylvania, Grant detached Phil Sheridan's 10,000 cavalrymen to move toward Richmond in order to draw out Jeb Stuart's riders. Sheridan's men carried deadly repeating carbines and their fine horses formed a column four-men wide and fourteen miles long. Jeb could manage to scrape together only 4,500 on worn down mounts. At Yellow Tavern, six miles outside the capital and not far from his family, Stuart had formed a sturdy line and for over three hours held off Sheridan's superior force. The Captain had known the likes of Stuart, Fitz Lee, Lomax, and Wickham well and had fought alongside every one of them many times before. On May 11, it was fortunate that the Captain was not with them as his old comrades were fighting stirrup to stirrup with Sheridan's overwhelming force. The fight raged into the late afternoon when suddenly at about 4 P. M, the South's most flamboyant and beloved cavalry commander was mortally wounded. Stuart's adjutant general, Major Henry B. McClellan, was by Jeb's side at Yellow Tavern.

*The enemy's charge captured our battery on the left of our line, and drove back almost the entire left...about eighty men had collected, and among these the general threw himself, and by his personal example held them steady while the enemy charged entirely past their position. With these men he fired into their flank and rear as they passed him...As they retired, one man who had been dismounted in the charge, and was running out on foot, turned as he passed the general, and discharging his pistol inflicted the fatal wound...As he was being driven from the field he noticed the disorganized ranks of his retreating men, and called out to them. "Go back! Go back! and do your duty, as I have done mine, and our country will be safe. Go back! Go back! I had rather die than be whipped"...On the morning of the 12th, he turned his eyes upward, and exclaimed earnestly, "God grant that they may be successful." Then turning his head aside, he said with a sigh, "But I must be prepared for another world." President Davis entered. Taking the general's hand, he asked, "General, how do you feel?" He replied; "Easy but willing to die, if God and my country think I have fulfilled my destiny and done my duty." The Rev. Mr. Peterkin visited him, and prayed with him. He requested Mr. Peterkin to sing "Rock of Ages" and joined in the singing of the hymn. During the afternoon he asked*

*Dr. Brewer whether it were not possible for him to survive the night. The doctor frankly told him that death was close at hand. He then said: "I am resigned if it be God's will; but I would like to see my wife. But God's will be done." Again he said to Dr. Brewer; "I am going fast now; I am resigned; God's will be done."*

Such was the dying declaration of General James Ewell Brown Stuart, killed at the age of 31. Only the death of beloved Stonewall Jackson unleashed a mightier wave of tears. "I can scarcely think of him without weeping," lamented Lee. Tributes came from adversaries like Union Captain Theophilus F. Rodenbough as well. "Deep in the hearts of all true cavalrymen, North and South, will ever burn a sentiment of admiration mingled with regret for this knightly soldier and generous man."

The day after the great cavalier spoke his final words, Leonard offered up words of his own written without the knowledge of the bloodshed in Spotsylvania, Longstreet's wounding and Stuart's death. Isolated on the coast of South Carolina, information on what was really going on was based on rumor, speculation, and hope.

*Camp Near Georgetown, S.C.*
*May 12, 1864*

*We are much elated with the glorious news of victory from all directions. Our joy is tempered by the possibility of erroneous or premature dispatches. Grant has certainly been terribly foiled so far in his purposes but the battle was indecisive and he may yet fight a greater battle. From the west the news is somewhat conflicting. I hope, however, everything may soon be confirmed. A merciful God assuredly blessed our efforts. The enemy have met with an unbroken series of disasters the entire year. The spirit of their army must be broken. The enlistments of 3 years troops expiring, their currency depreciating and the approaching presidential campaign will, I feel confident, bring out a very strong peace party, strong enough, I think, to elect a peace candidate for their next president. The condition of things are very auspicious and I begin to look forward at a time very distant when we will all be permitted to return to our peaceful homes. What a joy and relief to the soldiers who have been absent from houses for years to know that independence was won and that peace had dawned on the land and also to the wives, mothers, sisters and fathers whose lot it is to stay at home, toil and brood over the sad realities of war, a condition but little better than that of the soldiers'.*

*I can as yet, hardly understand the propriety of keeping troops in this part of the country. There is nothing to invite the enemy to land or to make an invasion. The rice plantations along the river are nearly deserted and the negroes moved back. This is the most uninteresting country I have ever seen and the most destitute. No one lives within half dozen miles of us. We can buy nothing to eat. The officers are living on half rations. They have to support themselves and boy on one ration. I and Stokes drew 2 lb. rice and 2/3 lb. bacon and 2 ¼ lb. flour, about half a pint of peas and 4 small no. 3 mackerel for the 3 days rations. We have managed by boiling corn and catching a mess or 2 of fish to get on tolerably well. I wrote home to Mr. Whitmire to buy for us about 30 lbs. of bacon and 50 lbs. of flour. He will send it about the 26th. If you can send me a parcel of red pepper, I wish you would put it in the box.*

*I hope this congress will do something for our relief. I am very pleasantly situated in a social point of view, we are near Capt. Keitt's company in which I have several friends from Newberry. I'm very anxious to hear from you. I shall look for a letter from you tomorrow. It seems a long time since I saw you. I hope your mother and Julia are well before this time. I shall direct this to you at Columbia as I do not expect you will start home before Monday. Write often and as soon as you get home. I want to know how things have been going on during your absence and tell Mr. Whitmire to write. My love to your father and all, tell Ned to send me word how all his crops are doing, oats, wheat, corn & c. I wrote to Mr. Whitmire to send me a few fishhooks. I wish he would have 3 or 4 lines made to send with them, about 10 ft. long about 8 threads of no. 10. I hope your cow and garden are prospering.*

*Yours affectionately*
*L. Williams*

As the Old Captain read on, he noticed that pencil had become pen. He had employed a new implement when he added two more paragraphs of instructions to Anna to the same letter over the next two days.

> *Tell me about the Irish potatoes at home and on the farm. I fear they were a good deal injured by the frost on the 4th or 5th inst. If William Mitts has not sent the peas up yet, ask Mr. Whitmire to do what he can in having them forwarded. You need them very much for your cow, with 5 bu. of peas, you could soon have as much milk as you could use and also butter, and give Ned a qt. or 2 to carry with him. I've never known what close living was before. It is true I have been without anything to eat scarcely for 2 or 3 days at a time, but I could always have good prospect of soon getting back to camp where there was plenty, but now I see no relief till Benson comes, which is yet 2 weeks off. You know I am not much of a hand for rice. Rice and peas and all the breadstuffs we get except 1 day's rations of flour in 9 days. Congress and Benson are now my hopes, but either relief is a good ways off. I fish now, not for amusement, but for necessity. There are some very fine fish in the waters near here. The officers are now restricted to one horse. I think I will send my gray to Richard Clary to keep till next fall and then rest the bay horse.*
>
> 

*13th May*

>
> *This morning is quite cool, almost like an October morning. Have had no rain since we have been here. I hope you have had some. If not, it is getting dry in the up country. Did the frost do much damage? The papers of yesterday contain no additional news from Va. except that Genl. Lee has repulsed a second attack near Spotsylvania C.H. on the 8th. I do not know what to think of the silence of the papers. Do, my dear Anna, write often. I never was more desirous to hear from you.*
>
> 

*Yours affectionately*
*L.W.*

In early June, at Cold Harbor six miles east of Richmond, Grant faced Lee once more, convinced that his opponent was on the brink of starvation and defeat. Just five miles from where Ephraim lost his life in the Seven Days Battles two years earlier, Lee's reinforced 59,000 outmaneuvered and outfought Grant's 109,000. In the first twenty minutes alone, the Union lost 7,000 in a hopeless frontal assault against the Confederate center. Despite the slaughter,

Grant never asked for a truce to care for his wounded or bury his dead. His writhing wounded seemed to make the slopes crawl. The macabre effect slowly came to an end, however, as cries for mercy gave way to the stench of death. For three days, they lay on the field as flies feasted on them. In the end, the Army of Northern Virginia was victorious, but never again would Lee win a large scale, decisive battle.

The Confederate "Gray Fox" had staved off defeat in the last engagements, but the Union "Bear" was on the verge of winning what had become a new kind of war. Previously pitched battles were fought and the loser retreated across the nearest river; now the two armies stayed in constant contact with one another. Shell shock, although the term was unknown at the time, was etched on the faces of the fought out men in the trenches. Stress and exhaustion were taking its toll on the officers, especially those in gray. Two of Lee's subordinates, A. P. Hill and Richard Ewell, succumbed to the pressure and ultimately Ewell was replaced by Jubal Early. Lee himself fell ill as his weak heart was pushed to the limit.

Because the first three years' marches and battles had so worn down the 2nd S. C. Cavalry and the unit had been relocated, it had been spared Grant's wrath. There was no Wilderness, Spotsylvania, or Cold Harbor for Captain Leonard Williams.

Years later, the Old Captain was still grateful that he had not taken part in that bloody spring. To this day, he firmly believed his transfer down to the Palmetto State just may have saved his life. The same could not be said for his cherished horse. It had been 35 harsh months since Ruby enjoyed the comforts of her hay-filled barn back in Greenville. Now, her ribs were visible from a distance, her stomach was distended, and her ulcerated throat was redder than her mane. The culprit was a diet of sheaf rice, the only fodder available for miles. It ate away her raw throat and stomach lining. It bound her up. Not only did the deadly feed make for an agonizing digestion process, it provided next to no nutritional value. Even Mid, who had recently rejoined the Captain, could do little more than keep the old horse watered, rested, and groomed. She had borne Virginia's ice, wind, and heat; now, the low country was killing her. Four horses of the 2nd S. C. Cavalry had died here already. Ruby seemed destined to join them.

The health of her 40-year old master had taken a downturn as well. So had his outlook. Being cut off from Anna and his old Legion tormented him. He was bored. He was exiled. He was full of unanswered questions. Why hadn't Anna written? Was she ill? How were Carrie and the crops? What was the purpose in guarding a coast that was not being invaded? Why were the papers with news of Grant and Sherman so tardy? Two days after the third anniversary of his enlistment, he wrote home for some answers.

*Camp Jackson*
*June 8, 1864*

*My Dear Anna*

*I have been looking with unusual anxiety for a letter from you. Your last was dated 31ˢᵗ May. I was very much in the hopes of hearing from you today. Your last letter left me under the impression that you were confined to the house. I am so anxious to hear that you are well and able to be out as usual. Do let me know how you are, I fear Auntie is not with you as you did not mention her in either of your last letters. I heard from Mr. Burgess today. He will, I think, get here tomorrow with the boxes. He got to Georgetown today, and if he can get a wagon, will be in tomorrow by noon. The boxes are looked for with eagerness and I feel at present like a tablespoon of the medicine you are sending me would do me good. I'm a little unwell today, but I think I will be all right tomorrow. I think we shall have good health here. My present ailing is the result of imprudence, being out on duty till 3 ock, took too much dinner which consisted first of hominy and a little meat and hominy and sorghum, which is evidence enough that I am in good health and appetite.*

*We are completely cut off from the public, as much so as if we were at Table Rock in Pickins Dist. We get a daily mail Sundays accepted but the next day after papers are published. The news from Va. continues favorable as Genl. Lee says, "under the blessings of God our successes are all we could expect." I would be glad to have such favorable accounts from Genl. Johnston though the state of things in Georgia are by no means disheartening. The Yankees so far, in all the various encounters, have been worsted and in addition to the army proper, the state troops of Georgia, I hear, number 40,000 men. I think we have troops enough to settle the fate of Sherman. As soon as we get things straight here, I shall begin to think of pulling the wires for a furlough.*

356

*Capt. McFie went home today. He lost one of his little children a few days ago. I think I will have to ask for a leave of absence about the 20th of July or 1ˢᵗ August. If nothing unusual prevents, I will be able to get another in the winter, at least officers in this department usually get 2 or 3 furloughs in the year and there seems to be no reason why they should not, for there is apparently no probability of any movements here. We have scouted the islands and find 200 Yankees on land, their blockades 2 or 3 miles distant. I held an election for 2ⁿᵈ Lieut. on the 6ᵗʰ. Sergt Blythe was elected. I have now 80 men in the company.*

*Thursday, June 9ᵗʰ*

*I think I shall get a letter from you today, how have the rains been? I hope the oats are still doing well, after they come in, you will need no corn for horses and cow, as William Mitts promised you corn. I should feel no hesitancy in writing him for it. Get about 15 or 20 bu. Tell me how the crops are doing. Write soon and let me know how you are getting on.*

*L. Williams*

Up in Virginia, the death of Jeb Stuart at Yellow Tavern meant that Lee's cavalry needed a new commander. Although his promotion wasn't made official until August 11, Wade Hampton almost immediately proved why he was such a worthy successor. Sheridan was raiding northwest of Richmond with 7,000 men and Lee ordered Hampton to pursue with 5,000. The Iron Scouts informed Hampton of Sheridan's movements and with young guns like M. C. Butler and Tom Rosser at his side, Hampton raced after Sheridan's imposing force. The Confederates rode all morning, rested only two hours, then leaped back in their saddles and galloped through the night. At midnight they halted for two more hours, then rode into the morning. Before dawn on June 11, Butler dismounted and hobbled over to fellow brigadier Tom Rosser.

"Butler," said Rosser, "what is Hampton going to do here today?"

"Damned if I know," replied Butler. "We have been up mounted since daylight and my men and horses are being worsted by nonaction."

"Let's ride down and inquire what Hampton's plans are," suggested Rosser.

As the two juniors approached, Hampton's big body stirred on the bench where he slept. Rising quickly, he greeted the two brigadiers.

"General," said Rosser, "what do you propose to do today, if I may inquire?"

357

"I propose to fight," replied Hampton succinctly.

For two days near Trevilian Station on June 11 and 12, Hampton slugged it out with Sheridan and Tom Rosser's West Point classmate General George Custer. Hampton picked off Yankees with his accurate revolver, and just as Custer was about to make off with 800 unprotected horses, the giant in gray whirled Rosser's men around and forced Custer to leave his prizes unclaimed. The next day, as Hart's South Carolina battery pounded them with shells, Sheridan attacked. Six times Sheridan's men charged. Six times Hampton's men held. So close were the two lines after reforming for the seventh time, that the Confederates could hear the Yankee bugles and see the enemy swigging whiskey to fuel their spirits. Near dusk, Hampton's men were so low on ammunition that his men had to search the wounded and dead laying out in the field for unspent bullets. As they did, the Federals formed for a final charge, and Hampton, Butler, and Rosser ordered their men to prepare for the worst. It came at sunset. Sheridan's men advanced smartly in close order, carbines blasting from their hips, as they neared Hampton's fence rails. The proverbial whites of their eyes were just yards away from the Confederates when Hampton's men suddenly unleashed a desperate, point-blank volley that turned the Federals back one last time. Somehow, Hampton's 5,000 had held off Sheridan's 7,000.

As Hampton cautiously pursued, he and his comrades were shocked to discover carcasses of horses shot by Sheridan's own men to save them from capture. They were fine, innocent mounts, and the sight of their still bodies sickened everyone who rode slowly by the fly-covered evidence.

Leonard did not have to bear witness to this cruelty, but on the following night he leaned down over poor Ruby who was now unable to stand. Rain poured over his brim and on to her ice cold withers. He looked into her sad brown eyes. Death was near. Mid knew it. Leonard knew it.

*Camp Jackson*
*June 13, 1864*

*My Dear Anna*

 *There has been several days of rains and for the last two days and nights it has rained almost without cessation and the prospect of continuance is very good. It is also very cool, fires at night indispensable for comfort. We are very comfortable, however. I have a sort of bed stead that keeps me high and dry and a good new tent with a piazza in front, that is a board shelter, very comfortable to sit under in the middle of the day. These dreary rainy days are not without their comforts; we are rid of the flies, mosquitoes and fleas, hope the latter are drowned out.*

*My poor horse is yet living, has eaten nothing in about a week, her throat terribly swollen, she is worse off. I think it is doubtful whether she gets well. I had just made arrangements to send her to Richard Clary's to be pastured and rested. She has been one of the best horses I ever saw. I hope she might live till after the war.*

*I recd your letter of the 8ᵗʰ and was glad you were able to write. I know you are suffering, though you have never mentioned it. Tell me how you are getting, whether you are improving or not. I have felt very uneasy about you. I hope you will not fail to let me know if you get very sick. I have been in good hopes that your sickness has been brought on by excitement and fatigue and that when you become rested and quiet at home, you would soon get well again. Let me know particularly how you are affected, and whether you are improving any.*

The Old Captain slowly placed the letter face up on his lap. He knew that there was more written on the back. He knew it without looking and remembered writing it like it was yesterday. Before he turned the page over, he reached for the handkerchief resting on the nightstand. He knew he'd need it. It was still damp from wiping away tears shed for Stonewall and Ephraim. As he adjusted his wire rims and carefully turned the letter over, he mused that while Jackson and his brother knew well the ultimate consequence of war, such was not the case for all the war's casualties.

*June 14, 1864*

*I am sorry to tell you my horse died last night. No one seems to know what was the matter. I think probably her throat was ulcerated of being fed on rough rice in the sheaf, but I know but little about horse diseases. This morning it has cleared up but the weather still looks unsettled. I hope it has not been so rainy in Greenville. Tell Ned when he commences to harvest to hire whatever help he needs. Have heard nothing more about moving to Adam's Run, hope it is not so. Under our present brigadier, there will be no difficulty in getting a furlough.*

*I have made up my mind to go home in August and see no difficulty about it. Hope you may be well and strong, long before then, so that you may go out with me on the farm.*

*There has not been much doing in Va. and Ga. for several days. I think Grant will keep quiet for some time. Sherman, I think, is obliged to do something and I look with a great deal of confidence to Johnson's success. Our condition, I regard satisfactory and full of hope; our monetary affairs too are improving, provisions, cheapening and the news of the growing crop encouraging. Write soon but do not overexert yourself by attempting too much. I feel your poultry yard does swarm with young broods, else you would give me a better, clearer idea of the number you have. You might say, for instance, between 60 or 70. I guess you have about 60, that is less the accidents, which may be half. I have no news. Write soon. My love to all.*

> *Yours affectionately*
> *L. Williams*

It is said that a life without suffering has no depth. The death of Ephraim, James' amputation, his own shoulder wound, and now, the agonizing death of poor Ruby…all were tragic, thought provoking events that altered the Captain's very being. Like millions north and south of the Mason Dixon Line, he sought to find meaning in that suffering and would continue to do so until his last dying breath. When hardship is shared, it becomes more tolerable. However, lost in the swarms of gnats and mosquitoes that attacked him daily, there were few with which to share his suffering down in the low country. Jeb and old Calhoun had already found that better place. Hampton, Butler, and many more fellow South Carolinians were up in Virginia battling Sheridan. Anna and Carrie, though tantalizingly in the same state, were clear across the other end of it. He still had junior officers Edward Stokes and Absalom Blythe, excellent brothers in arms since the beginning. Also joining him around the campfire was his commander Col. Thomas J. Lipscomb, friend and former classmate from South Carolina College. Less than a year ago, the two had ridden close to one another at Gettysburg, and when a Northern private charged their squadron yelling, "Oh damn you, I've got you now," T. J. calmly cocked his Colt revolver and drilled him square in the head. It had been months since he and Lipscomb had even heard a firearm discharged, and now cut off from the action, the Captain and his exiled inner circle found themselves suffering alone by the sea.

The suffering was only beginning up in Petersburg where Grant had determined to cut off the railroad and communications south of Richmond, in the hopes of choking both the capital and Lee's army, which was bound to defend it. On June 15, Manassas hero, Pierre Toutant Beauregard and 3,000 troops were Petersburg's only hope, and miraculously they held off Union General William "Baldy" Smith's bungled and sluggish attack. On the 16 and 18, Grant personally led two more attacks. Twice Beauregard's scratch force held then fell back as Confederate reinforcements poured into Petersburg. Uncharacteristically, Grant paused. He took an accounting. Finally, he came to the realization that his war of attrition, while brutally effective, was grinding down his own army in the process. Wisely, Grant laid his 70,000-man hammer down. Since May 4, 65,000 Federals had been killed, wounded, or missing. This staggering count represented sixty-percent of the losses suffered by the Army of the Potomac during the entire first three years of the war. Even Grant couldn't order any more to their deaths for now. As he had at Vicksburg, the stern general settled in for a sultry summer siege at Petersburg.

The Captain, meanwhile, found himself saddling a different mount each day for picket duty. Without Ruby or a suitable replacement, he employed borrowed mounts and rode the supply lines, guarded bridges, and kept his eye on Union gunboats. It was hard work and important work. On those hot summer rides, he thought always of the worsening affairs up in Virginia and across the state in Greenville. A part of him wished to be by Butler's side in the column. A larger part yearned to be seated by Anna on the porch rocker. His only recourse now was to do his best to manage his family and farm from down on the coast.

*Camp Jackson*
*June 18, 1864*

*My Dear Anna*

*I recd yours of the 12ᵗʰ two days ago and was glad to hear you were able to be up all day, but I know you are suffering still by your keeping to your room. I hope you are better, though you did not say, so you must tell me all about your sickness and how you are every day, whether getting better or worse. I wish I could be with you a month or two to nurse you and wait on you and provide you with whatever you could* eat, but this is impossible. *I can only advise to go to bed earlier and rise early. Take a little exercise soon in the morning and get whatever you think will agree with you for breakfast. Get Mr. Whitmire to buy you anything you fancy you would like. I believe people in feeble health ought to pay particular attention to their diet. They must take nourishment to gain strength and flesh and during the day take occasionally moderate exercise. I would leave off reading. Take an eggnog in the morning and before going to bed, a milk punch and also before dinner, take a stimulant. Encourage your appetite as much as possible by having prepared whatever you may fancy, provided it can be had.*

*We still hear rumors we are going to Adam's Run, but I hope will not be moved till after August. Under Genl. Trapier, there will be no difficulty in getting home, I think, before September. We are faring finely here since our boxes came. We frequently have messes of squirrels and fish and have several messes of venison and also of honey. The boys have found several bee trees which have turned out well, it can also be bought now a few miles off. I was glad to hear that Ned was getting along well with his crop, ask him to tell me particularly about the wheat, how much he thinks he will make and what arrangements he has made for cutting it. Tell him to use all means to save it. It may be he can house it in the field in the old house till he can have it threshed out and tell him as soon as the oats are cut and dry enough, to haul them home. That is his share. He can have one load a day, even while he is plowing, but if the crops permit, he had better haul it home at once.*

*I would like very much to be at home in August, for there I can tell pretty much what will be made and how much and what I will have to buy and make arrangements in time to get full supplies of everything. After the oats are gathered, you can make the cow give milk, oats are as good as peas. I expect your butter and milk is pretty scant. Have you written to Mr. Mitts for corn yet? I have no doubt yours is out.*

*There are several cases of chills and fevers in the companies that have been stationed here. But with us, there are no cases. I think this summer we shall have health, and I think next spring we will be moved to a field of active operations. We are at present puzzled to know where*

*Grant is and what he intends to do. So far he has been miserably beaten and thwarted. I wish that the same could be said of Sherman, but I am hopeful that things will turn out well with Johnson. Do not fatigue yourself with writing long letters, but write me a short letter everyday to say how.*

...

The Old Captain shook his head upon realizing that the rest of the letter was missing. It was remarkable that Anna had managed to save so many through such hard times. So much had been lost back then.

Preserving his army back in those days was the prime concern of Confederate General Joseph E. Johnston. To some he was dubbed "The Great Retreater," to others he was deemed the most brilliant defensive-minded tactician in the entire Confederate army. Regardless, the commander of all Southern forces in Virginia at the outset of the war now commanded the Army of Tennessee. His orders were straightforward: keep Atlanta out of Sherman's hands. For weeks, he had retreated adroitly with insignificant losses from one fortified position to the next while Sherman counter punched each time at locations like Resaca, Cassville, and Allatoona, sidling past Little Joe's flank down toward Atlanta, a critical Confederate supply point and railhead. The farther Sherman marched, however, the longer and more vulnerable his supply lines became. In his rear, running amok and wrecking havoc was Confederate General Nathan Bedford Forrest, a resourceful guerrilla style fighter who had tormented Grant earlier in the war. With the stealthy Forrest behind him and the cagey Johnston in front of him, Sherman headed toward Atlanta. All eyes now looked to Georgia.

Each evening around the campfire, Colonel Lipscomb and Captains McFie and Williams mulled over possible orders that might soon send them west to support Johnston or north to help defend besieged Petersburg. T. J. and Leonard argued the pros and cons of each option but both agreed that either assignment could cost them their lives. McFie said little. The death of his young son had long taken the fighting spirit away from him. The next morning, as Sherman marched steadily toward Atlanta, Leonard moved his pen slowly across a blank requisition form. There was little real news to report, but a real need to maintain contact with his family and home.

*Camp Jackson*
*June 20, 1864*

*My Dear Anna,*

*I write again by Mr. Burgess, who together with six others, leave tomorrow for home on a 15 day furlough to assist in harvesting their wheat. I was very glad to observe your cheerfulness in your last letter and I hope before this reaches you, your health may be much improved. We are getting on here quietly enough with but little to do and thanks to good friends at home, living very well. I've become as fond of rice as any low country man. Mr. Burgess' present prevented the disappointment you allude to and I can now look forward to your 2nd promise, recollect, a big eggnog. Mr. Whitmire sent me a lb. of ground coffee which is delicious. I indulge frequently in the evening in a flavorous cup. The Court Marshal is progressing, expect to get through tomorrow. There is on the court a Lieut. Ward, who lives in this district and his bro. Capt. Joshua Ward commands a company near here. Are they related to you? They are very wealthy, their father owns some 1,700 negroes. He gave his sons nearly all his property and his daughters nearly $40,000 each.*

*I have made no acquaintances scarcely and there seems to be no one living near here. We don't see a citizen in a month. I wrote you some time ago to get Auntie to make me a pair of pants. If they cannot be finished in time to send by Ferguson, you can send them by Burgess and also my horse cover. There is nothing else I need, but if you can get Osnaburgs to make Mid a shirt and pair of pants, I wish you would get them made for him. He's getting very ragged. Don't fatigue yourself about them, but if you can have them made, send them, he needs them badly.*

*We are anxious for the news, got no mail on Monday and yesterday's papers lead us to look for a battle in Va. and Ga. at any moment. I think our military condition altogether favorable and promising fine results. Forrest's victory is grand and astounding with his small army against such odds. Everywhere and on all occasions, we are successful. Grant has been worse beaten than any of his predecessors. He was their champion and par excellence, their great general, what will the Yankees do now?*

*I requested you in my last to write me a short letter every day. It will not fatigue you too much. I hope you will do so and tell me about your condition & c. Tell Ned to send me word how he is getting on harvesting and how much wheat he thinks he will make and also to get the oats home as soon as possible. I fear the cavalry passing may destroy it. Tell him to leave some at Mr. Watson's to feed on and save the trouble of hauling back. Let me know how everything is doing on the farm and garden. Rumors are still prevalent that we are to go to Adams Run but no orders. We have no news. Have you heard lately from James? My respects to all.*

*Yours affectionately*
*L. Williams*

Back in Greenville, Maum Fannie did what she could to scrape together meals for Anna, Carrie, and the servants. Lucy's slender black hands brushed Carrie's curls and mended her petticoats until the mistress could regain her strength. Mr. Whitmire kept an eye out for the rare bargain, putting aside necessities for Anna and occasionally sending a box down to the low country for his business partner. Bill and Clough became allergic to the plow. Steve wondered how he'd look in a new blue uniform. Loyal Ned hauled wheat by day and tended to the garden in the evenings. Southeast in Newberry, where the Williams boys were raised, James was navigating confidently now with the aid of his hard hickory cane. He was even contemplating a trip up to Greenville to visit his sister-in-law.

On the battlefront, Grant's soldiers had swapped their rifles for picks and shovels, digging in under the sweltering sun around Petersburg. Lee hoped that the siege would be of moderate duration, long enough to keep Grant bogged down thus threatening Lincoln's reelection bid in November, but not so interminable that his army would be unable to withstand it. For now, time was on the side that flew the Confederate battle flag. Despite Forrest's cavalry antics behind him, Sherman continued to push Johnston back as his 90,000-man army closed in on the trembling citizens in Atlanta. Captain Williams and his company of 80 men picketed the tropical coastline, patrolled the bays between Georgetown and Charleston, and swatted mosquitoes. The enemies now were shells from Federal gunboats and chills from the fever.

*Camp Jackson*
*June 23, 1864*

*My Dear Anna*

*I have just finished a good dinner, had a dish of excellent bean soup, bacon, peas and cornbread and as dessert, warm wheat hoe cake and molasses, nothing wanting but a mug of nice cool milk. By the way, let me mention that to make good pea soup requires long boiling, say 2 hours. I was very glad to hear by your letter of the 17th that you were going out a little. I hope you will by degrees, recover your strength. I am disappointed in the climate here. The weather here so far has been very pleasant, nights cool, find 2 blankets very comfortable.*

*Capt. Gary on North Island is being shelled today. We hear the guns. Last week our picket lines were shelled, but it occasioned no excitement among the old troopers, only a little nervousness with the recruits. The news is still exciting from Va. and Ga. I believe there is nothing so far discouraging. Grant is nearer Petersburg than I like, all the raiders are well punished and seem to be making their best speed to get into a safe place. Johnson seems to be satisfied with his position and all accounts agree in the fine condition and spirits of his army. His reserves at Atlanta are numerous. I do not look for any reverses in Ga., the first time I ever felt that perfectly easy about that army. I feel confident that that campaign will turn out well. In the meantime, while Grant, according to Yankee dispatches, is gaining victories, gold is steadily advancing and if the Yankees do not soon gain some successes, there is no telling where gold will stop.*

*I hope James and Alan will visit you. Tell them both to write to me. I would like very much to see them. Did James get his furlough extended and what does he think of doing? Tell Ned he must send me an account of his crops, how he got in the corn, does it need rain, and also how the sweet and Irish potatoes are doing & c and also how he is getting on harvesting and how he thinks the wheat crop will turn out. I recd the stamps but having been supplied, did not need them. Did you get those I sent you? The health of the troop continues good- my own health very good- though I have fallen off a good deal. I think, however, this took place before the box came, have lost no flesh since. My company have been unfortunate with horses, have lost 5 since coming here. We*

366

*lead a very quiet life here, I may say a lazy one. We have no news. I
begin to look forward to August with pleasant anticipation which by
the by, is only 6 weeks off. The mail is now waiting and I must close
with my love to all. Write very often and tell me how you are doing.*

*Yours affectionately*
*L. Williams*

One of Grant's underlings at Petersburg was General Ambrose Burnside,
former Commander of the Army of the Potomac, who had ordered fourteen
suicidal charges at Fredericksburg resulting in the worst defeat in the history of
the U. S. Army. On one steamy afternoon early in the siege, Colonel Henry
Pleasants, a mining engineer in command of a Pennsylvania regiment of coal
miners, approached Burnside armed with a sharp shovel and a bold plan. He
wished to have his men secretly dig a tunnel under the Confederate fortifications,
transport four tons of black powder to its end, and blow a hole right through the
rebel defenses. Burnside's boys could then charge through the gap and win the
day. To Burnside, the tunnel was a way for him to dig out from under his lingering
shame at Fredericksburg and become the champion of Petersburg. On June 25,
Pleasants' coal miners started to dig while Leonard began a new letter.

*Camp Jackson*
*June 25, 1864*

*My Dear Anna*

*I feel in great hopes of getting a letter from you this evening. I was
a good deal disappointed yesterday. For a week or two you had been
writing very punctually and had it in my mind to hear from you, am
much more anxious to hear from you now that you are sick and hope
you will write me a short letter every day. I do not wish you to write
enough to fatigue yourself. I'm very sorry to hear of Uncle Ephraim's
sickness. Tell me how he is. I hope James and Alan have visited you
before now and may spend a week or two in Greenville. Jim has had a
hard time during his imprisonment, hope he may enjoy his visit. The
weather is now getting quite warm and dry. I regret to hear of the
injury done the crop of small grain by long continuous rains. I
understand in the middle districts, wheat will be almost a failure, and
also that corn crops are almost overgrown with grass. It behooves all*

*to economize in everything and make the most of their crops they can.*

*Clough is a miserable pest. I wish he'd be put off 30 or 40 miles from home. I scarcely know what to advise to be done with him. Whenever he does anything that he deserves to be thrashed for, send for Martin and tell him to whip him severely and repeat it every time he deserves it and imprison him 2 or 3 days at a time, especially at night. Tell Ned to thrash the life nearly out of him or make him obey. I would like to have charge of him a month or two. I will try to get rid of him some way or other this summer. I forgot to mention to you that you must get Mr. Whitmire to return your bond to the tax collector. I hope it is not too late. Has Mr. Whitmire returned from Newberry?*

*Grant has more tenacity of purpose than any of his predecessors. I do not understand the situation of the armies very well now that they are this side of Richmond. They are in too close proximity to the RR to suit me and the fact that there were no telegrams from Richmond yesterday, favors the idea that the RR is already in their possession. I fear that it is so. Johnson seems to be still master of the situation in Ga. I look for news this evening. The cavalry in Va. have suffered pretty severely, but it must be remembered their ranks are full and a casualty of 20 per ct. makes a pretty heavy showing. We came off in a good time to get rid of hard fighting and heavy work, but we will have our turn again next spring if the war lasts.*

*Send me a Greenville paper, I would like to look over the district news now and then. I miss the map of Va. which I gave to you. Wish you would send it and send by Mr. Burgess or Ferguson. Without it, I cannot understand our positions and movements. I read yesterday the account of Capt. Smith's settlement at Jamestown, Va. and his explorations along the rivers of the peninsula, which possessed greater attractions by the familiarity with the localities, he ascended the James, York, Pamunkey, Chickahominy, Rappahannock...*

Again the rest of the letter was missing, so the Old Captain quickly reached for the next small envelope.

Atlanta had become a southern symbol of staunch resistance, yet its protector, Joseph Johnston, was not viewed the same way. That all changed on June 27 when Sherman faked yet another flanking movement and barreled into

Little Joe head on twenty miles above Atlanta at Kennesaw Mountain. In temperatures that neared the century mark, Johnston's army whipped a surprised Sherman. One sweaty rebel recalled the price that that victory exacted.

> *I never saw so many broken down and exhausted men in my life. I was as sick as a horse, and as wet with blood and sweat as I could be, and many of our men were vomiting with excessive fatigue, over-exhaustion, and sunstroke; our tongues were parched and cracked for water, and our faces blackened with powder and smoke, our dead and wounded were piled indiscriminately in the trenches.*

Morale in Johnston's army rose as high as Kennesaw Mountain itself, but up in the White House, spirits hit a new low. In the wake of 90,000 Union losses over the last eight weeks, Peace Democrats launched a new assault on Lincoln whose reelection was now in real peril. Worse, many a northern widow wished on the President the same fate that awaited Clough. But, there was plenty of fight left in "Uncle Billy's" vast army, and only 20 miles separated that army from its Atlanta prize. News of Johnston's stern stand and updates concerning Lee's siege predicament had not yet echoed down to the tidal basin. Something even more heartening had arrived, however, two envelopes bearing a Greenville postmark.

> *Camp Jackson*
> *June 28, 1864*
>
> *My Dear Anna*
>> *I was gladdened this evening by the receipt of two letters from you of the 22nd and 24th. The one of the 22nd was by some means delayed and gave me great anxiety about you. I have been greatly cheered by the accounts of your improvement and hope you will soon be well again. Hope you went to Henry's to dinner, would advise you to visit frequently. I'm very glad to hear that James and Alan have made you a visit, wish I could have been with them. Does James expect to go back to the army? What does he propose? Has Mr. Whitmire returned, you have not told me anything about the wheat. Will it be worth cutting? I hope you may get 3 or 4 barrels flour, expect flour will be high again.*
>> *We are in considerable anxiety in regard to the conditions of things around Petersburg. Have had no information from them since the 18th*

*and for the last 2 or 3 days, no intelligence from Genl. Johnson. I hope, however, that the interruption of communication with Genl. Lee's army and the south is not the result of any permanent foothold of the Yankees on the line of RR. I expect another great battle has been fought before this time. The present campaign will decide whether the war will close in a year or will last four more. I am hopeful of the best, but it may be my hopes as in the past are destined to be deferred. The Yankee tenacity seems to be developing to a more alarming extent than ever. After repeated chastisements, they seem not to relax in the least, but rather the more determined. I suppose we shall not be in suspense much longer. I think the next ten days must certainly terminate this campaign.*

*I see by the Yankee accounts Fernando Wood, Voorhees and other prominent men have been arrested and that Vallandigham has returned to Ohio and defies Mr. Lincoln. Their circumstances auger favorably of a pleasant state of things likely to culminate soon with them.*

*The weather has been extremely warm for a few days and it is getting somewhat dry. Last night a brisk breeze sprang up and still continues. It is not much warmer here than in Va. I hear of frequent cases of outrage and murder in the upper part of Greenville by deserters and tories. The government ought to spare no pains in ferreting out and shooting them. They are a greater nuisance than the same number of Yankees. We are enjoying our usual quiet and have no expectations of collision while we are here. I would like you to send me a Patriot or an Enterprise occasionally. I see the Charleston papers every day, Mondays excepted, the 2ⁿᵈ day after publication. Ferguson will start back around the 2ⁿᵈ. I fear you will not get this in time. I intended to tell you to send things to Mr. Grady's. If you fail to send by him, Mr. Burgess will leave about the 6ᵗʰ or 8ᵗʰ next month and will bring them for me. You had better inquire whether he can bring them or not and if he can send them to his house. Hope your mother will not disappoint you in the promised visit and also that the girls may find time to visit you this summer. Do write often. While you were ailing, I was so fearful about you. I wrote Auntie a day or two ago about you. Remember me to all.*

*Yours affectionately*
*L. Williams*

A year to the day after he ordered Pickett's ill-fated charge, Lee found himself surveying his fortifications around Petersburg. He wondered if and for how long his men could stand up to the wolf that lurked at his door. The horrors of this new kind of fighting, a precursor to the trench warfare of World War I, had worn Lee down. He gazed upon his hungry, barefoot soldiers and marveled that he still had an army at all. Thousands had been incinerated in the cruel Wilderness, bludgeoned to death at blood-spattered Spotsylvania, and blown to bits at Cold Harbor. Now in the Petersburg trenches, they once again clung to their shovels and their decimated dreams. Lee knew that in the months to come, they'd have to dig even deeper.

Captain Leonard Williams no longer had Ruby, but he was still riding on his dream. Lee would fight the good fight and God would lead the charge. If it was indeed their lot to lose, then he and his men of Company K would find a way to survive its final chapter. And, yes, he would sit once more with Anna by his side and Carrie on his lap, overlooking the Blue Ridge at Caesar's Head.

In the summer of '64, however, few dared to dream. Wives and mothers visited cemeteries. Husbands and fathers clad in blue and gray yearned for loved ones. Copperheads snapped. Lincoln stared at the casualty lists. In Petersburg, Lee winced at the sight of his boys digging what might prove to be their own graves. Underground, Pleasants' miners toiled in their secret tunnel. In Georgia, Sherman pushed angrily toward Atlanta and Johnston fell back again. The Captain, meanwhile, passed along an order to saddle up and ready the horses. Company K was headed for Charleston. Before breaking camp, however, he sat down to write home. In addition to alerting Anna of the coming change of station, Leonard wanted to encourage her as to the war's progress, and perhaps reassure himself.

*Camp Jackson*
*July 3, 1864*

*My Dear Anna*

> *I recd yours of the 28th yesterday, was very glad to hear you were still improving. Have no doubt the company you have had and the few visits you have made have benefited you. You must keep up your visits as often as you feel able and take the stimulating remedies I mentioned. Go to bed early and rise at daylight and as soon as the dew is off, take a short walk in the yard and garden. Have no doubt the bath will be*

*beneficial also. You will not, I fear, recover your strength fully during the hot weather. The weather is now extremely warm here, yesterday and today the warmest of the season. Have had as yet no cases of fever. There are, however, I understand, several cases among the troops who have been stationed here for 2 or 3 years, so I scarcely think we will have fever. This year am sorry to hear the wheat is turning out so badly. Did not expect much, tell Ned he must try to save it all and also the straw and chaff. Get it saved as soon as possible and also repeat him my wishes to have the oats hauled home as soon as possible to prevent marauding on them but to leave a few dozen in his house at Mr. Watson's to feed the mare on while at work there. How does the bacon hold out? I'm glad to hear the cow is giving you more milk, hope enough for all and to make you a little butter. Are your chickens big enough to fry; now is the time to use them while your appetite is weak.*

*We are under marching orders, do not yet know when we will start or where we will be going, I regret the move on one account only and that is the facilities to get furloughs here. I understand it is more difficult to get them in the other military districts and that they are given for ten days only. I still, however, hold on to my belief that I should get home in August or September, but if we stay here, I would ask for a furlough in a month. I understand the company Billy and Nath belong to has been disbanded. What do you know about it and when are they going home? I am sorry on their account as they seem to be well pleased. When did you hear from Uncle Ephraim?*

*I have seen the papers from the 1st inst. and from the general tone of the news everywhere, I feel much encouraged. Our affairs around Petersburg are not quite satisfactory. This may be owing to the fact that we know but little of the situation there. The best evidence as I can see of the waning condition of the Yankee's spirits and hopes consists in the steady depreciation of the currency, gold being quoted on the 24th in New York at $2.40. Sherman has met too with heavy losses while our loss was very light. The democrats of the U. S. are waiting the developments of the pending contests and if we can baffle the efforts of the Yankees till the latter part of summer, I feel very confident an unconditional peace man will be nominated for the presidency. Then, if our success lasts till November, I think he will be elected. May the*

*Lord enable us to pray fervently and with faith for such an end.*

*Your last two letters came to hand in proper time. I shall look for a continuance of energy in your letter writing. You need not fear telling anything too often. It never seems monotonous to me, but always fresh. Tell Henry and Mr. Whitmire to write me. My love to all.*

*Yours affectionately*
*L. Williams*

Leonard knew that Mt. Pleasant was not really a mountain but a sand dune stretch of coast above Charleston. With his boots firmly planted in that sand and field glasses pressed against his wise gray eyes, he could see clearly what used to be. He looked across to a harbor that not long ago teemed with ships stuffed with rice, indigo, and stout bales of King Cotton. Now, Federal gunboats patrolled off shore menacingly, their angry black guns trained on the marshy coastline. Out of field glass range, beyond the horizon, a handful of daring blockade runners still eluded the blockade, but each day more and more were captured or found watery graves. Charleston itself, the "Holy City," once the throne of southern culture, fine manners, and the birthplace of his dear wife, was now void of life, a gutted shell besieged by woe and war. He had spent the afternoon riding along its cobblestone streets and studying the blank faces of the refugees, orphans, deserters, and wandering slaves. Now, the city itself seemed to sigh, afraid to look back up at him. In the harbor entrance sat Fort Sumter where the first shots were fired. Although now a pile of rubble, to some it was still the mighty rock of defiance, to all it was the pebble that started the avalanche. The sun, now red as had been Ruby's mane, was soon to disappear. Charleston and life as he knew it already had.

All had arrived safely from Camp Jackson having gladly left behind its army of fleas, ticks, and mosquitoes. Although only slightly higher than the coast, Mt. Pleasant did catch the on shore breezes and picket duty was now indeed more pleasant. Soon, it was time for the Captain to leave his observation point and return to headquarters to see what Mid had rustled up for dinner. Later he would write Anna about what he had seen here.

*Mt. Pleasant*
*July 13, 1864*

*My Dear Anna*

*We are still at this place and may stay here a month. The enemy have failed in their assaults on John and James Islands. They've been driven back and I believe they have entirely left both islands. I went into the city yesterday. It's a dull place. It has undergone as great a change as Fredericksburg, Va., more than half the city is abandoned and the other part occupied in a great measure by vendors of vegetables, fruit & c., mostly foreigners. The part of the city now occupied is that with which I am least acquainted. I became lost at one time and was unable to recover my reckoning until I got into Anson opposite your old home. I stopped and looked in through the gate. My thoughts ran back to the time when everything was colored with the rays of hope and prosperity, when social and domestic happiness was undisturbed by the rude alarums of war.*

*I have not recd any letter from you other than the 2nd of July. I hope your health is still improving. Tell Ned to send me word how the wheat will turn out, since cutting it and also the oats. There is a good deal of chills and fever in the company, some 10 or 12 cases. The news from Va. and Ga. has been meager for several days. Mt. Pleasant has a fine breeze all the time and is free measurably from mosquitoes, fleas & c. The weather has been very warm for several days. Prices are, I believe, about as high as ever. Watermelons sell from $3 to $10. There was a great many pears and apples in market, did not price them. I wrote Mr. Whitmire a few days ago. Tell him he must write. I have not heard from him, I believe but once. I have no officer with me. Perry is with the regiment as commissary. Stokes and Blythe are sick at Georgetown. This keeps me pretty close in camp. The firing on the city and Fort Sumpter is much less frequent the last 2 or 3 days. The mail leaves at 7 ock and I have another letter to write. This will excuse the hurried and short letter I send you this time. My love to all. Shall look for a letter every 2 days.*

*Yours affectionately*
*L. Williams*

The Old Captain glanced at his pocket watch and counted the remaining envelopes, which now formed a thin stack about the thickness of his old leather reins. Only ten letters were left to be savored. In a short time he would carefully re-tie them all up snuggly with Anna's dainty apron string, enjoy a final pipeful, then don his uniform. Like those unread letters, the Confederacy was soon to be finished.

A decision that hastened its downfall was replacing Johnston with his subordinate John Bell Hood on July 17. Despite victory at Kennesaw Mountain, President Jefferson Davis had lost confidence in Johnston, and with Sherman in sight of Atlanta, he wanted a fighter. To be sure, Hood was more aggressive than his predecessor; the loss of his arm at Gettysburg and the use of his leg at Chickamauga making him even more feisty. Unlike the 45-year old Johnston, the 33-three year old Hood was an impetuous risk taker and fatally flawed. Soon Davis would regret placing Atlanta in Hood's lone and shaking hand. When intelligence reached the invaders that Hood now stood in their way, a gleam could be seen in Sherman's eye. News had already reached him that Nathan Forrest's cavalry had been repulsed at Tupelo and Forrest himself had been wounded. Now, with his supply line secure and the worthy Johnston demoted, Sherman marched at the double-quick to put the torch to Atlanta.

Captain Williams put a light to his briar pipe and ordered Company K to move out. After two days of marching in sweltering heat, the sad spires of Charleston had long vanished and the tiny village of Chisholmville lay around the bend. Chisholmville was situated not far from Green Pond, both towns resting near the Charleston and Savannah Railroad, southwest of Charleston. Four months duty of guarding this vital rail line awaited Leonard and his cavalrymen. He informed Anna of his new location, described the countryside, and expressed his hopes for better days ahead.

*Chisholmville near Green Pond, S. C.*
*July 20, 1864*

*My Dear Anna*

*I notified you on the 18th of our move from Mt. Pleasant. We arrived here an hour ago. I have not seen enough to tell you what sort of place it is. There have been 3 companies here for some time and they have had a good deal of sickness but I have no idea if it is more sickly than Georgetown. Mt. Pleasant was the nicest camp we ever had, hated very much to leave there. I am thus, early to write to you that you may know where to write to me. Direct to Green Pond. I have stood the march here very well, a good many were taken sick on the road. I left several in the hospital at Mt. Pleasant, though none were very sick. Stokes and Blythe are still at Georgetown, and still without any officer to assist me.*

*There is great monotony in the appearance of the country between Georgetown and this place. The land, however, is better this side of Charleston, except in the neighborhood of Georgetown, the country is much more thinly settled than I had supposed and a great deal of farmland uncleared. We had plenty of rain in Charleston, but it is a little dry here. Hope the seasons may continue good in the country.*

*I leave it to Mr. Whitmire's judgment to buy you a little corn to buy on the best terms. Use the wheat as soon as it can be threshed and also the oats can be used to feed the mare. I hope you will not have to buy much corn, the wheat crop will do quite as well as I expected. Mr. Whitmire says there was 60 doz. which will make 15 bu. It does very well. I am sorry to hear the potatoes are not likely to do well. You know they are my hobby, they have time yet to come out.*

*The papers give us no news for the last few days. What do the people think of Johnson's removal? We camped last night at Adams Run. It is a very good place. I presume now we may regard ourselves settled. If I can enjoy health, I am as well contented one place as another. The summer is half over and I hope I shall escape fever, am now in fine health. Hope you are still improving and that when I come home I shall find you as stout and hopeful as ever. I am still in hope of getting home before the summer is gone. My love to all.*

*Yours affectionately*
*L. Williams*

On the afternoon the Captain wrote his letter, and three days after taking command of the Army of Tennessee, Hood attacked a corps of Sherman's vast army in the savage Battle of Peachtree Creek, just four miles outside Atlanta. Citizens poured out of the city as the armies rained fire and shell upon one another. Hood was hammered but still hungry to fight. On the 22nd, he attacked with even more men and suffered half as many losses on that one day than Johnston had in ten weeks. In an eight-day period, the tactically impaired Kentuckian lost 15,000 of his 65,000 while Sherman forfeited a mere 6,000 of his 100,000. Simple arithmetic dictated that Atlanta's days were numbered.

While its defenders were on the brink of being overrun, the presses of the *Atlanta Intelligencer* were running overtime, spewing out rosy accounts of the city's staunch defiance in the face of constant bombardment. Editorials praised their heroic soldiers, declaring that Atlanta would never be taken by Sherman's or any other army. Such breast-beating, nationalistic dogma elated those who dared to believe it. Most, like Leonard, merely hoped against hope that what they read might be true. In his next letter he expressed some optimism, but as always he tried to concentrate on his family and the affairs back home.

*Chisholmville, S. C.*
*July 24, 1864*

*My Dear Anna*

*I have as yet recd but one letter directed to Charleston. I recd several sent in from Georgetown. It has been now 5 days since I have heard from you. I recd a letter from Mr. Whitmire day before yesterday. He told me you were not quite well, but up. As soon as Lt. Stokes gets back, I intend applying for a furlough. He is at home now on sick furlough. Blythe, I understand is better and will soon be here. We have a good deal of sickness and I fear but few will escape; the chills come on very suddenly at a time it is least expected. Mr. Whitmire gives an encouraging account of the corn crop. Our oat crop is certainly good and Mr. Watson agrees to let me have his share of them at a reasonable price. I've written to Richard Clary to engage wheat and peas for you. I hope you may be as fortunate in putting up vegetables for winter use as you were last year such as peas, beans, potatoes & c. When the oats are housed feed the cow liberally with them. She will then give you plenty of milk and butter. These are such a luxury to me, I wish everybody could have a good cow. With a good garden, milk and butter, plenty of breadstuffs, we can well afford to dispense with what are usually termed luxuries. Also try to save some cabbage for winter use. I hope Ned may have good luck with turnips. They make an excellent dish in the winter and spring as well as fine food for cows. Save all the beans that ripen. They are capital in hard times. I hope to get up to help Ned put in the turnip seed. Wish you could get a few rutabagas, say for 1/4 the patch.*

*We have just heard some delightful rumors from Genl. Hood that the fight was progressing most favorably. I trust it may be so and if true and Sherman can be driven back, Lincoln will have a hard time in raising his 500,000 troops. We are quiet here, picketing in very unhealthy localities on the Ashepoo and Combahee Rivers. You must keep up. Don't get low spirited, all things are going on well and will, I trust, soon end well.*

*July 25<sup>th</sup>*

*I have time to add this morning that I am quite well. Remember me to the neighbors and write often. Direct your letters to Green Pond. Had a fine rain yesterday. This morning is clear and bright. Let me know how the rains are.*

*Yours affectionately*
*L. Williams*

Life among the swamp tupelo and bald cypress was unsure and unsafe. The Charleston and Savannah Railroad was a critical line that could be attacked at any time, and an invasion on the coast against feeble defenses could be launched whenever the Federals wished. Up in Petersburg, the Union did attack, but they wish they hadn't. Burnside's tunnel was completed and the men lit the fuse. Seconds later, 200 feet of Lee's entrenchments were blown sky high, but instead of attacking the flanks near the blast, Burnside's troops poured in to the crater the blast created. Confederate artillery and mortars soon found their range and shot the trapped bluecoats like fish in a barrel. When it was over, all that was left was a massive hole and 4,000 Union casualties. Grant called the debacle one of the saddest affairs he had witnessed in the war. News of the ill-fated Federal assault reached Leonard in the local papers a week later. Before, he would celebrate such victories, but now this useless slaughter seemed merely to numb him even more. Like the Battle of the Crater, the war would leave a hole in the hearts of everyone, yet for now all was quiet around Green Pond, and he had plenty of time to relate what he knew and find out what he did not.

*Chisholmville near Green Pond*
*July 30, 1864*

*My Dear Anna*
*I recd yours of the 19<sup>th</sup> several days ago and of the 17<sup>th</sup> only day*

*before yesterday. I've been looking for a letter from you for several days. I fear you are not well enough to write. I've not written as usual, have been on picket, which prevented and will not be able to send this before Monday, as we have no Sunday mail. I am only waiting to get Stokes back or Blythe commissioned to ask for a furlough. I will need another horse. I find that the horse I have will not answer my purpose. I will make that a point in the application. I think I will send Mid home with the horse I have here and will try to swap him and to ride the one I get back. It may be 2 or 3 weeks before I can get off but I hope not so long. I think by the middle of Aug. I may be able to judge how much corn I may be able to make, how much wheat, molasses, potatoes & c and will know how much I will have to buy. I think it will be best to lay in a supply early. I wrote to Mr. Whitmire to find out and let me know how he could exchange salt for wheat, peas & c and to let me know. Ask him to write me about it as I wish to go to Charleston next week to buy 40 or 50 bu for the purposes of exchanging for supplies.*

*Our labor here is very light. The picket posts are on a tide water and generally a good breeze blowing. I had about as soon be on picket as in camp. Pickets have nothing to watch against but vessels. I think we shall stand this climate pretty well. Have had no new cases of fever for several days and all are getting well. I expect Sept. and Oct. are the sickliest months. If it was healthy I would like to own a farm in this section. The land is rich, the rice fields look beautiful now and also the corn crops are fine. I'm glad to hear that the up country has had fine rains and that the corn crops look prosperously. Hope an abundant corn crop can be made. I think you had better use the wheat as soon as it can be threshed. Corn is too high, I think. I can buy wheat at a less cost than corn is now bringing.*

*It is reported that Genl. S. D. Lee has joined Genl. Hood and that Kershaw's division is on the road to Atlanta. I trust it may be so. If Sherman can be routed and whipped back within the next 30 days, I think all will soon be well with us, gaining ground very rapidly. I'm in pretty good heart, looking to the prospects ahead. I want to see you all very much. You must hurry up and get well that you may travel about with me when I come. Would you like to go to Caesar's Head and Cedar Mountain?*

*I want to bring back with me 2 bu of Irish potatoes. Hope they will turn out better than Ned anticipates and also some dried beans. Has Ned hauled home any oats yet? I want him to leave a few dozen at Mr. Watson's to feed us while at work there and bring the rest home as soon as possible. I'm glad to get Mr. Watson's share, which together with mine will offer feed for the cow and horse for several months. You never told me anything about the sweet potatoes. Tell Mr. Whitmire to engage for me from the country people a half bushel of onions and also the same quantity of dried apples. I think, however, I shall be at home enough to get these things for myself. I wish Ned, just as soon as he can, should prepare his ground for turnips. I'm anxious to raise a good crop of turnips. I know of no better vegetable for winter and spring. Tell Ned if he needs help to hire. I will be disappointed if he fails to get the turnips planted. They will save a great deal of peas and corn in feeding the cow. If your mother does not go up to see you before I go up, I hope she will go up with me and the girls, I daresay, can take 2 or 3 weeks holiday and go to see you. Is your bacon all gone yet or do you expect to make it last you? I am sorry our prospect for next year is so bad. How are the young hogs doing and the calf and heifer?*

*So many men are greasing out of the war (as they term it). I expect it will be almost impossible to buy hogs or pork this fall or beef. Next year people and soldiers both will have to use still less meat. Now, have you succeeded with your poultry? There's a rumor, though it is not credited, that our regiment and Col. Black's are under orders for Atlanta. I hope not at least till I can get home. I do not believe it. The weather is quite warm but in the shade pleasant enough. The summer is nearly gone and in another month it will be fall. Time truly passes rapidly. I think that after another great battle, there will be but little more fighting, that is, if we are successful and I have the strongest hopes that such will be the issue.*

*Tell baby I'm glad to hear she goes to Sunday school and that she must learn her catechism and songs for me to hear when I go home to see her. I've written you a long letter on prosy subjects. I have so far enjoyed good health. Write soon and let me know how you are doing. Have you reached your weight of 108 lbs. yet? I believe you were*

[          ] *over to that figure. Tell me how much you weigh. Is Ferlines still teaching school? How is the potato crop? I shall be disappointed if I do not hear from you today, the 31ˢᵗ. I recd yesterday both your letters of the 25ᵗʰ and 26ᵗʰ. Was glad to hear your mother was with you. I think I will get the rice when I go to Charleston. My love to all.*

*Affectionately*
*L. Williams*

In August of 1864, the sweltering Petersburg trenches lay silent. Soldiers baked during the day and shook from the chills at night. Out in the west, Atlanta was shaking too. In the morning, Sherman launched his shells. In the evenings, Hood assessed the damage. The heat was also taking its toll on the men of the 2nd S. C. Cavalry down in Chisholmville. During the day dust and gnats covered them. Despite placing the latrine downwind, green head flies bit hard at sunset. At night, the mosquitoes always came. The unhealthy conditions finally caught up with Leonard and he became seriously ill. Unable to be cared for properly in camp, he was finally sent home on sick leave.

Laying up in bed in a pool of sweat, he glistened like the rebels in Lee's defenses. He trembled like the citizens of Atlanta. At first he believed the source of that sweat was his dusty, laborious ride home in the summer heat. Soon he realized that he had fallen victim to the much feared chills and fever of the low country. He had intended to spend his 30-day leave getting Anna and the farm in shape, now Anna nursed his fever and Lucy changed his sheets while Ned and Mid plowed on without him.

The mosquito-malaria relationship was unknown at the time. Little did he know that one of those little bloodthirsty insects, which had speared him along the Combahee River was responsible for his misery. Regardless, instead of fighting off Kilpatrick's Cavalry or Sherman's sharpshooters, he now waged a new battle between sharp fever and sudden chills. Quinine was the accepted remedy, but the naval blockade made its procurement nearly impossible. A small bottle of the precious fluid rested on his nightstand, however, thanks to the caring and well-connected Mr. Whitmire. While the cause of the illness was a mystery, its course was predictable. Every other day, the fever attacked and the shivering followed. One day tolerable, the next day hell. On the good days, he was able to drink a tall glass of Maum Fannie's buttermilk, pick at a small meal, and converse with Anna and Carrie. In a few weeks time, the quinine arrested the worst of the symptoms and the Captain improved enough to take short rides out to the fields or down to the mercantile. In the mornings, he sat on the porch reading St. Luke and Job with Anna, who was now completely immersed in the Holy Spirit. It guided her and strengthened her, and he too yearned for its soothing power, but now, either that Spirit hadn't knocked on his door or he was unwilling to let it in.

In the evenings, he scanned the *Greenville Enterprise* for developments along Lee's and Hood's lines. In early September, he read an account of how Sherman had lured Hood into thinking that he was retreating, only to flank him southward to destroy the last remaining railroad that fed Atlanta. Hoodwinked, John Bell responded too late when he discovered Sherman's true intentions, losing a pitched battle in Jonesborough. To avoid being trapped in the very city he was ordered to so vigorously defend, Hood had no choice but to evacuate it. The general who had already lost an arm and leg, had now lost Atlanta. On September 2, refugees poured out and Sherman marched in. The news was devastating for the Confederacy as the key railhead now belonged to Sherman. The Captain bitterly slammed the paper down. Buttermilk and broken glass covered the parlor floor. Fortunately, the quinine was capped. He knew then and there that Lincoln's reelection was virtually secured.

A few days later, Leonard's anger spiked higher than any of his fevers when he learned from a private, home on furlough, that he had been listed as absent without leave. Evidently, the Captain's message back to his Chisholmville headquarters had not been received. In it, he had conveyed the circumstances of his poor health and his plan to return to the low country as soon as he was strong enough to withstand the 200-mile journey back. Back at the Planter's Hotel, the Old Captain bristled anew. For years after the war, he fought to have this false designation rectified. Ultimately, he gave up in frustration and applied his energy to more pressing matters. To this day, his service records indicate that he had exceeded his 30-day furlough and was listed as absent without leave. Back then, he hastily crammed some mended clothes and two bottles of quinine into his saddlebag, kissed Anna and Carrie farewell, and spurred his new horse down to his old company of men and fleas.

Midway back to camp, in Columbia, he learned of some heartening news that to some small degree helped offset the loss of Atlanta. Yet again, Hampton's men had pulled off the unimaginable. In a daring raid, they slipped behind the Federals with their eyes trained on a prize far different than prisoners, cannon, or rifles. This time Hampton went after meat, over 2,500 head of fine enemy cattle to be exact. The rustlers were the usual suspects: Tom Rosser, Rooney Lee, and of course, Matthew Butler. Grant never knew what hit him. Rosser attacked first at 5 A.M. and those he didn't capture or kill ran for their lives. One-hundred and twenty shocked Federal guards were no match for Rosser's riders, who quickly drove nearly 2,500 steers back behind their lines. The raid was not without cost, as ten men were lost, but the operation netted close to two-million pounds of meat along with delicacies like sardines and pickles found in the sutler's wagons.

Twelve days after Hampton's grand cattle round up, the Captain rounded up a few sheets of paper. Mid was sick and duty was dull. Fall had arrived and he hoped Anna might be able to spend at least part of it with him. For now he would write her and let her know he was in better health and trying to make progress in his spiritual journey.

*Chisholmville, S. C*
*September 28, 1864*

*I have recd no letters from you since writing last. I feel a desire to chat with you though I commence without any definite topic to write about. I think of you continually and am better contented writing to you than at any other employment. Many a time I write without having anything to write about. I need not, however, tell you this. If I could find a boarding house in a mile or two of this camp after we change camps for winter qrs., what would you say to spending a month with me this winter and leave baby at home with Auntie or in Columbia. I would want her too very much but her coming would make it necessary for Lucy to come also which would be too expensive. I would expect to return home with you. I do not know of any house where accommodations could be had but I only submit the proposition to have your opinion provided arrangements could be made. I would be very agreeable if accommodations could be had in a mile of camp. Capt. McFie intends to rent a house and go to housekeeping, this however, is beyond my reach. The health of the company is improving. I attribute it to the use of medicated spirits. The men, however, look quite badly. I am a good deal reduced but have now a pretty good appetite and hope soon to recover. Mid yesterday for the first time was sick, he is about today but looks dull. I recd this evening yours of the 25th. Was glad to hear you were all getting on well except Lucy. I think it is only a cold. I'm also opposed to Sunday visiting-felt at the time it was not right but it was Billy's appointment as they had nothing to do on Sunday. I saw Nath today. He and Billy are quite well.*

*My dear Anna, I value very highly the deep interest you felt in the performance of promises made to you. I keep up my reading and feel that I am not unconcerned though I wish I felt a still deeper concern. I sometimes wish that I could have no quiet of mind until I felt converted, but I am not, though I feel a love and admiration for piety and virtue, a hatred of vulgar profanity and blasphemy and a love for truth, justice, charity and entertain neither malice, envy nor covetness, still I am not a Christian yet. I trust God in his good time, may vouch safe to me all the comforts of faith in the promises of the Gospel.*

*My health is very good now and Mid this morning, the 29th, is up and at his usual business. I hope he will escape a spell of the fever. We have nothing new, all dull enough in view of the state of the country. It is unfortunate that we have allowed our hopes of peace to run so high, that is the cause of the present despondency. My love to all and write soon.*

*Yours affectionately*
*L. Williams*

On all fronts, fortunes were fading fast in Confederate trenches. Sheridan thrashed General Jubal Early at Cedar Creek and Grant attacked at both ends of Lee's fortifications, forcing Lee to spread his men even thinner in order to hold a vast line that now stretched 35 miles between Richmond and Petersburg. Down in the Atlanta, Hood's army was marching into Tennessee where it hoped to link up with Forrest's. In doing so, Hood gambled that Sherman would leave Atlanta and pursue him. Sherman, however, had something far more devious up his deep blue sleeve. On the political front, none other than the hen himself, George B. McClellan, had received the Democratic nomination and would oppose Lincoln in November. Most of these developments, as always, were unknown to one Captain Williams who somehow managed to maintain a positive outlook.

*Chisholmville, S. C.*
*October 5, 1864*

*My Dear Anna*

*I have recd your letter of the 25ᵗʰ. I was glad to hear you were all about well again. Mid has had a spell of the fever and has been reduced a good deal. He has been clear of the fever now 2 or 3 days and is now walking about a little. Hope he will soon be well again. I did not know he was so useful until since he has been sick. I missed his services very much. I am now quite well, but have no guarantee that the fever will not return on me again. I believe everyone, black and white in the regiment, has been sick. There is less sickness now than at any time since coming here. I will be glad to see cold weather.*

*I think our military prospects encouraging. I think everything now in Va. looks hopeful. Hood certainly knows Sherman's strength at Atlanta. He has placed himself in Sherman's rear, which I think must soon compel the evacuation of Atlanta and subject Sherman to almost certain defeat. I have shared in the gloom, which has been hanging over the community but I am now in good spirits and hope this year's campaign will close with bright prospects.*

*You did not tell me how many bundles fodder Ned made. Tell me how much good and how much damaged by the rains. You speak of putting up hogs, put it off until corn is gathered. You will have only one to fatten. You ought to make every effort to get feed for the cow and not let her fall off any in quantity of milk. She will be hard to raise if you let her get down. Who will Ned get to grind his sugarcane? Mr. Watson intends to take toll, he intimated to me that he would not charge anything for the land, but I suppose he thinks I got too good of a bargain out of him in the oats. I hope your sweet potatoes will turn out better than you expected. These late rains will improve them very much. I am sorry to hear of the death of your uncle. I know it must make your father feel lonely. I expect but few of his boyhood friends are now living.*

*We have nothing new. Everything so far quiet. We are all getting on tolerably well. I had a few days ago a nice mess of venison, which Lieut. Jeffers complimented me with. I wish I could have shared it with you. If nothing prevents, this winter expect to get wild ducks frequently.*

*Give my respects to Uncle Whitmire and all the family and to all. Write often, I am now getting your letters punctually. Hope you will continue to be punctual. I recd Mr. Whitmire's letter of the 29th. I think your schedule comprehensive. I believe they are valued according to prices before the war, consequently, old furniture will be rated low. You must also include books. You and Mr. Whitmire can fix the prices, of course. Nothing is worth cost now.*

*Yours affectionately*
*L. Williams*

By the end of October, Phil Sheridan had smashed Jubal Early's army up in Virginia. Much of the lush valley was burnt and haystacks, crops, barns, and mills were destroyed. It was later said that even a crow flying across it would have to carry rations with him. Leonard had galloped across that very valley and led charges at the foot of the majestic Blue Ridge. Ruby had cooled off in the clear streams and survived on the rich clover and timothy. Stomped on, eaten out, and incinerated, the Shenandoah Valley now stood as a grim microcosm of Confederate fortunes. She had given all she had but now had nothing left. Discontent and prices were rising. In the Rebel ranks, dissatisfaction gave way to desertion. Starving refugees and displaced slaves wandered barefoot down dark roads patrolled by robbers and murderers. Loyalty could be bought. Allegiance was forsaken. The idyllic, moss-draped, magnolia-scented South was on the verge of collapse. As always, however, there was Dixie's eternal well of hope. Somehow it even managed to sustain a war weary Captain beset with malaria, an ailing wife, mounting debts, and fear.

*Near Green Pond*
*October 21, 1864*

*My Dear Wife*
*We have left Chisholmville some 5 miles and are now on the Rroad and have a very good quarters. It has been several days since I have written, owing to being on picket and the return of the chill and fever. I had only one. Have missed it two days by taking quinine. Mid is also sick. I am bad off at present. I will, however, report for duty tomorrow morning and hope Mid will soon be up. I recd yours of the 18th today, and was glad to hear you were well, but you do not tell me whether you*

*are improving. I see William Mitts was elected. Dick Clary will be compelled to join the army I expect. I see all the details are revoked. Our army needs strengthening and if all detailed men are sent in, it will add, I expect, 100,000 men to our forces. I am pleased with the proceedings of the meeting of Mr. Boyce's constituents in Columbia on the subject of his letter to Mr. Davis. They administer a just and deserving rebuke, which I hope will put a quiet to all such politicians.*

*I feel poor indeed. I know you are needing a great many things and are living on a very meager share of the necessities of life. I see it and know but cannot help it and what adds to the disagreeable reflection is that even the small stores drawn from Mr. Whitmire, exceeds, I fear, our share of his income. I will be able to pay for my horse without availing myself to preferred bonds, but I would advise that you send them to your father and get him to sell them for you and invest the proceeds in a cow. When I come home this winter, you and I will go into Pickens and spend a day or two and buy a good cow. Uncle Whitmire promised me a lot of peas and I can get more. Just think of it, plenty of milk and butter and bread. If I knew you had plenty of these, I assure you, I would feel very comfortable and also a bbl. of molasses. With these, a small ration of bacon or beef once a day would do you very well.*

*You seem to think Ned's farming has not amounted to much. He had made enough corn to feed his mare and fatten his hogs and hauled at least $500 worth of wood. His oat crop was worth $250 or $300. The shucks and fodder will winter the cows and mare. Suppose he only makes corn enough to feed the mare and fatten the hogs.*

| | |
|---|---|
| *20 bu to fatten the hogs* | *$200* |
| *Shucks for corn* | *$200* |
| *Wood* | *$600* |
| *Oats to the cow and hogs* | *$100 (which makes $ eleven hundred after feeding the horse)* |

*But I believe if I can hire Steve and Nan for corn next year, I will keep Ned at home and let him wagon about town. He can make money to pay taxes if it will not buy provisions and probably it will be the best. I will make an effort to get him in December and make arrangements for the next year to the best of my means and judgment.*

In his haste to complete the remaining letters before the reunion march, the Old Captain almost missed the paragraph added on the reverse side the next morning. It too was missing the final words.

*October 22ⁿᵈ*

*I do not think I will have another chill today. I am not taking quinine today but will take some tomorrow. All the attacks I have had have been every other day. Tomorrow is the day in course but I do not apprehend another at least*

...

Down on the coast, Leonard found himself free of duty sitting on the banks of the cool Combahee. The frogs croaked. In one hand he held a paper-thin yellow Jasmine. In the other, he held the Bible it had been pressed in. He was determined to sit there all day and read until he found the same religious strength that Anna had. In the book of Revelations, he hoped for a revelation of his own. Verse 6 caught his eye, because even though there was much he did not understand about the Holy Ghost, horses and swords were two things he knew intimately.

And I looked, and behold, an ashen horse;
and he who sat on it had the name Death
and Hades was following with him.
And authority was given to them…
To kill with sword and with famine and with
pestilence and by the wild beasts of the earth.

As Leonard sat waiting for God, the devil was coming. Soon he would scorch the earth, set Dixie ablaze, and release all of hell's fury.

# CHAPTER FIFTEEN
# END OF THE DREAM

*Where would you yet be struck,*
*you that rebel again and again?*
*The whole head is sick, the whole heart faint.*
*From the sole of the foot to the head*
*there is no sound spot:*
*Wound and welt and gaping gash,*
*not drained, or bandaged, or eased with salve.*
*Your country is waste, your cities burnt with fire...*
Isaiah 1:5

Satan goes by many names, but in 1864 his name was General William Tecumseh Sherman. On November 15, he put the torch to Atlanta. Flames raced through the streets. Arsenals exploded. Citizens ran for their lives. One third of the town was entirely destroyed. Behind him the Union commander could see the spirals of smoke and hear the distant screams, ahead of him 285 miles away, waited Savannah. In between, he would leave nothing behind except a swath of charred earth, tears, and death. "Total War" was his mantra. "I will make Georgia Howl!" was his battle cry. "The March to the Sea." would be his lasting legacy. When Sherman's soldiers left Atlanta, they took little with them but were full of resolve. His 62,000 men would live off the land and burn anything and everything they didn't eat or carry off.

Leaving behind the reliable Maj. Gen. George Thomas to deal with Hood and Forrest, Sherman set his sights on the complete demoralization of the southern people. To Sherman, breaking the will of Georgia's mothers, farmers and merchants would break the very heart of the Confederacy. Sherman termed it "Total War" and he was committed to it totally. From November 12, to December 22, Sherman's hoard swooped down and put the torch to towns, factories, farms, and mills. He invented the "Sherman Necktie" by twisting heated rails around telegraph poles and trees. Plantations were ransacked. Smokehouses, oatbins, and corncribs were emptied. Slaves were run off or fell in behind the raiders and joined in the pillaging. Rapes were reported. Sherman's pillagers marched twelve miles a day through waist-high swamp water and across rivers and fields, shooting militiamen in their path and leaving slaughtered livestock, burning barns, and ransacked houses in their wake.

As the three massive Yankee corps approached the sea, southern forces elsewhere were being hastily mustered together. Savannah could not be saved, but if Sherman could be detained from marching northward to hook up with Grant, then Lee's army just might have a chance. Leonard was one of those ordered to North Carolina to protect Fort Fisher and the key port of Wilmington. Perhaps here, a last stand could be made against the devil. Soon after arriving, Leonard wrote Anna with news of his visit to her family, his health, and his view that the war was far from over.

*Wilmington, N. C.*
*December 7, 1864*

*My Dear Anna*

*I arrived in camp today. The regiment is encamped about 7 miles from the city. Henry failed to meet me at 9 ock, he did not get my letter. I therefore, had to stop, went out to his house, took a chill, and stayed with him till Monday morning. Took medicine and had no chill since Friday the day I left home. I spent Monday night with your father and took the 11 ock. train for Kingsville, left Kingsville at dark, traveled and slept all night, and arrived at Wilmington at 9 1/2 this morning. I found all well at Henry's. At your father's, all inquired about you, they look for you in Columbia soon, Henry and Frances wish you to stop with them as you go up. I feel very dull at camp after staying at home so long. I left the flour sacks at Newberry and wrote Mr. Duckett that you would not be at home till Jan. and that if it suited him, not to ship the flour till then. I hope you will get it all safe. How does the cow do since you commenced feeding on beets? Give her 2 qts. meal at a feed with the beets and the seed turnips when you can get them. Give the fattening hog meal occasionally.*

*I forgot to tell Mr. Whitmire about the 2 7/8 yds. of plain woolen cloth I took for lining. Tell him to charge it to me. You will report the quantity of checked goods you used. I think probably when the hog is killed you had better have it packed away in the smokehouse. I feel it would not do to keep it in the basement room without daily air. Give Ned the key and tell him while you are away from home, it is my wish for him to stay 4 or 5 nights in the week at home. Tell Ned if the*

390

*weather keeps good to haul, if he can, wood this month to last as far as possible through the winter.*

*My dearest Anna, home is the pleasantest place in the world, though I am sometimes a little ill tempered, but I fear from present prospects, it will be a long time before I can return to its endearments. You must write to me often, at least till I get initiated into camp routine again. Remember me to Auntie, the girls and baby. My respects to Mr. Whitmire and family and tell him to write to me soon.*

*Yours affectionately*
*L. Williams*

Fifteen days later, on December 22, Sherman telegraphed the newly reelected president. He offered Lincoln the city of Savannah, with its 150 mighty guns, ammunition, and 25,000 bales of cotton as an early Christmas present. It was to be a grim Christmas indeed for the South. There would be no gifts for Carrie who sat quietly by the parlor window waiting in vain for her father to return. Anna, meanwhile, reread her husband's latest letter, placed it with the rest, then meticulously wrapped her apron string around her collection for safe keeping. For the fourth straight year, it was to be another bleak Yule for the Captain who sipped a bit of camp eggnog and shivered alone. No one, however, suffered more than the men huddling in Petersburg's frozen trenches. Winter winds ripped through the rags of the tattered men who were now subsisting on one-sixth rations. Scurvy and infection lingered among them. The day was for dying. The night was for burying. There was little Lee could do.

Savannah was doomed. Fort Fisher would fall. The men in gray were paying a steep price for their doomed rebellion. Now it was time for the first state that seceded to pay the ultimate price. South Carolina, the home of Leonard, Anna, Carrie, James, Ephraim, and the Laval's, was Sherman's next target. "The truth is," Sherman informed Halleck, "the whole army is burning with an insatiable desire to wreak vengeance upon South Carolina. I almost tremble at her fate, but feel that she deserves all that seems to be in store for her." On February 1, the devil raised his pitchfork and ordered his 65,000 torchbearers to march north to Columbia.

Leonard still clung to his dreams of hope and the unshakeable notion that Sherman would never reach the capital, but there was little good news, and no news at all when letters from home failed to arrive. The Captain was in a foul mood over the lack of mail from his wife, but a few days later, an envelope arrived and with it, his spirits rose. He immediately drafted a long reply venting his frustration and apologizing for his anger.

*Wilmington, N. C.*
*January 30, 1865*

*My Dear Anna*

*I have just recd yours of the 27th, which by your previous promises I looked for on the 25th and then on the 26th, 27th, 28th and 29th. I was induced to look for it not only on account of your promise but on your presumed leisure you would have in Columbia and I was all the more anxious because it was generally believed Wilmington would be at any day evacuated and all mail facilities cut off. Then again, when I knew the mail was being forwarded daily and it took only a little over a day for a letter to come through, but I will not quarrel, it is impolitic. I burned a long one I wrote two days ago because I was in a bad humor, but as I said, it is exceedingly impolitic to ever let it be known you are irritated by disappointments. A letter ought to be agreeable and fill the heart with joy, it must be self-prompted and spontaneous and must be written "con amore" uncompelled, a free will offering. I, therefore, promise not to complain anymore of neglect, and at the same time not to look for letters until I see them.*

*I was under the impression from the tenor of your letter of the 20th that the RR would begin to carry passengers through to Greenville in a short time, but I understand that the road has been washed away from Alston to Columbia and that it may be 2 months before it is finished. It is, therefore, impossible for you to go home the 1st of next month as I had hoped. Have you made arrangements at home to stay away so long? I fear your basement rooms and garret need ventilation, especially after so much rain. I am afraid your small parcel of meat will mould. It ought to be taken up and hung up to dry. The negroes must also have access to the corn and if Mr. Whitmire cannot furnish them beef, they must use the pork. If you did not leave the keys, you must send them up to Mr. Whitmire. You did not tell me what arrangements are being made for the negroes as you may be in*

*Columbia till March. By all means, give directions to have the basement rooms aired, the potatoes, pork, and corn are all liable to injury by dampness and may be entirely ruined. I am sorry I did not ask Mr. Duckett to send the flour at once but I thought you would leave home before it could get there and also this would be at home by the 15ᵗʰ of this month, so the thing has failed. I am glad you have a little anyhow. I intended to put in for one bag of it if it had all gone forward.*

*I do not think there is any possibility of our regiment going to S. C. We cannot be spared from this place unless this country is abandoned. If the enemy should ever get as far as Columbia, I will be glad to have an opportunity to strike him there, but I hope never to get into the low country. My men are still suffering with chills and fever contacted there and some dozen or 20 now in hospitals.*

*You wrote me such a long pleasant letter, I'm sorry I complained any. My opportunities for writing are better than yours and perhaps I am unreasonable in expecting to hear from you twice a week. It is always the case after a visit home, I am more anxious to hear from you and at the same time, while my anxiety is greatest, I hear the seldomer. The papers are full of peace rumors and of the commissioners sent to Washington, I confess I am not elated with the prospect. I fear it is a snare to entrap our people. I fear the Yankees will offer such terms as will divide our people and possibly carry the assent of some of the states. I cannot think the Yankees will offer an honorable adjustment unless they're influenced by an outside pressure we know nothing about.*

*The mails are coming through from Greenville. I do not see why you can't hear from home. I am done writing to Mr. Whitmire. I have not heard from him yet. William has not written me yet, nor James. I write no more. My correspondence is now limited to you alone and that is growing less by rapid degrees. It has been my chief pleasure since having been away to write and receive your letters. I have been irritated not little by the utter neglect of some, but I have a wonderful adaptability in my nature to acquiesce and not to suffer anything to impinge my feelings for any length of time. I am content to take things as I find them.*

*I do not think Sherman will get as far as Columbia. I hope and believe he will be beaten back. I hear the wheat crop in Greenville is nearly destroyed by the rains. You spoke of writing when your fingers were numb with cold. It is wrong you are staying too close to the house. I fear a long, continued stay in Columbia. Your health will suffer.*

*Yours affectionately*
*L. Williams*

Each day, Sherman and his marauding army moved further inland. Directly in their path was Columbia, where Anna was now visiting her parents. Leonard flung his tin cup into the fire. His wife was nearer the enemy than he. He jerked his picket pin from the hard ground, flung on his saddle, tightened up his pommel holster, and angrily galloped out to the lines. He wasn't the only trooper who contemplated a bolt for Columbia to defend his state, his capital, and his loved ones. Nothing lay between the Sherman's divisions and his family except swamp, rivers, and heavy rain. Lee, now Commander-In-Chief of all Confederate armies, was cornered by Grant and tethered to Richmond. Hood's force was routed by Thomas in Nashville. Only Forrest's brilliant generalship in retreat saved the Army of Tennessee from complete destruction. Ultimately, the beleaguered Joseph E. Johnston, soon to be restored to command yet again, would be ordered to delay Sherman.

Leonard Williams was one of only 15,000 or so that Johnston would sprinkle in the field to face Sherman's 65,000. Wade Hampton along with recently promoted Major General Matthew C. Butler and the boys put the spur to their mounts and raced to Columbia. Hampton had hoped that Charleston would be evacuated and its garrison, along with Hardee's infantry and Joe Wheeler's cavalry, might be united in order to halt Sherman in his tracks at Branchville, a key railroad junction south of Columbia. Instead, troops were ordered up to North Carolina leaving Beauregard and Hampton with a mere handful to defend the capital. Columbia was doomed and if Anna remained there, she was too.

Leonard knew this but he remained undaunted. Sheer will and bits of good fortune had seen the Williams family through before and they would now. Somehow, against all odds, he believed that Hampton's cavalry, militiamen, and determined town folk would shield Columbia, and Anna would be whisked away in the nick of time back to Greenville. Perhaps even peace would prevail in the spring. Anything else would be unthinkable. Since orders prevented him from defending his capital and saving his wife, the Captain did what he could do.  He could proclaim his devotion to her and offer solutions for preserving the farm through his letters.  To that end, he fashioned another long one with equal measures of blind optimism and practical advice.

*Wilmington, N. C.*
*February 8, 1865*

*I returned to camp today having been absent on duty for 8 days and was pleasantly surprised in finding 2 letters from you of the 30ᵗʰ Jan. and 5ᵗʰ inst. and also one from Mr. Whitmire of the 29ᵗʰ Jan.  You expressed some wonder at my construction of one of your letters.  I read your letter again and again and was unable to construct it otherwise and there were no explanatory remarks to modify the plain version of your letter.  It could not be interpreted otherwise than I did. It would have taken a more vivid imagination than I possess to have supplied the facts and circumstances which your subsequent letter furnished.  It is all clear enough now, the 2 letters taken together.  And now that I understand you, I can advise that if Sherman passes Branchville on his way to Columbia, that you start at once for Greenville at any cost of transportation.  Provided you can borrow enough and if there's no threatening of Columbia, that you wait till the cars run through and I hope that will be by the 1ˢᵗ of March.*

*Mr. Whitmire said he had not heard from you but intimated that it was time to commence gardening and you would soon be home. I wish you were home now to have manure spread over the upper part of the garden.  I wish Irish potatoes to be planted on the upper side and to plant the part that had grown potatoes two years in beans, squashes, cabbages, & c.  The ground for potatoes ought to be broken and manured now. I would like to get new seed.  Yours are deteriorating and I expect they will cost pretty high, but 1 1/2 or 2 bu. will be enough.  I hope you may have a better garden than ever but Lucy and Fannie will have to cultivate it.  Ned will not have the time to do more than plow it and assist in planting.  Mr. Whitmire says Mr. Duckett has sent the flour, he has in the store 10 sacks and I expect 6 barrels all that he promised. When you get home you must put it in the garret.  If you can, lend 2 bbls. of it to be paid back next fall.  You'd better do so.  It may be kept too long, inquire.  Henry will take 200 lbs. and pay back next summer* and probably Mr. Whitmire will take 1 bbl. Make the arrangement if you can now.

If you have a good cow, you would be well off, plenty of bread and milk. Mr. Whitmire did not say anything about the beef, he may have mentioned that in a letter that never reached me. He only spoke partially of some things, which he says he had already told me. I do not know what becomes of letters. He told me of the death of Mr. Goss. He has hired Steve to Mr. Holcombe of Pickens District for 75 bu. of corn but he furnishes no clothing and expects to hire Nan to Mr. Kirkpatrick for $150 and her clothing. He has her on trial and will send you by 1st opportunity my share of stock in the loom. I am anxious to get into operation as soon as possible, so that all hands may be doing something to make a support. Ned will have Bill and Clough and ought to make twice as much corn to raise hogs and with Steve's hire, you can exchange corn for bread. I think if you have no bad luck with the start you have, you ought to be able to get along, even if Mr. Whitmire's business failed.

I'm very much gratified at the result of the peace conference. The advocates of negotiation are now certainly satisfied. Parties can now be accurately defined. To counsel negociation now is to counsel submission to such terms as Mr. Lincoln may dictate. I think that all but few in the country so utterly craven spirited as to submit. My hopes revived when I saw the issue of the conference. I was afraid such terms would be offered as would divide and distract the Confederacy. If Sherman can be thwarted, the whole country will be reanimated.

It is growing late and I have to go into Wilmington early in the morning. I will, therefore, not be able to write you a long letter this time but I owe you one for the good length of your last. The initials of the Mr. Elliott you inquired about are different from those of the Elliott in our regiment, but he is the only one of that name here. His initials, I believe, are R. E. but I do not now remember. My best respects to all. I will write again next week but when I am in camp it is with difficulty. I'll refrain from writing every day. I, therefore, had better withdraw my promise of postponing it so long. By the by, could you give me a hint as to those absorbing tasks you have been imposing on yourself?

Yours affectionately

L. Williams

*You did not tell me about my coat. I need it.*

Taps. Lee took one last look into the fire-lit eyes of his gaunt and gallant men who had not deserted in Petersburg. Hampton made a final ride along his line and gazed down upon moonlit Columbia, soon to become a raging inferno. A Virginia gentleman named Wilmer McLean, whose prior house had been Beauregard's shelled headquarters at Manassas four years earlier, savored a last sip of wine in his parlor in a village called Appomattox Court House. Anna read the final words of the Twenty-Third Psalm. Mid swallowed the last remaining drop of quinine. The young captain packed his pipe with his last pinch of tobacco. The Old Captain opened his last envelope. The first word was *"I."* The last was *"family."* Soon they'd be reunited at last.

*Wilmington, N. C.*
*February 11, 1865*

*My Dear Anna*
*I have had 3 days of perfect quiet in camp but in a few miles of the roaring of artillery. The Yankees shell our lines every day and occasionally Ft. Anderson. I believe they have made no progress since the capture of Fort Fisher. I will probably go out again tomorrow. I will, therefore, write today. We are listening with deep anxiety to hear the news from our lines near Branchville. A general is sadly needed in S. C. I wish the president would place Dick Taylor in command of all our forces in S.C. and Ga. If I am correctly informed, we have troops enough in Charleston, Branchville and Augusta to meet and chastise Sherman. Our forces ought to be concentrated and thrown first on one and then another of Sherman's columns. It seems to be he ought to be whipped and if he is not, I shall be disappointed. If he should meet with a severe whipping, our cause would revive at once and confidence and hope be reestablished. Every effort ought to be made against Sherman and as we have in our power to choose the ground and fight under cover, he certainly ought to be whipped.*
*I think the proposition to put negroes in the field exceedingly unwise. During the first years of the war, negroes took every opportunity to fly to the enemy, but as soon as they found that they were put in the army, this running away stopped, and negroes now run from Yankees as their*

*worst enemies, simply from the fear of being enlisted. They prefer servitude from freedom, if freedom is to be won by risk of life. Let it once be understood amongst them that they are obliged to fight. I think it is very clear they will take sides with the enemy just as fast as they can get to him by running away or deserting. The Yankees can outbid us. They promise freedom to him and his kindred, in addition, our confiscated lands. I think if the measure is adopted it will put more negroes in the Yankee army than in our own and besides, we can scarcely feed our own army now and if 100,000 or 200,000 worthless soldiers were added, the difficulty would be much increased. We have white men enough. Bring in every able bodied man and bring absentees back. Let us all work together, forgo private interests, and send all our energies to one great end, our independence, and we will, I am confident, win success.*

*We have had very cold weather. Mr. Whitmire says it has been the coldest winter he ever saw and have had more rain. I am glad to hear that the RR will probably be completed in 2 or 3 weeks. I advised Mr. Whitmire to buy all the provisions he needed at once. As soon as the Rroad begins to run, the government will draw everything from the country in the shape of provisions for the use of the army. It will in a month or two be impossible to buy provisions. Everything that can be spared will be needed by the army. Mr. Whitmire did not mention how things are going on at home, only that Ned was unwell and the Dr. had advised for him to keep indoors. I recd yours of the 8th yesterday and was glad to hear you were all well. I have no idea if Columbia will be attacked and I am inclined to believe Greenville will be as safe a place as any part of the Confederacy and now since the old men have organized a company of artillery and one of infantry in the village, I have no fears of the tories and deserters.*

*I will be glad to hear of you being at home by the last of the month or as early as you can to begin to gardening. The turnip greens in the garden will be ready for use by the time you get home. Have the potato ground well manured and the walk on the upper side cleaned out and thrown over the ground. Get some cornfield beans for Ned to plant amongst the corn to gather after they dry. I would like for him to make 2 or 3 bu. and also increase your patch of butter beans in the garden.*

*Try to make enough to lay up 2 or 3 pecks and 1 peck for me. You gave me some of the Columbia prices but I did not understand whether you said fresh meats were worth $3 or $10 a lb. I could not make it out. In Wilmington, potatoes and corn sell at $50 a bu., pork and beef at $8 per lb., flour $10 a bbl., a small one horse cart of wood at $25. I was in Wilmington Wednesday. I wanted to buy a blackening brush and was told it was worth $35. Yarn is worth $85 per bunch, cotton cards the same.*

*It was very kind of Mr. Duckett to send you so much flour. I hope Mr. Whitmire will take good care of it till you get home. When you get home, if an opportunity occurs for us to remain stationary at any point accessible by RR, I would be proud to get 50 or 100 lbs. put in a box with a few peas and dried fruit. I have not eaten two meals of flourbread since I returned. We are using unsifted cornbread and marsh fed beef. I would like a change. The garret is the place for the flour where it will keep perfectly dry. You have enough to last till next fall and whatever wheat Ned makes you can keep over till the spring. I hope none of your pigs have been stolen. If you have good luck, they will make large hogs by next winter and will make you a good supply of bacon.*

*It looks like a spring day without. Clear and bright, but quite cool. Fires are very comfortable all day. I have very comfortable quarters with a good chimney and a homemade camp chair invented by Capt. Westfield. When I wrote you last, I could not put my hand on your letter. I send enclosed a small clipping from it. I have indicated by pencil marks the part I wish you to read. When do you think the cars will run? You have never said a word about my coat. Did you send it to Mr. Burgess? I have never heard anything from it. I will be glad to hear from Billy and Nath. Their battery, I expect, is actively engaged. I heard that one of their Lieuts., Lieut Kirby, was killed on the 3rd inst. but have heard of no other casualties. Have you seen or heard from James Blackburn? He belongs to Butler's command. My dear Anna, I confess to an exceeding blunder in permitting any expressions of dissatisfaction to appear in my letter. In regard to your tardy letters, I was probably in a peevish temper of mind. Your excuse was a good one and I would have you only write when you feel an inclination to do so. Tell me all about baby, what she says and does. Remember me to all the family.*

> *Yours affectionately*
> *L. Williams*

On February 17, two of Sherman's corps occupied South Carolina's evacuated capital. The next day, over half of Columbia lay in ashes. There is no doubt that smoldering cotton bales and gale force winds fed the blaze. There is, however, controversy that remains to this day as to the perpetrators. Sherman blamed Confederate cavalrymen for sparking the blaze. Hampton asserted that Union soldiers lit the torch. Others cast guilt upon vengeful Union prisoners, drunken Negroes, or the citizens themselves. Regardless, most witnesses agree that many Yankee troops labored harder and longer than anyone to contain the conflagration.

Spirals of smoke still feathered up from Columbia's rubble as Anna's train steamed into the depot. Ned was waiting for them. Carrie hopped off first, followed by her ashen-faced aunts, grandma, and Anna. The one-legged Major refused Ned's assistance and negotiated the steps with his cane. His Columbia home was now a mound of charred embers, but he still possessed a mountain of stubbornness. The proud Lavals were now forced to endure the last two months of the war on Augusta Street, living on scraps and what little else Anna's sparse garden and Mr. Whitmire could provide.

Lee's besieged troops were not only running out of food, they were running away. European recognition, perhaps always a distant fantasy, would never come. The Federal blockade ruled the seas and controlled all ports. Abraham Lincoln was firmly reseated in power and even firmer in his demand for unconditional surrender. President Davis was soon to pack his bags and flee, as Richmond, like Atlanta, Savannah, and Columbia before it, would soon be burnt to the ground. Marauders, refugees, deserters, and freed slaves roamed unchecked through gutted towns and unguarded plantations. Dixie lay in tatters, a wasteland of shattered dreams and broken hearts. The Confederate armies were on the brink, and Sherman was driving north to join with Grant to push them over the edge once and for all.

In late February and March, Leonard Williams and the 2nd S. C. Cavalry rode through the North Carolina countryside destroying bridges, interrogating captured prisoners, and scouting Sherman's advance. At Goldsborough, they picketed the roads and bridges from Fayetteville then fell back with the intelligence they had gathered. Johnston was planning a last ditch ambush and by March 19, Hampton had found the perfect spot to spring his trap. The place was Bentonville, and here Johnston planned to attack the strung out left wing of one of Sherman's corps. That crisp, sunny afternoon, Leonard once again rode with the venerable men he had fought with at the outset. Unshakeable Wade Hampton led one column. Hard-nosed Matthew Butler led another. Captain Leonard Williams rode just a stride ahead of Lieutenants Blythe and Stokes. Corporal McClanahan was next in line. Company K was rolling. Bentonville would be their last great battle.

On the first of the three-day fight, Johnston's infantry crushed the Federals' XIV corps, but five subsequent Confederate attacks were repulsed. With each passing hour, thousands of bluecoats poured into Bentonville, and it was just a matter of time before all three corps of Sherman's vast army would reach the arena. On the last day, on the verge of being completely surrounded, retreat was Johnston's only recourse. Back toward Raleigh they marched while Leonard and his company fought rear guard skirmishes during the day and slept fitfully in the saddle at night. Each morning, newspapers were passed around the campfire and with each hopeless headline, it became clear that the end was near...*A. P. Hill Killed at Petersburg...Sheridan Routs Pickett at Five Forks...Richmond in Flames!...Lee's Army Flees West*. A few days later, a lone courier arrived with intelligence that the exhausted Army of Northern Virginia had shrunk to 13,000 half-armed men, and Lee was soon to surrender. After an ill-fated breakout attempt, the defeated general had no choice but to do so.

Lee shook his head. "There is nothing left for me to do but go and see General Grant, and I would rather die a thousand deaths." On Palm Sunday, he entered the Wilmer McLean House in Appomattox. Belying the ragged condition of his army, a dress uniform adorned the weary general. On the brink of surrender, he still bore the coolness and nobility that his men had always cherished. Later, Grant arrived in his grimy campaign uniform and riding boots. Grant attempted some polite conversation, but Lee simply wished to attend to the matter at hand. "I suppose, General Grant, that the object of our present meeting is fully understood. I asked to see you to ascertain upon what terms you would receive the surrender of our army." This time, the terms of "Unconditional Surrender" Grant were most generous. If Lee's men would lay down their arms and pledge not to take them up again, they would receive their parole and return to their farms. Lee thought the terms more than fair, but asked the muddy-booted victor if Confederate cavalrymen and artillerists could be permitted to keep their horses. "I think we have fought the last battle of the war," Grant replied. "...it is doubtful whether they will be able to put in a crop to carry themselves and their families through the next winter without the aid of the horses they are now riding." They could keep their hungry horses and motley mules. The war was over...but not for everyone.

Lee's surrender was but an unconfirmed rumor down in North Carolina, and Leonard and his company were still under strict orders to guard the approaches to Cape Fear. Even as Lee was stoically riding Traveler back to what remained of Richmond, the Captain and his men were riding the picket line. One morning, as he rode back in to join Mid in a bit of breakfast, he perceived an odd stillness in camp. A moment later, he encountered his young servant, alone, head in his quivering hands, weeping by a dying fire. Mid shook uncontrollably as he informed his "Cap'n" that Mr. Lincoln had been murdered.

Eight days later, more tears streamed down the strained, weathered face of Wade Hampton as he exited the Bennett House outside Durham. U. R. Brooks, M. C. Butler's courier, recalled the dark day that Hampton finally laid down his sword.

> *On that morning of the 23rd of April, 1865, General Hampton's heart was very full, tears rose unbidden to the bronze cheeks of the Confederate chief, and the same good right hand that wielded the saber in the grand old Confederate cause was raised to brush away the tears that trickled down his cheek when in his anguish he contemplated the terrible duty assigned to him as an actor in that awful war which had cost the lives of so many gallant men.*

Now, his solemn task was to inform the troops that Johnston had surrendered to Sherman. Ironically, Sherman's conditions were even softer than those offered by Grant, and it wasn't until April 26 that terms previously deemed too lenient were agreed upon once and for all by both sides. Finally, the war was over for Captain Leonard Williams.

Now, so many years later in Columbia, the grand reunion march was about to get underway. While remembering the battle of Bentonville, the Old Captain had neatly stowed away his letters. As he envisioned Lee's final surrender, he had carefully buttoned up his pressed uniform pants and mended jacket. As he had on many a cold morning, he then attached his saber to his belt in one never forgotten, fluid motion. His unloaded Colt revolver slid silently once more into his smoothly worn holster. There was no time to put a quick shine to his once bright black cavalry boots. He lifted his frayed cap off the brass closet hook. He gave it a solid crack with the back of his hand. He placed it snuggly over his brow, the gray flannel blending invisibly with what was left of his sparse gray hair.

The slam of his hotel door was drowned out by the opening volley of cannon shot. Children covered their ears. Bugles sounded. The statehouse bells added to the glorious din. School children tossed bouquets of magnolia, tulip and dogwood high in the air. Horses snorted. Waving overhead, the old Stars and Bars seemed to smile, kissed by the gentle Columbia breeze. The order to mount up was given. Slowly this time, the Captain placed his foot in the covered stirrup and rose to the saddle for the last time. The horse he had been issued for the day stood firm amidst the clamor and color as if she too had been anticipating this magnificent moment.

The Captain's 79-year old heart raced like a new recruit's, eager for his first taste of action. He gazed down flower-bathed Lady Street and the vast assembly that lined its path. Then, instinctively, as he had so many times, at places like Williamsburg, Gettysburg, and Jack's Shop, he reached down to pat the neck of his mount to reassure her, calm her, before the charge they would soon make. Curiously, the mare raised her head as if she'd felt his comforting hand before. The Captain felt the connection too. He took a closer look and surveyed her more thoroughly. She was a sturdy, strong bay, obviously capable of pulling the plow for hours without complaint. He had seen those deep brown eyes before. Then he caught a flash of her rich, red mane and smiled knowingly. "Lets go old girl," he said. With a tug on the rein, and a nudge from his boot, Captain Leonard Williams, Company K, 2nd S. C. Cavalry, for the last time rode forward with the colors of the battle flags flashing in the sun.

# EPILOGUE
## CITIZEN WILLIAMS

*He shall judge between the nations,*
*and impose terms on many peoples.*
*They shall beat their swords into plowshares*
*and their spears into pruning hooks;*
*One nation shall not raise the sword against another,*
*nor shall they train for war again.*

Isaiah 2:4

Four months after the war ended, Wade Hampton received a letter from his former commander-in-chief, which concluded with the following words.

*It is over, and though the present is depressing and disheartening, I trust the future may prove brighter. We must at least hope so and each one do his part to make it so...That every happiness may attend you and yours is the earnest prayer of*

*Your friend,*
*R. E. Lee*

Almost the instant after completing his ten-day ride back to Greenville, Citizen Williams set out to "do his part to make it so" as well. His first priority was Anna. He joined her in long walks and helped oversee her diet and outlook. He read to her, attended Sunday services with her, and brightened her spirits in conversation. But just as she seemed to be as resilient and radiant as ever, the shy 26-year old was dealt a crushing blow. Her dear father Major William Laval died in August of 1865, only three months after her husband had returned. Once again, Anna's reconstruction took precedent over the rebuilding of his farm and community, and soon she was not only stronger, she was pregnant with the Captain's second daughter, Nancy. As the years progressed, the mercantile grew, the farm turned a handsome profit, and Leonard and Anna found themselves seated around a table with four daughters and a son. Life on Augusta Street was good. Anna wrote her cousin Eleanor to tell her so.

*My good husband has loaded me with good things, shawls, dresses, furs, knives, glass butter dish, ...and above all a new dining room, another company room downstairs, which is pretty often filled. Why I feel like Molly Spry when I go down now and find that cold basement as snug as a Charleston one...it is now like the upper story, four square rooms and entry through the middle, cold air shut out from the front by large glass doors. Oh! It is snug...Maum Fannie and I can sachez through it as often as we please...*

As his family and home expanded, so did Leonard's role in the revitalization of his city and state. A summary of his extensive civic work is included in James M. Richardson's <u>History</u> of <u>Greenville</u> <u>County</u>, <u>South</u> <u>Carolina</u>.

*As a merchant and farmer, "he conducted business on those high principles which ruled his life" and his influence was soon felt all over the entire upper part of the state. He was deeply interested in the various problems of the farmer and was one of the pioneers in practicing and encouraging intensive farming in Greenville County. With pen and by public speech he advocated the return, for taxation, "of all moneys, stocks, bonds, and such elusive property, so that the farmer might be relieved from the burden of unequal taxation." Captain Williams did not restrict his activities to matters of business, but was always concerned in public affairs. During the Sessions of 1870-72, he was a member of the House of Representatives from Greenville County, being one of the few Democrats to hold membership in that body during those troublesome times. In 1876 he bore a conspicuous part in the Hampton campaign. For four years he was auditor of Greenville County and for several terms was alderman of the city of Greenville. His part was large in the successful effort to bring the "Air Line," now the Southern Railway, through the upper Piedmont; and throughout the days of his activity he took a leading part in all enterprises which he felt would be for the uplift of his fellow citizens.*

As for the Captain's freed slaves it is known that Maum Fannie stayed with him long after the war. Free to go anywhere, it seems she never strayed far from the kitchen. Fannie's solid family loyalty is mentioned in many of Anna's letters to cousin Eleanor.

*Maum Fannie still is queen regent in the kitchen and sends her love to Miss Eleanor...Fannie is in the kitchen stirring up her hoe cake.*

In 1876, Anna, Leonard, and eldest daughter Carrie traveled up to Philadelphia to take in the Centennial celebrations. The route took them through Virginia where the Captain fixed his eyes again upon the familiar fields he and Ruby galloped across for three hard years. Anna wrote of the journey and the spectacular Centennial exhibitions.

*The trip to Philadelphia was delightful. We took the bay route to give Carrie an idea of water traveling. The Chesapeake was calm and lovely when we first crossed and the York River with its sweet Virginia scenery, a perfect treat. Philadelphia is a splendid city, Chestnut Street at night like a hundred King Streets at Fourth of July or Christmas.... It is a truly glorious exhibition...The sweet splashing of fountains, the hum of human voices mingled sweetly with it and when the organ ceased, the great band took up the strain and made you laugh again for joy. Fatigue is forgotten, the folly of fashion shamed into quiet in the presence of so much beauty and grandeur...and the gem of gems (surrounded by grounds rich with flowers-geraniums of every hue in full bloom) the Art Gallery. Ah! My heart turns to that. Oh! the wonders of art. You know nothing of statuary until you stand, in the presence of Italian sculpture. You forget everything, everybody, but the sweet pure, angelic voiceless thing- the creation of human hands but heaven born in its conception, more wonderful than painting or mosaic, the art of arts form, features, expression life-like, chiseled from a block of cold colorless marble- love, hope, fear, grief, mostly prayer all speaking, as it were, to you with startling effect from the cold marble lips and eyes. I would but say, if in this world so much beauty and so much glory can be enjoyed, what must heaven be?*

Three years later, she found out. Anna Olivia Laval Williams, the Captain's devoted wife of 21 years, died at the still young age of 39. The cause of her death is not cited, but it is most likely that she succumbed to hard times, frailty, and her generally weak constitution. In letters to Eleanor, dire economic circumstances and her waning health had always been the prime subjects.

> *My health has been poor all winter. I have not been to church in*
> *months, have drunk out all my money in cod liver oil and worn out*
> *porous plasters enough to plaster the house with. Well I have prayed*
> *for God to heal my diseases and to be merciful to me and I trust the*
> *means may be blessed with success for without the Great Physician's*
> *blessing all is in vain.*

Throughout the war, God had shielded her Captain from shot and shell and carried him safely home. In 1879, He called Anna home.

In 1880, a year after Anna's death, the 57-year old Captain married Anna's older sister, Harriet Julia Laval. While they had no children, they enjoyed a rich 28-year relationship, which lasted through the dawning of a new century. Together they watched Carrie earn her teaching degree and marry Baptist preacher W. J. Langston. Langston had three children from a previous marriage, but he and Carrie had none of their own. Carrie lived to be 85. Nancy married Isaac Mercer and raised three fine daughters. Son Davis married and moved to Kentucky where he trained thoroughbred horses. Daughter Julia never married and in her later years resided with the youngest of the Captain's daughters, Susan. Susan was the apple of her father's eye as Anna wrote Eleanor that:

> *This is the birthday of my little stranger. She is four today. She is*
> *quite fair and has bluish eyes for which we all idolize her. She is, too,*
> *very good, healthy, fat and as sweet as she can be- a pet with everyone,*
> *especially her father who thinks she is the prettiest, smartest, and most*
> *wonderful baby in town.*

Susie wed Thomas Mills Douglas, Postmaster of Chester, South Carolina. Her first son, Leonard, was named after her father, but sadly, he died in infancy. Her second was my father, Thomas Williams Douglas.

Leonard's younger brother James H. Williams, who had experienced both the nightmare of amputation and the squalid conditions of Point Lookout Prison Camp, must have been moved by the pain and suffering he had felt and witnessed. He became a doctor in South Carolina's Ninety-Six District.

As for the Captain himself, he had done his duty. How he came to terms with the defeat of the Confederacy, only he knows. To what degree he ever came to realize the cruelty of slavery and the immorality of subjugation rest with him as well. In the end, he was a simple man who lived in complex times. While Italian sculpture captivated Anna, the Captain found his art in life itself. He saw it in a freshly plowed field, a plump turnip, or a strong mare. He found it reflected in the bright, then terrified faces of the freckle-faced boys that rode next to him. He discovered it in the smell of gunpowder, a simmering frying pan, the fragrant Virginia clover, and the Lilies of the Valley-scented letters from Anna. He heard it in the clash of sabers, the roar of cannon, the laughter around the campfire, and the cries of the wounded in the Gettysburg rain.

To him the Lost Cause had not only been real, it had been righteous. It was an honor to serve with fellow South Carolinians Matthew Butler and gallant Wade Hampton. The sight of Jeb Stuart's peacock plumes spearheading another charge and Lee's stoic silhouette at Brandy Station remained strong, indelible, images long after the war was over. The Captain had honored his wife, family, city, county, and state before the war and after. He lived his times. He played his part. He gave and obeyed orders. But in the end what had all the blood been spilled for? The Civil War had claimed over 620,000 lives, one of them young brother Ephraim. What had this suffering, misery, and death achieved? To be sure, secession had been thwarted and slavery abolished, but what would this new, undivided nation ultimately become? For the four million slaves that were freed, a life of sharecropping awaited. Many of their children then toiled under a shadow of racism harsher than any overseer and distrust that ran deeper than any cotton furrow. For the white, Democratic south, the carpetbaggers were gone, but the scar of defeat and resentment would linger well into the next century.

The Twentieth Century had already come to Greenville. Farms prospered in large part due to the fair dealings of "Williams and Whitmire," the local mercantile down at the corner of Buncombe and Lawrence St. The region was growing, fed by the Southern Railway the Captain lobbied so tenaciously and articulately for in the state legislature. A day's ride to the east in Newberry, the school that he helped found now educated even more difference-makers. In the 1870's, Leonard was a mover and a shaker. In 1905, moving around was difficult and his hands trembled more than ever. The humble Captain was one month shy of his 82 birthday. He had outlived Generals Lee, Johnston, Sherman, and Grant. The surrender at Appomattox had taken place 40 years earlier. He sat beneath the magnolias on his wraparound porch pondering all that had taken place in the wake of the war and what was still to come.

What did come was a letter sent from James McClanahan. He remembered the name well. James had grown up in Greenville and they were mustered in together but he hadn't seen nor heard from him since the day Johnston surrendered. McClanahan was the young corporal who had fallen under his horse as the Yankees were closing in. Leonard and a few others galloped back and rescued him only seconds before he would have been captured. That was way back in 1862. Why, he wondered, would Jim be writing after all these years? The Old Captain opened the envelope with the same anticipation he had years ago when Anna's overdue letters would finally come to hand. With hands as unsteady as his heart, he unfolded it carefully, adjusted his spectacles and groaned a bit as he leaned back in the rocker.

*Westminster, S. C.*
*Nov. 20, 1905*

*Captain Leonard Williams*
*Greenville, S. C.*
*My Dear Captain:*

*Among my most pleasant recollections is the kindness with which you always treated me. When I was a boy, and was about your place of business, you treated me as a father. In our entire military service, I received at your hands nothing but the most tolerable and considerate treatment. I was greatly surprised in being made an officer upon the reorganization of the company in 1862. A position, even as humble as corporal, in a company where you had such material to select from, was worthy of the highest appreciation. You were the one member of company K who was always at his post. In the many engagements into which your company went you were always in command and always led them.*

*Don't you remember Jack's Shop where you charged the Yankees, outnumbering us at least ten to one? I can see you now as you gave the command, "About Wheel!" and placing yourself in advance of the first set of forty-five, rode as coolly at the Yankees as if on parade. The next morning you blushed when Gen. Stuart hunted up the squadron and told you that he had witnessed more cavalry charges than any man on this continent and that the one made by that squadron under your leadership was the best and most successful he had ever seen.*

*I have talked about you to my children, Captain, until they know you as well as I do. We are getting old, my dear friend, but it is pleasing to remember bygone events and to know that I, with all the ignorance of a boy, had the respect and kindly regard of the men whose good opinion I valued above all others. Had I been a younger brother, I could not have fared better at your hands.*

*I sincerely hope that we may meet again. If possible I will visit my old home before many months and will be sure to see you. With heartfelt thanks for all past kindnesses and with wishes for your health and prosperity, I am*

> *Very truly, your friend*
> *J. M. McClanahan*

Three years later, at 5:30 in the evening, perhaps in that very rocking chair, Leonard Williams died. The date was May 22, 1908. He was 84. His obituary appeared in *The Greenville Daily News* the next morning.

*Capt. Leonard Williams one of the boldest and best-known citizens of Greenville died at his home yesterday afternoon at 5:30. Capt. Williams was born in Newberry District in December 1823. His ancestors came from Wales to this country in the early part of the seventeenth century and received a large grant of land in Granville County, North Carolina. From there his grandfather moved to Newberry District, South Carolina where several of the family became noted partisan leaders in the Revolutionary War. Capt. Williams was graduated from the South Carolina College in 1844. He was advised by the faculty to open a classical school in the up country. He became principal of the Newberry Academy, which afterward merged into Newberry College. After several years of successful teaching he moved to Greenville County and was for years a leading merchant of this city. He was a man of great public spirit and had represented his county several terms in the State Legislature and has rendered efficient service in several county offices.*

*In June 1861 (at the call of his state), he joined the Brooks Troop of*

*Hampton's Legion. In 1862, he became captain of the troop, which he commanded during the remainder of the war. He led his men gallantly in many battles notably at Williamsburg, Seven Pines, and Gettysburg; was wounded in a hand-to-hand fight at Upperville, Va. After the engagement at Jack's Shop, he was publicly commended for conspicuous bravery by Gen. J. E. B. Stuart.*

*Captain Williams is survived by one brother, Dr. J. H. Williams of Ninety-Six, his wife and five children, namely; Mr. D. L. Williams of Georgetown, Ky., Mrs. I. M. Mercer of Rocky Mount, N. C., Mrs. T. M. Douglas of Chester, S. C., and Misses Carrie and Julia Williams of this city. The funeral will take place this afternoon at 5 o'clock at the Second Presbyterian Church of which Captain Williams was a member. The service will be conducted by the pastor, Dr. E. P. Davis and the interment will be in Christ Church Cemetery.*

*The active pallbearers will be his great nephews; L. Albert James, Hugh P. Williams, William M. James, W. Frank Riser, Joseph H. James and Chas. M. Riser. The honorary pallbearers are Prof. H. T. Cook, T. T. Ellison, J. P. Charles, H. W. Cely, J. C. Milford, J. C. Bailey, S. S. Crittenden, S. A. Townes, H. C. Markley, Capt. A. Blythe."*

A tribute submitted by fellow Company K cavalrymen Absalom Blythe and S. S. Crittenden appeared the next day.

*In Memoriam*
*Report of the Committee of Camp Pulliam on the death of Captain Leonard Williams.*

*Death has again invaded the ranks of our Camp, and taken from our midst one of our bravest and best as well as oldest and most beloved men. On Friday afternoon, the 22ⁿᵈ of May, at half past five o'clock, the spirit of our brother and comrade Leonard Williams, calmly and peacefully, and in perfect trust and confidence in the benign God and Father of us all who created it, took its flight to the eternal regions of immortal life. That our beloved friend and brother was well prepared for this great change we feel assured. He had lived to an old age as the average human life is considered. Through the vicissitudes of a long life of more than eighty-four years, in peace and in war, he discharged the duties of citizen and soldier in a manner to commend him to the highest respect of all who knew him. As a citizen he was honest, as a soldier brave, with all that these terms signify.*

*Be it therefore resolved: That we mourn the death of Captain Leonard Williams as a well beloved friend and comrade whose kindly heart, genial manners and generous disposition, as well as his well won reputation as a Confederate officer and soldier, have endeared him to us all. That we tender to the family of our departed friend our sincerest sympathy in their great loss, while we can but feel their loss is his eternal gain. Resolved: That our adjutant be instructed to inscribe a page in our minute book to the memory of Captain Williams, with a copy of these resolutions; also that a copy of them be transmitted to the family of our lost comrade.*

> *A. Blythe*
> *S. S. Crittenden*
> *Committee*

A second tribute from life-long friend John C. Bailey appeared in the May 27, 1908 edition of the *Greenville Daily News* entitled *"Judge John C. Bailey Pays Beautiful Tribute to His Late Comrade-Was a Man of Sterling Worth."*

*Editor the news: I have read with much interest in Saturday's paper your just and proper tribute to the life and character of our late fellow citizen, Capt. Leonard Williams, and also in the morning issue the paper adopted... "R. C. Pulliam Camp of Confederate Veterans", likewise bearing testimony to his worth.*

*After the publication, Mr. Editor, of two such able testimonials, it may seem superfluous of me to attempt to add hereto. However, being cognizant in a peculiar manner of the great loss of our State and Country have sustained in the death of Captain Williams, and further fact that I have known him since the days of boyhood, and also had him as a near neighbor for between three and four decades past, with your permission I will in some slight manner indicate my estimate of him as an upright and honorable citizen.*

*Captain Williams was a man of high mental and moral attainments, and gave evidence thereof by the select language he used every day of his life, his gentlemanly bearing on all occasions, the scope of his mind, the breadth of his opinions on all State and National questions, as well as the fullness of his comprehension of the problems of the times as discussed with men of equal calibre of mind. Although he enjoyed the advantage of instruction as imparted in the halls of the South Carolina College to full graduation, yet he was ever modest and gentle in advancing his opinions, done with great clearness of statement, as well as perspicacity of thought, using no verbiage of careless tantology. It was one of his well-known characteristics that he spoke unkindly of no fellow being, no matter the variance of degree in opinion.*

*Captain Williams' patriotism was positive and unequivocal, as evidenced by his readiness in entering the Confederate War in the year 1861, as a member of the Brooks Troop of cavalry from Greenville, remaining on the field of contest until the surrender of the army under Gen. R. E. Lee.*

*He showed equal zeal and ardour in the year 1876 in the state campaign that resulted in the election of Gen. Hampton as Governor of South Carolina. In 1880, when participating in State politics, Capt. Williams was again true to his convictions of what he conceived to be in the interest of the public welfare and did all that was in his influence for the success of the reform movement. As a member of the General Assembly from Greenville County, he was always alert and vigilant in furthering the public work and also it was as county auditor he proved his competency by his faithfulness and success in the performance of the duties required of him.*

*It is also as a neighbor that we wish to speak of the deceased. He was ever cheerful in his intercourse, his cordial greetings evincing a sincere interest in the well being of his fellow citizens. We unite with his bereaved family in their sorrow upon the death and burial of a beloved husband and father; notwithstanding he had reached the advanced age allotted to mankind. Feeling assured that he has entered upon a heavenly inheritance.*

*Respectfully,*
*John C. Bailey*

Today, the Captain rests in Greenville's Christ Church Cemetery. At his head is buried his true love. Her inscription reads, "Mother Anna Olivia, daughter of Wm. & S. C. Laval, wife of Leonard Williams, born in Charleston, S.C., Dec.-1839. Death is swallowed up in victory." Julia, his second wife, rests at his feet. "Harriet Julia, daughter of Wm. & S. C. Laval, wife of Leonard Williams, born in Charleston, S.C., March-1833. Peace perfect peace."

Between the Laval sisters rests the Captain. "Leonard Williams Co. K 2nd S.C. Cav. C.S.A., born in Newberry District, S.C., Dec.-1823, died in Greenville, S.C., May-1908. Christian-Patriot-Soldier."

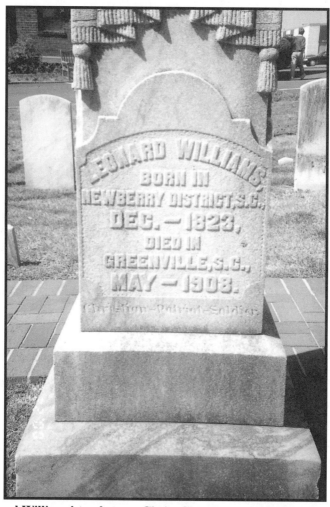

**Leonard Williams' tombstone, Christ Church Cemetery, Greenville, SC**
***Courtesy- Roy Christie***

**Williams House on Augusta Road, Greenville, S.C., circa 1880s**
*Courtesy- Greenville Historical Society*

# NOTES

## Chapter 2

p. 4     *The remnants of the Confederate Army..."* U. R. Brooks, *Butler and His Cavalry in the War of Secession*, (Guild Bindery Press, Germantown, TN, 1994), p. 481. This grand reunion march actually did take place in Columbia on May 13, 1903. Brook's collection includes the following passage: "...like God's sweetest benediction- fell the gentle rain from the heavens upon the gallant and battle-      scarred warriors of our great cause and upon the fair and dainty little children whose wee hands made of May's loveliest flowers a carpet from Lady street to the State House. Upon this fragrant pathway of flowers they marched again, clad in their suits of gray."

p. 5     *"As old Doctor Taylor would undo crusty, blood stained bandages..."* A portrait of Doctor W. B. "Watt" Taylor appears in Brook's *Butler and His Cavalry in the War of Secession*. He was Chief Surgeon for the 2nd S. C. Cavalry.

## Chapter 3

p. 9     *"Great grandfather John Williams emigrated from Shangallon, Wales, in 1700..."* James M. Richardson, History of Greenville County, South Carolina, (A. H. Cawston, Atlanta, GA, 1930), p. 190.

p. 9     *"From Virginia, his descendants moved to Granville County..."* Ibid., p. 190.

p. 9     *"Leonard's grandfather Daniel Williams had four sturdy sons..."* Ibid., p. 190.

p. 9     *"He too married a woman of patriotic stock..."* Ibid., p. 190.

p. 9     *"Leonard was born in the Newberry District..."* Ibid., p. 190.

p. 10     *"There he was introduced to a nineteen year old Charlestonian..."* Julia Gabrielle Williams, (Unpublished hand written family history owned by Anne Kesler Shields,

Winston- Salem), unnumbered. Julia was a daughter of Captain Leonard Williams. She never married and wrote a great deal concerning family events and genealogy. My mother stated that Julia told her that she would hide under the dining room table as a child in order to eavesdrop on animated family discussions about the war.

p. 10 *"For his valor at the capture of Pensacola in the War of 1812..."* Official document presented to Major William Laval signed by President James Madison and Actg. Sec. of War A. J. Dallas "for gallant and meritorious conduct at the capture of Pensacola, and provided protection from sunburn." Many times soldiers used the havelock as a strainer or a rag to clean pots and utensils.

p. 17 *"Yesterday was the Fourth of July..."* Anna Laval Williams, *The Diary of Anna Williams,* July 5, 1861 entry, owned by Anne Kesler Shields, Winston-Salem.

p. 17 *"President Davis, an old cavalryman himself, watched proudly..."* Ron Field, *The Hampton Legion Part 1: Regimental History,* (Design Folio, Gloucestershire, England, 1994), p. 4.

p. 18 *"'Move out there, you...'"* E. Prioleau Henderson, *Autobiography of Arab,* (Fox Books, Guild Bindery Press, 1997), p. 16.

p. 18 *"The new troopers found that their horses learned the drills..."* Robert Paul Jordan, *The Civil War,* (The National Geographic Society, New York, NY, 1969), p. 55.

p. 19 *"The whole cavalry force of the legion is now here but Taylor's..."* Leonard Williams letter dated July 21, 1861. In *Giant in Gray* (p. 51), Manly Wade Wellman writes, "Matthew Calbraith Butler, a handsome twenty-five year old lawyer, rode in with the Edgefield Hussars, and Captain Thomas Taylor reported with a fourth troop." In his Regimental History (p. 9), Ron Field writes, "Companies A, B, and C of the cavalry left Ashland for Manassas on 22 July and rejoined the infantry of the Legion at 'Camp Johnson' eight days later. The Congaree

Troop, which had been 'left at Ashland for the purpose of perfecting its drill,' rejoined the battalion on 26 August." Captain John Lanneau is the source quoted by Field.

p. 19     *"...were ordered to remain behind at Ashland under Major Griffin for more drilling."* Major James B. Griffin was the Legion's original major serving under Lt. Col. Benjamin J. Johnson and Colonel Wade Hampton. When Johnson was killed at Manassas, Griffin replaced him as Lt. Col.

p. 19     *"After two sweltering days in freight cars..."* Ron Field, *The Hampton Legion Part 1: Regimental History,* (Design Folio, Gloucestershire, England, 1994), p. 4.

## Chapter 4

p. 22     *"Unable to stand the suspense, one of Hampton's men rose up to peek..."* Ron Field, *The Hampton Legion Part 1: Regimental History,* (Design Folio, Gloucestershire, England, 1994), p. 5.

p. 22     *"Here the Legion suffered its first casualties..."* Ibid., p. 5.

p. 22     *"It was by this volley that Lieutenant Colonel Benjamin Johnson..."* Charleston Mercury, (August 5, 1861, col. 5), p. 1. In his regimental history, Ron Field noted that Johnson was about 45 years old and hailed from the Beaufort District when he joined the Legion.

p. 23     *"Inspired by Jackson's boldness, Bee's men halted their retreat..."* Confederate Military History, Volume 3, Chapter III, (Broadfoot, Wilmington, NC, 1987).

p. 23     *"We advanced to the Spring Hill farm house..."* Official Report of Colonel Wade Hampton, *O.R.'s,* Series I, Volume 2, p. 567.

p. 24     *"The road back to Centerville was clogged with correspondents..."* Ralph Selph Henry, *The Story of the Confederacy,* (Garden City Publishing, Garden City, NY, 1931), p. 59.

p. 24    *"The defeated Federals streamed back to Washington with frenzied eyes..."* Albert Riddle, quoted in Samuel S. Cox, *Three Decades of Southern Legislation, 1855-1885,* (Providence, RI, 1885), p. 158.

p. 25    *"A gentleman made a present today of a horse to Austin..."* Leonard Williams letter dated July 21, 1861. Private J. N. Austin would not ride that horse very long, however, as Williams mentions in a letter dated May 9, 1862 that, "Jno Austin of our company died last week near Richmond."

p. 26    *"On last Thursday 18ᵗʰ a battle was fought at Fairfax..."* Anna Olivia Laval Williams, *The Diary of Anna Williams,* July 25, 1861 entry, owned by Anne Kesler Shields, Winston-Salem.

p. 27    *"The defeated troops commenced pouring into Washington..."* www.civilwarhome.com/cmhistmanassas.htm.

p. 27    *"The dead were sent south in narrow boxes of rough plank..."* T. C. DeLeon, *Four Years in Rebel Capitals,* (The Gossip Printing Company, Mobile, AL, 1890), p. 97.

p. 29    *"There was an atmosphere of triumph in the camps..."* Ibid., p. 112.

p. 30    *"The Confederates captured 26 pieces of artillery..."* *Confederate Military History, Volume 3,* Chapter III, (Broadfoot, Wilmington, NC, 1987).

p. 30    *"One, two, or three others reached here the day before yesterday and were guests of the Davis Guards."* Leonard Williams letter dated July 27, 1861. In his Hampton Legion Regimental History, Ron Field points out that the Davis Guards (Greenville) were a light infantry unit that comprised Company F when the Hampton Legion was first assembled.

p. 31    *"A great many letters were found with words of caution as to the health when they got to a southern climate especially at N. O."* Ibid. "N. O." is most likely a reference to New Orleans, Louisiana. Oppressive southern heat and the unknown diseases associated with it were a concern to many Union troops and commanders.

p. 31      *"We have now reached the naborhoods of the enemy and hard times are looked for."* Ibid., "Naborhoods" was a common spelling of "neighborhoods."

p. 32      *"It is now reported that we will go in a few days to Leesburg..."* Leonard Williams letter dated July 27, 1861. Leesburg was the site of Lee's famous crossing into Maryland where he would face McClellan at Sharpsburg (Antietam) a year later.

p. 32      *"On August 16, the Legion was ordered from Camp Johnson..."* O. R.'s Series I, Volume 5, 778-779, Verner to Mother, *Verner Letters,* August 17, 1861 entry, (Atlanta, Georgia Dept. of Archives & History). Brentsville is located 6 miles from Manassas. Bacon Race Church is located 9 miles from Manassas.

p. 32      *"A regular old Methodist looking building..."* Major James Conner, *James Conner to Mother,* August 29, 1861 entry, Mary Conner Moffett, ed., R. L. Bryan Co., Columbia, SC, 1950), p. 55.

p. 32      *"The surroundings seemed custom-made for the Legion..."* *Charleston Daily Courier,* October 9, 1861, column 4, p. 1.

p. 33      *"Maj. Perry will probably leave tomorrow and I write to send by him."* Leonard Williams letter dated August 29, 1861. A "Maj. Perry" was not listed in Williams' company as such. W. H. Perry, a first lieutenant, is the only "Perry" designated on the Roll of the troop. "Major" may refer to Perry's rank in the militia.

p. 34      *"You must pay attention to the cleanliness of the room the negroes sleep in..."* Leonard Williams letter dated August 30, 1861. Williams never capitalized the word "negroes" in any of his letters.

p. 34      *"I am now wearing a pair of Brogans..."* Ibid., "Brogans" were ankle-high black shoes that laced in front. Most were taken from Union soldiers, as they were standard issue for

Federal troops. Brogans were more comfortable than cavalry boots because they were lighter and easily put on and taken off. One drawback, however, is that Williams later states that Brogans fit poorly into stirrups.

## Chapter 5

p. 36     *"Genl Johnson says that we occupy the most important post on the river..."* Leonard Williams letter dated September 9, 1861. "General Johnson" is actually General Joseph E. Johnston, commander of the Confederate forces around Richmond. After his wounding at Seven Pines, Johnston would be replaced by General Robert E. Lee. In later letters, "Johnson" is the incorrect spelling of General Joseph E. Johnston.

p. 36     *"Twenty-five men from each company had been handpicked by Major Butler..."* Ron Field, *The Hampton Legion Part 1: Regimental History,* (Design Folio, Gloucestershire, England, 1994), p. 10.

p. 37     *"Matthew C. Butler, to Leonard then and even more so now..."* U. R. Brooks, *Butler and His Cavalry in the War of Secession,* (Guild Bindery Press, Germantown, TN, 1994), p. 54. Brooks' work is an excellent source for biographical and anecdotal information concerning the heroic cavalry commander and United States Senator.

p. 37     *"Leonard was sure that he had more horses shot from under him..."* Ibid., p. 19.

p. 37     *"A former West Pointer who had graduated in 1825..."* Ralph Selph Henry, *The Story of the Confederacy,* (Garden City Publishing, Garden City, NY, 1931), p. 64.

p. 38     *"Such was the case at Cheat Mountain where Lee failed to defeat..."* Ibid., p. 65.

p. 38     *"He is quite well now but after the great battle and fatiguing marches and exposure has taken sick and went to near Culpepper."* Leonard Williams letter dated September 9, 1861. "Culpepper" is actually spelled

"Culpeper" and is a north central county and town in Virginia. Like most of the surrounding counties, Culpeper was the site of many skirmishes and battles and was the gathering place of Lee's army prior to the Gettysburg Campaign. Brandy Station is located just northeast of the town.

p. 39     *"Get Mr. Whitmire to save you twenty- five pounds..."* Leonard Williams letter dated September 9, 1861. Mr. William Whitmire was Williams' business partner at the local Greenville mercantile. After the war, they remained partners for a time. Later the mercantile became known as "Williams and Feaster's." "Billy" and "Nath" are mentioned often in Williams' letters. Both are either sons or nephews of Whitmire's.

p. 40     *"I would like for you to write me twice a week and tell me about your affairs, whether you are supplied with the table necessaries, poultry, mutton, beef & c..."* Leonard Williams letter dated September 10, 1861. "& c" is a symbol often employed in Williams' letters. Further use in subsequent letters reveals that "& c" simply means "etcetera."

p. 41     *"Bacon Race Church, Camp Griffin, Virginia"* Undated letter of Leonard Williams. This letter is undated and contains no salutation.

p. 42     *"Henry wrote me that the baby has teeth..."* Ibid., Both Williams and his wife had brothers or cousins named "Henry." Often times it is difficult to determine which "Henry" is being referred to throughout the letters.

p. 43     *"I wrote you by Moore and also Lieut. Gaillard..."* Leonard Williams letter dated September 16, 1861. First Sergeant J. P. Moore and First Lieutenant S. S. Gaillard are listed in Dr. M. B. Harrison's *Roll of Brooks Troop.*

p. 44     *"The strategic triangle of northern Virginia shielded invasion routes."* Maurice Matloff, *The Civil War, A Concise Military History of the War Between the States,* (David McKay Company, Inc., New York, NY), p. 13.

p. 46       *"On 17 September 1861, Lieutenant-Colonel Griffin was struck by lightning..."* Ron Field, *The Hampton Legion Part 1: Regimental History,* (Design Folio, Gloucestershire, England, 1994), p. 10. See Field's note section as well.

p. 47       *"The first fight of the artillery branch took place on December 26..."* Ibid., p. 10.

p. 47       *"Finally Lee gave the order to fire and shelling forced the side-wheel tug 'U. S. Jacob Bell'..."* Ibid., p. 11. John Mills Bigham, 'Guidon Bearer', Pvt. Louis Sherfesee, *Hart's South Carolina Artillery* in *Military Images,* (Volume IX, No. 6, May-June, 1988), p. 14.

p. 49       *"The tomatto catsup as usual was lost..."* Leonard Williams letter dated September 26, 1861. "Tomatto" is an alternate spelling for "tomato." Lost foodstuffs, clothing, whiskey, etc. in transit was commonplace as bags and trunks were apparently relieved of their precious contents by sorters in Richmond or cold, hungry, and thirsty couriers. Most goods sent to and from the front arrived late but with their contents untouched, however.

p. 49       *"On October 4, 1861, the entire Legion advanced on Pohick Church..."* Ron Field, *The Hampton Legion Part 1: Regimental History,* (Design Folio, Gloucestershire, England, 1994), p. 11. "Pohick" Church is also spelled "Pohieck" Church in other writings.

p. 49       *"Both the Legion's Artillery and cavalry started off at two o'clock in the morning..."* Ibid., p.11. *Charleston Daily Courier,* November 19, 1861, column 3, p. 3.

p. 52       *"...and occupy with Lieut. Prince a tent by ourselves."* Leonard Williams letter dated October 12, 1861. In a newspaper clipping from *The Greenville Daily News* (date unknown) handed down in our family, a Roll of Brooks Troop contains the following entry: "Second Lieutenant W. G. Prince (died in 1861)."

p. 52       *"When news of the defeat and Lee's arrival on the coast reached the Legion, the men wished to return to South Carolina as a unit..."* Hutson, *Hutson Papers,* Hutson to

Father, November 9, 1861, continuation of November 8, 1861 letter. Hutson's words appear in Field's Regimental History, (p.11): "We are longing to hear orders from the Legion to proceed to the scene of action in South Carolina." In John Lanneau's diary, it is mentioned that their request was denied.

## Chapter 6

p. 59     *"Camp Wigfall, located near the village of Occoquan, was in essence the first and last true winter quarters..."* E. Prioleau Henderson, *Autobiography of Arab,* (Fox Books, The Guild Bindery Press, 1997), p. 20.

p. 63     *"You have no idea how the men brighten up now when I go among them..."* Albert Riddle quoted in Samuel S. Cox, *Three Decades of Southern Legislation, 1855-1885,* (Providence, RI, 1885), p. 158.

p. 66     *"I and Alex Payne occupy a large sybley tent and have a good chimney..."* Leonard Williams letter dated January 22, 1862. In James I. Robertson Jr.'s *The Civil War: Tenting Tonight* (Time Life, Chicago, IL, 1984, p. 45), the following appears: "...the Sibley tent, named for its inventor, Henry H. Sibley, who later became a Confederate brigadier general...[is described as] a large cone of canvas, 18 feet in diameter, 12 feet tall and supported by a center pole, the tent had a circular opening at the top for ventilation, and a cone-shaped stove for heat."

p. 67     *"How well I remember to this day that sight..."* E. Prioleau Henderson, *Autobiography of Arab,* (Fox Books, The Guild Bindery Press, 1997), p. 25.

p. 67     *"A few weeks later, Hampton again led four cavalry companies out toward the enemy."* Ibid., p 26.

p. 70     *"Inactivity and confinement soon led to boredom."* Bell Irvin Wiley, *The Life of Johnny Reb,* (Louisiana State University Press, Baton Rouge, LA, 1978), p. 63.

p. 71     *"You need not send me the papers except one Mercury each week...*" Leonard Williams letter dated February 2, 1862. The newspaper he is requesting weekly is *The Charleston Mercury.*

p. 71     *"Paper is scarce here. I write on one of my blanks."* Ibid. A "blank" is one of Williams' morning report forms that had not been filled in. On it are columns and spaces where Williams would list the number of privates, sergeants, etc. available for duty as well as those away on leave or unaccounted for. This is his only letter written on a blank morning report.

p. 72     *"At Fort Donelson, when asked what his terms for surrender were, he sent his famous message: 'No terms except unconditional...'"* Maurice Matloff, *The Civil War: A Concise Military History of the War Between the States,* (David McKay Company Inc., New York, NY, 1978), p. 33.

p. 75     *"We remained several weeks at Catlett's..."* E. Prioleau Henderson, *Autobiography of Arab,* (Fox Books, The Guild Bindery Press, 1997), p. 29.

p. 75     *"When Virginia seceded, the Federals had hurriedly but only partially destroyed the new steam frigate U. S. S. Merrimac..."* Craig L. Symonds, *The Battlefield Atlas of the Civil War,* The Nautical and Aviation Publishing Company of America, Annapolis, MD), p. 27.

p. 76     *"The two circled one another, got in close, and then fired away..."* Bruce Catton, *This Hallowed Ground,* (Doubleday & Company, Garden City, NY, 1956), p. 431.

p. 76     " *'Prince John,'* as he was called, loved attending the theater..." David Donald, *Divided We Fought,* (The MacMillan Company, New York, NY, 1953), p. 41.

p. 76     *"...along with those dreaded 'quaker guns' convinced..."* "Quaker guns" were really not guns at all. They were merely tree trunks positioned and sometimes painted so as to deceive the enemy into believing they were cannon. This tactic enabled Magruder to give the impression that he possessed far more men and artillery than he actually had.

*425*

p. 76    *"'Old Joe's' forces were brought south slowly by way of Trennis Crossroads..."* E. Prioleau Henderson, *Autobiography of Arab,* (Fox Books, The Guild Bindery Press, 1997), p. 30.

p. 77    *"The distance was about fifty miles, over the worst roads..."* Ron Field, *The Hampton Legion Part 1: Regimental History,* (Design Folio, Gloucestershire, England, 1994), p. 15. *Charleston Daily Courier,* June 21, 1862, column 2, p. 4.

p. 77    *"When a soggy General Johnston finally arrived to inspect what Magruder..."* Johnston to Robert E. Lee, April 22, 1862, *O. R.'s,* Series 1, Volume 11, Part 3, p. 456. Johnston actually stated that, "No one but McClellan would have hesitated to attack."

p. 78    *"Our election has not yet come off..."* Bell Irvin Wiley, *The Life of Johnny Reb,* (Louisiana State University Press, Baton Rouge, LA, 1978), p. 20.

p. 79    *"I did not approve of throwing good and tried officers out..."* E. Prioleau Henderson, *Autobiography of Arab,* (Fox Books, The Guild Bindery Press, 1997), p. 30.

## Chapter 7

p. 83    *"It makes sassafras tea drinks as well as [    ] or rye..."* Leonard Williams letter dated April 3, 1862. Brackets represent an undecipherable word. Material in the letters marked with parentheses are words that Williams himself placed in parentheses.

p. 84    *"While spearheading that afternoon charge, Confederate commander Albert Sydney Johnston..."* T. C. DeLeon, *Four Years in Rebel Capitals,* (The Gossip Printing Company, Mobile, AL, 1980), p. 166.

p. 85    *"Grant answered him sharply, 'Retreat? No. I propose to attack...'"* Bruce Catton, *Grant Moves South,* (Little, Brown and Company, Boston, MA, 1960), p. 241.

p. 85    *"I saw an open field, in our possession on the second day...*" Robert Paul Jordan, *The Civil War,* (The National Geographic Society, New York, NY, 1969), p. 83.

p. 85     *"The President replied, 'I can't spare this man; he fights.'"* Ibid., p. 83.

p. 86     *"Thomas Jonathan Jackson was a quirky loner who kept to himself..."* Clarence C. Buel and Robert U. Johnson, eds., *Battles and Leaders, Stonewall Jackson in the Shenandoah, Volume II,* (New York, NY, 1888), p. 297.

p. 86     *"Between March 23 and June 9, with as little as 4,200..."* Robert Paul Jordan, *The Civil War,* (The National Geographic Society, New York, NY, 1969), p. 90.

p. 86     *"Throughout those remarkable weeks, Jackson came to be revered by his men..."* James M. McPherson, *Battle Cry of Freedom,* (Oxford University Press, New York, NY, 1988), p. 456.

p. 88     *"As Butler rode through the cobblestone streets of old Williamsburg..."* U. R. Brooks, *Butler and His Cavalry in the War of Secession,* (Guild Bindery Press, Germantown, TN, 1994), p. 71.

p. 88     *"He was a true cavalier and dressed the part."* James M. McPherson, *Battle Cry of Freedom,* (Oxford University Press, New York, NY, 1988), p. 463.

p. 88     *"'See them across that valley,' yelled Jeb."* E. Prioleau Henderson, *Autobiography of Arab,* (Fox Books, The Guild Bindery Press, 1997), p. 82.

p. 90     *"Thornwell of the Congarees was wounded..."* Leonard Williams letter dated May 8, 1862. The Congarees were named for the South Carolina river and hailed from the Richland area. Originally they formed Company D of Hampton's cavalry battalion.

p. 90     *"First Butler ordered his command to form platoons..."* E. Prioleau Henderson, *Autobiography of Arab,* (Fox Books, Guild Bindery Press, 1997), p. 83.

p. 90     *"Go ahead Major Butler, we will follow you to hell."* Ibid., p. 35.

p. 90     *"The day before yesterday a considerable fight took place with the enemy that were landed at West Point on the York River."* Leonard Williams letter dated May 9, 1982. See *I Rode With Jeb Stuart* (p. 50) for a more detailed account of this fight in which the Federals tried to turn the Confederate right flank by landing "Franklin's Division at Eltham's Landing on the York River."

p. 92      *"Jno Austin of our company died last week..."* Leonard Williams letter dated May 9, 1862. A Roll of Brooks Troop contains the following entry: "[Private] Austin, J. P. (Died in 1862)."

p. 92      *"I was sent with fifteen men to picquett the roads leading toward the James River."* Leonard Williams letter dated May 10, 1862. "Picquett" is a form of the word "picket." "Picquet" is another variation. To "picket" is to patrol the areas surrounding an encampment. A "picket" is a soldier performing that duty. The "picket line" is the camp's perimeter. Troopers took turns picketing as the edges of camp had to be watched morning and night. Williams himself was responsible for posting the picketing duty schedule and determining what rider or riders would be placed as guards and sentries.

p. 93      *"The only sad occurrence being the loss of our fellow trooper Mr. Boggs..."* Ibid. In an undated family newspaper clipping from *The Greenville Daily News,* a Roll of Brooks Troop contains the following: "Boggs, G. W.B., (first man in company killed in battle at Williamsburg, Va.)."

p. 93      *"5 of our regiments were sent to meet them."* Ibid., Concerning the affair at Eltham's landing, H. B. McClellan writes the following in *I Rode With Jeb Stuart,* (p. 50): "...two brigades of Whiting's Division, Hood's and Hampton's, attacked the enemy and drove him under the cover of the fire of his gun-boats."

p. 93      *"Since then (now Sunday) our rear has been comparatively unmolested except on Friday Genl. Stewart's cavalry were attacked and lost several men."* Ibid. "Genl. Stewart" is actually General James Ewell Brown Stuart. Many times in his letters, Williams inexplicably fails to correctly spell the name of the Confederate cavalry commander.

p. 96　　*"The enemy in their haste to escape over a very rough boggy place were piled three deep..."* Ron Field, *The Hampton Legion Part 1: Regimental History,* (Design Folio, Gloucestershire, England, 1994), p. 15.

p. 96　　*"Indeed, it was John Lanneau who 'at the first blow, severed the head of a Hessian.'"* Ibid., p. 15. Captain John P. Lanneau first assembled the Brooks troop in Greenville in 1861. During the reorganization of 1862, Leonard Williams was elected to replace Lanneau as captain.

p. 97　　*"In early May, Beauregard had 70,000 men there, many still recovering..."* James M. McPherson, *Battle Cry of Freedom,* (Oxford University Press, New York, NY, 1988), p. 416.

p. 98　　*"Some 7 or 8 from the Butler Guards..."* Leonard Williams letter dated May 20, 1862. The Butler Guards comprised Company B of the 2nd South Carolina Infantry Regiment, which was attached to Kershaw's Brigade. The Butler Guards were almost exclusively Greenville natives.

p. 99　　*"Lieut. J. P. Moore is at home now..."* Leonard Williams letter dated May 21, 1863. In the family newspaper clipping of the Roll of Brooks Troop the following entry appears: "First Sergeant J. P. Moore (elected 3$^{rd}$ lieutenant to succeed Alex McBee)."

p. 100　　*"...as Dr. Long, discharged, leaves this morning."* Leonard Williams letter dated May 24, 1862. In a newspaper clipping from *The Greenville Daily News* the following entry appears: "John T. Long , R. D. (with company first year)."

p. 101　　*"The plan for his bold counter stroke was to assault..."* Joseph P. Cullen, *The Peninsula Campaign 1862,* (The Stackpole Company, Harrisburg, PA, 1973), p. 54.

p. 101　　*"Assaulting columns were indecisive and disjointed, and attacks came in drips and drabs."* Maurice Matloff, *The Civil War: A Concise Military History of the War*

*Between the States,* (David McKay Company Inc., New York, NY), p. 45.

p. 101    *"If either side gained an edge it was the Union which suffered 1000 less casualties."* James M. McPherson, *Battle Cry of Freedom,* (Oxford University Press, New York, NY, 1988), p. 462.

p. 101    *"What a scene- the roads for miles, blocked with artillery and ambulances..."* E. Prioleau Henderson, *Autobiography of Arab,* (Fox Books, The Guild Bindery Press, 1997), p. 36.

p. 102    *"Probably no one in service carried more lead in his belly than Joseph E.Johnston."* Frank E. Vandiver, *Their Tattered Flags,* (Harper and Row, New York, NY, 1970), p. 138.

p. 104    *"You know he was wounded in the battle of the 31ˢᵗ."* Leonard Williams letter dated June 12, 1862. "The battle of the 31ˢᵗ" refers to Seven Pines.

p. 105    *"I am staying with a family named Randolph, a relation of the celebrated Jno. Randolphs, a very pleasant family."* Leonard Williams letter dated June 15, 1862. Sir John Randolph (1693-1737) was instrumental in the formation and growth of Colonial Williamsburg. When Williamsburg was incorporated, he served as one of its original alderman and later Attorney General. Randolph was a knighted member of The House of Burgesses and later served as burgess of the College of William and Mary.

p. 105    *"Captain Gary of Edgefield and Captain Henry Smith..."* Ibid. Capt. J. W. Gary from Pickens is listed in Brooks' *Butler and his Cavalry in the War of Secession,* p. 537. After the reorganization, J. Wister Gary is listed as Captain of Co. G, 2nd S.C. Cavalry.

p. 106    *"As superintendent at West Point..."* Lee became superintendent of West Point in 1852 and oversaw the development of future Union and Confederate Civil War officers.

p. 107    *"George McClellan cackled at the appointment, berating*

Lee as 'cautious and weak...'" Shelby Foote, McClellan quoted in *Civil War, Volume 1*, (Vintage, New York, NY, 1958), p. 465.

p. 107  *"To that end, he dispatched General J. E. B. Stuart, with twelve hundred cavalry..."* Ralph Selph Henry, *The Story of the Confederacy*, (Garden City Publishing, Garden City, NY, 1931), p. 152.

p. 108  *"With visions of heroic headlines in his head, Stuart rode out..."* James M. McPherson, *Battle Cry of Freedom*, (Oxford University Press, New York, NY, 1988), p. 463.

p. 108  *"...and tormented Union cavalry officers for four days."* One of those embarrassed was Jeb's own father-in-law, Philip St. George Cooke, a Virginian who remained loyal to the Union.

p. 108  *"The Old Captain remembered how disgruntled many of the Legion cavalrymen..."* E. Prioleau Henderson, *Autobiography of Arab*, (Fox Books, The Guild Bindery Press, 1997), p. 37.

p. 109  *"I hope you will send me by Mr. Greenfield or Robt. Adams the articles I wrote for [      ] the hat, shoes..."* Leonard Williams letter dated June 21, 1862. Brackets signify an undecipherable word.

p. 109  *"Our squadron will soon have an ascension of two companies, Capt. Lipscomb's..."* Ibid. In *Giant in Gray*, (p. 85), Manly Wade Wellman writes, "The Second South Carolina Cavalry was formed of several smaller units, the four troops of the old Legion, four more of Easley's Squadron, Captain A. H. Boykin's Rangers, and the Bonham Light Dragoons, Captain Thomas J. Lipscomb."

p. 110  *"I alas bought the cotton undershirts and a pair of cassimere pants."* Ibid. "Cassimere" was a common spelling of "cashmere", the soft material made from goat's wool. He uses "cassimere" again in his July 19, 1863 letter.

p. 110  *"He would move swiftly, with great strength and at great risk."* Bruce Catton, *This Hallowed Ground*, (Doubleday & Company, Garden City, NY, 1956), p. 139.

p. 113    *"The Hampton Legion Cavalry battalion was commanded by Captain Thomas E. Screven..."* Ron Field, *The Hampton Legion Part1: Regimental History,* (Design Folio, Gloucestershire, England, 1994), p. 19.

p. 113    *"Throughout nearly every day of these critical Richmond fights, one commander known for his poise..."* James M. McPherson, *Battle Cry of Freedom,* (Oxford University Press, New York, NY, 1988), p. 466.

p. 114    *"We received the command forward and immediately thereafter the command to charge."* Report Of Colonel James D. Nance, *O.R.'s,* Number 290, Chapter XXIII, p. 735.

## Chapter 8

p. 116    *"Ephraim was one of the 20,614 men Lee lost..."* Mark Grimsley, *Battle Chronicles of the Civil War: Robert E. Lee Volume 6,* (MacMillan Publishing, New York, NY, 1989), p. 122.

p. 116    *"On July 11, he plucked overall Federal command..."* Joseph P. Cullen, *The Peninsula Campaign 1862,* (The Stackpole Company, Harrisburg, PA, 1973), p. 176.

p. 118    *"I have come to you from the West, where we have always seen the backs of our enemies..."* Ralph Selph Henry, *The Story of the Confederacy,* (Garden City Publishing, Garden City, NY, 1931), p. 171.

p. 120    *"Pay was meager and never regular."* In 1861, the wage earned by a Confederate private was eleven dollars per month. In early 1864, his pay had risen to eighteen dollars and by midyear reached twenty dollars. As a captain, Williams earned $90 per month in 1864. Soldiers were supposed to be paid every two months, but often times more than half a year would pass between payroll issues. Williams and his fellow cavalrymen were paid in Confederate currency, which plummeted in value as the war wore on.

p. 120    *"The wounded in the late battles have died and are still dieing fearfully."* Leonard Williams letter dated July 14, 1862. "Dieing" is an incorrect spelling of "dying."

p. 121    *"We are attached temporarily to the Jeff Davis Legion, Col. Martin."* Ibid. Colonel William Martin commanded the Jeff Davis Legion.

p. 121    *"July 19ᵗʰ...I am again disappointed, no letters yet."* Leonard Williams letter dated July 19, 1862. This letter contains no location or salutation. The previous and following letter, however, cite "Camp in Hanover County" as the location, so it is assumed this is the location from which he wrote the letter of July 19, 1862.

p. 122    *"We have just heard of the brilliant performance of the Arkansas."* Ibid. The *Arkansas* was a Confederate ironclad that menaced the Union fleet on the Mississippi around Vicksburg. See *The Story of the Confederacy,* p. 165.

p. 125    *"I am very much in need of a hat..."* Leonard Williams letter dated July 24, 1862. The sky blue kepi cap with a dark blue band was the hat designed for the Confederate soldier but few were ever issued and even fewer were worn. Lighter felt hats and soft brimmed "slouch caps" were the order of the day. Caps and hats were often gathered up during and after skirmishes and Williams came away with one after the Battle of Jack's Shop in 1863.

p. 126    *"The braggart must be suppressed..."* Mark Grimsley, *Battle Chronicles of the Civil War, Robert E. Lee, Volume 6,* (MacMillan Publishing Company, New York, NY, 1989), p. 123.

p. 126    *"On August 9 at Cedar Mountain, he rode out in front of his troops..."* James M. McPherson, *Battle Cry of Freedom,* (Oxford University Press, New York, NY, 1988), p. 526.

p. 128    *"The battle of the 9ᵗʰ was a larger matter than we thought."* Leonard Williams letter dated August 19, 1862. "The battle of the 9th" refers to Cedar Creek.

p. 128    *"The weather now will soon begin to change and I expect a severe winter, the last few winters being so mild..."* Ibid.

The remainder of this letter is lost.

p. 129    *"to get out of this scrape himself...[If] Pope is beaten..."*
Roy C. Basler, ed., *The Collected Works of Abraham Lincoln, Volume 5*, (New Brunswick, NJ, 1952-5), p. 399, *McClellan to Ellen McClellan, McClellan Papers*, August 22, 1862.

p. 130    *"...McClellan and Burnside have baulked in effecting a junction with Pope."* Leonard Williams letter dated August 26, 1862. "Baulked" is a common spelling of "balked."

p. 131    *"'Surrender hell!' thundered Col. Gary."* *Charleston Daily Courier*, September 11, 1862, Column 3, p. 4. Ron Field, *The Hampton Legion Part 1: Regimental History*, (Design Folio, Gloucestershire, England, 1994), p. 22. Martin Witherspoon Gary was born in Cokesbury, South Carolina in 1831 and was educated at the South Carolina College and Harvard. He advocated secession as a Congressman and began the war as Captain of the Watson Guards in the Hampton Legion. Gary led his men in many battles and rose to the rank of Brigadier General. Near the end, as Lee was surrendering at Appomattox, Gary had no intentions of doing the same. Instead, he brazenly cut his way through Union lines and rode toward Greensboro where he took command of about 200 men. Gary's column then escorted a fleeing President Davis back to Cokesbury, where the Confederate cabinet met for one final time in Gary's mother's house. The bold fighter died in Edgefield on April 9, 1881, 16 years to the day after Lee's surrender.

p. 131    *"The exhausted Southern line bent and nearly collapsed..."* James M. McPherson, *Battle Cry of Freedom*, (Oxford University Press, New York, NY, 1988), p. 531.

p. 132    *"McClellan rode forward to meet his retreating army."* Ralph Selph Henry, *The Story of the Confederacy*, (Garden City Publishing, Garden City, NY, 1931), p. 179.

p. 132    *"I plan and work with all my might to bring the troops..."* Mark Grimsley, *Battle Chronicles of the Civil War, Robert E. Lee, Volume 6*, (MacMillen Publishing, New York, NY,

1989), p. 131.

p. 133    *"Our men have been nearly worn and punished out but now resting and eating Johnny Cake."* Leonard Williams letter of September 7, 1862. "Johnny Cake" is cornbread meal shaped into a flat patty and fried on a griddle or frying pan.

## Chapter 9

p. 136    *"We left the North Anna near Hanover C. H..."* Leonard Williams letter dated September 28, 1862. See Wellman's *Giant in Gray* for a more detailed account of the route and action on the way to Sharpsburg as Stuart and Hampton guarded passes, scouted McClellan's movements and screened Lee's advance.

p. 137    *"The skirmish in Frederick was most spirited..."* Major Henry B. McClellan, *I Rode With Jeb Stuart,* (Da Capo Press, New York, NY, 1994), p. 114. McClellan was the nephew and aide to the famous Confederate cavalry general.

p. 137    *"The Frederick fight was unremarkable in the grand scheme of things, but remarkable indeed was the extraordinary discovery made..."* Mark Grimsley, *Battle Chronicles of the Civil War, Robert E. Lee, Volume 6,* (MacMillan Publishing, New York, NY, 1989), p. 125.

p. 138    *"'Here', he boasted to one of his generals, 'is the paper which if I cannot...'"* John Gibbon, *Personal Recollections of the Civil War,* (New York, 1928), p. 73.

p. 138    *"The Cobb Legion this time engaged".* Leonard Williams letter dated September 28, 1862. The Cobb Legion was commanded by hard-fighting, 25-year old Georgian, Pierce Manning Butler Young.

p. 139    *"Joe Hooker tore down the Hagerstown Turnpike then slashed..."* William C. Davis, *The Battlefields of the Civil War,* (Salamander Books Ltd., London, England, 1990), p. 76.

p. 140　　*"Jackson, Longstreet, and later A. P. Hill fought until it was pitch black..."* James M. McPherson, *Battle Cry of Freedom,* (Oxford University Press, New York, NY, 1988), p. 544.

p. 140　　*"On September 23, President Abraham Lincoln issued..."* William A Frassanito, *Antietam: The Photographic Legacy of America's Bloodiest Day,* (Charles Scribner's Sons, New York, NY, 1978), p. 50.

p. 141　　*"I had to leave Douglas Holloway of my co. at Frederick."* Leonard Williams letter dated September 28, 1862. An undated clipping from *The Greenville Daily News* of the Roll of Brooks Troop contains the following entry: "Company went to Virginia about first of July 1861 and was joined by the following during year indicated...Holloway, D. G. 1862."

p. 143　　*"Stuart personally led the brigade as they splashed across the Potomac..."* Author unknown, *Cavalry Sketches in Brook's Confederacy,* (Columbia, 1912), p. 68.

p. 144　　*"Soldiers! You are about to engage in an enterprise..."* U. R. Brooks, *Butler and His Cavalry in the War of Secession,* (Guild Bindery Press, Germantown, TN, 1994), p. 80.

p. 145　　*"'Blackford, we are going to lose our rear guard.'"* Ibid., p. 82.

p. 145　　*"To the surprise of everyone, the mired and worn out Union horses..."* Major Henry B. McClellan, *I Rode With Jeb Stuart,* (Press of Morningside Bookshop, Dayton, OH, 1988), p. 159.

p. 147　　*"I am grateful at your accounts of her smartness and sociability and hope you will be able to restrain her temper within proper limits and mould her disposition..."* Leonard Williams letter dated October 9, 1862. "Mould" is an incorrect spelling of "mold."

p. 148　　*"Occasionally and far more frequently as the war wore on, some would flee..."* Bell Irvin Wiley, *The Life of Johnny Reb,* (Louisiana State University Press, Baton Rouge, LA,

1978), p. 89.

p. 149    *"He took advantage of the darkness to recross."* Leonard Williams letter dated October 21, 1862.

p. 150    *"'How are ye, boys?' called a Yankee late in October."* Manly Wade Wellman, *Giant in Gray,* (Press of Morningside Bookshop, Dayton, OH, 1988), p. 100.

p. 152    *"The young ladies made me a haversack and when I left filled it..."* Leonard Williams letter dated October 21, 1862. A "haversack" is a leather, cloth, or canvas bag about 12 inches square with a shoulder strap. Soldiers employed the often rancid smelling bags to carry utensils and food. Grease and juices from left over meat would rot the haversacks, which had to be replaced often.

p. 153    *"There were feisty showdowns at Berryville, Flint Hill, and Barbee's Crossroads."* E. Prioleau Henderson, *Autobiography of Arab,* (Fox Books, The Guild Bindery Press, 1997), p. 53. Henderson states the location for the Skirmish as "Barber's Crossroads." The correct name is "Barbee's Crossroads."

p. 154    *"At the skirmish at Barbee's Crossroads, a Confederate private named Eldrid Simkins..."* Ibid., p. 53.

p. 155    *"'Stand by General Burnside as you have stood by me and all will be well.'"* James M. McPherson, *Battle Cry of Freedom,* (Oxford University Press, New York, NY, 1988), p. 570.

p. 155    *"It would be an arduous one full of unexpected twists and turns..."* Ralph Selph Henry, *The Story of the Confederacy,* (Garden City Publishing, Garden City, NY, 1931), p. 206.

p. 157    *"This time the leader of the brash expeditions wasn't Jeb Stuart, it was his second in command, Wade Hampton..."* Wade Hampton rose to the rank of brigadier general but unlike other high-ranking officers and West Pointers, he did so without any formal military training before the war.

p. 157    *"He was more than commonly large and strong by nature..."* Manly Wade Wellman, *Giant in Gray,* (Press of Morningside Bookshop, Dayton, OH, 1988), p. 20.

p. 157      *"He would pursue bears with a pack of hounds."* Ibid., p. 84. Hampton's record of "bears slayed by hand" still stands in South Carolina. Perhaps if former Chicago Bear defensive tackle William "The Refrigerator" Perry, a resident of Aiken, SC, would take up the pursuit, he just might break Hampton's record!

p. 158      *"Stuart seemed a god of battles to his comrades, and perhaps to himself."* Ibid., p. 84.

p. 158      *"Hampton often sent them off behind enemy lines under the leadership of Sergeants Bill Mickler and Jack Schoolbred."* Ibid., p. 101. Both sergeants were members of the famed "Iron Scouts."

p. 160      *"Burnside was on the march to Fredericksburg..."* William C. Davis, *The Battlefields of the Civil War,* (Salamander Books Ltd, London, England, 1990), p. 93.

p. 163      *"Fog veiled the plain in the early morning hours as many divisions of Federal troops..."* Bruce Catton, *This Hallowed Ground,* (Doubleday and Company, Garden City, New York, NY, 1956), p. 189.

p. 163      *"It is well,"* he said *"that we know how terrible war really is..."* William C. Davis, *The Battlefields of the Civil War,* (Salamander Books Ltd., London, England, 1990), p. 103.

p. 163      *"A chicken could not live on that field when we open fire on it."* Mark Grimsley, *Battle Chronicles of the Civil War, Robert E. Lee, Volume 6,* (MacMillan Publishing Company, New York, NY, 1989), p. 128.

p. 163      *"Swarming out of the Fredericksburg streets, Burnside's men..."* Bruce Catton, *This Hallowed Ground,* (Doubleday and Company, Garden City, NY, 1956), p. 189.

p. 163      *"His name was Sgt. Richard Kirkland of the 2nd South Carolina..."* Robert Paul Jordan, *The Civil War,* (The National Geographic Society, New York, NY, 1969), p. 108.

p. 164      *"One overwhelmed mother was found in her cottage surrounded by bodies..."* Ralph Selph Henry, *The Story of the Confederacy,* (Garden City Publishing, Garden City,

NY, 1931), p. 213.

p. 164    *"'We had really accomplished nothing', Lee later lamented."* Mark Grimsley, *Battle Chronicles of the Civil War, Robert E. Lee,* (MacMillan Publishing Company, New York, NY), p. 128.

p. 166    *"He said if the Major knew of it that we were setting by the fire..."* Leonard Williams letter dated December 20, 1862. When he speaks of "the Major," Colonel Black is referring to William Laval, Anna's father.

## Chapter 10

p. 171    *"An enthusiastic band of Union musicians..."* Robert Paul Jordan, *The Civil War,* (The National Geographic Society, New York, NY, 1969), p. 111. Perhaps the most colorful of all Confederate musicians was "Sweeny," Jeb Stuart's sidekick who it is said actually strummed his banjo during skirmishes. In the evenings in camp, Sweeny and his merry band of players were nearly always regaling Stuart and his staff. Both Henry McClellan's and W. W. Blackford's books mention Sweeny.

p. 172    *"Northern privates ate little more than salt pork and hardtack..."* Hardtack was a biscuit, bread, or cracker made with only flour and water. Quartermasters distributed hardtack in half-inch-thick, three-inch-square crackers that the men called "teeth dullers" because of their legendary hardness.

p. 173    *"Genl's Hampton and Stuart have taken about 10 men from every company and are now beyond Dumfrees."* Leonard Williams letter dated January 1, 1863. The correct spelling of "Dumfrees" is actually "Dumfries."

p. 173    *"Butler was leading a detachment of 150 men toward Bacon Race Church..."* U. R. Brooks, *Butler and His Cavalry in the War of Secession,* (Guild Bindery Press, Germantown, TN, 1994), p. 88.

p. 174     *"I sent by Harvey Gaillard a hundred dollar note..."* Leonard Williams letter dated January 1, 1863. A Roll of Brooks Troop contains two "Gaillards." S. S. Gaillard is listed as a first lieutenant before the reorganization and J. H. Gaillard is listed as a private.

p. 175     *"Stonewall Jackson's headquarters were below Fredericksburg..."* E. Prioleau Henderson, *Autobiography of Arab,* (Fox Books, Guild Bindery Press, 1997), p. 56.

p. 175     *"So did crooked merchants filled with goods and greed called sutlers..."* Sutlers were merchants who followed armies around in order to sell provisions out of their wagons. While some were honest purveyors, many more were not.

p. 175     *"Exorbitant fees for ginger cakes, half- moon pies, dried fruit..."* Bell Irvin Wiley, *The Life of Johnny Reb,* (Louisiana State University Press, Baton Rouge, LA, 1978), p. 100.

p. 177     *"Murfreesboro was a brutal affair..."* This battle, also known as Stones River, took place from Dec. 31, 1862 to Jan. 2, 1863.

p. 177     *"Thirteen thousand of Bragg's screaming men descended upon the Yankees..."* Shelby Foote, *The Civil War, Vol. 2,* (Vintage, New York, NY, 1963), p. 87.

p. 177     *"Old Rosy' was at his tenacious best..."* James M. McPherson, *Battle Cry of Freedom,* (Oxford University Press, New York, NY, 1988), p. 580.

p. 178     *"This was the second time in only three short months..."* Ibid., p. 582.

p. 179     *"I sleep with Sergt. Beattie, Lieuts. Perry and Stokes..."* Leonard Williams letter dated January 8, 1863. In Dr. M. B. Harrison's *Roll of Brooks Troop,* Second Sergeant Wm. Beattie, First Lieutenant W. H. Perry, and Second Lieutenant E. F. Stokes are listed.

p. 179     *"We have plenty of blanketts..."* Ibid. "Blanketts" was a common spelling of the word "blankets".

p. 179     *"I used to when a boy almost shed tears in reading about*

*Marion's men dining on potatoes...* " Ibid., "Marion" refers to famed South Carolina General Francis Marion, the "Swamp Fox," who fought against the British in the Revolutionary War.

p. 179     *"Bragg's fight in Tenn. has turned out as have all the western battles..."* Ibid. The battle in Tennessee is a reference to Murfreesboro (Stones River).

p. 181     *"No less than four generals in the 6ᵗʰ corps went directly to Lincoln..."* James M. McPherson, *Battle Cry of Freedom,* (Oxford University Press, New York, NY, 1988), p. 584.

p. 181     *"All are [          ]."* Leonard Williams letter dated January 9, 1863. Word is undecipherable.

p. 181     *"...except the purpose of the French Emperor to recognize the Confederacy."* Ibid., The French emperor at the time was Louie Napoleon.

p. 182     *"Wheels were stuck up to their axles..."* David Donald, *Divided We Fought,* (The MacMillan Company, New York, NY, 1953), p. 148.

p. 183     *"Our scouts report that Genl. Slocum...& also that Milroy..."* Leonard Williams letter dated January 23, 1863. General Henry Slocum commanded the Union XII Corps at Chancellorsville. Federal Brigadier General Robert H. Milroy suffered a disastrous defeat at Winchester in June of 1863 and was brought before a court of inquiry on charges of cowardice. The "Gray Eagle" was acquitted of all charges and resigned from the army in 1865.

p. 184     *"The very sight of the name 'Calhoun Sparks'..."* Sparks was a famed member of the "Iron Scouts" and since he too mustered in at Greenville, he must have been at least an acquaintance of Leonard Williams.

p. 184     *"Mind, I am going on a running, not a fighting trip this afternoon..."* E. Prioleau Henderson, *Autobiography of Arab,* (Fox Books, Guild Bindery Press, 1997), p. 77.

p. 187     *"On one dark night early in 1863, Isaac Curtis..."* U. R. Brooks, *Butler and His Cavalry in the War of Secession,*

(Guild Bindery Press, Germantown, TN, 1994), p. 90.

p. 189      *"...by one of Capt. Westfield's men who is entitled to a discharge..."* Leonard Williams' letter dated February 5, 1863. In the *Roll of Brooks Troop*, Captain John Westfield is listed as the Captain of Company E, 2nd S.C. Cavalry.

p. 193      *"I overtook Capts. Clark and Screven..."* Leonard Williams letter dated March 22, 1863. In *Butler and His Cavalry in the War of Secession*, Brooks notes that T. H. Clark from Edgefield was Captain of Company I in the 2nd S.C. Cav. and Thomas E. Screven from Beaufort was Captain of Company B in the 2nd. S. C. Cav. In Williams' letters and other books, Screven is also spelled "Scriven."

p. 194      *"He sent corrupt quartermasters packing, upgraded rations..."* James M. McPherson, *Battle Cry of Freedom*, (Oxford University Press, New York, NY, 1988), p. 585.

p. 195      *"...diseases ranging from glanders and farcy to distemper and hoof rot."* Glanders is a usually fatal equine disease caused by bacteria and communicable to other mammals including humans. Swollen lymph nodes, skin ulcers and nasal discharge were the common symptoms. Farcy is a chronic form of glanders that affects the skin.

p. 196      *"...and send them by Sergt. Benson who is at home on furlough."* Leonard Williams letter dated March 31, 1863. In the *Roll of Brooks Troop,* W. K. Benson is listed as Fourth Sergeant, Commissary of Company K.

p. 197      *"It is shelled corn and perhaps you had better perhaps get 2 barrels and [          ].* Ibid. Bracketed word is undecipherable.

p. 198      *"If we can baffle them in their various designs this year..."* Robert E. Lee to his wife, April 19, 1863, Clifford Dowdey and Louis H. Manarin eds., *The Wartime Papers of R. E. Lee,* (New York, NY, 1961), p. 438.

p. 199      *"Three days prior to writing that letter, Charleston Harbor was shelled..."* Union Rear Admiral Samuel DuPont began a series of attacks and sieges with eight ironclads. Beauregard's Fort Sumter defenses had been reinforced, however, sinking one ship and disabling two more. DuPont withdrew.

p. 201      *"May God have mercy on General Lee, for I will have none..."* William C. *Davis, The Battlefields of the Civil War,* (Salamander Books Ltd., London, England, 1990), p. 126.

p. 201      *"First, General George Stoneman would lead 10,000..."* David Donald, *Divided We Fought,* (The MacMillan Company, New York, NY, 1953), p. 157. Donald David adds that Hooker told Stoneman, " Let your watchword be, fight, fight, fight. If you can not cut out from [the enemy's] columns large slices, the general desires that you will not fail to take small ones." Stoneman's raid was largely ineffective as little damage was inflicted. He was relieved of his command on July 18,1863 for seven months and later given command of the XXIII Corps under Sherman.

p. 201      *"Our enemy must ingloriously fly, declared Hooker..."* O. R.'s, Series 1, Vol. 25, Part 1, p.171.

p. 204      *"The night before, while seated on a couple of rickety old cracker boxes..."* Mark Grimsley, *Battle Chronicles of the Civil War: Robert E. Lee, Volume 6,*(MacMillan Publishing Co., New York, NY, 1989), p. 130.

p. 204      *"Early was still outnumbered..."* James M. McPherson, *Battle Cry of Freedom,* (Oxford University Press, New York, NY, 1988), p. 641.

p. 205      *"Suddenly, a shell struck one of the porch pillars..."* Ralph Selph Henry, *The Story of the Confederacy,* (Garden City Publishing, Garden City, NY, 1931), p. 250.

p. 205      *"He lay between the lines on the edge of a road..."* Ibid., p. 248.

p. 205      *"No, no,' he murmured. 'let us pass over the river..."* Ibid., p. 251.

p. 206      *"I have heard of but few of the casualties at the fight at Fredericksburg."* Leonard Williams letter dated May 11, 1863. The fight at Fredericksburg refers to Chancellorsville.

p. 207     *"It was a brilliant achievement of Forrest's near Rome, Georgia."* Ibid. Confederate Commander Nathan Bedford Forrest cut Grant's communications by tearing up railroads and telegraph lines.

p. 207     *"'My God! My God!' lamented Lincoln..."* Ibid., p.137.

p. 208     *"The 17,000 union casualties amounted to roughly fifteen percent..."* William C. Davis, *The Battlefields of the Civil War,* (Salamander Books Ltd., London, England, 1990), p. 137.

p. 210     *"Dear Henry...I received your favor through the hand of Ct. Lanneau..."* Leonard Williams letter to older brother Henry dated May 16, 1863. This letter was actually found in order with the rest of his letters to Anna. Williams' daughter Julia G. Williams, ardent caretaker of the family history, was most likely to have saved it. Twice in the letter he refers to "Fredericksburg," which is actually Chancellorsville.

p. 211     *"I am anxious to see the progress and result of Vallandigham's trial."* Ibid., Burnside had Vallandigham arrested at his Dayton home for disloyalty to the Union. He was found guilty but Lincoln commuted his sentence from imprisonment to exile in Canada.

p. 212     *"McGowan's brigade suffered 452 casualties. The 14th had 8 killed..."* Casualty numbers provided by Jim Fox, historian and bookseller, Camden, SC.

p. 213     *"If you can get any Linsey..."* Leonard Williams letter dated May 19, 1863. "Linsey" or "linsey-woolsey" is a coarse fabric woven from linen or cotton with coarse wool filling.

p. 215     *"To be sure, the sight of so many magnificent horses and men..."* Lt. Col. W. W. Blackford served under Stuart. In his work, *War Years with Jeb Stuart,* (p. 212), he provided this vivid, eyewitness description of the first grand review at Brandy Station. " ...there were nearly a hundred horsemen, all officers, dashing through the field. Then the lines broke into a column of squadrons and marched by at a walk, making the entire circuit; then they came by at a trot, taking the gallop a hundred yards before reaching the reviewing stand; and then the "charge" at full speed past the reviewing stand, yelling just as they do in a real charge, and brandishing their sabers over their heads. The effect was thrilling, even to us…"

p. 215     *"Eight thousand cavalry passed under the eye of their commander…"* Eric J. Wittenberg, *Brandy Station Seminar, Part 1,* www.gdg.org/brandy.html.

p. 215     *"It was observed that General Stuart's personal charms never showed to better advantage…"* Ibid. unnumbered.

p. 216     *"There is no doubt Grant's army has been severely cut up by Kirby Smith."* Leonard Williams letter dated June 8, 1863. General Edmund Kirby Smith harassed Grant whenever possible and commanded his own virtual empire in western Mississippi. Smith was the Trans-Mississippi Dept. commander from March of 1863 to May of 1865 and led the last Confederate operational unit to surrender.

p. 219     *"The Second South Carolina Cavalry, commanded by M. C. Butler…"* Official Report of Major Thomas J. Lipscomb, June 11,1863, O. R.'s, Number 570 entry.

p. 219     *"A few minutes later, Frank Hampton finally arrived with 36 men."* U. R. Brooks, *Butler and His Cavalry in the War of Secession,* (Guild Bindery Press, Germantown, TN, 1994), p. 165.

p. 219     *"Just as he was about to close back and unite with the 4th Virginia…"* Major Henry B. McClellan, *I Rode With Jeb Stuart,* (DaCapo Press, New York, NY, 1994), p. 289.

p. 220     *"In a moment they were swept to the side of the road…"* Ibid., p. 289.

p. 220     *"His big, handsome face was slashed terribly by a saber."* Manly Wade Wellman, *Giant in Gray,* (Press of Morningside Bookshop, Dayton, OH, 1988), p. 109.

p. 220     *"While panic apparently possessed the 4th Virginia Regiment…"* Major Henry B. McClellan, *I Rode With Jeb Stuart,* (Da Capo Press, New York, NY, 1994), p. 289.

p. 220    *"Our horses were facing in opposite directions, mine facing the enemy..."* U. R. Brooks, *Butler and His Cavalry in the War of Secession,* (Guild Bindery Press, Germantown, TN, 1994), p. 155.

p. 221    *"We went to Captain Farley...He was very cool..."* Major Henry B. McClellan, *I Rode With Jeb Stuart,* (Da Capo Press, New York, NY, 1994), p. 292.

p. 222    *"The 2nd South Carolina Cavalry had single-handedly halted..."* W. W. Blackford, *War Years with Jeb Stuart,* (reprint, Scribner, New York, NY, 1945), p. 227.

p. 222    *"The Rebels were going to have a review of their cavalry that day..."* Eric J. Wittenberg, *Brandy Station Seminar, Lesson 6: The Aftermath,* www.gdg.org/brandy.html, p. 1.

p. 222    *"This battle...made the Federal cavalry..."* Ibid., p. 1.

p. 223    *"Nearly all our forces and perhaps 15,000 Yankee cavalry were engaged..."* Leonard Williams letter dated June 11, 1863. Actually, about 12,000 Union cavalry faced 10,000 Confederate cavalry on June 9th at Brandy Station.

p. 224    *"I had the misfortune to lose one of my own, Jno Ligon..."* Ibid. *The Roll of Brooks Troop* contains the name John T. Ligon (private).

p. 225    *"Genl.Hampton, with his brigade, was near Brandy and I have no doubt rescued the day."* Ibid. Hampton's men did indeed play a key role as a charge supported by Hart's Battery helped scatter Gregg's force from Fleetwood Hill in the decisive waning moments of the battle.

## Chapter 11

p. 226    *"Vincent's brigade, over 1,500 strong..."* Major Henry B. McClellan, *I Rode With Jeb Stuart,* (DaCapo Press, New York, NY, 1994), p. 308.

p. 227    *"Well," observed Hampton soberly, 'I am afraid Hart has lost a gun this time..."* Manly Wade Wellman, *Giant in Gray,* (Press of Morningside Bookshop, Dayton, OH, 1988), p. 110.

p. 227 *"One was Angus P. Brown of the 1st South Carolina..."*
U. R. Brooks, *Butler and His Cavalry in the War of Secession*, (Guild Bindery Press, Germantown, TN, 1994), p. 178. Brown was the captain of Company K, 1st S.C. Cavalry. In Brooks' *Butler and His Cavalry in the War of Secession* (p. 496), Captain Brown writes of the horrid conditions and cruel treatment he and his fellow prisoners received at Point Lookout, Maryland, the same facility where Leonard's brother James was housed before he was paroled.

p. 227 *"'First North Carolina, follow me!' he thundered..."*
Manly Wade Wellman, *Giant in Gray,* (Press of Morningside Bookshop, Dayton, OH, 1988), p. 111.

p. 227 *"As I reached the ditch, I nearly rode upon a Federal dragoon..."* U. R. Brooks, *Butler and His Cavalry in the War of Secession,* (Guild Bindery Press, Germantown, TN, 1994), p. 181.

p. 228 *"Two troopers from Leonard's company were not as fortunate..."* Ibid., p. 177.

p. 228 *"We had the most terrific day's work of it on the 21ˢᵗ."*
Leonard Williams letter dated June 24, 1863. That work was done at Upperville.

p. 228 *"Joel Ketchum, slightly wounded in the leg..."* Ibid., Privates Joel and Charles Ketchum are listed in the *Roll of Brooks Troop.*

p. 229 *"Soldiers were surviving on quarter rations..."* James M. McPherson, *Battle Cry of Freedom,* (Oxford University Press, New York, NY, 1988), p. 635.

p. 229 *"It was a bold undertaking that fueled Southern hopes..."*
T. C. DeLeon, *Four Years in Rebel Capitals*, (The Gossip Printing Company, Mobile, AL, 1890), p. 253.

p. 231 *"I think Genl. Lee's army can go through the W. S. or wherever Genl. Lee may wish to carry it."* Leonard Williams letter dated June 30, 1863. "W. S. might be an abbreviation of "Western States..

p. 232 *"On the 30th of June, Stuart, bogged down by his captured trains...*" W. W. Blackford, *War Years with Jeb Stuart,* (reprint, Scribners, New York, NY, 1945), p. 225.

p. 232     *"Two days later, Custer confronted Stuart, Hampton..."* In *I Rode with Jeb Stuart* (p. 331), Henry B. McCLellan provides Wade Hampton's account of the fighting at Hunterstown. "General Hampton states that after some skirmishing the enemy attempted to charge, which was met in front by the Cobb Legion, and on either flank by the Phillips Legion and the 2nd South Carolina Cavalry."

p. 234     *"We...moved forward...and as soon as the brigade commenced ascending the hill..."* Report of Colonel Abner Perrin 14th S. C. V. I., O. R.'s, Number 557, Chapter XXXIX, p. 661.

p. 237     *"Still dazed and smarting from a nasty head wound..."* Manly Wade Wellman, *Giant in Gray*, (Press of Morningside Bookshop, Dayton, OH, 1988), p. 118.

p. 237     *"Row upon row of galloping horses bore down,..."* Ibid., p. 119.

p. 237     *"Columnhead drove into columnhead at a gallop..."* Ibid., p. 119.

p. 238     *"At one point Hampton was separated from the rest of his force..."* Edward L. Wells, *Hampton and His Cavalry in '64*, (The B. F. Johnson Publishing Company, Richmond, VA, 1907), p. 75.

p. 238     *"General, general, they are too many for us..."* U. R. Brooks, *Cavalry Sketches in Brooks' Confederacy,* (Columbia, S. C., 1912), p. 175.

p. 238     *"The fighting was hand to hand now..."* Major Henry B. McClellan, *I Rode With Jeb Stuart,* (DaCapo Press, New York, NY, 1994), p. 340.

p. 238     *"Scattered over the fields adjacent to the Rummel barn..."* Ibid, p. 346.

p. 239     *"'General, shall I advance?' asked Pickett..."* Ralph Selph Henry, *The Story of the Confederacy,* (Garden City Publishing, Garden City, NY, 1931), p. 282.

p. 239     *"Stop Pickett immediately and replenish your*

*ammunition...* " Ibid., p. 282.

p. 241   *"'It's all my fault,' said Lee as he rode among his men..."* Clifford Dowdey, *Death of a Nation: The Story of Lee and His Men at Gettysburg,* (New York, NY, 1958), p. 341, Shelby Foote, *The Civil War, Volume II,* (New York, NY, 1958), p. 567.

p. 241   *"One brief month ago we were apparently at the point of success..."* John B. Jones, *A War Clerk's Diary,* ed. Earl Schenck Miers, (New York, NY, 1958), p. 238; Betty L. Mitchell, *Edmund Ruffin: A Biography,* (Bloomington, 1981), p. 231; Frank E. Vandiver ed., *The Civil War Diary of General Josiah Gorgas,* (University, AL, 1947), p. 50.

p. 241   *"In a torrential downpour, a seventeen-mile long procession..."* Ralph Selph Henry, *The Story of the Confederacy,* (Garden City Publishing, Garden City, NY, 1931), p. 286. In *War Years with Jeb Stuart* (p. 235), W. W. Blackford wrote, "In crossing even on horseback the cavalry got almost as wet as the infantry, and they were worse off afterwards, for they had to sit in wet saddles..."

p. 242   *"I visited the battleground...when the evidences of the horrid carnage..."* Sophronia Bucklin, *Vast Sea of Misery,* http://www.cee.indiana.edu/gopher/Turner-Adventure-Learning?Gettys.../Vast-Sea-of-miser, March 29, 1999.

p. 245   *"Dear Annie...Yours of the 24th was received..."* Letter dated July 14, 1863 from "Aunt L. M." to niece Anna Olivia Laval Williams. "M" could possibly stand for "Martin" as the last name is prevalent in the letter. Bracketed word is undecipherable.

p. 247   *"For seven straight days, the enemy demonstrated near Hedgesville forcing back Baker's Brigade..."* Major Henry B. McClellan, *I Rode With Jeb Stuart,* ( DaCapo Press, New York, NY, 1994), p. 369. "Baker's Brigade" was formerly commanded by Hampton, who was away recuperating from his wounds.

p. 248   *"We hear the sadness of the fall of Vicksburg, Port Hudson, and the probable fall of Charleston."* Leonard Williams letter dated July 19, 1863. Vicksburg surrendered on July 4, 1863. Port Hudson, 240 miles south of Vicksburg on the river, surrendered almost immediately after. Charleston held out until February of 1865 when the Confederates abandoned Fort Sumter.

p. 248     *"Dum spiro spero..."* Ibid., "Dum spiro spero" is the latin form of the South Carolina state motto. Its translation is "While I breathe, I hope."

p. 249     *"At Chambersburg, I was superceded in my Colonelcy by Maj. Screven."* Leonard Williams letter dated July 29, 1863. Williams never attained the rank of colonel but he may be referring to the fact that he commanded over 300 men at the time.

p. 250     *"Captain Nesbit, of the 1ˢᵗ Regt. and myself, each with about 50 men..."* Ibid., In Brooks' *Butler and his Cavalry in the War of Secession,* Niles Nesbit is listed as a major in the 1st S.C. Cavalry while Miles Nesbit is listed as Captain of Company B in the 1st S.C. Cavalry.

p. 250     *"...and held them in check until a regiment of infantry came to our relief."* Ibid. The "regiment of infantry" he refers to was more than likely dismounted cavalry.

p. 250     *"I regret our failure to rout and destroy Hooker's army."* Ibid. "Hooker's army" was now commanded by General George Meade. This change in Federal command prior to Gettysburg was apparently unknown to Captain Williams.

p. 251     *"I recd yesterday all your letters by Beattie and Thompson..."* Ibid., Second Sergeant Wm. Beattie is listed as "wounded and disabled at Pony Mountain" on the *Roll of Brooks Troop.* Before the reorganization in 1862, W. H. Thompson was     listed as a Fourth Corporal on the roll.

p. 252     *"On the 1st day of August, the enemy crossed at the railroad bridge..."* E. Prioleau Henderson, *Autobiography of Arab,* (Fox Books, Guild Bindery Press, 1997), p. 119. The battle termed "The Second Battle of Brandy Station" fought on August 1, 1863 is in actuality "The Third Battle of Brandy Station." Most refer to it as the "second" in books, obituaries, etc. so I did the same for uniformity.

p. 253      *"I regret to tell you Lieut. Williams...Cunningham and Day...Cooley and Thornburg...Campbell Williams and Stephen Smith..."* Leonard Williams letter dated August 2, 1863. In the *Roll of Brooks Troop,* Third Lieutenant Pierce B. Williams (no relation) is listed as "killed 1st August, 1862." The year of his death should be cited as 1863. Privates John and Samuel Cunningham, Private Elias Day, Fourth Sergeant N. W. Cooley, Private J. W. Thornburg, Privates T. B., George, and S. C. Williams, and Privates E. C. and W. S. Smith are listed on the roll. This letter contained no closing.

p. 254      *"After long and trying marches, endured with the fortitude..."* General Order Number 76, From His Excellency Jefferson Davis, O. R.'s Volume XXXIX, The Gettysburg Campaign, p. 301.

## Chapter 12

p. 258      *"I think you had better dsy your white cow..."* Leonard Williams letter dated August 8, 1863. "Dsy" is an abbreviated form of "destroy", as he mentions having the cow fattened then killed in the following sentence.

p. 258      *"I suppose you have heard of the death of Capt. Pulliam..."* Ibid. Captain Robert C. Pulliam was a member of the 2nd South Carolina Infantry Regiment at Gettysburg. Pulliam was killed during the second day of battle near the Peach Orchard. In *Gettysburg: The Second Day,* (p. 254), (University of North Carolina Press, Chapel Hill, NC, 1987), Harry W. Pfanz included the following passage, which quotes Pvt. John Coxe of the 2nd S.C.V.I. "O the awful deathly surging sounds of those little black balls as they flew by us, through us, between our legs, and over us! Captain Robert C. Pulliam was one of those killed by this hail of pellets." A memorial ribbon from the U. C. V. at "Camp Pulliam" was presented to the Williams family upon the death of Leonard.

p. 259      *"Wade Hampton and Fitz Lee were both promoted to Major General..."* Manly Wade Wellman, *Giant in Gray,* (Press of Morningside Bookshop, Dayton, OH, 1988), p. 129.

p. 260      *"M. C. Butler, the South Carolinian; Pierce Young, the Georgian; and Tom Rosser, the Virginian..."* Ibid., p. 142.

p. 261      *"It is believed Genl. Hampton is promoted to Maj. Genl. and Gen. Hood is Lieut. Genl. over all the cavalry."* Leonard Williams letter dated August 13, 1863. General Jeb Stuart remained commander of all cavalry during the reorganization. After Stuart's death in 1864, Wade Hampton would assume overall command of the Confederate cavalry.

p. 262      *"The horse is, in active campaign, saddled on an average about fifteen hours out of the twenty four..."* Charles Francis Adams, *About the Cavalry Horse,* Website of the 17th Pa. Volunteer Cavalry Co. E. www.geocities.com/~mando2802/horse.html.

p. 263      *"I have hopes Charleston will stand against all their attacks even if Fort Sumpter..."* Leonard Williams letter dated August 18, 1863. "Sumpter" is a misspelling of "Sumter" and Williams continues to use this spelling of the famous Charleston fort throughout his letters home to Anna. The fort was abandoned on February 18, 1865, the day after the occupation of Columbia. On April 14, 1865, the stars and stripes were raised over the fort once more by Maj. Gen. Robert Anderson who had lowered the flag just four years earlier.

p. 265      *"The camp newspaper, The Rapid Ann, written in pen and pencil by the soldiers..."* Ralph Selph Henry, *The Story of the Confederacy,* (Garden City Publishing, Garden City, NY, 1931), p. 300.

p. 266      *"What's the matter here? What's all this confusion about? he asked..."* Ibid., p. 301.

p. 267      *"Mr. Whitmire, Uncle Adam, your mistress and everybody who writes..."* Leonard Williams letter to Ned dated August

22, 1863. "Ned" was Williams' most reliable house servant and quite possibly the oldest. "Your mistress" refers to Anna, who counted on Ned constantly in light of her husband's prolonged absences throughout the war. The letter contained no closing or perhaps the remainder of the letter was lost.

p. 272    *"I am now wearing a wool hat of the commonest kind looking pretty seedy, such as Steve used to wear."* Leonard Williams letter dated September 5, 1863. "Steve" refers to his young house servant Steve who was a constant source of stress to Williams. Apparently Steve was a shirker in the eyes of his master and required Anna's and Ned's constant supervision.

p. 273    *"Out in Tennessee, prospects were darker still as Rosecrans..."* James M. McPherson, *Battle Cry of Freedom,* (Oxford University Press, New York, NY, 1988), p. 670.

p. 273    *"Lee had no choice but to dispatch Longstreet and 12,000 of his sorely needed men..."* Ibid., p. 671.

p. 274    *"On September 13, Meade's army, supported by a large cavalry force, advanced toward Culpeper County..."* Major Henry B. McClellan, *I Rode With Jeb Stuart,* (DaCapo Press, New York, NY, 1994), p. 373.

p. 274    *"We were in another severe fight on the 13th."* Leonard Williams letter dated September 15, 1863. In *War Years with Jeb Stuart* (p. 238), W. W. Blackford writes, "On the morning of the 13th Stuart received orders from General Lee to make a reconnaissance towards Catlett's Station on the Orange and Alexandria R. R. He immediately sent Lomax on to Auburn..., and Stuart followed soon after with seven guns under Beckham and two brigades of cavalry, Funsten's and Gordon's." Williams' squadron was attached to Gordon's Brigade.

p. 275    *"That night, rescue workers tripped over corpses while searching for the wounded..."* Ralph Selph Henry, *The Story of the Confederacy,* (Garden City Publishing, Garden

City, NY, 1931), p. 309.

p. 275    *"At the Battle of Chickamauga, Confederate General Braxton Bragg lost 20,000 killed..."* John S. Blay, *The Civil War: A Pictorial Profile,* (Bonanza Books, New York, NY, 1958), p. 218.

p. 277    *"Gibbs of my company was sent out with another man..."* Leonard Williams letter dated September 19, 1863. The *Roll of Brooks Troop* lists S. S. Gibbs as First Corporal before the reorganization.

p. 277    *"I understand Smith and Campbell Williams, who were taken on the 1ˢᵗ August are held with 20 other South Carolinians as hostages for the rendition of the negroe prisoners taken at Charleston and now in Gov. Bonham's hands."* Ibid., "Gov. Bonham" is General M. L. Bonham, commander of the first brigade to leave South Carolina for the war. He was later governor of SC.

p. 278    *"Buford took 2,500 troopers and headed down the old Blue Ridge Turnpike."* The Battle of Jack's Shop occurred at what is today Rochelle, Virginia. A written account of the battle is found in McClellan's *I Rode With Jeb Stuart,* (p. 374). McClellan makes no mention of Devin's force and cites Wilcox (not Trimble) as the commander of Stuart's supporting infantry. I based my account on an interview and personal tour provided by an esteemed local historian. Stuart made no official report of the action.

p. 281    *"Jos. Knotts was severely wounded in the neck."* Leonard Williams letter dated September 25, 1863. In the *Roll of Brooks Troop,* Private J. E. Knotts is listed as "wounded at Jack's Shops" [sic].

p. 282    *"My squadron behaved gallantly and recd the commendations of our col. and also Col. Gordon commanding..."* Leonard Williams letter dated September 25,1863. "Our col." is Colonel P. M. B. Young who was commanding Butler's Brigade. Colonel Gordon is Colonel James B. Gordon. Williams also received a personal commendation from Stuart himself shortly after the clash at Jack's Shop. An account of that honor bestowed upon Williams and his squadron is included in the epilogue.

p. 286    *"Meanwhile, Lomax had discovered a large body of Federals..."* Francis Trevelyan Miller, *The Photographic History of the Civil War,* (A. S. Barnes & Co., New York, NY, 1957), p. 92. Brigadier General L. L. Lomax commanded a cavalry brigade in Fitz Lee's Division.

p. 287    *"Soon after we captured the prisoners..."* E. Prioleau Henderson, *Autobiography of Arab,* (Fox Books, Guild Bindery Press, 1997), p. 122.

p. 287    *"A part of my programme is commenced."* Leonard Williams letter dated October 8, 1863. "Programme" was a common spelling of "program."

p. 288    *"Tell Julia and Susan, they must stay with you..."* Ibid. "Julia" and "Susan" are Anna's sisters.

p. 289    *"The enemy's picket at Russell's Ford was driven back..."* Major Henry B. McClellan, *I Rode With Jeb Stuart,* (DaCapo Press, New York, NY, 1994), p. 376.

p. 289    *"On October 13, the usually steady General A. P. Hill..."* Mark Grimsley, *Battle Chronicles of the Civil War, Robert E. Lee, Volume 6,* (MacMillan Publishing Company, New York, NY, 1989), p. 138.

p. 289    *"When Lee's cannon opened fire, Stuart's men sprung into action."* Ibid. p. 394.

p. 290    *"We have just concluded another arduous campaign"* Williams letter dated October 22,1863. The campaign referred to is Lee's Bristoe Campaign. Meade's Mine Run Campaign would follow.

p. 290    *"I hear Genl. Hill is under arrest."* Leonard Williams letter dated October 22, 1863. Hill received a rebuke from Jefferson Davis after his ignominious defeat at the Battle of Bristoe Station fought on October 14, 1863. In *A. P. Hill: Lee's Forgotten General* (p. 180), (reprint, University of North Carolina Press, Chapel Hill, NC, 1962), William Woods Hassler wrote of Lee's reaction to Hill's poor generalship. "Lee characteristically refrained from direct criticism of Hill, preferring instead to express disapprobation of the proud, sensitive commander's precipitate action in a far more poignant manner. The morning after the battle he rode with Hill over the corpse-strewn field. After listening gravely to Hill's account of the affair, he commented tersely, 'Well, well, General, bury these poor dead men and let us say no more about it.'" Lt. Gen. Hill was killed at Petersburg, April 2, 1865, just one week before Lee's surrender.

p. 291     *"I lost one of my men, John Green..."* Ibid., In the *Roll of Brooks Troop,* Privates A. J. Green, G. S. Green and Jno. C. Green "killed in battle at Cedar Mountain" are listed.

p. 293     *"There is considerable excitement in the regiment on account of a prospect of exchanging with Aiken's Regt."* Leonard Williams letter dated October 26,1863. Colonel Hugh K. Aiken commanded the 6th S. C. Cavalry. His regiment, along with Colonel John Dunovant's 5th and Colonel B. H. Rutledge's 4th, replaced the depleted 1st and 2nd S. C. Cavalry Regiments. M. C. Butler returned to action with a cork foot to command the three new units, which became known as "Butler's Brigade." In *Giant in Gray* (p. 169) Manly Wade Wellman wrote of the death of Aiken. "With Wheeler and Butler, Hampton had some 4,000 effectives as, on February 24 [1865], he opposed the Yankees [Sherman's army] at Kellytown. Colonel Aiken was shot dead as he led a charge."

p. 296     *"On November 3, General Wade Hampton reported for duty..."* Manly Wade Wellman, *Giant in Gray,* (Press of Morningside Bookshop, Dayton, OH, 1988), p. 130.

p. 297     *"That skirmishing was coming from Parker's Store..."* Ibid., p. 131.

p. 299     *"At the cemetery, the president sat shivering on a crowded platform..."* John S. Blay, *The Civil War: A Pictorial Profile,* (Bonanza Books, New York, NY, 1958), p. 211.

p. 299     *"Lincoln spoke in a squeaky voice and three minutes later..."* Burke *Davis, The Civil War: Strange and*

*Fascinating Facts,* (The Fairfax Press, New York, NY, 1960), p. 152.

p. 299     *"Later that same day, after Lincoln had delivered what he considered..."* Ibid., p.152.

p. 301     *"On November 26, General George Meade launched his Mine Run Campaign."* W. W. Blackford, *War Years with Jeb Stuart,* (reprint, Scribner, New York, NY, 1945), p. 242.

p. 301     *"Hampton's Division, supported by the advance of Hill's Corps..."* Major Henry B. McClellan, *I Rode With Jeb Stuart,* (DaCapo Press, New York, NY, 1994), p. 397.

p. 304     *"Camp near Fredericksburg, Va., Louisa County, December, 1863"* Leonard Williams letter dated December, 1863. The exact date in December was torn and thereby undecipherable.

p. 304     *"It has been [       ] since I wrote you..."* Ibid., Bracketed material is torn and undecipherable. The same is true for the additional bracketed material in this letter.

p. 307     *"In late December, the soldier becomes the builder..."* Carlton McCarthy, *Detailed Minutiae of Soldier Life,* (Carlton McCarthy and Company, Richmond, VA, 1882), p. 84.

p. 308     *"I am very glad you paid my relations a visit on your way to Columbia..."* Leonard Williams letter dated December 23, 1863. Newberry, SC was the probable location visited for it was there where Williams was born and raised.

## Chapter 13

p. 313     *"Fifty- two thousand Confederates would ultimately limp through its doors." Point Lookout Camp Conditions,* http://tripod.com/~PLPOW/Prisonhistory.htm., p.1.

p. 313     *"It was over crowded with morphine-addicted sick..."* Ibid., p. 1.

p. 313     *"Once proud fighters now roamed aimlessly about the grounds..."* Ibid., p.1.

p. 316    *"Sergt. Mickler had left Sparks to hold the three horses..."*
E. Prioleau Henderson, *Autobiography of Arab,* (Fox Books, Guild Bindery Press, 1997), p. 82.

p. 316    *"The body of Leonard's close friend and one of Hampton's best scouts..."* Ibid., p. 83.

p. 316    *"I have heard nothing of my application..."* Leonard Williams letter dated January 20, 1864. My "application" refers to his request for a leave of absence.

p. 316    *"I have been suffering from the worst attack of dysentery."* Ibid. Dysentery is an infectious intestinal disease causing cramping and diarrhea. It was reported that as many as 70% of all soldiers suffered from dysentery at one time or another.

p. 321    *"If victorious, we have everything to look forward to in the future..."* Clifford Dowdey, *Lee's Last Campaign: The Story of Lee and His Men Against Grant- 1864,* (Boston, 1960), p. 60.

p. 322    *"Soldiers huddled by fires stirring their cush."* "Cush" or "coosh" was a mixture of cornmeal and bacon grease.

p. 324    *"As Lee ruminated in his drafty headquarters, 136,000 Union soldiers re-enlisted..."* James M. McPherson, *Battle Cry of Freedom,* (Oxford University Press, New York, NY, 1988), p. 720.

p. 324    *"You must sometimes cast your thoughts on the Army of Northern Virginia..."* Robert Paul Jordan, *The Civil War,* (The National Geographic Society, New York, NY, 1969), p. 151.

p. 325    *"Does Dr. Watson want Clough;..."* Leonard Williams letter dated February 27. Clough was one of Williams' black field hands. Like Steve, the Captain considered him an unreliable servant at times. Clearly, Ned was the overseer of Williams' small group of slaves. This letter is the most revealing as to the prevailing Southern belief that slaves were mere property to be dealt with most severely at times.

p. 326    *"On February 28, the dead calm was momentarily interrupted..."* Manly Wade Wellman, *Giant in Gray,*

(Press of the Morningside Bookshop, Dayton, OH, 1988), p. 133.

p. 326    *"Hampton ordered 100 of his troopers to dismount and the rest to split up ... "* Ibid., p. 134., Ned Bradford, *Battles and Leaders of the Civil War, IV,* (The Fairfax Press, New York, NY, 1888), p. 95.

p. 326    *"All the yells that throats could furnish were to be poured forth..."* Manly Wade Wellman, *Giant in Gray,* (Press of Morningside Bookshop, Dayton, OH, 1988), p. 134.

p. 330    *"Four days later, on March 9, President Abraham Lincoln made a fateful decision..."* John S. Blay, *The Civil War: A Pictorial Profile,* (Bonanza Books, New York, NY, 1958), p. 233.

p. 331    *"First, forty-four year old fellow Ohioan, General William Tecumseh Sherman..."* Ibid., p. 233.

p. 332    *"I bought some cloth yesterday from the Qr. Master for pants."* Leonard Williams letter dated March 12, 1864. Quartermasters were the officers in charge of procurement and supply for army units. Corruption among quartermasters was commonplace throughout the war.

p. 333    *"If Meade does not take the initiative, I expect General Lee will..."* Leonard Williams letter dated March 15, 1864. Meade retained command of his army but Grant now assumed its overall control.

p. 333    *"I was very glad our authorities took a stand not to negotiate with Butler."* Ibid. Union Major General Benjamin Butler occupied New Orleans and Southerners dubbed him "The Beast" because of corruption, harsh treatment and high taxes they believed him responsible for. Butler now commanded the Army of the James.

p. 333    *"I saw Col. Black a few days ago."* Ibid. Colonel John L. Black commanded the 1st South Carolina Cavalry and was apparently a friend of Anna's father and brother, (the Lavals). Black was wounded in the Gettysburg cavalry fight.

p. 335    *"Confederate farriers and a handful of skilled veterinary surgeons...*" Farriers were responsible for the everyday care of horses. Their duties were generally limited to changing shoes, repairing tack, and stitching small wounds.

p. 335    *"Newspaper accounts revealed that affairs were even worse..."* Ralph Selph Henry, *The Story of the Confederacy,* (Garden City Publishing, Garden City, NY, 1931), p. 333.

p. 336    *"Dear Henry..."* Leonard Williams letter dated March 18, 1864. Henry was Leonard's older brother. This letter was found with Leonard's letters to Anna. Williams' daughter, Julia Gabrielle Williams, is more than likely responsible for keeping it and placing it in order with the rest.

p. 336    *"There is at present a rumor and general impression that the 1ˢᵗ and 2ⁿᵈ regiment will be ordered to S.C. and 2 or 3 fresh regiments brought out here in our stead."* Ibid. The 1st and 2nd South Carolina Cavalry Regiments were indeed ordered back to South Carolina to guard the coast. Toward the end of the war, the depleted units rejoined General Joseph E. Johnston's army in North Carolina.

p. 336    *"I have some fears of sickness on the coast..."* Ibid. The sickness referred to by Williams is malaria. Malaria was termed "the fever" or "the chills" by the men. The infectious role played by the mosquito was unknown at the time and quinine was the standard medicine prescribed for treatment.

p. 337    *"...France will recognize us as a political necessity toensure success in her Mexican schemes."* Ibid. Louis Napoleon ruled at the time and his French army had captured Mexico City and overthrown Benito Juarez. European recognition never came.

p. 338    *"Major Screven from Beaufort assures me..."* Leonard Williams letter dated March 19, 1864. Major Thomas E. Screven was originally Captain of Company B in the 2nd S.C. Cavalry. When the regiment was sent south, Screven became a Major serving under Colonel Thomas J. Lipscomb.

## Chapter 14

p. 343     *"When I reached here I found your mother quite sick and low spirited with cold, the glands about her jaw very much swoolen."* Leonard Williams letter dated April 24, 1864. "Swoolen" was a colloquialism for "swollen."

p. 343     *"General Grant was contemplating calling a halt to all prisoner exchanges."* James M. McPherson, *Battle Cry of Freedom,* (Oxford University Press, New York, NY, 1988), p. 793. Dr. McPherson points out that this course of action was in response to the South threatening to "re-enslave or execute captured black soldiers and their officers." Also, paroled Confederates were back in the field within a few weeks.

p. 345     *"Miraculously, three days later, James was exchanged at City Point..."* James' parole date is stated in "Confederate Abstract," a document provided by Patrick McCawley, Reference Archivist at the South Carolina Archives and History Center. It also states that he was paroled at Hammond General Hospital, Point Lookout, Md. on April 27, 1864. He was furloughed home on May 5, 1864. City Point is located in Virginia where the James and Appomattox Rivers meet. Grant headquartered there later in the war.

p. 345     *"On May 4, 1864, Grant's bluecoats swarmed across the Rapidan."* David Donald, *Divided We Fought,* (The MacMillan Company, New York, NY, 1953), p. 299.

p. 346     *"The roads were rutted, narrow, and surrounded by dense tangles..."* Noah Andre Trudeau, *A Frightful and Frightening Place,* Civil War Times Illustrated, May, 1999, Volume XXXVIII, (Primedia, Inc., Harrisburg, PA), p. 45.

p. 346     *"Forest fires raged...; the dead were roasted..."* Ibid., p. 49.

p. 346     *"I knew he meant to kill himself in case of fire..."* John Hennessy, *A Heart-Chilling Walk in Hell's Woods,* Civil War Times Illustrated, May, 1999, Volume XXXVIII, (Primedia Inc., Harrisburg, PA), p. 26.

p. 346     *"Yet another of Grant's men remembered the victim's 'shrieks, cries, and groans..."* Ibid., p. 26.

p. 346     *"Years before, as a youth, hunting small animals the mere sight of blood..."* William Conant Church, *The Armies and Their Leaders,* Miller, Editor in Chief, p. 32.

p. 346     *"One soldier remembered that as the wounded wailed, the eerie screeches..."* John Hennessy, *A Heart-Chilling Walk in Hell's Woods,* Civil War Times Illustrated, May, 1999, Volume XXXVIII, (Primedia, Inc., Harrisburg, PA), p. 24.

p. 346     *"These birds seemed to mock at our grief and laugh at the groans..."* Ibid., p. 24.

p. 346     *"Like Stonewall before him, and less than two miles from where Jackson fell..."* Ralph Selph Henry, *The Story of the Confederacy,* (Garden City Publishing, Garden City, NY, 1931), p. 353.

p. 347     *"On May 7, both generals raced towards Spottsylvania Court House..."* John S. Blay, *The Civil War: A Pictorial Profile,* (Bonanza Books, New York, NY, 1958), p. 287. In many old texts and on many old maps, Spotsylvania is spelled "Spottsylvania."

p. 347     *"We passed near Indian Town, crossed the Black River, camped on Black Mingo and are now on the Sampit in sight of Winyaw Bay."* Leonard Williams letter dated May 7, 1864. These towns and rivers are located in eastern and southeastern South Carolina. Today "Winyaw" Bay is spelled "Winyah" Bay.

p. 348     *" ...but address me directed in the care of Capt. McFie."* Ibid. Captain James P. McFie was from Richland and led Company H of the 2nd S. C. Cavalry.

p. 348     *"I propose to fight it out on this line if it takes all summer..."* David Donald, *Divided We Fought,* (The MacMillan Company, New York, NY, 1953), p. 304.

p. 348    *"For two days, he vainly endeavored to cave in his own skull..."* Ralph Selph Henry, *The Story of the Confederacy,* (Garden City Publishing, Garden City, NY, 1931), p. 356.

p. 349    *"In the end, the Bloody Angle overflowed with corpses and Grant's burial squad..."* Bruce Catton, *A Stillness at Appomattox,* (Doubleday & Company, Boston, 1968), p. 127.

p. 349    *"Between May 5 and May 12, the Union suffered 32,000 casualties..."* James M. McPherson, *Battle Cry of Freedom,* (Oxford University Press, New York, NY, 1988), p. 732.

p. 350    *"We heard of the commencement of the battle on the Rappahannock..."* Leonard Williams letter dated May 9, 1864. The "battle on the Rappahannock" refers to the bloody Wilderness battle, which had taken place south of the river. The day before this letter was written Grant met Lee at Spotsylvania.

p. 351    *"While the most ferocious fighting of the entire Civil War shook the ground..."* John S. Blay, *The Civil War: A Pictorial Profile,* (Bonanza Books, New York, NY, 1958), p. 288.

p. 351    *"The enemy's charge captured our battery on the left of our line..."* Major Henry B. McClellan, *I Rode With Jeb Stuart,* (DaCapo Press, New York, NY, 1994), p. 416.

p. 352    *"I can scarcely think of him without weeping..."* Ralph Selph Henry, *The Story of the Confederacy,* (Garden City Publishing, Garden City, NY, 1931), p. 358.

p. 352    *"Deep in the hearts of all true cavalrymen, North and South..."* Francis Trevelyan Miller, *The Cavalry: The Photographic History of the Civil War,* (A. S. Barnes and Company, New York, NY, 1957), p. 113.

p. 352    *"...I feel confident, bring about a very strong peace party, strong enough, I think, to elect a peace candidate..."* Leonard Williams letter dated May 12, 1864. That candidate would be former Union general, Democrat George McClellan, and Lincoln would beat him soundly.

p. 353     *"...we are near Capt. Keitt's company..."* Ibid. "Capt. Keitt's company" refers to Company B, 19th Cav. Bn., commanded by Capt. E. S. Keitt. Keitt and his men had been assigned to coastal defense duty.

p. 354     *"...Lee's reinforced 59,000 outmaneuvered and outfought Grant's 109,000."* James M. McPherson, *Battle Cry of Freedom,* (Oxford University Press, New York, NY, 1988), p. 733.

p. 354     *"Despite the slaughter, Grant never asked for a truce to care for his wounded..."* Ralph Selph Henry, *The Story of the Confederacy,* (Garden City Publishing, Garden City, NY, 1931), p. 363.

p. 355     *"Previously pitched battles were fought and the loser retreated..."* James M. McPherson, *Battle Cry of Freedom,* (Oxford University Press, New York, NY, 1988), p. 734.

p. 356     *"I would be glad to have such favorable accounts from Genl. Johnston..."* Leonard Williams letter dated June 8, 1864. General Joseph E. Johnston was retreating toward Atlanta in the face of Sherman's superior numbers. Though he fought defensively and gave ground, Johnston did so by design so as to preserve his troop strength.

p. 357     *"Sergeant Blythe was elected."* Ibid. Sergeant Blythe is most definitely Sergeant Absalom Blythe, a close friend of Williams. Blythe helped pen a testimonial upon the Captain's death, which appears in the epilogue.

p. 357     *"'Butler,' said Rosser, 'what is Hampton going to do here today?'"* Manly Wade Wellman, *Giant in Gray,* (Press of Morningside Bookshop, Dayton, OH, 1988), p. 146.

p. 358     *"Six times Sheridan's men charged."* Ibid., p. 149.

p. 358     *"As Hampton cautiously pursued..."* Ibid., p. 149.

p. 360     *"Oh damn you, I've got you now..."* U. R. Brooks, *Butler and His Cavalry in the War of Secession,* (Guild Bindery Press, Germantown, TN, 1994), p. 546.

p. 361     *"Since May 4, 65,000 Federals had been killed, wounded, or missing."* James M. McPherson, *Battle Cry of Freedom,* (Oxford University Press, New York, NY, 1988), p. 742.

p. 361      *"Camp Jackson...June 18, 1864"* Leonard Williams letter dated June 18, 1864. Remainder of letter missing.

p. 362      *"Under Genl. Trapier, there will be no difficulty in getting home..."* Ibid. In Brooks' *Butler and his Cavalry in the War of Secession* (p. 381), a mention of Trapier appears. "When Columbia, S. C., was evacuated, the battalion was again organized with Lieutenant-Colonel Trapier of the regular C. S. A. in command, and Adjutant Holmes again at his post. On reaching Charlotte, N. C., the men were remounted and reported to their companies, except Adjutant Holmes, who was assigned to the staff of Brigadier-General E. M. Law, commanding the remounts of both Butler's and Young's brigades, until the cavalry under General Hampton was overtaken, the night before Kilpatrick's camp near Fayetteville, N. C., was attacked."

p. 364      *"Forrest's victory is grand and astounding with his small army..."* Leonard Williams letter dated June 20, 1864. The victory referred to is Brice's Crossroads. Forrest was a resourceful, highly regarded general and was also the founder of an organization that later became the Ku Klux Klan.

p. 366      *"Capt. Gary on North Island is being shelled today."* Leonard Williams letter dated June 23, 1864. North Island was east of Leonard's position, 40 miles south of what is today Myrtle Beach. "Company F, from Pickens, Capt. J. W. Gary" appears in Brook's *Butler and his Cavalry in the War of Secession.*

p. 367      *"On one steamy afternoon early in the siege, Colonel Henry Pleasants..."* John S. Blay, *The Civil War: A Pictorial Profile,* (Bonanza Books, New York, NY, 1958), p. 294.

p. 368      *"...he ascended the James, York, Pamunkey, Chickahominy, Rappahannock..."* Leonard Williams letter dated June 25, 1864. Remainder of letter lost.

p. 369      *"I never saw so many broken down and exhausted men in my life."* Sam R. Watkins, *Company Aytch: A Sideshow to the Big Show,* (Collier Books, New York, NY, 1962), p.

160.

p. 370　　*"I expect another battle has been fought before this time."* Leonard Williams letter dated June 28, 1864. There had not been a great battle fought around Petersburg. Burnside's men were digging their tunnel while Grant maintained his siege.

p. 370　　*"I see by the Yankee accounts Fernando Wood, Voorhees, and other prominent..."* Ibid. Fernando Wood was the mayor of New York and an advocate for peace. He even promoted the separation of New York City from the Union in order to allow for free trade with the South. Wood was an ardent McClellan supporter in the coming election. Clement Vallandigham was a radical, abolitionist Democrat. Ultimately, he would be banished to Canada and after the war, the attorney accidently shot and killed himself while handling a firearm at a murder trial.

p. 370　　*"I would like you to send me a Patriot or an Enterprise occasionally."* Ibid. By *Patriot*, Williams is referring to *The Patriot and Mountaineer.* The *Enterprise* he requests is *The Greenville Enterprise.* Both newspapers were published in his hometown of Greenville.

p. 372　　*"Sherman has met too with heavy losses..."* Leonard Williams letter dated July 3, 1864. Williams is referring to Sherman's casualty count at Kennesaw Mountain, the battle fought against General Joseph E. Johnston's Confederates in the Atlanta Campaign.

p. 374　　*"The enemy have failed in their assaults on John and James Islands."* Leonard Williams letter dated July 13, 1864. John, James, Morris, and Folly Islands are located just south of Fort Sumter. The fortified islands were loosely connected by swamp and bayou and integral to the Charleston Harbor defenses.

p. 375　　*"A decision that hastened its downfall was replacing Johnston with his subordinate John Bell Hood on July 17."* John S. Blay, *The Civil War: A Pictorial Profile,* (Bonanza Books, New York, NY, 1958), p. 254.

p. 375      *"...the loss of his arm at Gettysburg and the use of his leg..."* Ibid., p. 254.

p. 376      *"What do the people think of Johnson's removal?"* Leonard Williams letter dated July 20, 1864. Williams is referring to Jefferson Davis' bold decision to replace Joseph E. Johnson with John Bell Hood in the defense of Atlanta.

p. 376      *"...Hood attacked a corps of Sherman's vast army in the savage Battle of Peachtree Creek..."* John S. Blay, *The Civil War: A Pictorial Profile,* (Bonanza Books, New York, NY, 1958), p. 254.

p. 378      *"Seconds later, 200 feet of Lee's entrenchments were blown sky high..."* James M. McPherson, *Battle Cry of Freedom,* (Oxford University Press, New York, NY, 1988), p. 760. In *Battles and Leaders, Volume IV,* William H. Powell provides a detailed account of the Battle of the Crater.

p. 378      *"Grant called the debacle one of the saddest affairs he had witnessed..."* John S. Blay *The Civil War: A Pictorial Profile,* (Bonanza Books, New York, NY, 1958), p. 294.

p. 379      *"It is reported that Genl. S. D. Lee has joined Genl. Hood..."* Leonard Williams letter dated July 30, 1864. Lee, along with Alexander P. Stewart and Benjamin F. Cheatham, were Hood's 3 corps commanders.

p. 380      *"There's a rumor, though it is not credited, that our regiment and Col. Black's are under orders for Atlanta.* Ibid., The 2nd S.C. Cavalry and Col. Black's 1st S.C. Cavalry never went to aid in the defense of Atlanta. Both regiments remained on coastal duty in South Carolina. The 2nd later joined Bragg near Wilmington.

p. 380      *"I believe you were [    ] over to that figure."* Ibid., Bracketed word is undecipherable.

p. 382      *"A few days later, Leonard's anger spiked higher than any of his fevers when he learned from a private, home on furlough, that he had been listed as absent without leave."* In Williams' compiled service records, he was listed as AWOL at this time. More than likely he was in transit and returned to his regiment late.

p. 383      *"This time Hampton went after meat, over 2,500 head of fine enemy cattle..."* Manly Wade Wellman, *Giant in Gray*, (Press of the Morningside Bookshop, Dayton, OH, 1988), p. 157. Wellman provides a wonderful account of Hampton's famed "Beefsteak Raid."

p. 384      *"Sheridan thrashed General Jubal Early at Cedar Creek and Grant attacked..."* John S. Blay, *The Civil War: A Pictorial Profile*, (Bonanza Books, New York, NY, 1958), p. 301.

p. 386      *"It was later said that even a crow flying across it..."* Ralph Selph Henry, *The Story of the Confederacy*, (Garden City Publishing, Garden City, NY, 1931), p. 411.

p. 387      *"I am pleased with the proceedings of the meeting of Mr. Boyce's constituents in Columbia on the subject of his letter to Mr. Davis."* Leonard Williams letter dated October 21, 1864. South Carolina Congressman William Boyce spearheaded an anti-Jefferson Davis caucus in Columbia. Boyce doubted Davis' ability to lead the new Confederacy almost from the start and had written him on the subject of removing certain ineffective generals from the Southern armies.

p. 388      *"Tomorrow is the day in course but I do not apprehend another at least..."* Leonard Williams letter dated October 22, 1864. Remainder of letter missing.

## CHAPTER 15

p. 389      *"Flames raced through the streets. Arsenals exploded. Citizens ran for their lives."* John S. Blay. *The Civil War: A Pictorial Profile*, (Bonanza Books, New York, NY, 1958), p. 255.

p. 389      *"'Total War' was his mantra."* The notion of "Total War" was first put forth by Prussian officer Karl Maria von Clausewitz who served in the French Revolutionary Wars.

p. 389      *"'I will make Georgia howl!' was his battle cry."* David Donald, *Divided We Fought*, (The MacMillan Company,

New York, NY, 1953), p. 410.

p. 391    *"Fifteen days later, on December 22, Sherman telegraphed the newly re-elected president."* William C. Davis, *The Battlefields of the Civil War,* (Salamander Books Ltd., London, England, 1990), p. 242.

p. 391    *"Winter winds ripped through the rags of the tattered men..."* Ralph Selph Henry, *The Story of the Confederacy,* (Garden City Publishing, Garden City, NY, 1931), p. 452.

p. 391    *"'The truth is,' Sherman informed Halleck, 'the whole army is burning...'"* David Donald, *Divided We Fought,* (The MacMillan Company, New York, NY), p. 419.

p. 392    *"...I was all the more anxious because it was generally believed Wilmington would be at any day evacuated..."* Leonard Williams letter dated January 30, 1865. Wilmington was evacuated in February of 1865, a month after Fort Fisher was taken by Federal forces.

p. 392    *"I am afraid your small parcel of meat will mould."* Ibid. "Mould" was a common spelling for "mold." Certainly, this is the concern of Williams here as he suggests in the following sentence that the meat be "taken up and hung up to dry."

p. 393    *"I do not think Sherman will get as far as Columbia."* Ibid. Two corps of Sherman's army occupied South Carolina's capital on February 17 and the next day Columbia was in flames.

p. 396    *"I'm very much gratified at the result of the peace conference."* Leonard Williams letter dated February 8, 1865. The meeting was held on February 3, 1865 on the Union steamer *River Queen* near Hampton Roads. At this conference, Davis was represented by Alexander H. Stephens, R. M. T. Hunter and John A. Campbell, while Lincoln appeared in person with William Seward. Lincoln insisted on surrender, not an armistice, adamant that the Union be maintained. Davis' representatives were not empowered to discuss cessation of fighting on those terms and no agreement was reached. Williams was satisfied at the result because he, like most Southern soldiers, didn't want Lincoln to dictate war-ending terms that did not provide for recognition of the Confederacy or a separate South.

p. 396     *"To counsel negociation now is to counsel submission..."* Ibid. "Negociation" may have been an alternate form of today's spelling.

p. 397     *"The Yankees shell our lines every day and occasionally Ft. Anderson."* Leonard Williams letter dated February 11, 1865. Fort Anderson is located on the west bank of the Cape Fear River midway between Fort Fisher and Wilmington. Its remains were restored and today is a state park.

p. 397     *"I wish the president would place Dick Taylor in command..."* Ibid., Richard Taylor was the son of former President Zachary Taylor and was the Confederate commander in Louisiana.

p. 397     *"I think the proposition to put negroes in the field exceedingly unwise."* Ibid. While the Federals placed many Negro troops in the field, the South never did. Davis did advocate their recruitment and black troops were drilling in the streets of Richmond in early 1865. The war ended before any Confederate Negro troops could serve.

p. 398     *"I have no idea if Columbia will be attacked."* Ibid. Six days later, Columbia fell into Union hands despite the efforts of Confederate Generals Hampton and Beauregard.

p. 400     *"There is, however, controversy that remains to this day as to the perpetrators."* David Donald, *Divided We Fought,* (The MacMillan Company, New York, NY, 1953), p. 419.

p. 401     *"There is nothing left for me to do but go and see General Grant..."* Craig L. Symonds, *The Battlefield Atlas of the Civil War,* (The Nautical and Aviation Publishing Company, Annapolis, MD), p. 101.

p. 401     *"I suppose, General Grant, that the object of our present meeting..."* Ibid., p. 103.

p. 402     *"I think we have fought the last battle of the war..."* Robert

Paul Jordan, *The Civil War*, (The National Geographic Society, New York, NY, 1969), p. 181.

p. 402     *"On that morning of the 23rd of April..."* U. R. Brooks, *Butler and His Cavalry in the War of Secession,* (Guild Bindery Press, Germantown, TN, 1994), p. 288.

p. 402     *"Ironically, Sherman's conditions were even softer than those offered by Grant..."* John S. Blay, *The Civil War: A Pictorial History,* (Bonanza Books, New York, NY, 1958), p. 329.

## EPILOGUE

p. 404     *"It is over, and though the present is depressing and disheartening..."* Manly Wade Wellman, *Giant in Gray,* (Press of Morningside Bookshop, Dayton, OH, 1988), p. 196.

p. 404     *"My good husband has loaded me with good things..." Letter From Anna Williams to Cousin Eleanor,* dated January 9, 1875, owned by Anne Kesler Shields, Winston-Salem.

p. 405     *"As a merchant and farmer, 'he conducted his business...'"* James M. Richardson, *The History of Greenville County, South Carolina,* (A. H. Cawston, Atlanta, GA, 1930), p. 191.

p. 406     *"Maum Fannie still is queen regent in the kitchen..." Letter From Anna Williams to Cousin Eleanor,"* dated March 20, 1873, owned by Anne Kesler Shields, Winston-Salem.

p. 406     *"The trip to Philadelphia was delightful..." Letter From Anna Williams to Cousin Eleanor,* dated October 15, 1876, owned by Anne Kesler Shields, Winston-Salem.

p. 407     *"My health has been poor all winter..." Letter From Anna Williams to Cousin Eleanor,* dated March 20, 1873, owned by Anne Kesler Shields, Winston-Salem.

p. 407     *"This is the birthday of my little stranger..." Letter from Anna Williams to Cousin Eleanor,* dated January 9, 1875, owned by Anne Kesler Shields, Winston-Salem.

p. 407     *"Leonard's younger brother James H. Williams..."* James is referred to as "Dr. J. H. Williams of Ninety-Six" in Leonard Williams' obituary.

p. 408     *"Farms prospered in large part due to the fair dealings of Williams and Whitmire..."* Anne K. McCuen, a local Greenville historical researcher, provided varied photocopied materials concerning the site of this mercantile. A Coca-Cola bottling plant was later built on the lot and demolished years later. Other newspaper excerpts contain advertisements and sales pertaining to the "Williams and Whitmire" establishment.

p. 409     *"Among my most pleasant recollections is the kindness..."* Transcribed letter from Corp. James M. McClanahan, 2nd S.C. Cavalry, to Capt. Leonard Williams, 2nd S. C. Cavalry, dated November 20, 1905, owned by Anne Kesler Shields, Winston-Salem.

p. 410     *"Captain Leonard Williams one of the boldest and best-known citizens..."* Obituary of Captain Leonard Williams, *The Greenville Daily News,* dated May 23,1908.

p. 411     *"...was wounded in a hand-to-hand fight at Upperville..."* Ibid. Williams was wounded at the Second Battle of Brandy Station, August 1, 1863. Subsequent accounts concerning the wounding of Williams were based on this obituary and are thus innately flawed.

p. 411     *"In Memoriam...Report of the Committee of Camp Pulliam..."* A. Blythe and S. S. Crittenden, *Tribute to Captain Leonard Williams, The Greenville Daily News*, exact date unknown. Both Absalom Blythe and S. S. Crittenden, submitters of this tribute, are listed in the *Roll of Brooks Troop.*

p. 412     *"Judge John C. Bailey Pays Beautiful Tribute..."* Judge John C. Bailey, *Tribute to Captain Leonard Williams, The Greenville Daily News*, dated May 27, 1908. This tribute was found in photocopy form. Smeared material was bracketed and the final lines were ink-blotched and rendered unreadable.

# SELECTED BIBLIOGRAPHY

Basler, Roy C. ed. <u>The Collected Works of Abraham Lincoln, Volume V</u>, New Brunswick: 1952-55.

Billings, John D. <u>Hard Tack and Coffee: The Unwritten Story of Army Life</u>, Lincoln: University of Nebraska Press, 1993.

Blackford, Lt. Col. W. W. <u>War Years with Jeb Stuart</u>, reprint, New York: Scribner, 1945.

Blay, John S. <u>The Civil War: A Pictorial Profile</u>, New York: Bonanza Books, 1958.

Bradford, Ned. <u>Battles and Leaders of the Civil War: Volume IV</u>, New York: The Fairfax Press, 1888.

Brooks, Ulysses R. <u>Butler and His Cavalry in the War of Secession</u>, Germantown: Guild Bindery Press, 1994.

_____ <u>Cavalry Sketches in Brooks' Confederacy</u>, Columbia: 1912.

Catton, Bruce. <u>A Stillness at Appomattox</u>, Boston: Doubleday & Co., 1968.

_____ <u>Grant Moves South</u>, Boston: Little, Brown and Co., 1960.

_____ <u>This Hallowed Ground</u>, Garden City: Doubleday & Co., 1956.

Cox, Samuel S. <u>Three Decades of Southern Legislation</u>, Providence: 1885.

Cullen, Joseph P. <u>The Peninsula Campaign 1862</u>, Harrisburg: The Stackpole Company, 1973.

Davis, Burke. <u>The Civil War: Strange and Fascinating Facts</u>, New York: The Fairfax Press, 1960.

Davis, William C. <u>The Battlefields of the Civil War</u>, London: Salamander Books Ltd., 1990.

De Leon, T. C. <u>Four Years in Rebel Capitals</u>, Mobile: The Gossip Printing Company, 1890.

Donald, David. <u>Divided We Fought: A Pictorial History of the War 1861-1865</u>, New York: The MacMillan Co., 1953.

Dowdey, Clifford. <u>Death of a Nation: The Story of Lee and His Men at Gettysburg</u>New York: 1958.

Dowdey, Clifford and Manarin, Louis H.  <u>The Wartime Papers of R. E. Lee</u>,  New York: 1961.

Dowdey, Clifford.  <u>Lee's Last Campaign: The Story of Lee and His Men Against Grant</u>, Boston: 1960.

Dupuy, R. Ernest, and Trevor N. <u>The Compact History of the Civil War</u>, New York: Warner Books, 1993.

Field, Ron.  <u>The Hampton Legion Part 1: Regimental History</u>, Gloucestershire: Design Folio, 1994.

Fonvielle, Chris E., Jr.  <u>The Wilmington Campaign: Last Rays of Departing Hope</u>, Mechanicsburg: Stackpole, 1997.

Foote, Shelby.  <u>The Civil War, Volume 2</u>,  reprint,  New York: Vintage, 1986.

Frassanito, William A.  <u>Antietam: The Photographic Legacy of America's Bloodiest Day</u>,  New York: Charles Scribner's Sons, 1978.

Freeman, Douglas Southall.  <u>Lee</u>, New York: Scribners, 1934.

Furgurson, Ernest B. <u>Chancellorsville 1863</u>, New York: Alfred A. Knopf, 1992.

Gibbon, John.  <u>Personal Recollections of the Civil War</u>, New York, 1928.

Grimsley, Mark.  <u>Battle Chronicles of the Civil War: Robert E. Lee, Vol.VI</u>,  New York: MacMillan, 1989.

Hassler, William Woods.  <u>A. P. Hill: Lee's Forgotten General</u>,  Chapel Hill:  reprint, University of North Carolina Press, 1962.

Henderson, E. Prioleau.  <u>Autobiography of Arab</u>, Camden: Fox Books, Guild Bindery, 1997.

Hennessy, John.  "A Heart-Chilling Walk in Hell's Woods," <u>Civil War Times Illustrated</u>,  Volume XXXVIII, Harrisburg: Primedia, Inc., May, 1999.

Henry, Ralph Selph. <u>The Story of the Confederacy</u>, Garden City: Garden City Publishing, 1931.

Jordan, Robert Paul, ed.  <u>The Civil War</u>, New York: The National Geographic Society, 1975.

Longacre, Edward G. <u>The Cavalry at Gettysburg</u>, Rutherford: Fairleigh Dickinson University Press, 1986.

Matloff, Maurice.  <u>A Concise Military History of the War Between the</u>

States, New York: David McKay Co., Inc., 1978.

McCarthy, Carlton.  Detailed Minutiae of Soldier Life, Richmond: Carlton McCarthy and Co., 1882.

McClellan, Major Henry B.  I Rode With Jeb Stuart, New York: Da Capo Press, 1994.

McFeely, William S. Grant: A Biography, New York: Norton, 1981.

McPherson, James M.  Battle Cry of Freedom, New York: Oxford University Press, 1988.

Miller, Francis Trevelyan.  The Cavalry: The Photographic History of the Civil War, New York: A. S. Barnes & Co., 1957.

Nolan, Alan T.  Lee Considered: General Robert E. Lee and Civil War History, Chapel Hill: University of North Carolina Press, 1991.

Persico, Joseph E.  My Enemy My Brother, New York: MacMillan, 1977.

Pfanz, Harry W. Gettysburg: The Second Day, Chapel Hill:  University of North Carolina Press, 1987.

Richardson, James M.  History of Greenville County, South Carolina, Atlanta: A. H. Cawston, 1930.

Robertson, James I., Jr. Soldiers Blue and Gray, Columbia: University of South Carolina Press, 1988.

_____ The Civil War: Tenting Tonight, Chicago: Time Life Books, 1984.

Sears, Stephen W.  Chancellorsville, Boston: Mifflin Company, 1996.

Sifakis, Stewart.  Compendium of the Confederate Armies: South Carolina New York: Facts on File, E577S53, 1995.

Smith, Gene.  Lee and Grant, New York: McGraw-Hill, 1984.

Symonds, Craig L.  The Battlefield Atlas of the Civil War, Annapolis: The Nautical and Aviation Publishing Company of America, 1983.

Taylor, Walter H.  Four Years with General Lee, New York: Bonanza Books, 1962.

Trudeau, Noah Andre.  "A Frightful and Frightening Place," Civil War Times Illustrated, Volume XXXVIII, Harrisburg: Primedia, Inc., May, 1999.

Vandiver, Frank E. ed.  The Civil War Diary of General Josiah Gorgas, Alabama: University, 1947.

_____ Their Tattered Flags, New York: Harper and Row,

1970.

Watkins, Sam R. <u>Co. Aytch: A Side Show to the Big Show</u>, New York: Collier Books, 1962.

Wellman, Manly Wade. <u>Giant in Gray</u>, Dayton: Press of the Morningside Bookshop, 1988.

Wells, Edward L. <u>Hampton and His Cavalry in '64</u>, Richmond: B. F. Johnson, 1907.

Wheeler, Richard. <u>Sherman's March</u>, New York: Crowell Publishers, 1978.

Wiley, Bell Irvin. <u>The Life of Johnny Reb</u>, Baton Rouge: Louisiana State University Press, 1978.

Williams, Anna Laval. <u>Letters to Cousin Eleanor</u>, Unpublished: Owned by Anne Kesler Shields, Winston-Salem.

_____ <u>The Personal Diary of Anna Laval Williams</u>, Unpublished: Owned by Anne Kesler Shields, Winston-Salem.

Williams, Julia Gabrielle. <u>Personal Family History</u>, Unpublished, Owned by Anne Kesler Shields, Winston-Salem.

Woodworth, Steven E. <u>Jefferson Davis and his Generals</u>, Lawrence: University Press of Nebraska, 1990.

## INDEX